THE PERVERSION OF NORMALITY

FROM THE MARQUIS DE SADE TO CYBORGS

THE PERVERSION OF NORMALITY

FROM THE MARQUIS DE SADE TO CYBORGS

KERRY BOLTON

ARKTOS
LONDON 2021

ISBN	978-1-914208-20-1 (Paperback)
	978-1-914208-21-8 (Hardback)
	978-1-914208-22-5 (Ebook)
EDITING	Constantin von Hoffmeister
COVER & LAYOUT	Tor Westman

🌐 Arktos.com   ⬛ fb.com/Arktos   🐦 @arktosmedia   📷 arktosmedia

CONTENTS

INTRODUCTION XI

DE SADE & FREUD 1
    De Sade: Paragon of Liberal Virtue   12

CULTURAL MARXISM: ORIGINS, DEVELOPMENT AND SIGNIFICANCE 17
    Definition of Cultural Marxism   18

FREUDO-MARXIAN SYNTHESIS 23

NEW SCHOOL & FRANKFURT SCHOOL 25
    Patronage   29

FUNDING FOR SOCIAL SCIENCES 31
    Social Science Research Council   33
    Motives   38
    London School of Economics & Political Science   42
    Carnegie Corporation   44
    An American Dilemma   49

'SOCIAL CONTROL' & 'SOCIAL ENGINEERING' 53
    Sorokin's Critique of Sociological Methodology   56

BEHAVIOURISM 59
    Pavlov and Lenin   63
    Konrad Lorenz's Critique   65

PATHOLOGISING MORALITY 69

'CONSPIRACY THEORY' AS PERSONALITY DISORDER? 83
    Defining 'Conspiracy'   86
    Cycles of History   88
    Congressional Investigation   91
    Left-Wing Red Herring: Lyndon LaRouche   94
    Soviets Condemn Cultural Marxism   97

PSYCHIATRY & DISSENT **101**

MK-Ultra & the CIA 102

'Pathology of Normalcy' 103

Wilhelm Reich's Sexual Reductionism 105

VICTIMISING DISSENT **111**

'Siberia Bill' 112

Goldwater on the Couch 116

Trump on the Couch 121

MARGINALISING DISSIDENTS **125**

Institute for Strategic Dialogue 127

COLD WAR AGENDAS **135**

Anti-Soviet Analyses 136

Foundation Funds 140

Role of Social Sciences 143

The Non-Communist Manifesto: Rostow's Dialectics 149

DECONSTRUCTING THE 'PRIMARY TIES' **153**

Organic 'Freedom' vs. Rootless 'Freedom' 156

Organic Community versus Contractual Society 158

Individuation 162

The Individual and 'Collective Norms' 164

The Danger of 'Freedom' 165

MOTHER, CHILD, FASCISM **167**

Children as Consumers 171

'Patriarchal Repression' 176

LESSONS FROM SAMOA: MARGARET MEAD **185**

Role in Revival of Freudianism 195

PERENNIAL CHARACTER OF PRIMARY TIES **199**

Jung & Nietzsche 200

DIALECTICS OF CRITICAL THEORY **209**

Fromm's Bastards 217

Jewish Factor 218

Marcuse & the New Left 221

Increased Production: Meaning of Life 228

New Conceptions of Family Bonding 230

Self-Actualising with Charles Manson 230

SPAWNING THE NEW LEFT. 235
   'Materialization and Quantification of Values'   241
   Tyranny Means 'Freedom'   243

LASCH DISSENTS 249
   The Left Reacts   260

SEXOLOGY 265

ALFRED KINSEY 269
   Role of the Kinseyan Sexual Dialectics   280

WILHELM REICH'S 'SEX-POL'. 287

IDENTITY POLITICS. 295
   Gramscianism   296
   Proletariat Reductant as Revolutionary Factor   298
   Role of Marcuse   302

RECONSTRUCTING GENDERS. 307
   Magnus Hirschfeld: Father of Transvestism and Transgenderism   311
   House of World Cultures: Cold War Origins   317
   Gate-Crashing the APA   319

RECONDITIONING CHILDREN. 325
   Indoctrination in the Schools   326
   What is 'Relationships and Sexuality Education' (RSE)?   327
   Revolution in Morals   329
   Deconstruction of Language   331
   Imposed and Enforced   332
   Awareness Raising   333
   Remoulding Generations   335
   No Choice   336

PROGRESSIVE REGRESSION 337
   Return of the Eunuchs   337
   Toxicity of 'Traditional Masculine Ideology'   341
   Feminism   347
   Role of Feminism in Post-Cold War Globalism   350

INTERSECTIONALITY — THE POLITICS OF BEDLAM, OR, 'WHERE RIGHTS COLLIDE' . . . 353
   Gays versus Queers   355
   TERFing   357

'Just an Exiled Old White Woman'   359
Muslims versus Gays   360
Political Agendas   361
Straight White Leftists   363

THE MYTH OF 'WHITE PRIVILEGE' 365
Engels of British Poverty   365
Redlegs   369
The South and the White Worker   371

POPULATION CONTROL 377
Soviet Eugenics   380
Confluence   381
Rockefeller's Population Council   386
Hugh Moore and International Capitalism   389
Draper Committee 1959   393
Sanger & Planned Parenthood   396
Equality of Exploitation   398
Marx & Malthus   399
Birth Control 'Pivotal'   401
Intersectionality with the New Left   403
Frederick Jaffe Memo   406
Good Club: Buffett, Rockefeller Gates, et al.   411

ROLE OF THE UNITED NATIONS ORGANISATION.................... 415
United Nations Global Migration Compact   417
Nature of U.N. Declarations and Covenants   417
Labour Market Fodder   422
Indoctrination   423
What is Behind the U.N. Global Compact?   425
Universal 'General Will'   428

JULIAN HUXLEY'S BRAVE NEW WORLD 433
UNESCO Doctrine   436
Global Aesthetics: Formless, Rootless   437
Classifying Castes   439
Family Remains the Target   442

SOROS' 'BRAVE NEW WORLD' 447
'Piecemeal Social Engineering'   454

SOCIAL DECONSTRUCTION THROUGH ETHNIC DIVERSITY 457

Reality Not on Side of Globalists — 459
Putnam Study — 460
Unity in Diversity? — 462
The Review — 464
Nature of Discrimination — 467
Discrimination as Cognitive Development — 468
The Corporation Ideal — 468
Meta Estimated — 470
Conclusion — 474

BEHAVIOUR MODIFICATION 475

NTL Institute for Applied Behavioral Science — 477
Tavistock Institute of Human Relations — 478
'Racial Confrontation as Transcended Experience' — 480
'Unconscious Bias' — 482
Rev. Jones' Socialist Paradise Based on Group Therapy — 487

TRANSHUMAN 493

'Naturalistic', Universal Religion — 495

POSTHUMAN 501

Cyberfeminism & Postgender — 501
Postgender — 506

CONCLUSION 511

BIBLIOGRAPHY 515

❝ Kerry Bolton's book is the most thorough analysis of "Cultural Marxism". It is a sweeping study bursting with insights about the origins, trajectory, intellectual sources, financial sponsorship, and incredible influence of Cultural Marxism over every facet of Western society within both the Left and the mainstream Right.'

— RICARDO DUCHESNE, Ph.D. Social & Political Thought; Professor (retired), Department of Social Science, University of New Brunswick; author, *The Uniqueness of Western Civilization: Studies in Critical Social Sciences, Faustian Man in a Multicultural Age, Canada in Decay: Mass Immigration, Diversity, and the Ethnocide of Euro-Canadians, Defending the Rise of Western Culture Against its Multicultural Critics*; founder of the Council of European Canadians.

❝ When Éliphas Lévi composed the image of Baphomet, he tattooed the words *solve* and *coagula* or "dissolve" and "coagulate" on the inner right and left forearms of the idol. In *The Perversion of Normality*, Kerry Bolton does a remarkable job of surveying these twin policies of subversion (the dissolving factor) and perversion (the coagulating factor), which "leftist" storm troopers have been spearheading for many decades, whether consciously or not, at the behest of an international plutocratic oligarchy. The breadth and depth of the ideological assault against all that was healthy, sane, and functional in traditional Western civilization has been in need of a thorough investigation for quite some time. Bolton's latest book answers the call of the hour and is a must-read.'

— DR. OLIVER HEYDORN, author of *Social Credit Economics, The Economics of Social Credit & Catholic Social Teaching, and Social Credit Philosophy*. He graduated *summa cum laude* with a Ph.D. in philosophy, and has taught philosophy at three institutions in three countries.

Introduction

THE WORLD'S legends are replete with tales of those who sought to defy the gods — from Prometheus to Maui to Doctor Faustus — and to themselves become godlike, whose *hubris* brought destruction rather than their visions of sublimity. Within the West, for generations there have been those who imagine through their wealth or some other ego-inflated attribute, that they can, godlike, remake 'mankind' in an image more palatable with their own visions.

Believing that man is infinitely malleable, or 'perfectible' as was the word used in the much-vaunted Age of Enlightenment, from whence the trash today called 'modern' emerged, and can be reshaped at a whim, an array of individuals, ideologies and movements sought to deconstruct and rebuild humanity to serve some new purpose. In so doing, millennia of traditions and customs, of what is regarded as *normal* for having been formed and accumulated through generations by an array of historical processes, along with races, peoples, cultures, nations and states, are expected to disappear on command, to clear the way for something proceeding from nothing, or from the abyss at most. Such grand new visions have indeed resulted in something from the abyss, or at least from the darkness of cerebral recess, creating 'hell on earth', but always in the name of high ideals.

The West has suffered under such grandiose schemes in the name of 'liberty, equality, fraternity', *la droit humaine*, 'humanity', 'progress', behind the inspired leadership of the Marquis de Sade, Marat, Robespierre, Marx, Trotsky, Pol Pot, Mao, Jim Jones, Soros,

Rockefeller, Julian Huxley, Musk, Zuckerberg, Bill Gates; with the expectation that to reach the utopia that seems to become ever more distant, any sense of permanence and duration — what Soros disparages as the *organic*, and the Critical Theorists condemn as 'repressive primary ties,' of family, homeland, and faith — are discarded as *passé*.

The Perversion of Normality examines an array of individuals, doctrines and movements, most claiming to serve behind the banners of science, progress, and humanity. What seem to be divergent converge by what Dr Richard Spence, a genuine scholar, calls 'connecting the dots'. What emerges is a movement over the course of several hundred years, pushing forward an artificial construct in the name of 'humanity', but for the benefit of a self-anointed elite of oligarchs and technocrats. In hellish pandemonium normality is toppled on its head, in the name of 'normality', and the absurd, sick and destructive become the new normal.

De Sade & Freud

... If you envisage men as being only men, you are bound to see human society, not in Christian terms as a family, but as a factory-farm in which the only consideration that matters is the well-being of the livestock and the prosperity or productivity of the enterprise. That's where you land yourself. And it is in that situation that western man is increasingly finding himself.

— Malcom Muggeridge

THE IMPACT OF Sigmund Freud, father of psychoanalysis, on Western civilisation and, via globalisation, increasingly upon every region of the world, has been one of the primary influences of the modern epoch. It is not that Freud himself is necessarily recognised as the primary influence, but his teachings have permeated social theory and politics, even if his name is not evident. Freudianism, combined with Marxism and heavily revised, has been a lethal formula for deconstructing the primary customs, ethos, traditions and faith of the West. This was enabled due to the cultural crisis of the modern epoch of Western civilisation that starts with the Reformation and the Renaissance, proceeds through the Age of Enlightenment, the American and French Revolutions against the vestiges of the traditional Western social order, and through the Industrial Revolution, Bolshevism, and the world-expansive liberal-democratic-capitalism that is today called globalisation.

Marx and Freud were both products of the same *Zeitgeist* or spirit of the age, where the old certainties of faith had been destroyed by rationalism and *scientism* and, as Marx said, the bourgeoisie had replaced the aristocracy, the financier became lord, and God was replaced by 'reason'. Richard LaPiere,[1] a dissenter among social scientists, stated of this, 'Sigmund Freud was a product of the nineteenth century, who had the unusual distinction of providing the twentieth century with a new and very radical idea of man, and of living to see that idea rise to a position of dominance in the thought of Western peoples'.[2]

The Freudo-Marxian world revolution has been more enduring and encompassing than Bolshevism, while 'conservatives' were worrying about a 'Moscow plot'.

LaPiere wrote, about a decade prior to Freudo-Marxism becoming the basis of the 'New Left' student revolt, that

> Freudianism has become ... more than a theory of the causes of mental disorders and a therapy claimed to resolve them. It has become, as Freud so obviously hoped that it would, a doctrine on the nature of man that its adherents believe applicable to all mankind. And it has of late years become remarkably popular with both laymen and scientists, particularly here in the United States.

> Those less beguiled by Freudianism have been inclined to find the explanation for its popularity in its exotic content; and a few observers have related its popularity, vaguely but perhaps with some validity, to the current American ethos with its liberality toward self-indulgence and irresponsibility. ...[3]

It is notable that LaPiere refers to the reception Freudianism received in the USA because of the liberal hedonism that marks America's modernist ideology. The Freudo-Marxian synthesis, known as *Critical Theory*, was brought to the USA by the faculty of the Frankfurt Institute for Social Research, fleeing Hitlerism. It is notable that this

---

1   Richard LaPiere: Professor of Sociology, Stanford University.
2   Richard LaPiere, *The Freudian Ethic*, p. 33.
3   Ibid., vii, viii.

synthesis was resolutely rejected by the orthodox Communists in Germany and the regime in Moscow, while gaining enduring influence in the USA. It is also of note that this 'Frankfurt School' arose during the era of the Weimar regime in Germany in the aftermath of World War I, where moral and social experimentation were the product of social decay.

LaPiere referred to the fracture of the traditional order by Freudianism:

> The growing popularity of Freudianism as an explanation of and justification for human conduct is only one of many social changes, but it is a change of paramount significance; for Freudianism provides a unique idea of the nature of man, of his potentialities, and of his relations to society. Those who adopt this new idea and act upon it *ipso facto* regard themselves and the world about them in a way that **differs radically from the traditional view. They are perforce constrained to renounce many established values and sentiments** and to accept, as logical correlates of the Freudian idea of man, a new set—values and sentiments that are, for convenience and with an eye to precedent, here designated as the 'Freudian ethic'.[4]

LaPiere refers to a period of subversion of the social sciences, which we are able to readily trace to the *Critical Theorists*:

> The Freudian invasion of contemporary social psychology and sociology has been less spectacular and considerably less forthright [than pre-Freudian psychology]. Freudian concepts have seeped into these disciplines in fragments and, often, have been camouflaged by the use of non-Freudian terms. The result is a partial retreat from the behavioristic orientation that dominated these fields from about 1925 to 1945 to a modified version of the kind of instinctivism that was popular in the years just preceding 1925. **In this version, the antisocial character of man's presumed instincts is not stressed, but it is frequently assumed and stated that man comes into this world with a variety of psychological needs that can be fulfilled only under special social circumstances. Thus the small-group approach in social psychology stresses the desirability of a 'democratic atmosphere'**

---

4   Ibid., viii. Emphasis added.

in the individual's work, study, and other life circumstances on the grounds that 'autocratic' authority violates the innate need for self-fulfillment, self-expression, and self-determination. Those social psychologists who are much concerned with the 'tension-producing' conditions of modern life—and who purport to be able to explain everything from divorce to war in accordance with their tensional system of interpretation—likewise assume that there is a common if not universal conflict between the individual's innate psychological needs and the social demands made upon him.[5]

While LaPiere does not name *Critical Theory*, the doctrines he is describing are those of the Frankfurt School, where the therapeutic state is propounded as necessary to ensure the mental health of mass society, in need of freedom to express instincts that are repressed by the authoritarian patriarchal family.

The focus of this neo-Freudianism is on the individual detached from society. It is therefore a means of deconstructing and fracturing the social organism, which is why the Marxian theorists who created the Frankfurt Institute in 1923 found Freudianism to be such a useful ingredient in creating a new revolutionary synthesis. The organic bonds of family, state, faith and ethos, disparaged as 'primary ties' in need of cutting, were portrayed as injurious to the individual well-being and as repressing the individual's path to self-actualisation. LaPiere called Freudianism 'a doctrine of social irresponsibility and personal despair'.[6] In the pursuit of individual meaning through liberation from traditional social bonds, the result is not the universal bliss of oneness with humanity, as the *Critical Theorists* promise, but the despair of nihilism, of the detached individual who goes toward the light with the promise of eternal fulfilment, only to find that it is one of obliteration within a void.

---

5   Ibid., p. 47. Emphasis added.
6   Ibid., p. 53.

Freud's concern, both as a therapist and as a theorist, was with the individual. His data, if so they may be described, were dredged up from the hypothesized unconscious of his neurotic patients; moreover, he delved into this unconscious with a preconceived notion of what he would find there. Both what he looked for and what he found were inevitably **biased in favor of the individual and against society. The patients saw themselves as victims of society; they were poor, misunderstood, mistreated creatures in search of someone who could comprehend their troubles and sympathize with them.** Such are the common characteristics of neurotics. They are people who have failed, to a significant degree, to make their peace with society; and they believe that society has failed them. Never, in the mind of the neurotic, has he failed society.[7]

We might discern here, decades before the rise of 'identity politics', what has become the manifestation of a mass of neurotic individuals, socially fractured and re-clustering into aggrieved 'minorities', who are open to manipulation. The *Critical Theorists* sought to create these aggrieved minorities as revolutionary vanguards. LaPiere continues:

What Freud secured from his patients might justly have been used to demonstrate how the neurotic individual regards himself and his relation to society. Freud used it, however, as evidence in favor of his humanistic but completely unrealistic idea that the **individual is inevitably and inescapably repressed by the inhuman dictates of organized social life. Freud, like his patients, believed that they were victims of social circumstances; and, like them, he was in all respects antagonistic toward society.** So strong, apparently, was that antagonism that Freud never pondered the question: If man is by nature contrasocial, how can it be that men have evolved the social systems by which man lives?[8]

The critique of 'organised social life' as repressing the individual became the basis of *Critical Theory*. Erich Fromm called 'organised social life' the 'primary ties' from which the individual must be freed.

---

7   Ibid., p. 53. Emphasis added.
8   Ibid., p. 53. Emphasis added.

His colleague Herbert Marcuse, father of the New Left and of 'identity politics', explained the Freudian method of *Critical Theory*:

> The concept of man that emerges from **Freudian theory is the most irrefutable indictment of Western civilization** and at the same time the most unshakable defense of this civilization. According to Freud, the history of man is the history of his repression. Culture constrains not only his societal but also his biological existence, not only parts of the human being but his instinctual structure itself. However, such constraint is the very precondition of progress. **Left free to pursue their natural objectives, the basic instincts of man would be incompatible with all lasting association and preservation: they would destroy even where they unite.** The uncontrolled *Eros* is just as fatal as his deadly counterpart, the death instinct. **Their destructive force derives from the fact that they strive for a gratification which culture cannot grant: gratification as such and as an end in itself, at any moment.** The instincts must therefore be deflected from their goal, inhibited in their aim. Civilization begins when the primary objective — namely, integral satisfaction of needs — is effectively renounced.[9]

Here Marcuse distilled the premises of *Critical Theory*. Freud and his dissident protégé Carl Jung said that culture depends on the extent to which the atavistic urges are redirected, or *canalised* as Jung termed it; which the philosopher Nietzsche called *sublimation*, but which Marcuse and other *Critical Theorists* condemned as 'deflection from the goal of satisfaction of instinctual needs'. The post-Freudians depart company from their father-figure (an *Oedipal* conflict?) and contend that in the name of *self-actualisation* the individual must liberate himself from the constraints of custom, law, family, religion, and morality and give free reign to his instinctual drives. Marcuse listed a dichotomy between atavistic impulse and *sublimation*:

---

9   Herbert Marcuse, *Eros and Civilization*, Chapter I: 'The Hidden Trend in Psychoanalysis'. Emphasis added.

FROM:	TO:
immediate satisfaction	delayed satisfaction
pleasure	restraint of pleasure
joy (play)	toil (work)
receptiveness	productiveness
absence of repression	security

The *Critical Theorists* aim to regress culture to that of the instinctual drives in the name of 'freedom'. That which prevents this is called 'authoritarian' and even 'Fascist'. What concerned Fromm was that individuals when given a choice prefer 'security' rather than the 'absence of repression'. This repressive tendency, which one would expect to be an instinctual survival drive, was claimed by Marcuse and other post-Freudians, such as Wilhelm Reich, to be the result of sexual repression. These doctrines became the premises of the New Left, but have been mainstreamed to become the new normal.

Marcuse *et al* claimed to be rejecting conventional society and rebelling against capitalism. However, the self-indulgent, unrestrained individualism that demands immediate ego gratification and objects to any form of 'delayed satisfaction' as the result of repression, oppression, suppression, racism, misogyny, or homophobia, *ad infinitum*, became the ideology of capitalism. The expectation of 'immediate satisfaction' is the basis for ever-expanding markets. It is the old game established by Freud's nephew Edward Bernays, father of public relations, when, employed by the tobacco industry, he promoted cigarettes as 'torches of freedom' for 'the modern women'. Hence the 'liberated women' became a vast new consumer market for the tobacco industry.

Richard LaPiere described the manner by which Freudianism became the method for expanding consumer markets:

> The advocates of the Freudian view of man and of the ethic that stems from that view have recently been augmented by a host of bright young men whose ostensible task is to aid in the shaping of advertising and other promotional endeavors. A generation ago it was the assumption along Madison Avenue that people buy goods for their use or prestige values.

Market researchers, as they were then called, endeavored by interview and survey studies to ascertain what people wanted to buy or why they bought what they did buy rather than something else. From such studies the 'wants' of men were determined, and the advertising copy writer then slanted his appeals toward the satisfaction of these wants. If it appeared that people wanted economy in their automobiles, he claimed that his car was the most economical; if they seemed to want speed, he claimed the highest speed; etc.

Of recent years, however, market researching has given way to a more complex, impressive, and costly operation called 'motivational research.' The motivational researchers proceed on the assumption that people do not know why they buy what they buy; therefore it is futile to ask them what they want to buy or why they bought what they did. One must, they believe, probe behind the obvious to the real — dig down through the public's conscious self to its unconscious motivations. To this end a sample of the population must be subjected to depth interviews, and the interview materials must then be analyzed to determine the hidden, unconscious motives that have been inadvertently revealed. When the psychoanalysts of the public have made their diagnoses, the advertising copy writer, or the political propagandist, can then pitch his appeals to the real rather than the ostensible motives of men. The motivational researchers have become, it would appear, a considerable power in advertising and related circles. **An increasing proportion of advertising is slanted toward such 'unconscious' motivations as the need for emotional security, ego gratification, guilt release, and—inevitably—thwarted sexual desires**. Whether the new appeals actually fool the buying public is debatable, but the fact that the advertising fraternity believe they do suggests that advertisers have taken over the Freudian idea of man and have made the public in its image.[10]

The social sciences provided a doctrine for the rationalisation of instant 'ego gratification' that is the premise for expanding consumerism, and the fad of the new. Traditional — medieval — Western societies, with their religious foundation and repudiation of avarice as sinful, prohibited mercantile competition, advertising and marketing, without which modern capitalism could not function. This was the

---

10   Richard LaPiere, pp. 77–78. Emphasis added.

basis of the pre-capitalist organic social community. The Left, with its cult of the new, have played a role in expanding consumerism, all the while, like Edward Bernays, assuring consumers that they are exercising a healthy 'freedom'. This is why ostensibly 'radical' leftist institutions such as the New School for Social Research, and the London School of Economics have a close relationship with capitalism.

The first institution that requires destruction in the name of 'freedom' is the 'patriarchal family' as the seedbed of repression and 'authoritarianism'. Marcuse states of this: 'The primal father, as the archetype of domination, initiates the chain reaction of enslavement, rebellion, and reinforced domination which marks the history of civilization'.[11] Karl Marx's *class struggle* as the impelling force of history, is replaced by a post-Freudian *Oedipal struggle* against the perennial father-*Führer*-god figure.

After World War II Max Horkheimer, Theodor Adorno and others of the Frankfurt School, undertook studies, sponsored by the American Jewish Committee, to determine the degree to which individuals are constrained by the *primary ties*, and particularly by the family, which supposedly measured their 'authoritarian personality' on an 'F' (for Fascism) scale. The stronger one's bond to parents, church and homeland, the more authoritarian and neurotic one was deemed. LaPiere stated:

> Unlike Marx, who also hated society—but the society of his times rather than society in general—Freud did not counsel general revolt from social restraints. Nevertheless, he implied the wisdom and justice of individual evasion of those restraints by designating (as have all psychoanalysts since) **social repression as the cause of the difficulties experienced by his patients. And if he did not directly advise the patient to evade the authority of the feared and hated parent or desert the intolerable wife, his doctrine certainly does nothing to foster submission to the requirements of society and everything to cast society into disrepute.**[12]

---

11   Herbert Marcuse, *Eros and Civilization*, Ch. I.
12   LaPiere, p. 54. Emphasis added.

It is here that the *Critical Theorists* have made their seminal contribution to the modern epoch. With the use of Marx's dialectical method of historical struggle they politicised Freudianism as the modern form of struggle that replaced class war. Rather than two contending classes vying for domination over the forces of social production, there would be a multiplicity of fractured interests each with its own demands on the social organism. Why then, do oligarchs sponsor what appears to be a revolt against their rule? LaPiere gives part of the answer in that Freudianism is the basis of 'motivational research' which examines the consumption habits of mass society and how these might be manipulated. Analogous to this, *Critical Theory* provides the analytical methodology for determining how aggrieved minorities can be manipulated. The studies of the *Critical Theorists* in what was published as *The Authoritarian Personality* provided data for social engineering and control, an example being the way this was used to 're-educate' Germany after World War II.

We can find the origins of these doctrines in the Age of Enlightenment, where 'reason' and 'science' questioned faith and tradition. Jean-Jacques Rousseau wrote of the need to overthrow King and Church and return man to what he supposed to be a 'state of nature', where he imagined perfect freedom prevailed. Donatien Alphonse Francois Marquis de Sade expounded on libertine sexuality, abortion, and the end of marriage for the sake of perfect freedom. The English liberal philosopher John Locke had written in 1690 a treatise on government where he imagined mankind had lived in a perfect state of equality before civilisation intervened:

> To understand political power right, and derive it from its original, we must consider, what state all men are naturally in, and that is, a state of perfect freedom to order their actions, and dispose of their possessions and persons, as they think fit, within the bounds of the law of nature, without asking leave, or depending upon the will of any other man.
>
> A state also of equality, wherein all the power and jurisdiction is reciprocal, no one having more than another; there being nothing more evident, than

that creatures of the same species and rank, promiscuously born to all the same advantages of nature, and the use of the same faculties, should also be equal one amongst another without subordination or subjection, unless the lord and master of them all should, by any manifest declaration of his will, set one above another, and confer on him, by an evident and clear appointment, an undoubted right to dominion and sovereignty.[13]

These were the precursors of today's 'progressive' intelligentsia, social scientists, and oligarchic 'philanthropists', who all aim — like the Jacobins and the Bolsheviks — to reshape Man according to ideological assumptions. These doctrines culminated in the 1789 Jacobin Revolution in France, which ushered in the current epoch of liberalism, with capitalist and socialist derivatives.

Professor Edelstein, in his aptly named study *Terror of Natural Right*, states that with the destruction of the Church the ideal of returning man to a supposed state of Nature legitimised the revolutionary terror.[14] Inspired by Enlightenment philosophers, such as those named above, Saint-Just and Robespierre regarded transgressors of Jacobin law as contravening 'Nature' herself, who forfeited their right to live in the revolutionary idyll of *Liberté, égalité, fraternité*.[15]

Rousseau had given ideological justification for mass terror in his concept of the 'general will' and the 'social contract'.[16] The concept is now called 'international law', and dissidents still find themselves liable to imprisonment, under an ideology that is neo-Jacobin, while 'rogue nations' are targeted for destruction by advanced technical warfare, again in the name of a nebulous 'international community'.

---

13 John Locke, *Second Treatise of Civil Government* (1690), Chapter II: 'Of the State of Nature', Section 4.

14 Dan Edelstein, *Terror of Natural Right: Republicanism, the Cult of Nature, and the French Revolution*, pp. 4–5.

15 Dan Edelstein, *Terror of Natural Right*, pp. 14–15.

16 J. J. Rousseau, *The Social Contract* (1762).

De Sade: Paragon of Liberal Virtue

With the triumph of Jacobinism and the overthrow of the remnants of traditional society, de Sade was released from an asylum in 1790 and assumed a role in Revolutionary France. His synthesis of sexual *sadism* as the impelling force of humanity makes de Sade the real father of *Critical Theory*, and allied movements such as 'population control', feminism, and liberalism. Despite his infamy as a brutaliser of women, especially among the poor, de Sade was elected to the National Assembly, where he aligned with the most extreme wing of the Revolution, led by Marat.[17] His doctrine of sex and death preempted Freud's premise of *Eros* and *Thanatos* as the primary motivators of human behaviour. Antedating Freud, de Sade wrote in *The 120 Days of Sodom* that '[s]exual pleasure is, I agree, a passion to which all others are subordinate but in which they all unite'.[18]

In *Philosophy in the Bedroom*,[19] de Sade condemned 'insipid moralists' in the name of 'Nature'. He called maidenly virtue 'absurd' and a product of 'dangerous bonds', imposed by 'a disgusting religion', and 'imbecilic parents'. He pre-empted the disparagement by the Bolsheviks and *Critical Theorists* of familial bonds as 'repressive':

> Then listen to me, Eugénie. It is absurd to say that immediately a girl is weaned she must continue the victim of her parents' will in order to remain thus to her dying day. **It is not in this age of preoccupation with the rights of man and general concern for liberties** that girls ought to continue to believe themselves their families' slaves, when it is clearly established that these families' power over them is totally illusory.[20]

---

17 After Marat died in 1793, de Sade fell afoul with the regime and was jailed during 1793–94. Under Napoleon's regime he was returned to an asylum in 1803.

18 Donatien Alphonse François de Sade, *The 120 Days of Sodom, or the School of Libertinage* (1785). First published 1904.

19 Donatien Alphonse François de Sade, *Philosophy in the Bedroom* (1795).

20 Ibid., Dialogue the Third.

De Sade anticipates the condemnation of the 'patriarchal family' by *Critical Theory* and feminism:

> Let us consult Nature upon so interesting a question as this, and may the laws that govern animals, in much stricter conformance with Nature, provide us for a moment with examples. Amongst beasts, do paternal duties extend beyond primary physical needs? Do not the offspring of animals possess all their parents' liberty, all their rights? As soon as they are able to walk alone and feed themselves, beginning at this instant, are they any longer recognized by the authors of their days? And do the young fancy themselves in any sense beholden to those whence they have received breath? Surely not. By what right, hence, are other duties incumbent upon the children of men? And what is the basis of these duties if not the fathers' greed or ambition?[21]

While de Sade touchingly anticipates feminism with his call for the 'liberation' of girls from their parents, his motives, true to form, soon follow: to 'liberate' girls so that they might be abused by male psychopaths such as himself:

> ... Begin, therefore, with the legitimacy of these principles, Eugenie, and break your shackles at no matter what the cost; be contemptuous of the futile remonstrances of an imbecile mother to whom you legitimately owe only hatred and a curse. If your father, who is a libertine, desires you, why then, go merrily to him: let him enjoy you, but enjoy without enchaining you; cast off the yoke if he wishes to enslave you; more than one daughter has treated thus with her father. ...[22]

In proto-feminist mode de Sade counsels, through the character of a fictitious woman, to discard all familial kinship and abjure marriage as a burden, in order that women might be liberated to copulate without moral, religious or legal restraints, leaving women to be subjected to the 'freedoms' according to the utopian Republic of Nature:

---

21 Ibid.

22 Ibid. The language descends further along the road of puerility...

... I require her to trample upon all the prejudices of her childhood, if I prescribe to her the most formal disobedience to her family's orders, the most arrant contempt for all her relatives' advice, you will agree with me, Eugénie, that among all the bonds to be burst, I ought very surely to recommend that the very first be those of wedlock.[23]

While de Sade, who regarded France as in need of depopulation, an attitude to which the Jacobins agreed with bloody results, refers to methods of birth control, he soon resorts to recommending sodomy as the best method; again anticipating the 'new normal' of the modern world. De Sade also predates Dr. Alfred Kinsey and Magnus Hirschfeld as the 'father of sexology' when writing of 'buggery', 'Absurd to say the mania offends Nature; can it be so, when 'tis she who puts it into our head? Can she dictate what degrades her? No, Eugénie, not at all; this is as good a place to serve her as any other, and perhaps it is there she is most devoutly worshipped'.[24]

De Sade also establishes himself as the father of 'population control', preceding Margaret Sanger by 120 years:

MADAME DE SAINT-ANGE — Do you know, Dolmancé, that by means of this system [mass buggery] you are going to be led to prove that totally to extinguish the human race would be nothing but to render Nature a service?

DOLMANCE — Who doubts of it, Madame?[25]

Child-birth and child-rearing are to be abhorred as infringing on women's freedom, and abortion and infanticide are 'no crimes of Nature'. Again we hear the distant echo that has become the thunderous rage of gender politics, and the sickness that has been normalised:

MADAME DE SAINT-ANGE —... propagation is in no wise the objective of Nature; she merely tolerates it; from her viewpoint, the less we

---

23 Ibid.
24 Ibid.
25 Ibid.

propagate, the better; and when we avoid it altogether, that's best of all. Eugénie, **be the implacable enemy of this wearisome child-getting**, and even in marriage incessantly deflect that perfidious liquor whose vegetation serves only to spoil our figures, which deadens our voluptuous sensations, withers us, ages and makes us fade and disturbs our health; get your husband to accustom himself to these losses; entice him into this or that passage, let him busy himself there and thus keep him from making his offerings at the temple; tell him you detest children, **point out the advantages of having none**. Keep a close watch over yourself in this article, my dear, for, I declare to you, **I hold generation in such horror** I should cease to be your friend the instant you were to become pregnant. If, however, the misfortune does occur, without yourself having been at fault, notify me within the first seven or eight weeks, and I'll have it very neatly remedied. **Dread not infanticide; the crime is imaginary: we are always mistress of what we carry in our womb...**[26]

De Sade invents the clichés and slogans of feminism in his defence of abortion. 'We are always mistress of what we carry in our womb', says this liberal champion of 'women's health issues'. He compares the child to excrement that might be purged with no more meaning than a daily toilet routine.

... as we are of the nails we pare from our fingers, or the excrements we eliminate through our bowels, because the one and the other are our own, and because we are absolute proprietors of what emanates from us.

Here is the liberal creed of freedom laid bare and unequivocal. With **exactitude** we find the doctrine of *Critical Theory* and other forms of Freudo-Marxism that condemn the family as the incubator of 'Fascism', and the 'primary ties' as the obstacles to 'self-realisation'. In the name of 'Nature', de Sade wrote, 'destruction' was one of her 'chief laws', under which 'nothing that destroys can be criminal'. 'Murder' was 'altering forms'. Man was matter, without spirit, and Nature was 'conflict'.[27] Under the Republican utopia of Nature, there would be

26 Ibid., Emphasis added.
27 Ibid.

few actions that are 'criminal',[28] when the foundations of society are 'liberty and equality'.

With de Sade we have the range of today's leftist doctrine, which has been mainstreamed in the name of 'progress', as the new 'normal'. Simone de Beauvoir, seminal feminist and social critic, for example, acknowledged this, writing, 'Intuitions such as these allow us to hail Sade as a precursor of psychoanalysis'.[29] De Sade struck the right chord for the 'modern age'; his time had dawned. He anticipated the

- Dialectical materialism of Karl Marx

- Psychoanalysis of Sigmund Freud

- Sexology of Alfred Kinsey

- Feminist birth control and abortion of Margaret Sanger

- Critical Theory of Marcuse, Fromm, Adorno et al.

---

28   Ibid.

29   Simone de Beauvoir, *Must we Burn De Sade?*

Cultural Marxism: Origins, Development and Significance

'**C**ULTURAL MARXISM' is the ideological buttressing of anything that subverts traditional values and cultures, such as globalism; open borders; transgenderism; formlessness in arts, music, architecture; a hellish formlessness in general. The purpose is to deconstruct any vestiges of tradition in the name of 'progress', the goal is to establish a nebulous mass humanity devoid of identity in regard to ethnos, land, and even gender, ironically called 'identity politics'. Dialectically, this push toward universal homogenisation is promoted in the name of being 'different'. Society becomes so fractured where there is even a 'sliding scale of gender', and individuals can change their identity at will, that any really organic identity, requiring a sense of **permanence** is destroyed. The Left and its globalist sponsors **deconstruct** in order to reconstruct.

There is a common outlook between the Left and capitalism, which sees the two as part of the same historic process of internationalism. Detachment and rootlessness allow for the unhampered movement of labour, so that people become economic units, as part of a global production process. This is why the Left are useless as opponents of globalisation: when the Left attack any restrictions on immigration as 'racism', 'xenophobia', and 'Fascism', they are following the party-line of international capitalism. This 'Left' is funded by George Soros' Open Society Foundations, the National Endowment for Democracy, the Rockefeller Foundation, Movements.org and hundreds of other NGOs and foundations.[1]

As the philosopher-historian Oswald Spengler observed nearly a century ago, leftist movements operate in the interests of money' (plutocracy); so-called 'people's revolts' have served oligarchic interests since the Gracchus revolt in Rome.[2] Bolshevism was funded by oligarchs.[3] The situation remains.[4]

Definition of Cultural Marxism

Professor Jerome Jamin of the Political Science Department, University de Liège, Belgium, defines Cultural Marxism as synonymous with Critical Theory:

> From a philosophical point of view, Cultural Marxism, as Critical Theory, considers culture as something that needs to be studied within the system and the social relations through which it is produced, and then carried by the people. So, according to Kellner (2013, p. 10),[5] the 'analysis of culture is intimately bound up with the study of society, politics, and economics'. This theory means that the culture does not have an autonomous life next to the daily concrete lives of individuals and their social relations. It also states that, as a consequence, cultures are built to help the dominance of powerful and ruling social groups. Within the Marxist tradition, which sees dominant ideology as the ideology of the bourgeoisie to control the proletariat and the working class, Cultural Marxism considers cultures and ideologies as inextricably linked to the economic, social, and political context: they are tools in the hands of the powerful to control the people.[6]

---

1   K. R. Bolton, *Revolution from Above*, passim.

2   Oswald Spengler, *The Decline of the West*, Vol. 2, pp. 402, 464.

3   Richard B. Spence, *Wall Street and the Russian Revolution 1905–1925*, passim.

4   Bolton, *Revolution from Above*, passim.

5   D. Kellner, 'Cultural Marxism and Cultural Studies' (2013), https://pages.gseis. ucla.edu/faculty/kellner/, Lind W. (2000), as cited by Jerome Jamin.

6   Jerome Jamin, 'Cultural Marxism: A Survey', *Religion Compass*, 2018, p. 4.

The Left, despite the above assumption, is sponsored by 'powerful and ruling social groups', the aim being social control, through social engineering. This has been enabled because Marx and others of the Left were responding to bourgeois economic control in a limited sense, and did not detach themselves from the same 19th century *Zeitgeist* as the bourgeoisie. They were, simply, two sides of one coin. Hence the Marxists and neo-Marxists see traditional bonds as nothing more than bourgeois moral and social institutions, without an organic, perennial character. As the former Critical Theorist Professor Christopher Lasch contended against the Left, these supposedly 'repressive' 'primary ties' are the organic bonds that predate capitalism, that sustain communities, based around the family and the home, and one's native land. The Left, in undermining these as 'repressive bourgeoisie morality', serve the aims of capitalist globalisation, which also sees these 'primary ties' as a hindrance to the global economic process. Between the Left and global capitalism there is a confluence of worldviews because both have the same preoccupation with the 'laws of social production' rather than with the organic laws of history and society. As referred to above, Spengler pointed this confluence out a century ago.

Cultural Marxism is the will-to-destroy as it pertains to these traditional cultural and societal bastions. *The Communist Manifesto* is a handbook for the destruction of whatever remains in this late epoch of the West, of organic bonds such as family, marriage, faith and the pre-capitalist attachment to village, church, and land. Rather than decrying the destruction of these organic bonds by capitalism and industrialism, Marx regarded the passing away of these so-called 'bourgeois' institutions as a necessary part of the progress of dialectical history. Those who resisted this dialectic were vehemently denounced in *The Communist Manifesto* as 'reactionists'.[7]

What the orthodox Marxists seek with the destruction of the organic bonds of traditional society, the Cultural Marxists seek by

---

7   K. R. Bolton, 'Marx Contra Marx: A Traditionalist Conservative Critique of the Communist Manifesto'.

broadening their subversion beyond economic critiques, and working class mobilisations, which have been largely unsuccessful. The proletariat has remained generally conservative and dangerously inclined to 'populism'. Consider how the media pundits ridiculed the alleged lack of college graduates among Donald Trump's supporters, while the privileged Hillary Clinton sneered at them as the 'deplorables'? Such elitist attitudes express the fear and the contempt the leftist intelligentsia and the oligarchy have towards 'the people', which they hide behind slogans about 'social justice', 'human rights' and 'equality'. A commentator analysed the election of the 'populist' Trump, and the demographic studies of voting patterns, finding that

> Economic discontent defined this election, and a populist won it. But bare economics do not appear to have played a leading role in how voters cast their ballots. The proportion of people who held a bachelor's degree or higher was the primary correlate in how a county voted, far more than how much money the average townsperson made, or how many had lost a job.[8]

Amidst the perplexity and literal tears of the liberal bourgeoisie, intelligentsia, and oligarchy as to how someone such as Trump could have won, with the news media against him, and without money from the usual sources, one explanation could be that the divide was between the *plebs* who see the world in unencumbered reality, and those who see it through the distorted lenses of the education system. Frankly, what proportion of those going through a tertiary education, where the perimeters of enquiry and thought are strictly confined, are going to have the determination and independence to question established leftist orthodoxy?

Against such dangers from populist reaction, disaffected minorities have to be found or **created**, so that the social order will split apart under a multiplicity of factions, all seeking their 'rights' as separate

---

8   Andrew McGill, 'America's Educational Divide Put Trump in the White House', *The Atlantic*, 27 November, 2018; https://www.theatlantic.com/politics/archive/2016/11/education-put-donald-trump-in-the-white-house/508703/.

and alienated identities. Hence, 'identity politics' is fractured by ever-increasing, newly-discovered 'genders', each with its own rights and grievances, and even its own flags, symbols, and *lingua franca*.

The aim is to fracture traditional, organic identities that are barriers to globalisation and social control, by creating artificial identities that can be manipulated and subjected to social engineering.

However, to the above quoted Jamin such a definition is part of a widespread 'right-wing conspiracy theory' with undertones of 'racism'. He writes of this 'right-wing conspiracy theory' as though it is conspiracy, alluding to 'confidential journals':

> If Cultural Marxism, as a school of thought, dates from the 1930s, Cultural Marxism, as a conspiracy theory, has appeared in conservative and radical American literature from the beginning of the 1990s. It has been regularly expressed in articles published in confidential journals, some of which have either ceased to exist or are no longer published.[9]

Jamin reiterates the association between Cultural Marxism and 'Critical Theory':

> Cultural Marxism, and Critical Theory more generally with which it has a close signification, have both a direct link with the Frankfurt School and its Marxian theorists. Initially called the 'Institute for Social Research' during the 1930s, and taking the label the 'Frankfurt School' by the 1950s, the designation meant as much an academic environment as a geographical location. ...[10]

The Frankfurt School began as the Institute for Social Research in 1923, founded by members of the German Communist Party at Frankfurt University.[11] Influenced by Antonio Gramsci, the theoretician of the Italian Communist Party, they concluded that a radical subversion

---

9   Jamin, p. 5.

10   Ibid., p. 4.

11   Patrick J Buchanan, *The Death of the West*, pp. 78–96.

of the cultural mores and institutions of a society must precede a Communist state.[12] The founding endowment for the Frankfurt School was provided by the international grain speculator, Herman Weil, father of one of the Institute's moving spirits, Felix Weil.[13]

Max Horkheimer, who became the institute's director in 1930,[14] adopted the Gramscian analysis and strategy that a subtle revolution must be made through the penetration and transformation of cultural traditions and institutions.[15] At that time, music critic Theodor Adorno and psychologists Erich Fromm and Wilhelm Reich joined the Frankfurt School.[16] However, in 1933 this largely Jewish group was exiled from Germany with the rise of Hitler. They and other leftist academics left Germany and further afield *en masse* for the USA. With them came the future guru of the New Left, Herbert Marcuse, a graduate student. They re-established the Frankfurt School at Columbia University,[17] where Franz Boas and the school of cultural anthropology had long been ensconced.

12   Ibid., p. 77.
13   Rolf Wiggershaus, *The Frankfurt School: Its History, Theories, Political Significance,* passim.
14   Ibid.
15   Ibid.
16   Ibid.
17   Ibid.

Freudo-Marxian Synthesis

PSYCHOANALYST SIGMUND FREUD laid the premise for Critical Theory in stating that between the individual and society there is a conflict: civilisation rests on the need to repress innate impulses and the demands for instant gratification. Not only a civilisation, but any society with its customs and taboos, must restrain the total freedom of the individual to act on instinct, such as rape and murder. The individual must find outlets for his repressed instincts, which are classifiable into two types: *Thanatos* (death/destruction) and *Eros* (sex). The 'sublimation' of those instincts is expressed as culture. The repressed psychical energy, called *libido*, is redirected into pursuits other than orgasm or aggression. This theory culminated in Freud's influential book *Civilisation and its Discontents*, published in 1930. Freud considered modern civilisation to have reached a crisis point, concluding:

> The fateful question of the human species seems to me to be whether and to what extent the cultural development in it will succeed in mastering the derangements of communal life caused by the human instinct of aggression and self-destruction. ... Men have brought their powers of subduing the forces of nature to such a pitch that by using them they could now very easily exterminate each other to the last man. They know this — hence arises a great part of their current unrest, their dejection, their mood of apprehension. And now it may be expected that the other of the two 'heavenly forces' — immortal *Eros* — will put forth his strength so as to maintain himself alongside of his equally immortal adversary.[1]

---

1   Sigmund Freud, *Civilization and Its Discontents*, pp. 143–144.

To Freudian psychoanalysis the Critical Theorists combined the doctrine of Marx on class struggle. The result was that the individual, rather than the class, must be freed from the oppression and repression of 'bourgeoisie society', and that this primarily involved the free expression of Eros. This reached such dogmatism that by the time *The Authoritarian Personality* was published shortly after World War II, one's mental health was judged on the extent to which one identified with left-wing attitudes. This required a hi-jacking of Freud.

Freud had not claimed that psychoanalysis could heal society. While Freud said that the way neuroses are diagnosed in an individual might be used to diagnose collective or social neuroses, it 'behoves us to be very careful' when using analogies between the individual and society. He thought that diagnosis of 'social neuroses' would not be of use 'since no one possesses power to compel the community to adopt the therapy'. Nonetheless, Freud expected that some day someone would try to diagnose social neuroses.[2] The latter became the purpose of Critical Theory and social science research. Social engineering became the 'therapy'; 'social control' the aim.

---

2   Ibid., p. 142.

New School & Frankfurt School

As a group, these leading intellectuals helped transform the social sciences
and philosophy in this country.

— The New School for Social Research

I
N 1933 A LARGELY Jewish group of academics left Europe for the
USA. This so-called 'University of Exile' was initially employed by
the New School for Social Research (NSSR) in New York, while others
from the Frankfurt School were employed at Columbia University.

The University of Exile, funded by 'enlightened philanthropists
like Hiram Halle[1] and the Rockefeller Foundation,'[2] formed the faculty
of the New School's Graduate Faculty on Political and Social Science.
The NSSR implemented the Rockefeller Foundation's Emergency
Program for European Scholars, 'selected by the [Rockefeller]
Foundation'. The U.S. State Department was consulted and indicated
its complete satisfaction with the project.[3] 'While some of these refugees remained at the New School for many years, others moved on
to make an impact on other institutions in the United States'. Some
became government advisors. 'Others helped transform the social

---

1 Hiram Halle was an owner of Gulf Oil, one of the *Seven Sisters* world oil companies, which merged with David Rockefeller's Standard Oil (Chevron) in 1984.

2 New School, 'History', http://www.newschool.edu/nssr/subpage.aspx?id=9064.

3 'Emergency Program for European Scholars, 1940–1945', Rockefeller Foundation
   Archives, http://74.125.155.132/search?q=cache:tXK4eQ50XbAJ:www.rockarch.
   org/collections/rf/refugee.php.

sciences and philosophy of this country'.[4] The Rockefeller Foundation explains of these Cultural Marxists that upon their arrival each was provided with a teaching post.

> In the case of a scholar received by the New School, it was not expected that he would remain there permanently; the New School aimed merely to be the springboard for his American adventure. Every effort was made to expose scholars to other opportunities; a scholar was transferred immediately upon receipt of an invitation from another institution offering a position with some assurance of permanency. .... Fifty-two scholars actually reached America and assumed teaching.... The total cost of the Emergency Program was, therefore, $437,659.[5]

Andrew Woods,[6] in his attempt to expose and repudiate so-called 'conspiracy theories' on Critical Theory, questions the intimate association between the Frankfurt School and the New School. He sees this as a fallacy of the Right, citing this author's 2011 book *Revolution from Above,* Woods using the tactic of the straw man argument and *reductio ad absurdum* throughout:

> Several decades later, Dewey's brood of American socialist intellectuals were joined by what Bolton calls 'the German counterpart of Fabianism,' The Frankfurt School (otherwise known as the Institute for Social Research).[7] Although only one member of the Frankfurt School — Erich Fromm — actually taught at The New School, Bolton sees the 'University of Exile' facilitating the integration of 'Frankfurtian Marxists' into American intellectual life.[8]

---

4   Ibid.

5   Ibid.

6   Woods is as of writing a doctoral candidate at the Center for the Study of Theory & Criticism, Western University, and a Doctoral Fellow at the Centre for the Analysis of the Radical Right.

7   Woods citing Bolton, *Revolution from Above*, p. 101.

8   Andrew Woods, 'A Secret Invasion: The University in Exile and Conspiracy Theories', Public Seminar, The New School, 20 May 2019; https://publicseminar.org/essays/a-secret-invasion/, citing Bolton, p. 108.

Revolution from Above does not use descriptions such as 'brood'. Woods presumably implies that such terminology is used to give the impression that the book is an extremist polemic rather than meeting standards of scholarship to the extent of being shortlisted as recommended reading by Professor Richard Spence in his book *Wall Street and the Russian Revolution*. Secondly, 'the University of Exile', the sundry academics brought from Europe to the USA courtesy of the Rockefeller Foundation and State Department, is not used in *Revolution from Above* as a euphemism for the Frankfurt School. Rather, the 'University of Exile' is described as a 'large number of socialist intellectuals' fleeing Hitler, who formed the Graduate Faculty of Political and Social Science at the New School.[9] Thirdly, it is the New School that boasts of its relationship with the Frankfurt School, stating:

> The New School for Social Research believes that research and pedagogy should advance economic justice, promote an understanding of change, and train the next generation to influence public debate. **Its commitment to progressive values, academic freedom, rigorous scholarship, and critical theory in the tradition of the Frankfurt School lies at the heart of The New School's history and draws upon the vital legacy of the University in Exile.**[10]

Woods correctly states that *Revolution from Above* cites former White House communications aide and presidential candidate Pat Buchanan's book *The Death of the West* as a reliable secondary source for a brief historical outline of the Frankfurt School:

> Bolton would not be the first to infer a firmer connection between the two institutions of 'social research.' Citing Pat Buchanan's 2002 *The Death of the West*,[11] Bolton claims that the thinkers of the Frankfurt School travelled to

---

9   Bolton, *Revolution from Above*, p. 107.

10   The New School, 'About Us', https://www.newschool.edu/nssr/about-us/. Emphasis added.

11   Patrick J. Buchanan, *The Death of the West*.

America in the 1930s to besmirch traditional American values and destroy Western Civilization.[12]

Just how influential these academics are in the social sciences in the USA, and across the Western world, is again described by the New School:

> From the beginning, The New School maintained close ties to Europe. Its founders had modeled the school in part after the *Volkshochschulen* for adults established in Germany. Then, during the 1920s, Alvin Johnson, The New School's director, became co-editor of the *Encyclopedia of the Social Sciences*. While working on this massive undertaking, Johnson collaborated regularly with colleagues in Germany and elsewhere in Europe. … With the financial support of philanthropist Hiram Halle and the Rockefeller Foundation, he obtained funding to provide a haven in the United States for scholars whose careers (and lives) were threatened by the Nazis, called the University in Exile. This institution was given a home at The New School and sponsored more than 180 individuals and their families, providing them with visas and jobs. Some of these refugees remained at The New School for many years and some moved on to other institutions in the United States, but **the influx of new people and new ideas had an impact on the U.S. academy far beyond any particular university or institute.** …[13]
>
> **As a group, these leading intellectuals helped transform the social sciences and philosophy in this country,** presenting new theoretical and methodological approaches to their fields. …[14]

---

12 Woods, 'A Secret Invasion'.
13 Ibid. Emphasis added.
14 The New School, 'Our History', https://www.newschool.edu/nssr/history/. Emphasis added.

Patronage

Revolution from Above focuses on the bogus character of the primary issues that preoccupy the Left, both past and present, and specifies the funding of these causes and movements by plutocracy. Such associations, which Professor Richard Spence of Idaho University, a specialist on such matters, calls 'connecting the dots', is disparaged mostly with baseless ridicule by apologists, such as Andrew Woods lampooning *Revolution from Above*:

> The New School's Board of Trustees is crammed full of globalist plutocrats who plan to use these left-wing scholars as ground-troops in their assault on 'Tradition.' Under plutocratic control, higher education is intellectual warfare. The unlikely cooperation of Marxist scholars and philanthropists is a key dynamic of what Bolton calls 'dialectical capitalism'.[15]

Woods' allusion, 'The New School's Board of Trustees is crammed full of globalist plutocrats', is supposedly an assertion that is so ridiculous it needs no refutation. As if there could possibly be collusion. Woods is therefore presumably implying, without need for argument, that the Board of Trustees is *not* 'crammed full of globalist plutocrats'. Pages 108 and 109 of *Revolution from Above* cite the affiliations of the trustees at the time, including Salomon Bros., Chevron, Wesco Finance, et al. The New School states of its board:

> The New School is governed by a board of trustees drawn from the ranks of leaders in civil society. The trustees' capacity to chart a course for the university's future is exemplified by the roles they have in business, education, philanthropy, government, media, and other fields. The board meets regularly throughout the year and participates actively in the rich array of public programs, performances, and university ceremonies that characterize The New School.[16]

---

15 Bolton, p. 9, cited by Woods.

16 The New School, 'Board of Trustees', https://www.newschool.edu/about/university-leadership/board-of-trustees/.

Past and present affiliations of current Board members include: Stanley M. Proctor Company, Hudson Executive Capital, Debevoise & Plimpton LLP, Grosvenor Capital Management, Susquehanna International Group, Deutsche Bank, Durst Organization, Newmark Family Properties, Tioga Downs Casino, Vernon Downs Casino, Stone Run Capital LLC, Capital Group Companies, Extell Development Company, DMA Consulting Group, Moelis & Company, Lazard, Salomon Brothers Inc., Shearman & Sterling LLP, Abercrombie & Fitch Co., Life Insurance Company of Boston and New York, AMC Networks, Perry Ellis International, Acertas LLC, Commonwealth Capital Partner, Senturion Forecasting LLC, Davis Polk & Wardwell LLP, Allen and Company, BLS Investments LLC, et al.[17]

Is everyone supposed to remain wilfully blind, to keep up the orthodox pretence that plutocracy and the Left are antithetical, *Emperor's New Clothes* style? Of particular irony, the 'sponsor' of *Public Seminar*, the New School journal where Woods' article is published, is Michael E. Gellert,[18] 'Mr Gellert is a general partner and co-founder of Windcrest Partners, an evergreen venture capital and private equity partnership. He is also a director of Dalet Technologies, director emeritus of Seacor Holdings, and chairman of the board of Smith Barney Worldwide Special Fund NV and numerous private companies'.[19] Woods could not see what was under his own nose.

---

17   The New School, 'Board of Trustees', ibid.

18   Public Seminar, 'Sponsors', https://publicseminar.org/resetpass/.

19   The New School, 'Board of Trustees'. Smith Barney is part of Morgan Stanley.

Funding for Social Sciences

Aid will be given for objective studies on selected problems of realistic importance in social control.

— Rockefeller Foundation, 1934

THE INTEREST OF the oligarchs in the social sciences as a means of social engineering starts well prior to the Hitlerian crisis in Europe. The year 1923 is significant for the social sciences in both Europe and the USA. That year the Institute for Social Research was established as an affiliate of the Johann Wolfgang Goethe University at Frankfurt with an endowment from Hermann Weil,[1] the world's leading grain speculator.[2] Weil had been political adviser to Kaiser Wilhelm II.[3] After the war he secured grain imports from the Ukraine by establishing connections with the new Soviet Government during 1921–1922. Shortly before his death, Hermann was awarded a doctorate *honoris causa* from the Institute for his endowments. His son Felix was a founding member of the Institute and continued to provide funding. Prior to Hitler's assumption to government, Felix Weil settled in Argentina, where his father had established the international grain business. Here Felix diversified the family's commerce:

---

1   Jack Jacobs, *The Frankfurt School, Jewish Lives and Antisemitism*, p. 2.
2   Gebrüder Weill und Partner (Weill Brothers & Co.).
3   John Abromeit, *Max Horkheimer and the Foundations of the Frankfurt School*, p. 56.

> Before Hitler became Chancellor of Germany, Weil left again for South
> America because his family's old company lacked leadership and lost its
> leading position on the international markets. Weil decided to stop the
> trade of grain across the Atlantic and to diversify his own and other family
> members' wealth. Ingeniously he established a net of companies and trust
> companies, and recruited trustworthy men to run all these businesses on a
> daily base. His genius in handling money was greater than he himself was
> willing to recognize.[4]

Felix continued to combine commerce with Communism, as have
others, financing the Argentine Communist Party, acting as adviser
to the Minister of Finance, and in 1933 published a book on tax col-
lecting, and instructed tax collectors. Weil 'commissioned the erec-
tion of a new Art-Déco skyscraper and reserved the highest floor for
himself', but settled in New York City soon after. In New York Max
Horkheimer, head of the Frankfurt Institute, introduced Felix to the
daughter of a banker from Stuttgart, who became his third wife.[5]

In reviewing *Grand Hotel Abyss*,[6] Benjamin Cunningham makes
some pertinent comments about the Left-capitalist nexus of the
Critical Theorists:

> Marxists without Party, Socialists Dependent on Capitalist Money

> No doubt the Frankfurt School thinkers harbor at least as many contra-
> dictions as they diagnosed in the society surrounding them. Their initial
> funding came from Hermann Weil, a capitalist if there ever was one and
> the world's largest grain trader. This led the playwright and Frankfurt
> School opponent Bertolt Brecht to come up with the following joke: 'A rich
> old man dies, disturbed by the poverty in the world. In his will, he leaves a
> large sum to set up an institute which will do research on the source of this
> poverty. Which is of course himself'.

---

4   Christian Fleck, 'Heufelder, Argentinischer Krösus', *Serendipities: Journal for
the Sociology & History of the Social Sciences*, Vol. 3, No. 1, 2018.

5   Ibid.

6   Stuart Jeffries, *Grand Hotel Abyss: The Lives of the Frankfurt School*.

Most of the Frankfurt School criticized the capitalist system while enjoying pleasures delivered by that same system. Starting with their American exile years, it was institute policy to discourage the use of Marx's name in writing so as to not threaten funding. During World War II, Marcuse and others worked for the OSS (precursor to the CIA). Upon returning to Germany the Frankfurt School conducted research for the Federal Republic. Even as they doubted scientific truth was possible in an environment poisoned by ideology, they thought themselves uniquely capable of seeing through mist to interpret the world as it is. As Jeffries notes, the Frankfurt School was comprised of 'Marxists without party, socialists dependent on capitalist money, beneficiaries of a society they sniffily disdained and without which they would have had nothing to write about'.[7]

When the Frankfurt Institute was relocated to Columbia University, with sponsorship from the Rockefeller Foundation and the State Department, 'one of the main reasons why the affiliation went smoothly was the abundance of funds the institute had at its disposal and was transferring to these shores'. Friedrich Pollock, a founder and director of the Institute (1928–1930), outlined in a letter the exact financial background of the Institute, which included in 1934 an endowment of 5 million Swiss francs, a considerable sum at the time of the Great Depression. The institute's budget for 1935, according to Pollock, was $100,000.[8]

Social Science Research Council

In the USA from 1922, Rockefeller money, through the Laura Spelman Rockefeller Memorial (LSRM),[9] started funding the social sciences. In 1923, 'social scientists came together to organize the Social Science Research Council, and the Council—under the Memorial's developing agenda—became an early and prominent recipient of Rockefeller

---

7 Benjamin Cunningham, 'Myth over Math', *Aspen Review*, No. 4, 2017; https://www.aspen.review/article/2017/myth-over-math/.

8 Judith T Marcus and Zoltan Tar (eds.), *Foundations of the Frankfurt School of Social Research*, Introduction.

9 The Memorial was consolidated into the Rockefeller Foundation in 1929.

support. Well into the final years of the Second World War, Rockefeller funds provided more than ninety percent of the financing at the Council.[10] Rockefeller money was instrumental in forming the SSRC:

> Charles Merriam, President of the American Political Science Association, first promoted the idea of a research council that would work toward 'the closer integration of all the social sciences' and develop interdisciplinary approaches for the solution of social problems. Beardsley Ruml, President of the Laura Spelman Rockefeller Memorial (LSRM), worked with Merriam and others to establish the Social Science Research Council (SSRC) for this purpose in 1923.[11]

The Rockefeller Foundation states that,

> with support first from LSRM and then the RF (along with other foundations such as Russell Sage and the Carnegie Corporation), **SSRC rapidly became an operating arm of the foundation world** similar to the role played in science by the National Research Council and in the humanities by the American Council for Learned Societies.[12]

The Rockefeller Foundation's annual report for 1934 brazenly stated that this interest was a matter of 'social control' and of managing the problems of international capitalism:

> **In the field of social science aid will be given for objective studies on selected problems of realistic importance in social control**, through the methods of direct factual study, training of personnel, and basic research. In many such fields, the work is beset with great difficulties, the stakes are so large that their attainment is worthy of tremendous effort. International relations form a case in point. Objective studies in the problems relating to economic security will be fostered, both those relating to the business

---

10 Rockefeller Foundation Digital History, 'Social Science Research Council', https://rockfound.rockarch.org/social-science-research-council.

11 Ibid.

12 Ibid. Emphasis added.

cycle and those arising from attempts to ameliorate the effects upon the individual of economic instability.[13]

The Encyclopaedia of Social Sciences was funded by the Rockefeller Foundation from 1932.[14]

The social sciences programme has an international scope, with the Foundation supporting both its own fellowships and those of the Social Science Research Council: 'The award of fellowships to advanced scholars has been a principal element in the social science program from its beginning.'[15] In 1932, for example, throughout the world 'there were 167 active fellows under Foundation supervision.'[16] Institutions in the USA and overseas received funding, with the London School of Economics being regarded as particularly important.[17]

Despite occasional assumptions as to why the Foundations fund supposedly 'anti-capitalist' causes, the oligarchy has never lost control over its funds. At the time the president of the Rockefeller Foundation was Owen D. Young, industrialist, founder of RCA, head of General Electric, counsel to U.S. presidents, and author of the Young Plan on German reparations after World War I. Chairman of the Board of Trustees was John D. Rockefeller Jr.

The influence of the Foundations on the social sciences was explained in an article by Dr. Maribel Morey, a specialist in the history of philanthropy:

Of course, the individual research priorities, preferences, and prejudices of the SSRC's leadership and teams of scholars help explain the Council's

---

13 Rockefeller Foundation, Annual Report, 1934, p. 12; https://assets.rockefeller-foundation.org/app/uploads/20150530122121/Annual-Report-1934.pdf.

14 Rockefeller Foundation, Annual Report, 1932, p. 270; https://assets.rockefel-lerfoundation.org/app/uploads/20150530122117/Annual-Report-1932.pdf.

15 Rockefeller Foundation, Annual Report, 1934, p. 267.

16 Ibid., p. 268.

17 Ibid., p. 271.

decisions at these separate junctures. But read together, they also betray the **critical influence of another group of actors in shaping research priorities in the social sciences and even more specifically at the Council: leading private foundations.** This is to say that the SSRC's intellectual history should be understood not only as a story about networks of social scientists and these individuals' idiosyncratic research preferences but also as one about the Council's developing relationships with philanthropies and these organizations' varying fortunes and research priorities over the years. For today's Council, and US social scientists more broadly, this history furthermore should suggest the need for continuing self-reflection on **how their own research agendas might be influenced by funders.** And this self-reflection is important. After all, we all would benefit from living in a world where social scientists are acutely aware of how their **research priorities might be echoing what leading funders want** rather than what they as scholars find vitally important to investigate or even what their societies need most from their social scientists.[18]

Among the present directors of the Social Science Research Council is Michael Gellert, who, as we have seen, is a trustee of the New School. Other interesting associations on the SSRC board include: William H. Janeway, a director of Warburg Pincus international investment firm; Peter Nager, Principal of Skyview Ventures, a venture capital investment firm, and formerly a partner with the investment banking firm James D. Wolfensohn Inc., and Deutsche Bank; José A. Scheinkman, vice-president in the Financial Strategies Group of Goldman, Sachs & Co.; Vishakha N. Desai, president and CEO *emerita* of the Asia Society (founded by John D. Rockefeller III in 1956, to promote the economic penetration of Asia), and a director on the corporate board of Mahindra and Mahindra, 'one of the five largest global companies in India'.[19]

18   Maribel Morey, *Items (Social Science Research Council)*, 8 January 2019; https://items.ssrc.org/insights/rockefeller-carnegie-and-the-ssrcs-focus-on-race-in-the-1920s-and-1930s/.

19   Social Science Research Council, 'Board of Directors', https://www.ssrc.org/about/board-of-directors/.

The president (*ex officio*) of the SSRC is Alondra Nelson, recipient of Ford Foundation funding for her research on Black studies,[20] which seems to have a decidedly 'activist' approach, indicated by one of her books, *Body and Soul: The Black Panther Party & the Fight Against Medical Discrimination*, in which she argues for the Black Panthers' 'broader struggle for social justice'.[21] The SSRC vice-president of programs is Ronald Kassimir, who took time off from the SSRC during 2005 to 2013 to become a prominent staff member of the New School, as associate dean and associate professor in the Department of Politics, associate provost for research and special projects, and co-chair of the New School's committee on the reaccreditation process.[22]

The 'visiting committee', the advisory group for the SSRC, includes: Cheng Li of the Brookings Institution, the influential Washington think tank; Mark Kingdon of Kingdon Capital Management; Peter Nager of Egret Capital Partners; Joseph Schull, founder of Corton Capital; Marina Whitman, formerly of General Motors; Michael Gellert, and others from academia, and from law firms concerned with global investing.[23]

The Rockefeller Foundation remains a primary patron of the New School.[24] In 1980 George Soros was awarded an honorary doctorate by the New School.[25] The NSSR's social research conferences initiated in 1988 are funded by Open Society, the Rockefeller Foundation, Rockefeller Financial Services, etc., with institutional collaboration

---

20 Ibid.

21 Alondra Nelson, http://www.alondranelson.com/books/body-and-soul-the-black-panther-party-and-the-fight-against-medical-discrimination.

22 SSRC, https://www.ssrc.org/staff/kassimir-ronald/.

23 SSRC, 'Visiting Committee', https://www.ssrc.org/about/visiting-committee-to-the-social-science-research-council/.

24 The New School, http://blogs.newschool.edu/news/2017/12/new-school-col-laboratory-call-for-projects/#.Win3UfmWaM8, https://www.newschool.edu/pressroom/pressreleases/2009/desis.aspx.

25 Steven G. Koven and Frank Götzke, *American Immigration Policy: Confronting the Nation's Challenges* (Springer, 2010), p. 91.

from the Open Society Institute, Asia Society (Rockefellers), etc.[26] The New School's economic research department was founded and is chaired by Bernard Schwartz, a senior fellow with the Council on Foreign Relations and Brookings Institute, and former chief executive of Loral, the defence industry contractor.[27]

Motives

Why do some of the wealthiest businessmen support the Left with what is termed 'philanthropy'? Caroline Glick, a strategist of wide experience,[28] writing of George Soros, explains:

> The first thing that we see is the megalomaniacal nature of Soros's philanthropic project. No corner of the globe is unaffected by his efforts. No policy area is left untouched. On the surface, the vast number of groups and people he supports seem unrelated. After all, what does climate change have to do with illegal African immigration to Israel? What does Occupy Wall Street have to do with Greek immigration policies? But the fact is that Soros-backed projects share basic common attributes.... They all work to weaken the ability of national and local authorities in Western democracies to uphold the laws and values of their nations and communities. ... In other words, their goal is to subvert Western democracies and make it impossible for governments to maintain order or for societies to retain their unique identities and values. ... The notion at the heart of the push for the legalization of unfettered immigration is that states should not be able to protect their national identities. ... Parallel to these efforts are others geared toward rejecting the right of Western democracies to uphold long-held social norms. Soros-supported groups, for instance, stand behind the push not only for gay marriage but for unisex public bathrooms. ... the peoples of the West need to recognize the common foundations of all Soros's actions. They need to realize as well that the only response to

---

26 Social Research Conference Series, https://www.newschool.edu/cps/conference-series/.

27 'U.S. Competiveness in the 21st Century', Schwartz Forum, Brookings Institute, 19 April 2006; https://www.brookings.edu/wp-content/uploads/2012/04/20060428.pdf.

28 *Jerusalem Post*, http://www.jpost.com/Author/Caroline-B-Glick.

these premeditated campaigns of subversion is for the people of the West to stand up for their national rights and their individual right to security. They must stand with the national institutions that guarantee that security, in accordance with the rule of the law, and uphold and defend their national values and traditions.[29]

The Rockefeller Foundation explains that it is about global 'integrated economies'. In the U.S. the issues have 'primarily centered on marriage equality and, more recently, public attention to the experiences of transgender people'. Speakers at a 2014 Rockefeller Foundation seminar 'emphasized that funding and policy focus largely remains on health and human rights issues, which neglects the ways in which both areas are interrelated with economic wellbeing'.[30]

A basic error of so-called 'right-wing' critics of the tax-exempt foundations in sponsoring Cultural Marxism is to assume that the dichotomy is one of 'free enterprise versus collectivism', and that these oligarchic funds have been infiltrated and taken over by Marxists who are using the wealth of their enemies to destroy capitalism. For example in an early exposé of the left-wing orientation of the social sciences, conservative researcher Zygmund Dobbs wrote:

> Academic leftists were experts in the technique of separating millionaires from their money while simultaneously vociferating that the wealthy were an evil element that had to be eliminated. In the ensuing years, the socialists accomplished the amazing feat of getting control of the giant foundations, all founded by men who had devoted their lives to the free enterprise system and owed to it their enormous fortunes.[31]

Dobbs had little understanding of the factors involved.

---

29 Caroline B. Glick, 'Our World: Soros' Campaign of Global Chaos', *Jerusalem Post*, 22 August 2016, http://www.jpost.com/Opinion/Our-World-Soross-campaign-of-global-chaos-464770.

30 'Inclusive Economies, Sexual Orientation, and Gender Identity Expression', Rockefeller Foundation, 15 August 2014, https://www.rockefellerfoundation.org/blog/inclusive-economies-sexual-orientation/.

31 Z. Dobbs, *The Great Deceit: Social Pseudo-Sciences*, p. 195.

Rather it is plutocracy that has been manipulating the Left in promoting an integrated economy by the use of Leftist doctrines that break down barriers to such an economy. It is the same strategy that was used by Edward Bernays, father of public relations (which he termed 'engineering consent') when, hired by the American Tobacco Company, he promoted cigarettes as the 'symbol of the liberated woman' for the purpose of expanding the market. Consider how this same principle is used for the causes that are promoted as 'progressive' and funded by oligarchic wealth. The following description of how women were manipulated into becoming consumers of tobacco in the name of 'emancipation' could be applied to the sundry causes of so-called 'social justice' that are funded by plutocracy:

When the Irish born American *femme fatale* Lola Montez had her photograph taken at a Boston studio in 1851, neither she nor anyone else could foresee the future symbolic value of the cigarette as a sign of emancipation for women and the tragic development that we are now facing with women as the next wave of the tobacco epidemic. ...So widespread was the social stigma attached to women smoking that as late as 1908 a woman in New York was arrested for smoking a cigarette in public, and in 1921 a bill was proposed in the US Congress to ban women from smoking in the District of Columbia.

It is therefore remarkable that within 50 years of the invention of the mass produced cigarette, smoking among women in North America and northern Europe has become socially acceptable and even socially desirable. This was due not only to the dramatic changes in the social and economic status of women over this period, but also to the way in which the tobacco industry capitalised on changing social attitudes towards women by promoting smoking as a symbol of emancipation, a 'torch of freedom'. This message is still being promoted today by the tobacco industry around the world, particularly in countries which have recently undergone or are undergoing rapid social change.

... The First World War proved to be a watershed in both the emancipation of women and the spread of smoking among women. During the war many women had not only taken on 'male' occupations but had also started to wear trousers, play sports, cut their hair, and smoke. Subsequently attitudes towards women smoking began to change, and more and more women started to use the cigarette as a weapon in their increasing challenge to traditional ideas about female behaviour.

Another important element in the company's campaign to change the image of smoking was to challenge the social taboo against women smoking in public. In 1929 there was the much publicised event in the Easter Sunday parade in New York where Great American Tobacco hired several young women to smoke their 'torches of freedom' (Lucky Strikes) as they marched down Fifth Avenue protesting against women's inequality. This event generated widespread newspaper coverage and provoked a national debate. As Bernays reflected later, 'Age old customs, I learned, could be broken down by a dramatic appeal, disseminated by the network of the media'.[32]

Just as the American Tobacco Company hired Bernays to promote smoking by women as a symbol of their emancipation, 'age old customs' are broken down by Critical Theorists and other leftist academics with oligarchic sponsorship. Two female scholars who authorised a paper published in *Tobacco Control* allude to the way tobacco is now spreading among women in countries that have 'recently undergone or are undergoing rapid social change'. These are the countries that have experienced the 'colour revolutions' promoted by Soros, Ford, Rockefeller *et al*, where feminism, pushed along with programmes for 'women's reproductive rights', has made hitherto traditional states into what Soros calls 'open societies', open, that is, to globalisation in the name of 'human rights'.[33]

---

32 Amanda Amos, Margaretha Hagland, 'From Social Taboo to "Torch of Freedom" : The Marketing of Cigarettes to Women', *Tobacco Control*, Vol. 9, No. 1; https://tobaccocontrol.bmj.com/content/9/1/3.

33 On the 'colour revolutions' see Bolton, *Revolution from Above*, pp. 213–244.

London School of Economics & Political Science

David Rockefeller and George Soros attended the London School of Economics. They imbibed the free market economics of Hayek, who taught there (1931–1950)[34] at the same time as eminent Fabian socialist Harold Laski (1926–1950). Rockefeller and Soros were instructed in classical liberalism in an institution founded by Fabian socialists, funded from the start to the present day by international financiers, and still associated with the Fabian Society.[35]

As pointed out in *Revolution from Above*, the London School of Economics (LSE) was founded by the Fabians for the purpose of training the public servants that would administer a world state, with endowments from international financiers.[36] Affiliated with the University of London, the commerce degree was initiated with an appeal for funds from The City of London; i.e. the centre of international finance. Additionally, 'a large sum' was given by Sir Ernest Cassel, from which £150,000 came in 1920 to endow commerce training, and grants for modern languages and scholarships.[37] A biographical sketch

---

34 'Friedrich von Hayek', London School of Economics, http://www.lse.ac.uk/about-lse/lse-people/Friedrich-von-Hayek.

35 Today, the society and the LSE continue to work closely together, Fabian Society, 'Our History', https://fabians.org.uk/about-us/our-history/.

36 Bolton, *Revolution from Above*, pp. 98–100.

37 William H. Beveridge, *The London School of Economics and Its Problems 1919–1937*, pp. 15–16. Beveridge was director of the LSE from 1919–1937. Like Fabian directors Sidney and Beatrice Webb, George Bernard Shaw, H. G. Wells, and other Fabian eminences, Beveridge was an enthusiast for eugenics, to curtail the breeding of undesirable elements of the proletariat. Beveridge, credited as the father of Britain's 'welfare state', contended in 1909, 'those men who through general defects are unable to fill such a whole place in industry, are to be recognised as "unemployable". They must become the acknowledged dependents of the State… but with complete and permanent loss of all citizen rights — including not only the franchise but civil freedom and fatherhood'. See: Dennis Sewell, 'How Eugenics Poisoned the Welfare State', *Spectator*, 25 November 2009; https://web.archive.org/web/20101203124517/http://www.spectator.co.uk/essays/all/5571423/part_4/how-eugenics-poisoned-the-welfare-state.thtml.

of Cassel, from a reputable Jewish source (hence, not liable to charges of 'anti-Semitism'), states:

> From 1884 until 1910 Cassel was an independent merchant banker in London, building a vast web of international finance that included investments in Latin America, South Africa and the United States (which most Anglo-Jewish bankers avoided). He also held domestic finance concerns, for instance for Vickers, the armaments manufacturers. Cassel became one of the closest friends of the Prince of Wales (later King Edward VII) … and was an exemplar of the Prince's 'Jewish Court'...[38]

The association between the Rockefellers and the LSE has been close since 1923. David Rockefeller studied there during 1937–1938 under Lionel Robbins and Friedrich von Hayek, eminences in the theory of free market economics. In his eulogy Professor Michael Cox describes David Rockefeller's association with the LSE, the pivotal role played by the Rockefellers in funding the LSE, and the important role of LSE alumni throughout the world:

> After the First World War, the Rockefellers began to take the social sciences increasingly seriously and, led by the remarkable Chicago-trained political psychologist Beardsley Ruml, contributed enormously to the School, both in terms of LSE's actual fabric and in supporting serious research across the board. Although not the School's only source of income in the interwar period, the Rockefeller support (notably between 1923 and 1937) was certainly of great importance in helping LSE to become regarded as a world class research institution by the end of the 1930s — one which to the present day seeks to use the knowledge it creates to understand the causes of things and improve society.

> Furthermore, the Rockefellers' connection to LSE tells us much about the wider and invaluable relationship the School has always had — and continues to have — with the United States. Put simply, LSE has welcomed many thousands of brilliant American students and faculty to Houghton Street over the years.

---

38 'Ernest Cassel', Jewish Lives Project, https://www.jewishlivesproject.com/profiles/ernest-cassel.

Throughout the School's history, US alumni have left Houghton Street and gone on to influence government, politics and society. David Rockefeller was one such person — a prominent and distinguished inter-war American LSE alumnus who left an indelible mark on the world.[39]

Carnegie Corporation

The first of the great tax-exempt foundations established for reconstructing society was that of Andrew Carnegie, owner of the Carnegie Steel Company. Having retired and with what he regarded as an excess of wealth, he founded the Carnegie Corporation in 1911 to dispense his fortune in perpetuity. The establishment of the trust was suggested by Carnegie's friend, Senator Elihu Root, Wall Street lawyer, Secretary of War, and Secretary of State under Presidents Theodore Roosevelt and William McKinley.

There is much about Andrew Carnegie's social philosophy for disposing of vast wealth that seems commendable, almost in the style of the European aristocrat's *noblesse oblige*. However, Carnegie explained his 'gospel of wealth' as one of unrestrained economic competition in the 19th century sense of Social Darwinism; an economic free-for-all and survival-of-the-fittest. He was an exponent of classical liberalism. Carnegie explained:

> The price which society pays for the law of competition, like the price it pays for cheap comforts and luxuries, is also great; but the advantages of this law are also greater still, for it is to this law that we owe our wonderful material development, which brings improved conditions in its train. But, whether the law be benign or not, we must say of it, as we say of the change in the conditions of men to which we have referred: It is here; we cannot evade it; no substitutes for it have been found; and while the law may be sometimes hard for the individual, it is best for the race, because it insures the **survival of the fittest** in every department. **We accept and welcome therefore, as conditions to which we must accommodate ourselves, great**

---

39 Michael Cox, 'David Rockefeller', LSE, 3 April 2017; https://blogs.lse.ac.uk/condolences/2017/04/03/david-rockefeller/. Emphasis added.

inequality of environment, the concentration of business, industrial and commercial, in the hands of a few, and the law of competition between these, as being not only beneficial, but essential for the future progress of the race.[40]

This Social Darwinism as the engine of 'progress' was the rationalisation for the unrestrained free market capitalism of the 19th century, and was widely acclaimed as the epitome of human achievement. In a sense, it is also the outlook of Karl Marx in stating that 'great inequality of environment, the concentration of business, industrial and commercial, in the hands of a few, and the law of competition between these', are essential for progress as a phase in the cycle of historical materialism. While Marx saw such steps as leading inexorably to socialism, Carnegie saw these as the progressive development of capitalism toward more concentrated forms. Carnegie rejected 'socialism', but both he and Marx saw the future, in the name of 'progress', as one of increasing economic concentration.

Carnegie's doctrine was that vast wealth created by the free market can be used to reconstruct society, but it must be done not by the state but by those best fitted to organise the redistribution of wealth; those who create it, the oligarchy. The oligarchy constitutes an elite that should dispense wealth towards projects above and beyond states, transcending national interests and traditional bonds. The laws of Social Darwinism forge this elite through economic struggle:

Having accepted these, it follows that **there must be great scope for the exercise of special ability in the merchant and in the manufacturer who has to conduct affairs upon a great scale. That this talent for organization and management is rare among men is proved by the fact that it invariably secures for its possessor enormous rewards, no matter where or under what laws or conditions.** The experienced in affairs always rate the MAN whose services can be obtained as a partner as not only the first

---

40 Andrew Carnegie, 'Wealth', *North American Review*, Vol. CXLVIII, June 1889. Reprinted in Andrew Carnegie, *The Gospel of Wealth and Other Timely Essays*. Emphasis added.

consideration, but such as to render the question of his capital scarcely worth considering, for such men soon create capital; while, without the special talent required, capital soon takes wings. Such men become interested in firms or corporations using millions; and estimating only simple interest to be made upon the capital invested, it is inevitable that their income must exceed their expenditures, and that they must accumulate wealth. Nor is there any middle ground which such men can occupy, because the **great manufacturing or commercial concern which does not earn at least interest upon its capital soon becomes bankrupt. It must either go forward or fall behind: to stand still is impossible.** It is a condition essential for its successful operation that it should be thus far profitable, and even that, in addition to interest on capital, it should make profit. It is a law, as certain as any of the others named, that **men possessed of this peculiar talent for affair, under the free play of economic forces, must, of necessity, soon be in receipt of more revenue than can be judiciously expended upon themselves; and this law is as beneficial for the race as the others.**

…Not evil, but good, has come to the race from the accumulation of wealth by those who have the ability and energy that produce it. …[41]

Carnegie advocated graduated tax on wealth; particularly tax on inherited wealth. This might seem a puzzling contradiction for an exponent of free market Social Darwinism. Rather, it is an example of the 'socialism' of the oligarchy. Carnegie wrote:

The growing disposition to tax more and more heavily large estates left at death is a cheering indication of the growth of a salutary change in public opinion. The State of Pennsylvania now takes—subject to some exceptions—one-tenth of the property left by its citizens. The budget presented in the British Parliament the other day proposes to increase the death-duties; and, most significant of all, **the new tax is to be a graduated one. Of all forms of taxation, this seems the wisest.** Men who continue hoarding great sums all their lives, the proper use of which for — public ends would work good to the community, should be made to feel that the community, in the form of the state, cannot thus be deprived of its proper share. **By**

---

41   Andrew Carnegie, 'Wealth', ibid. Emphasis added.

taxing estates heavily at death the state marks its condemnation of the selfish millionaire's unworthy life.[42]

Karl Marx had listed in *The Communist Manifesto* ten premises for establishing Communism, including: (2) a heavy progressive or graduated income tax; (3) abolition of all right of inheritance.[43] Oligarchs with the immense wealth of Carnegie or Rockefeller could establish tax exempt foundations. What might be viewed as 'outsiders', wealthy but not part of the oligarchy centered on Wall Street, could be eliminated by taxation. Carnegie was unequivocal in stating that the dispensing of wealth on social agendas would rest with the oligarchy; not with the state:

> There remains, then, only one mode of using great fortunes; but in this we have the true antidote for the **temporary unequal distribution of wealth**, the reconciliation of the rich and the poor—a reign of harmony—another ideal, differing, indeed, from that of the Communist in requiring only the further evolution of existing conditions, not the total overthrow of our civilization.[44]

Carnegie is being disingenuous in referring to the 'temporary unequal distribution of wealth'. He had explained his doctrine as being one of Social Darwinism and the free market that left in the gutter those who could not 'survive', until mitigated, lest the danger of revolt arise, by the charity of the oligarchs. Carnegie reiterates that industrial civilisation is founded on 'the most intense individualism'. Carnegie mentions the 'ideal state'; and he made it clear that this state will be the creation of the oligarchic elite, with the strategic use of wealth. With the use of *doublespeak* Carnegie assures his readers that oligarchic wealth will become 'public' wealth, but that this will be based entirely on its administration by the oligarchy through the tax exempt foundations.

---

42 Ibid. Emphasis added.

43 Karl Marx, *The Communist Manifesto* (1848), Ch.: 'Proletarians and Communists'.

44 Andrew Carnegie, 'Wealth'. Emphasis added.

The oligarchy will assume power by circumventing the state with the dispensing of its wealth where it sees fit, for the benefit of the mass of plebeians, who will be grateful for it:

> It is founded upon the present most intense individualism, and the race is projected to put it in practice by degree whenever it pleases. Under its sway we shall have an ideal state, in which the surplus wealth of the few will become, in the best sense the property of the many, because administered for the common good, and **this wealth, passing through the hands of the few**, can be made a much more potent force for the elevation of our race than if it had been distributed in small sums to the people themselves. Even the poorest can be made to see this, and to agree that great sums gathered by some of their fellow-citizens and spent for public purposes, from which the masses reap the principal benefit, are more valuable to them than if scattered among them through the course of many years in trifling amounts through the course of many years.
>
> Thus is the problem of Rich and Poor to be solved. **The laws of accumulation will be left free; the laws of distribution free. Individualism will continue, but the millionaire will be but a trustee for the poor; intrusted for a season with a great part of the increased wealth of the community, but administering it for the community far better than it could or would have done for itself.**[45]

When Carnegie died, his position as chairman of the board of the Carnegie Corporation was assumed in 1919 by Elihu Root. Dr. Spence refers to Root as 'a perfect embodiment of American plutocracy'.[46]

Root was an early and influential exponent of American global hegemony. He was the primary author of the Platt Amendment on Cuba.[47] The Root Commission went to Russia in the aftermath of the March 1917 Revolution. Like the American Red Cross Mission

---

45   Ibid. Emphasis added.

46   Richard B. Spence, *Wall Street and the Russian Revolution 1905–1925*, p. 163.

47   The Platt Amendment was imposed with the ostensible intention of 'protecting Cuban independence', an early example of the U.S. justification for global intervention.

in the same period,[48] the Root Commission was mostly comprised of Wall Street interests, seeking investment opportunities with the Revolutionary Provisional Government.[49]

The Carnegie Corporation became one of the primary patrons of the social sciences, established two years prior to his friend John D. Rockefeller establishing the Laura Spelman Memorial. Carnegie became a primary funder of the Social Science Research Council.

An American Dilemma

One of the Research Council's most influential projects was the sponsoring of the Swedish economist Gunnar Myrdal, to lead a study on the negro in the USA. This was published as *An American Dilemma*. The Carnegie Corporation states of this:

> In the fall of 1938, Myrdal and his family arrived in New York City from Stockholm and he soon met with the SSRC's Donald Young who, at the request of Carnegie Corporation president Keppel, would help coordinate and staff the project. Early in the spring of 1939, Young assisted Myrdal in organizing a three-day conference in order to bring together a key group of staff members, including black political scientist Ralph Bunche, who had just recently returned to the United States after a two-year SSRC fellowship abroad. Indeed, Young would play a critical role in guiding Myrdal through the planning of research projects. ...[50]

Maribel Morey, a specialist on the history of U.S. philanthropies, and editor of *HistPhil*, in describing the Rockefeller and Carnegie funding of research on the American negro, comments that these foundations, through their funding, were able to set the agendas of the social sciences, writing of the

---

48 Richard B. Spence, pp. 167–171.

49 Ibid., pp. 162–163.

50 Gunnar Myrdal, *An American Dilemma: The Negro Problem and Modern Democracy*, x.

critical influence of another group of actors in shaping research priorities in the social sciences and even more specifically at the Council: leading private foundations. This is to say that the SSRC's intellectual history should be understood not only as a story about networks of social scientists and these individuals' idiosyncratic research preferences but also as one about the Council's developing relationships with philanthropies and these organizations' varying fortunes and research priorities over the years. For today's Council, and US social scientists more broadly, this history furthermore should suggest the need for continuing self-reflection on how their own research agendas might be influenced by funders. And this self-reflection is important. After all, we all would benefit from living in a world where social scientists are acutely aware of how their research priorities might be echoing what leading funders want rather than what they as scholars find vitally important to investigate or even what their societies need most from their social scientists.[51]

In assessing the importance of *An American Dilemma*, Dr. Shari Cohen, writing for the Carnegie Corporation, states that the publication 'has been called one of the most important works of social science of the twentieth century.'[52] Myrdal based his moral argument on the discrepancy between the existence of segregation and the ideal of the 'American Creed'. A primary element was the dilemma of having fought 'Nazi racism', while racism remained in American institutions. Cohen writes that a 'key facet of Myrdal's argument was to set the study in an international context, predicting that Americans, having defined World War II as a struggle for liberty and equality and against Nazi racism, would force a redefinition and reexamination of race in the United States.'[53]

---

51   M. Morey, 'Rockefeller, Carnegie, and the SSRC's Focus on Race in the 1920s and 1930s', Social Science Research Council, 8 January 2019; https://items.ssrc.org/insights/rockefeller-carnegie-and-the-ssrcs-focus-on-race-in-the-1920s-and-1930s/.

52   Shari Cohen, 'The Lasting Legacy of an American Dilemma', *Carnegie Results*, Carnegie Corporation of New York, Fall 2004.

53   Ibid.

Eliminating the vestiges of race separatism would enhance the USA's world prestige: 'Myrdal also thought that the treatment of blacks in the U.S. would affect its international prestige and power'. Cohen, quoting David Southern,[54] writes of the long-term influence on policy-makers and the impact of the social sciences, that '[w]ith the increase in teaching of social sciences after the war "a generation of future racial reformers in the Kennedy and Johnson administrations of the 1960s grew up on an academic diet of Myrdal"'. Martin Luther King lauded Myrdal for making race relations 'a moral issue'. Perhaps most far-reaching, the Supreme Court, in *Brown vs. Board*,[55] the landmark case on school desegregation, cited the book.[56]

When writing of the excessive wealth that would be used for philanthropy, Dr. Carrol Quigley, the liberal-internationalist Harvard and Georgetown senior historian, who had on his own account studied the institutions of the international financial 'network', said that 'to some extent' the spending of excess wealth on philanthropy included a 'realization that the position and privileges of the very wealthy could be preserved better with superficial concessions and increased opportunity for the discontented to blow off steam than from any policy of blind obstructionism on the part of the rich'. Quigley mentions the Carnegie Foundation in this process.[57] Quigley also mentioned that the Carnegie and Rockefeller Foundations 'were themselves

---

54 David W. Southern, *Gunnar Myrdal and Black-White Relations*, p. 111.

55 Brown vs. the Board of Education of Topeka, Kansas. The Supreme Court unanimously ruled on 17 May 1954 that school segregation was unconstitutional. In September 1957, President Eisenhower sent the 101st Airborne Division to Central High School in Little Rock, Arkansas, to enforce desegregation at bayonet point, in a domestic enforcement of the 'American Creed', that is increasingly played out over the world in the name of global human rights, democracy, and equality,

56 Shari Cohen.

57 Carrol Quigley, *Tragedy & Hope: A History of the World in Our Time*, pp. 75–76.

interlocking groups controlled by an alliance of [J. P.] Morgan and Rockefeller interests in Wall Street'.[58]

---

58 Carrol Quigley, ibid., pp. 946–947. Quigley was here commenting on the 1951 Senate investigation into the role of the Institute of Pacific Relations (IPR) in the fall of China to Mao Zedong. Most of the funding for the IPR came from the Carnegie and Rockefeller Foundations, and associated Wall Street interests such as Standard Oil, ITT, Chase, National City Bank. (p. 947). Quigley is disparaging about the right-wing conspiracy theories on Communist infiltration of the IPR and the fall of China, and states that what is usually supposed to be the work of Communist agents, is that of an 'international network' that works similar to Communist subversion, the operations of which Quigley had studied for 20 years, and whose papers he examined in the 1960s. Quigley explained that he had 'no aversion to most of the aims' of this network, and had worked 'close to it' for much of his life. Quigley's main difference of opinion with it was 'that it wishes to remain unknown, and I believe its role in history is significant enough to be known.' (p. 950).

'Social Control' & 'Social Engineering'

Complete control over the physical and psychical and social structure of the individual or the group.

— CHARLES MERRIAM, Social Science Research Council

CHARLES MERRIAM of the Social Science Research Council was a proponent of social control and social engineering to direct human development and evolution. He envisioned a brave new world overseen by social scientists, who would form a new humanity. He redefined politics in terms of social science, 'the new politics which is to emerge in the new world: that of the conscious control of human evolution...'[1] Technology would create 'international obligations', and 'the ancient idea of the state' would be destroyed or modified.[2] A 'new world of science' would allow 'a new race of beings' to 'master nature' on a universal scale.

Merriam announced the dogmatic breach between the social and biological sciences, stating that 'social training and the environment' can transcend any superficial differences. If genetics shows otherwise, then eugenics can eliminate undesirable traits,[3] while psychoanalysis has a large role to play in 'intelligent social control',[4] and in the future

---

1   Charles Merriam, *New Aspects of Politics*, xvi.
2   Ibid., p. 5.
3   Ibid., pp. 81–82.
4   Ibid., p. 84.

the understanding of biochemistry might enable the bio-engineering of individuals and populations (aided by social psychology).[5] The study of chromosomes might allow for induced variations by conditioning; 'this is the key to social training'.[6] The study of child behaviour will enable the social scientist to determine the 'political attitudes and interests of the later citizen'.[7] Foreshadowing *The Authoritarian Personality* and other studies of the Frankfurt School *et al,* Merriam suggested that one's politics might be predicted by charting one's 'traits, habits, responses, behavior', and allow for the possibilities of being 'controlled or modified'.[8]

These gains in science will replace the laws and customs of tradition. This is the new 'democratic' science that replaces the former questions as to whether a group is an 'organism', or has a 'spirit' or 'soul',[9] with the study of humanity as 'units of measure and comparison'.[10] The counting-house mentality came to dominate science; English utilitarianism and materialism had overthrown the few remaining vestiges of tradition. It is here that the dichotomy between Tradition and Modernism becomes most apparent; between Right and Left, organic community versus civil society.

Darwinian evolution would eventually destroy whatever vestiges remained of traditional societies. Because evolution is based on 'variation and adaptation' as part of a 'ceaseless process',[11] humanity will be placed in a continual state of flux, without the roots that tradition maintains. The world is one of 'unceasing reorganization and readjustment'.[12] This requires the elimination of cultural heritages and

---

5   Ibid., p. 89.
6   Ibid., p. 144.
7   Ibid., p. 85.
8   Ibid., p. 92.
9   Ibid., p. 94.
10 Ibid.
11 Ibid., p. 141.
12 Ibid., p. 159.

customs that are a hindrance to the 'new world'. The maintenance of institutions in the past and the present has 'depended on a backward look, upon an assiduous cultivation of traditions and habits transmitted to each new generation by the old as the accumulated wisdom of the group... Perhaps some magic was necessary to produce social and political cohesiveness, and prevent perpetual turmoil'. However, with the new social sciences it is possible to quickly 'create customs'. It is possible to 'materially modify the whole attitude of the group' within about twenty years. If necessary 'new values, interests and attitudes' can be created 'by the educational and social process'.[13] God is just a type of 'magic', and is now displaced by the new faith in science.[14]

It might be discovered 'what type of environment' is required to produce a 'specific type of man'.[15] The new social science transcends time and place and universalises all in the name of 'democracy', a word used often by Merriam, even when he is discussing ways in which humans can be modified. A 'calamity of the first order' awaits should the new insights of science fall into the 'hands of medievalists', 'with the tremendous possibilities in the way of thoroughgoing social and political control of individuals'. The urgent task is for 'the social and political education of the next generation', forming 'a new majority with an entirely new political education, with new political values, attitudes, interests, capacities. We would re-create the world politically within some twenty years, were we minded and equipped to do so'.[16] It is up to social science to determine what constitutes a good citizen in this new world.[17] The new world will be one that goes beyond the League of Nations [precursor to the United Nations Organisation] and results in the 'interpenetration of national cultures',[18] or globalisation as it is

---

13   Ibid., p. 242.

14   Ibid., p. 243.

15   Ibid., p. 150.

16   Ibid., p. 203.

17   Ibid., p. 205.

18   Ibid., p. 237.

now called, in a 'new world', 'governed under a system of social and political control',[19] sustained by a 'trained electorate', a government of technocrats, and 'the science of social control',[20] 'co-ordinating, class, races and groups of human beings' across the world.[21]

The question Merriam asked of his fellow social scientists and financial patrons was as to 'what use' shall be made of this 'complete control over the physical and psychical and social structure of the individual or the group..?'[22]

It does not matter whether any of this is called a 'conspiracy'. The facts are that the oligarchic foundations launched and promoted the social sciences under the auspices of Merriam, and others, whose doctrine was that of world-wide control through social engineering. That this doctrine accords with the policies and outlook of the foundations that backed these academics can be readily ascertained by perusing their publicly available annual reports. There was and remains a convergence of aims and ideologies, and the social sciences continue to receive the funding to promote these.

Sorokin's Critique of Sociological Methodology

In 1954 the social sciences came under critical scrutiny by the congressional investigation of the tax-exempt foundations chaired by Congressman B. Carroll Reece. Several dissident sociologists testified before the committee and others submitted letters, as to the dubious methods being used by social scientists. The most famous of these was the sociologist Pitirim Sorokin, who was at the time of the Reece hearings president of Harvard University. Reece committee counsel Rene Wormser paraphrased in his book *Foundations: Their Power and Influence* Sorokin's written testimony:

---

19   Ibid., p. 238.
20   Ibid., p. 241.
21   Ibid., p. 240.
22   Ibid., p. 160.

Professor Sorokin, in his *Fads and Foibles in Modern Sociology*, puts it this way: 'Most of the defects of modem psychosocial science are due to a clumsy imitation of the physical sciences. Most of the numerous 'experimental' studies in sociology and psychology are pseudo-experimental, and have a very remote relationship, if any, to real experimental method. We should by all means use a real experimental method in our studies wherever it can be applied, and the more it is used the better. But we should not fool ourselves and others. They do not and cannot contribute to the real knowledge of psychosocial phenomena. If anything, they corrode the real experimental method and psychosocial science itself". ...

Professor Sorokin ridicules the wide use of the poll-taking method of operation, calling it unscientific, vague, indeterminate and, more often than not, 'hearsay' in its product.

Even their 'hearsay' material is ordinarily collected not by the investigators themselves, but by their assistants and hired pollsters. Imagine physicists or chemists operating in this fashion and then tabulating the collected opinions and giving the results in the form of various statistical tables and other paraphernalia to point to the 'objectivity' of their 'scientific' and 'operational' techniques. Moreover, says Professor Sorokin, 'what is true or false cannot be decided by majority vote'.

'The tidal wave' of the quantitative, empirical method of research is now so high, says Professor Sorokin, 'that the contemporary stage of the psychosocial sciences can be properly called the age of quantophobia and numerology'.

The 'comptometer compulsion', the 'fact-finding mania' of these foundation-supported 'social scientists' induce them to accept the principle of moral relativity — that moral laws are only relative — 'the facts' speak for themselves and must dictate moral law; whatever 'the facts' disclose is right.

As with the vilification of Senator Joseph McCarthy during this era, Reece and his witnesses also endured much. Congressman Reece stated before Congress the year following the conclusion of his investigations that 'the number of interruptions and the intensity of the vituperations heaped upon these witnesses', and on members of the committee, by Congressman Wayne Hays, who had stymied the committee's investigations into the funding of sexologist Dr. Alfred Kinsey, 'was without precedent in the history of Congressional investigations'.[23] For a time the oligarchy went into a panic and still recall the era with anxiety.

---

23   Hon. B. Carroll Reece, U. S. Congressional Record, 23 February 1955, A1184.

Behaviourism

Sooner or later, research animals will be replaced by humans, and scientists will become the social engineers of the human psyche.

— Hub Zwart, Professor of Philosophy

BEHAVIOURISM PROVIDED the social engineers with a pseudo-scientific arsenal. Behaviourism came into vogue in the USA through the experiments of John B. Watson and B. F. Skinner. In a paper examining the parallels between Marxism and Behaviourism, Dr. Stephen P. Forster[1] wrote:

> In both Marxism and behaviorism man's role becomes that of interpreter of the forces that shape him. This is accomplished by analyzing the disposition and dynamics of material forces. For Skinner: 'The task of a scientific analysis is to explain how the behavior of a person as a physical system is related to conditions under which this individual lives.'[2] For Marx: 'The first premise of all human history is, of course, the existence of living human individuals. Thus the first fact to be established is the physical organization of these individuals and their consequent relation to the rest of nature.'[3][4]

---

1 Stephen P. Foster, 'Marxism & Behaviorism: Ideological Parallels', Wright State University, *Dialogue*, Vol. 21, No. 1, October 1978.

2 B. F. Skinner, *Beyond Freedom and Dignity*, p. 14; cited by Foster, p. 3.

3 Marx, 'The German Ideology', in Karl Marx, Friedrich Engels: *Collected Works* (1976), Vol. 5, p. 31; cited by Foster, p. 3.

4 Stephen P. Foster, p. 3.

Foster described Skinnerian Behaviourism as 'a behavioural technology' with a political purpose, that of 'control':

> This view, however, has a significant political implication. Scientific understanding provides the possibility of prediction and control and thus leads to a technology of human affairs. This technology in Marxist terms is a revolutionary activity, in Skinnerian terms a behavioral technology. The scientific objective detachment of Marx and Skinner is linked to social-political commitment. Indeed, the social goals are the ultimate justifications for both systems.[5]

Skinner was an advocate of Behaviourism as a means of 'control' to prevent 'the catastrophe toward which the world seems to be inexorably moving'.[6] It has a familiar ring for today. Skinner was a recipient of CIA funding.[7] Foster describes Skinner's aims for Behaviourism, which can be seen as the aims of 'social control' and 'social engineering' advocated by Charles Merriam:

> Skinner's ultimate purpose in this respect is to formulate all human problems into technological problems. Then man can establish a process of identifying causal relations of human behavior to antisocial and destructive activities and a technique of adjusting those causes to obtain an extinction of the unwanted behavior. The domain of human affairs which has been traditionally considered ethical is thus transformed into a strict scientific one and thus man, in effect, delivers himself without obstacle to his own scrutiny, which is capable of identifying and eliminating his own imperfections.[8]

What Foster ascribes to Behaviourism is the doctrine that came into eminence in the 'Age of Enlightenment', the 'perfectibility of man', the doctrine of Rousseau, of the Jacobin Revolution, of the *Perfectibilists* (as the Order of the Illuminati were also called), of liberalism,

---

5   Ibid.

6   B. F. Skinner, *Beyond Freedom and Dignity*, p. 11; cited by Foster, p. 4.

7   David Price, p. 205.

8   Stephen P. Foster, p. 5.

Marxism, and the modernist social doctrines that aim to replace traditional ethics, morality and religion with social engineering. Foster
shows the parallels between Marxism and Behaviourism in this quest
for perfection through social change:

> Skinner's proposed transformation of morality into technology is very
> much analogous to Marx's vision of the withering away of the state once
> the productive capacities of society have been transformed. Implicit in
> both views is the idea that the greatest human goods will be realized when
> man acknowledges his being acted upon and shaped by the material world
> and also acknowledges that by rearranging material conditions (for Marx,
> the termination of commodity production, for Skinner, a more consistent
> system of distributing pleasure and pain) a better world will come into
> existence.[9]

Foster stated that in both Marxism and Behaviourism, 'there is the
assumption that the quality of human social experience will be sig-
nificantly improved because social institutions will be based on the
recognition and satisfaction of genuine human needs and these institutions will be more knowledgeably and efficiently administered'.[10]
What these 'human needs' are is determined by the social scientists in
research that is financed by the oligarchy.

Skinner was introduced to Behaviourism via its primary salesman,
John B. Watson, who had a double career as vice-president of the J.
Walter Thompson advertising agency in New York City.[11] Watson's
lectures at Columbia University in 1913, 'Psychology as the Behaviorist
Views It', were published as the *Behaviorist Manifesto*. Applying
Behaviourism to advertising, Watson stated that three basic emotions,
'fear, rage and love' can be utilised to sell a product to the consumer,
by appealing to a 'deep psychological or habit need'. For example to

---

9   Ibid., p. 5.

10   Ibid.

11   C. James Godwin, *A History of Modern Psychology*, p. 295.

sell Johnson & Johnson baby powder, fear of infection was the message 'to scare young parents'.[12]

While Watson was applying Behaviourism to capitalist marketing, he also lectured on Behaviourism to the New School for Social Research, and supervised research on infants, funded by the Laura Spelman Rockefeller Memorial Fund.[13]

Watson's dictum that there are no inherited human traits remains a pervasive dogma that separates the social sciences from genetics. Hence, although Behaviourism might not seem to retain the domination of psychology it once had in the USA, this dogma remains the basis of the social sciences, and of social policy throughout the West and further afield. Watson wrote in his seminal book, *Behaviorism*, that 'there is no real evidence for the inheritance of traits'. A baby born from a long line of crooks, thieves, murderers and prostitutes, raised in another environment 'would have a favorable outcome'.[14] He added:

> Give me a dozen healthy infants, well-formed and my own specified world to bring them up in and I'll guarantee to take any one at random and train him to become any type of specialist I might select — doctor, lawyer, artist, merchant-chief and, yes, even beggar-man and thief, regardless of his talents, penchants, tendencies, abilities, vocations, and race of his ancestors.[15]

Here we have the same type of dogma used to justify the mass terror of the Jacobin state and then the Bolshevik state, and the 'soft dictatorship' of contemporary Western societies, where states are guided by the principles of Behviourism in assuming that all social problems can be eliminated by social engineering. This is also the underlying doctrine that one can recreate individuals at will, according to the production and marketing requirements of international capital. It

---

12   Ibid., p. 296.

13   Ibid.

14   John. B. Watson, *Behaviorism* (1924), p. 103; cited by Godwin, p. 296.

15   John. B. Watson, p. 104, cited by Godwin, ibid.

accords with Critical Theory, with its doctrine that there are no 'primary ties' that should not be eliminated to reconstruct the individual.

Pavlov and Lenin

Behaviourism was pioneered in Russia by the physiologist Dr. Ivan Pavlov. Despite his misgivings about Bolshevism, when the Bolsheviks assumed control, Pavlov was treated as part of a privileged class. Pavlov sought to induce conditioned reflexes in dogs by a system of signals and rewards. Zwart describes Pavlov's laboratory as 'a pathogenic environment, a totalitarian regime that cared for its animals but exploited their bodies as production factors ...'[16] That is to say, it was a Communist state in microcosm. Despite the intentions of Pavlov himself, his research was seen to reflect

> the philosophy and *zeitgeist* of a particular political ideology (an ideological universe even), namely communism as a twentieth-century creed ... The conditioned reflex provides a **powerful tool for social engineering**. Sooner or later, research animals will be replaced by humans, and **scientists will become the social engineers of the human psyche.**

> Pavlovian psychology ... is a style of research driven by interest. It is interested in developing effective, evidence-based tools for **manipulation and exploitation. Ideally, society as a whole becomes structured as Pavlov's laboratory** (i.e. Pavlov's laboratory as a small-scale, anticipatory model of an ideal state, **a window into the communist future**).[17]

Zwart states of Lenin's interest:

> ... After speaking with Pavlov, Lenin proclaimed his desire to re-educate the Russian people as an animal trainer would. In October 1919, Lenin allegedly paid a secret visit to Pavlov's laboratory to find out how the work

---

16   Hub Zwart, 'Conditioned Reflexes and the Symbolic Order: A Lacanian Perspective of Ivan Pavlov's Experimental Practice', *Vestigia (Journal of the International Network of Psychoanalytic Practices)*, Vol. 1, No. 2, Summer 2018, p. 60.
     Zwart is dean of the School of Philosophy at Erasmus University, Rotterdam.

17   Ibid., p. 71. Emphasis added.

on conditional reflexes might help communism to control human behaviour. The ultimate aim of communism was to improve human beings and to transform human nature. Although Pavlov was critical of communism, he was patronized by the Bolshevik regime. Lenin spoke of Pavlov's work as hugely significant for the revolution and Trotsky saw the production of a new, improved version of humankind as the great task of communism, using current humanity as raw material, or as a semi-manufactured product.[18]

As will be seen below when discussing eugenics and population control, Trotsky described the creation of the 'new Soviet man' by using Nietzsche's term *Übermensch*, which if used by anyone else would be greeted with wails about 'Nazism' by today's intersectional, transsexual Trotskyites. Trotsky was also interested in applying Freudian psychoanalysis to Marxism, placing him along the same path as the Critical Theorists:

> In 1923, Trotsky wrote to Pavlov arguing that, whereas Freudians assumed an artistic stance towards human existence, Pavlov opted for an experimental, physiological approach, so that his reflex doctrine might provide a physiological substructure to Freudian theories. Despite its literary tendencies, he argued, psychoanalysis could be encompassed as a special case of doctrine of conditioned reflexes. Later, however, Pavlovian psychology became the official doctrine and in 1949 it was formally declared that Pavlov had demolished 'the Freudian houses of cards'. On January 24, 1921, a formal Decree was published on Pavlov's research indicating that, in view of Pavlov's outstanding scientific services, which were of tremendous importance to the working people of the world, a special committee was established to guarantee the best conditions for research. While 'the academician Pavlov's laboratory' would be furnished with every possible facility, Pavlov and his wife would receive a special food ration, equal in caloricity to two normal academic rations. ...[19]

Particularly interesting is that Zwart alludes to the analogous character of the USSR and capitalist USA in that both aimed to reconstruct

---

18   Ibid., p. 73.
19   Ibid., p. 73.

humanity according to economic factors, and as seen above in regard to the USA, both used *behaviourism* as a method of social engineering with,

> ... the Soviet Union as decidedly science-based, relying on physics, dialectical materialism and social engineering. **A similar wave of social engineering and human resources management could be discerned in capitalism as well,** however, notably in the form of Taylorism,[20] Fordism[21] and other instances of Americanism. While Pavlovian knowledge could provide scientific input for communism, Pavlov's work could be regarded as the realisation or condensation of an ideology of social engineering ...[22]

Konrad Lorenz's Critique

Ethologist Konrad Lorenz contended that the universal acceptance of Behaviourism was achieved because it offered a method to circumvent the difficulties of instinct and the unconscious. The social engineer could affirm that every individual is born 'as a completely blank page and that all he thinks, feels, believes and knows is the result of his "conditioning"'.[23] If that is the case, he can be re-conditioned. Liberals saw it as a 'liberating and democratic principle'. If everyone was born *tabula rasa,* then, raised under ideal and equal conditions, humanity could be reshaped according to an ideal.

Lorenz pointed out that the rulers and policy makers in the USA, China and the USSR were unanimous in their insistence on the conditionality of human behaviour. Lorenz described the behaviourist doctrine as 'pseudodemocratic', 'inhuman' and 'satanic', as it enables

---

20 Taylorism: method of scientific business management, aimed at the most effective methods for achieving worker productivity.

21 The method of modern mechanised mass production named after Henry Ford. It is interesting that Aldous Huxley in his dystopian novel *Brave New World* refers to a global society in which Communism and capitalism have been synthesised, and in which both Lenin and 'Our Ford' are venerated.

22 Zwart, p. 74. Emphasis added.

23 Lorenz, p. 86.

the 'dehumanization' and 'manipulation' of mankind. This is the crux of the matter:

> It is equally important to the capitalist mass producer as to the Soviet functionary to condition people into uniform, unresisting subjects, not very different from those described by Aldous Huxley in his terrifying novel *Brave New World*.[24]

Lorenz warns that if a doctrine based on 'a lie' about human behaviour is universally accepted, then the effects will be 'disastrous'. This doctrine, Lorenz contends, is responsible for much of the 'moral and cultural collapse that threatens the Western world'.[25] Lorenz saw the methods used by 'various "establishments"' — whether capitalist or Communist — to recondition people into their own preconceptions of the ideal, as 'substantially the same throughout the world'. 'We, ostensibly free, Western civilized people are no longer conscious of the extent to which we are being manipulated by the commercial decisions of the mass producers'. While crafts disappear in the mass (global) consumer society, we are increasingly conditioned to consume according to the production requirements of mass manufacturers, and are not aware of our manipulation.[26] Science itself has been conditioned to what is fashionable. Environmental conditioning is the fashion within science as it is within politics.

However, Lorenz states that this fallacious science does not **cause** the West's 'cultural diseases', but is the product of them.[27] That is to say, the position of the social engineers is enabled by a pre-existing weakness in the social organism. If the social organism had not succumbed to age and disease in the first instant, it would have the stamina to resist and repel the social pathologies that are able to enter. The rise of the oligarchy, for example, occurs during the late epoch

---

24 Ibid., p. 87.

25 Ibid., p. 88.

26 Ibid., p. 89.

27 Ibid., p. 98.

of a civilisation, as explained by Oswald Spengler in *The Decline of the West*,[28] and Brooks Adams in *The Law of Civilization and Decay*.[29] The cultural diseases of the West are the cause of the dehumanising impact of modern science, and not the effect.[30] If the West had not succumbed to social decay, it would have the vigour to resist.

---

28 Oswald Spengler, *The Decline of the West*.

29 Brooks Adams, *The Law of Civilization and Decay*.

30 Lorenz, p. 98.

Pathologising Morality

The Authoritarian Personality had a tremendous influence on … liberal intellectuals, because it showed them how to conduct political criticism in psychiatric categories, to make those categories bear the weight of political criticism. This procedure excused them from the difficult work of judgment and argumentation. Instead of arguing with opponents, they simply dismissed them on psychiatric grounds.

— Christopher Lasch[1]

According to Critical Theorists, 'conspiracy theorists' are 'right-wing extremists' with paranoid delusions leading to 'Fascism' and hence to genocide. While it requires a leap in logic, it is the theory that was popularised by the Critical Theorists since before World War II and given a clinical guise with the publication of *The Authoritarian Personality*, which remains a seminal text in academia.[2]

---

1   Casey Blake and Christopher Phelps, 'History as Social Criticism: Conversations with Christopher Lasch', *The Journal of American History*, Vol. 80, No. 4, March 1994. Lasch, an eminent historian, initially influenced by Critical Theory, discarded the Left and sought out a genuine conservatism that would uphold pre-capitalist, pre-industrial organic traditions; especially the primacy of the family. Failing to find this amongst American conservative defenders of 'free enterprise', he came to a position that he considered 'beyond Left and Right', and identified with 'communitarianism', which includes critiques of immigration, free trade liberalism and globalisation as destroyers of organic communities.

2   See for example: Michael J. Wood, Karen M. Douglas, Robbie M. Sutton, 'Dead and Alive: Beliefs in Contradictory Conspiracy Theories', *Social Psychology &*

The Authoritarian Personality sought to characterise traditional institutions and attitudes as latently 'F' for 'Fascist', based on surveys that rated individual mental health according to the scale. 'F' designated the 'Fascist' tendencies of individuals according to how they scored on attitudes, such as respect for parents, and a strong sense of morality.[3] Hence, if question 23 on the 'F scale' ('He is, indeed, contemptible who does not feel an undying love, gratitude, and respect for his parents') elicits a positive response, this is a symptom of 'authoritarian submission', and 'authoritarian aggression'.[4] The Frankfurt School theory towards the family is summarised by Jay Martin in a semi-official history of the institution: 'Even a partial breakdown of parental authority in the family might tend to increase the readiness of a coming generation to accept social change'.[5]

The Authoritarian Personality formulates a theory about family that defines healthy and unhealthy familial relationships on the basis of the degree of submission to a father figure. Authoritarian family relationships are thereby judged to breed Fascism and prejudice. Thus, according to the conclusions of Else Frenkel-Brunswik's surveys, prejudiced individuals were likely to be so according to the level of 'dominance and submission in contradistinction to equalitarian policies' within a family.[6] This dominance includes 'fearful subservience', and impulse suppression by parents towards children, said to be characteristic of a 'highly conventional' parental outlook. Repressed hostility towards parents externalises through exaggerated idealization,

---

Personality Science, 25 January 2012.

3   T. W. Adorno, Else Frenkel-Brunswik, Daniel J Levinson and R. Nevitt Sanford, *The Authoritarian Personality*.

4   Ibid., pp. 231, 232.

5   Martin Jay, *The Dialectical Imagination: A History of the Frankfurt School and the New School for Social Research*.

6   Else Frenkel-Brunswik, 'Parents and Childhood as Seen through the Interviews', in Adorno et al., Vol. 1, Chap. 10, p. ibid., p. 385.

which manifests itself again in conformist attitudes towards authority and social institutions.[7]

The logical conclusion is that individual and societal health can only be achieved — and prejudice, 'Fascism', and genocide, prevented — by reorientation away from traditional norms, particularly parental authority.

The hypothesis upon which *The Authoritarian Personality* is based is that an individual's politics is a reflection of deep-seated personality traits. The primary concern of Adorno et al. was to establish what personality traits made up the 'potentially fascistic individual'.[8] These personality traits are developed from the earliest stages within 'a setting of family life', which is 'profoundly influenced by economic and social factors'. Therefore, 'broad changes' of social conditions will affect the types of personalities within a society.[9]

Frenkel-Brunswik arrives at the question of sexual attitudes in Chapter XI, the studies and surveys having established in the preceding chapters of *The Authoritarian Personality* the pathological nature of prejudice shaped via the authoritarian structure of the family. These chapters present case studies based on the scales of 'Projective Questioning' analysis devised by Frenkel-Brunswik.[10] The methodology was to devise tests that could be statistically analysed in regard to social backgrounds, and how these correlated to 'potential fascism' by means of 'surveying opinions, attitudes, and values'.[11] In order to 'generalize' patterns of prejudice to arrive at a predictive method, it was necessary to examine both individual and group surveys. Adorno explained: 'Individuals were studied by means of interviews and special clinical techniques for revealing underlying wishes, fears, and

7   Ibid., p. 386.

8   Ibid., p. 1.

9   Ibid., p. 6.

10   Max Horkheimer, ibid., Preface, xi.

11   Adorno, et al., ibid., pp. 11–12.

defenses; groups were studied by means of questionnaires'.[12] Survey questions included:

6. It is only natural and right that women be restricted in certain ways in which men have more freedom.

23. He is, indeed, contemptible who does not feel an undying love, gratitude, and respect for his parents.

24. Today everything is unstable; we should be prepared for a period of constant change, conflict, and upheaval.

46. The sexual orgies of the old Greeks and Romans are nursery school stuff compared to some of the goings-on in this country today, even in circles where people might least expect it.

66. Books and movies ought not to deal so much with the sordid and seamy side of life; they ought to concentrate on themes that are entertaining or uplifting.

73. Nowadays when so many different kinds of people move around so much and mix together so freely, a person has to be especially careful to protect himself against infection and disease.

75. Sex crimes, such as rape and attacks on children, deserve more than mere imprisonment; such criminals ought to be publicly whipped.[13]

In the sexual analyses, the 'restricted type of prejudiced person manifests, in the main, explicit anti-id moralism....' 'Unprejudiced individuals', on the other hand, have 'integrated' sex better into their social relations. The least prejudiced tend to be 'less repressed' and 'manifest more acceptance of the id'.[14]

Males who place priority on morality among women and scorn premarital sexual relations 'lack integration of sex and affection'.[15] This is said to be based not on respect for woman, but to the contrary

---

12   Ibid., p. 12.

13   Ibid., pp. 226–227; 'The F Scale, Form 78'.

14   Frenkel-Brunswik in Adorno et al., ibid., p. 395.

15   Ibid., p. 398.

on an 'ambivalent underlying disrespect' and 'resentment against the opposite sex'.[16] Expressions by male subjects about women, such as 'sweet, kind and generous' and 'wholesome' are deemed to signify 'authoritarian personalities' seeking to place women in a submissive role.[17]

As for the authoritarian woman, the 'unrealistic search for a great romantic love' is seen as the yearning to 'restore a successful early relation with a parent based on nurturance and succorance'. The healthy personality is one with a 'liberal' (sic) attitude in a relationship.[18]

In summary, Frenkel-Brunswik finds that, as in relationships with parents, relationships with the opposite sex for the authoritarian type are based on 'a lack of real object relationship'. This is often a manifestation of disappointment with 'their first-love relations, those with their parents'. In attitudes towards both parents and the opposite sex, there is an ambivalent 'surface admiration, combined with underlying resentment'. This manifests in gender 'stereotypes'.[19]

In terms of outlook on social morality, the authoritarian type scores high on 'moralistic condemnation'.[20] This is often buttressed with a religious outlook.[21]

Emphasis on gender differentiation and self-identity is said to derive from 'threatening parental figures'.[22]

By now a generalised picture should have emerged: that in the view of these authors, traditional Western attitudes towards the sexes and relationships are all signs of deep pathological traits that go to make up the 'authoritarian personality'; the 'Fascist' type. All of this is said to stem from parental relations, and particularly from patriarchy.

---

16   Ibid., p. 399.
17   Ibid., p. 400.
18   Ibid., p. 401.
19   Ibid., p. 404.
20   Ibid., p. 406.
21   Ibid., p. 408.
22   Ibid., p. 428.

The question of political ideologies was addressed in Chapter V by Daniel J. Levinson.[23] Since the extreme Left, epitomised by Communism, and the Right, epitomised by Fascism, were regarded by the researchers as not having reached a significant level of support in the USA, they instead focused on 'liberalism' and 'conservatism'[24] as the foundations from which the extreme polarities might arise in times of crisis. However, it is clear that the categories did include the extremes, such as those 'liberals' who favour not just 'mild reforms' but a 'complete overthrow of the status quo'.[25] The aim then was to establish a scholarly method upon which to predict what personality types would be susceptible to Communism and Fascism, with the implication being that societal changes would have to be made in order to prevent the significant emergence of extremism.

Not surprisingly, those of 'liberal' persuasion, or the 'Left', are considered to be low scorers on the personality tests and surveys for determining the 'authoritarian personality'. Therefore, liberals, including socialists, are psychologically healthy in contrast to conservatives. However, the definitions of 'Left' and 'Right', or 'liberalism' and 'conservatism' are reliant on those provided by the authors, and since they came from left-wing persuasions, one might question their objectivity. The ideological definitions once made are then neatly fitted into the survey data to show predictable results.

In Chapter XVII Adorno returns to the Levinson survey data on political and economic attitudes, intervening chapters having provided the necessary data to show that those with 'conservative' views are afflicted with the 'authoritarian personality', which arises from dysfunctional parent-child relations in the patriarchal family; in comparison to the healthy and individuated 'liberal' or 'socialist'.

---

23   Daniel J. Levinson, ibid., pp. 153–206.

24   Ibid., p. 152.

25   Ibid., p. 154.

The primary objective of the study is to determine a 'potentially Fascist character',[26] as a means of preventing the widespread re-emergence of such a sociopathy. The emergence of this personality is reinforced by 'our general cultural climate', the implication being that in order to reach optimal social health, society must be changed. The possibility of a mass 'antidemocratic movement' arising must be addressed by psychological 'diagnosis'.[27] The intentions of the study are clear:

> The importance of this diagnosis, if it should be corroborated sufficiently by our data, is self-evident, its most immediate implication being that the fight against such a general potential cannot be carried through only educationally on a purely psychological level, but that it requires at the same time decisive changes of that cultural climate which makes for the overall pattern.[28]

Adorno emphasises that the focus needs to be on changing the 'supra-individual social forces operating in our society'.[29]

The necessary conclusions are drawn by Maria Hertz Levinson (Chapter XXII) when stating that if adherence to ideologies is related to personality, then one would expect 'ideology to be related to various kinds of mental disturbance'.[30] Here, of the numerous 'variables', the one found to be the most unambiguous in a survey of mental patients was that 'high scores' for 'authoritarian personality' or 'potential fascist' were related to unhappy childhood and family relationships. There was also found to be a strong relationship with ethnocentrism. The results are said to agree with the study as a whole, that 'low scorers' for 'potential fascism' were able to acknowledge parental issues

---

26 Adorno, ibid., p. 655.

27 Ibid., p. 655.

28 Ibid.

29 Ibid.

30 Maria Hertz Levinson, ibid., Chapter XXII, 'Psychological Ill-Health in Relation to Potential Fascism: A Study of Psychiatric Clinic Patients', p. 891.

freely, whereas 'highs scorers', the 'potential fascists', rationalised such relationships and idealised their families.[31]

In concluding the study as a whole, M. H. Levinson stated that the 'high scorers' for 'potential fascism' 'have rigid, constricted personalities', 'stereotyped, conventionalised thinking', and an extreme reaction against whatever 'reminded them of their own repressed impulses'.[32] 'Their range of experience, emotionally and intellectually, is narrow'.[33]

> It is as if they can experience only the one conventionally correct attitude or emotion in any given situation. Everything else is suppressed or denied, or if another impulse breaks through, it is experienced as something which is completely incompatible with the conception of the self, and which suddenly overwhelms the ego. In part, this high degree of ego-alienness probably derives from the fact that the impulses emerging from repression are so primitive and, especially in the women, so very hostile.[34]

Repression is the primary basis for the psychopathy of the 'authoritarian personality type'. Levinson explains this in regard to men in their relation to women, and respect for women and motherhood as deriving from repressed anxieties:

> High scorers — particularly men — also seem to have strong but repressed passive-dependent desires, but these appear to be differently organized in the personality than is the case with the low scorers. Whereas in the low scorers these tendencies are expressed directly in interpersonal relationships, in the desire to be loved and in the fear of being rejected in a very personalized way, the high-scoring men's passivity and dependency probably is mainly a reaction to their extreme castration anxiety. The high-scoring men often seek protection from this anxiety in a motherly woman, but without having a very differentiated relationship to this woman as a person.[35]

---

31   Ibid., p. 939.
32   Ibid., p. 965.
33   Ibid., p. 966.
34   Ibid.
35   Ibid., p. 967.

One could envisage, for instance, such a Freudo-Marxian analysis of the Western medieval concept of knightly chivalry as being nothing other than a symptom of 'extreme castration anxiety'. Western high culture might be analysed as a method of denigrating whatever traditional vestiges remain in contemporary society, diagnosed as vestigial repression that requires exorcising from the social organism. Hence, the need for social engineering, and for politicised analysts, sociologists, social anthropologists, psychiatrists and psychologists to provide the necessary social panacea to cure societal ills.

What Adorno *et al.* call 'conservative' outlooks on gender roles seems reducible in these terms: 'The interpersonal relationships of high scorers ["potential fascists"] appeared to be much weaker, less personal, more conventional, and more often expressed in terms of dominance-submission'.[36]

A difference in outlook between 'conservative' and 'liberal' mental patients is ascribed to differences in types of dysfunction, the liberal dysfunction seemingly being of a preferable type since it does not result in a 'fascist' disposition:

> Our results indicate, however, that the way a person thinks is always conditioned, to a greater or lesser degree, by emotional dispositions. The capacity for rational functioning, in which needs and affects play a positive rather than a negative (distorting, inhibiting) role, is part of what we and others have called a strong ego. While ego strength seems higher, on the average, in the low than in the high scorers, it must be emphasized that irrationality has been found to some degree in both; however, it is qualitatively different in the two groups and impels the individuals in antipodal directions.[37]

In conclusion, Levinson states that the repressed individual will find outlets in ethnocentrism and other forms of personality disorder:

---

36 Maria Hertz Levinson, p. 967.

37 Ibid., p. 968.

In the high scorers, extensive repressions and *countercathexes*[38] have hindered the ego's development. The ego remains rather primitive, undifferentiated, and completely isolated from a large portion of the deeper layers. When the unresolved unconscious conflicts become intensified and come closer to consciousness, the ego, totally unprepared, feels overwhelmed and shocked. This may lead merely to strong anxieties with or without somatic symptoms. In more extreme form, however, it may lead to depersonalization, withdrawal from reality, denial, projections, and other psychotic manifestations. Given a sufficiently supporting environment, highly ethnocentric individuals achieve a sense of 'comfort' and 'adjustment'; but they frequently lack the productiveness, the capacity for love, and, in times of stress, the grip on reality, which are more characteristic of the anti-authoritarian individuals.[39]

Behind the charts and data, the conclusions are intended to have a political application. The authors of *The Authoritarian Personality* state that the aim is to 'fight' 'potential fascism', the diagnostic warning signs of which are 'conservative' attitudes towards gender and familial relations. These attitudes are manifested politically in one's attitude towards issues such as defence, and what respondents thought of President Franklin Roosevelt's 'New Deal'. It is not sufficient, however, that such dysfunctional individuals be treated through re-education. It is society and culture that need changing.

The Authoritarian Personality has recently been invoked against those who have voted for the presidency of Donald Trump. So far from being 'poor White trash' of bourgeois–liberal stereotype, it transpires that Trump supporters are generally a resurgent lower middle class possessing the authoritarian personality traits. In a recent study on the *authoritarian personality* for the Trump era, Matthew MacWilliams[40] states:

---

38 The *libidic* (sexual) energy invested in maintaining a repressed complex.

39 Maria Hertz Levinson, p. 970.

40 Founder of MacWilliams Sanders, a political communications firm, and Ph.D. candidate in political science at the University of Massachusetts, writing his dissertation about authoritarianism.

If I asked you what most defines Donald Trump supporters, what would you say? They're white? They're poor? They're uneducated? You'd be wrong. In fact, I've found a single statistically significant variable predicts whether a voter supports Trump—and it's not race, income or education levels: It's authoritarianism. …

My finding is the result of a national poll I conducted in the last five days of December under the auspices of the University of Massachusetts, Amherst, sampling 1,800 registered voters across the country and the political spectrum. Running a standard statistical analysis, I found that education, income, gender, age, ideology and religiosity had no significant bearing on a Republican voter's preferred candidate. Only two of the variables I looked at were statistically significant: authoritarianism, followed by fear of terrorism, though the former was far more significant than the latter.[41]

Although *The Authoritarian Personality* is not cited by MacWilliams, there is an implicit reference, and it must be assumed that this is the premise for his doctoral thesis.

Authoritarianism is not a new, untested concept in the American electorate. Since the rise of Nazi Germany, it has been one of the most widely studied ideas in social science. While its causes are still debated, the political behavior of authoritarians is not. Authoritarians obey. **They rally to and follow strong leaders. And they respond aggressively to outsiders, especially when they feel threatened.** From pledging to "make America great again" by building a wall on the border to promising to close mosques and ban Muslims from visiting the United States, Trump is playing directly to authoritarian inclinations. Indeed, 49 percent of likely Republican primary voters I surveyed score in the top quarter of the authoritarian scale—**more than twice as many as Democratic** voters.

… [M]y poll asked a set of four simple survey questions that political scientists have employed since 1992 to measure inclination toward authoritarianism. **These questions pertain to child-rearing**: whether it is more important for the voter to have a child who is respectful or independent;

---

41   Matthew MacWilliams, 'The One Weird Trait That Predicts Whether You're a Trump Supporter, and It's Not Gender, Age, Income, Race or Religion', *Politico Magazine*, 17 January 2016; https://www.politico.com/magazine/story/2016/01/donald-trump-2016-authoritarian-213533.

obedient or self-reliant; well-behaved or considerate; and well-mannered or curious. Respondents who pick the first option in each of these questions are strongly authoritarian.

Based on these questions, Trump was the only candidate—Republican or Democrat—whose support among authoritarians was statistically significant.

It is time for those who would appeal to our better angels to take his insurgency seriously and stop dismissing his supporters as a small band of the dispossessed. Trump support is firmly rooted in American authoritarianism and, once awakened, it is a force to be reckoned with. That means it's also time for political pollsters to take authoritarianism seriously and begin measuring it in their polls.[42]

The focus on questions of child-rearing maintains the focus on the family as the incubator of 'authoritarianism'. The implication is that in order to expunge this danger from society it is best that children are inculcated with the dominant ideology; i.e., liberalism or 'political correctness', and that contrary ideas, including especially those of parents, are repressed as 'thought crimes'.

One might conversely ask:

1) If the 'authoritarian personality' follows a 'strong leader', does this imply that liberals, including Democrats, follow a weak leader? Was Hillary Clinton selected as the Democratic contender for the presidency against Trump on the basis of her gentleness and tolerance? Was the mass weeping and histrionics when she was defeated for the presidency a sign of mature psychological adjustment?

2) Is **not** responding to outsiders, especially when one feels threatened, a normal reaction? How should one interpret the widespread verbally abusive and physically violent reactions against Trump supporters before and after the presidential election?

---

42 Matthew MacWilliams, Emphasis added.

3) Given that MacWilliams reacts 'aggressively' to the perceived 'threat' of Trump, isn't he projecting his own 'authoritarian personality' onto 'the other'?; those whom Clinton dehumanised as 'the deplorables':

Hillary Clinton sparked a controversy after suggesting that half of Donald Trump's supporters belonged in "a basket of deplorables", which she described as consisting of "the racist, sexist, homophobic, xenophobic, Islamaphobic — you name it." She went to note "some of those folks — **they are irredeemable, but thankfully they are not America"**.[43]

In the Clinton liberal narrative the political opponent becomes an *outsider*, not American, indeed 'un-American', and not capable of becoming part of America by 'redemption'. Stereotypical labels are used to dehumanise the perceived 'threat' to 'real Americans'. Whatever flaws Trump had as president, calling his 'America First' foreign policy, at odds with Hillary Clinton's aggressive U.S. global interventionism when Secretary of State, 'not America', requires a national forgetfulness of the Americanist tradition established by George Washington in his 1796 'Farewell Address to the American People', where he warned on the necessity of America keeping aloof from foreign quarrels and the importation of foreign ideologies (at that time, Jacobinism). The loss of collective national memory is an important element in social engineering, which was why the genuine national heroes and founders of nations must today be vilified and then consigned to the memory hole in the name of 'progress'. This has taken symbolic form in the dismantling of statues of American heroes, a process of hysteria and purging that soon spread from the USA to Britain and the Antipodes. It is within the same context as

---

43 Ben Jacobs, 'Hillary Clinton Calls Half of Trump Supporters Bigoted 'Deplorables', *The Guardian*, 10 September 2016; https://www.theguardian.com/us-news/2016/sep/10/hillary-clinton-trump-supporters--bigoted-deplorables. Emphasis added.

the destruction of cultural monuments by utilitarian fanatics, from Egyptian scribes eliminating all traces of a former Pharaoh or deity out of favour with the new regime, to the Jacobins seeking to eliminate all vestiges of monarchy and Catholicism, or the Taliban destroying museum antiquities that offend *Wahhab* fanaticism.

'Conspiracy Theory' as Personality Disorder?

WHILE PSYCHIATRY AS a means of repressing political dissent was well-known for its use in the USSR, this also occurred in the West, and particularly in the USA. While the case of the poet Ezra Pound is comparatively well-known, not so recognised is that during the Kennedy era in particular there were efforts to silence critics through psychiatry.

Since the study on the *Authoritarian Personality,* social scientists have remained occupied with creating new approaches for the de-legitimizing of dissident opinions. Among the primary targets are those who have in recent years been termed *conspiracists.* The term is used to induce a Pavlovian behavioural reflex in nullifying dissident views on a range of subjects, additional to the use of words such as 'racist', 'Fascist', 'sexist', 'homophobe', 'White supremacist'.

Recently a group of psychologists studying the allegedly contradictory nature of conspiracy beliefs were able to furnish mind-manipulators with a study that can be used to show that anything called 'conspiracy theory' can be relegated to the realm of mental imbalance. The paper was published as 'Dead and Alive: Beliefs in Contradictory Conspiracy Theories'.[1] The abstract reads:

---

1   Michael J. Wood, Karen M Douglas, Robbie M Sutton, 'Dead and Alive: Beliefs in Contradictory Conspiracy Theories', *Social Psychology & Personality Science,* 25 January 2012, http://m.spp.sagepub.com/content/early/2012/01/18/1948550611434786.full.pdf.

Conspiracy theories can form a monological belief system: A self-sustaining worldview comprised of a network of mutually supportive beliefs. The present research shows that even mutually incompatible conspiracy theories are positively correlated in endorsement. In Study 1 (n ¼ 137), the more participants believed that Princess Diana faked her own death, the more they believed that she was murdered. In Study 2 (n ¼ 102), the more participants believed that Osama Bin Laden was already dead when U.S. special forces raided his compound in Pakistan, the more they believed he is still alive. Hierarchical regression models showed that mutually incompatible conspiracy theories are positively associated because both are associated with the view that the authorities are engaged in a cover-up (Study 2). The monological nature of conspiracy belief appears to be driven not by conspiracy theories directly supporting one another but by broader beliefs supporting conspiracy theories in general.[2]

The conclusion is that conspiracy theorists have a generalized suspicion of all authority, and thereby believe that any event is the product of a conspiracy by authority. Several categories were used to score contradictory attitudes in regard to conspiracy. The subjects were chosen from 137 undergraduate psychology students. Five questions were asked regarding conspiratorial beliefs in Princess Diana's death.[3] The results 'suggest that those who distrust the official story of Diana's death do not tend to settle on a single *conspiracist* account as the only acceptable explanation; rather, they simultaneously endorse several contradictory accounts'.[4]

There are several factors to consider:

1) The small number of subjects drawn from the same background.

2) Whether the belief in contradictory theories is rather the willingness to accept several alternatives rather than being bound to a single explanation.

---

2   Ibid., p. 2.

3   Ibid., p. 4.

4   Ibid., p. 5.

3) The tests appear to be of a 'tick the boxes' character, and do not seem to offer the subjects opportunity to explain their views.

4) The tests therefore seem to be nothing other than very limited statistical surveys from which a generalised theory is postulated in regard to *conspiracism*.

In is of interest that Wood, Douglas and Sutton draw on *The Authoritarian Personality* in creating a psychological profile of *conspiracists* that will accord with leftist assumptions on *conspiracists* as 'Fascists' and 'anti-Semites': 'There are strong parallels between this conception of a monological belief system and Adorno et al's (1950) work on prejudice and authoritarianism'.[5] The purpose of the study can be discerned from this passage:

> If Adorno's explanation for contradictory antisemitic beliefs can indeed be applied to conspiracy theories, conspiracist beliefs might be most accurately viewed as not only monological but also ideological in nature. Just as an orthodox Marxist might interpret major world events as arising inevitably from the forces of history, a conspiracist would see the same events as carefully orchestrated steps in a plot for global domination. Conceptualizing conspiracism as a coherent ideology, rather than as a cluster of beliefs in individual theories, may be a fruitful approach in the future when examining its connection to ideologically relevant variables such as social dominance orientation and right-wing authoritarianism.[6]

Conspiracism is identified as an inherently 'right-wing authoritarian' ideology. The authors, Wood, Douglas, and Sutton, thereby show themselves to be ideologically biased and agenda-driven; as were Adorno, et al. Moreover, in ascribing *conspiracism* to 'right-wing ideology' there seems to be ignorance as to the diversity of *conspiracists*.

---

5   Ibid., p. 6.

6   Ibid., p. 6.

Defining 'Conspiracy'

How should one designate Dr. Carroll Quigley, other than as a liberal, Professor of History at Harvard and Georgetown University Foreign Service School, whose academic magnum opus, *Tragedy & Hope*, is often quoted by *conspiracists*? This includes several dozen pages describing an 'international network' of bankers whose aim is to bring about a centralised world political and financial control system.[7] Despite the relatively few pages on this network in Quigley's 1300 page tome, he regarded the role of this network in history, over the course of several generations, as not only pivotal, but also as laudable (apart from its 'secrecy').[8]

Wood, Douglas and Sutton begin their paper with the definition: 'A conspiracy theory is defined as a proposed plot by powerful people or organizations working together in secret to accomplish some (usually sinister) goal'.[9] Based on that definition, it would seem difficult to conclude anything other than that Quigley was describing conspiracy, insofar as it is:

1) 'Secret', which Quigley laments as being the primary cause of his disagreement with the 'network'

2) Composed of powerful people and organisations

3) Aims to accomplish a world financial system under the control of international bankers.

The only question is whether 'it' should be considered 'sinister'. However, Wood *et al.* state that 'conspiracies' are *usually* regarded as 'sinister', which presumably means that it is not an essential ingredient. Obviously, the word 'sinister' is subjective. Quigley regarded 'it' as being composed of highly cultured and intelligent men with good

---

7   C. Quigley, p. 51.

8   Ibid., pp. 950–956. See also: Bolton, *Revolution from Above*, pp. 24–26.

9   Michael J. Wood, et al, p. 2.

intentions for the world, although he seemed to have doubts towards the end of his life, when the lecture circuit had been denied to him, and his textbook *Tragedy & Hope* was inexplicably suppressed by his publisher.[10]

What should one make of the 'warning' to the American people by Dwight Eisenhower, during his 'farewell speech', in which he referred to the 'military-industrial complex', which became a favourite expression of the New Left? Eisenhower pointed out its wide ramifications, not only on economic and political but also on moral and cultural levels:

> In the councils of government, we must guard against the acquisition of unwarranted influence, whether sought or unsought, by the military-industrial complex. The potential for the disastrous rise of misplaced power exists and will persist....
>
> The prospect of domination of the nation's scholars by Federal employment, project allocations, and the power of money is ever present and is gravely to be regarded. Yet, in holding scientific research and discovery in respect, as we should, we must also be alert to the equal and opposite danger that public policy could itself become the captive of a scientific-technological elite.[11]

Here are the primary elements for 'conspiracy theory' in Eisenhower's address:

1) There is a threat that is 'secret', or at least not above board, otherwise Eisenhower would not see the need to make it a feature of his final words as president.

2) This threat involves a cabal: 'the military-industrial complex', and a technocratic 'elite'.

10　Robert Eringer, *The Global Manipulators*, pp. 9–10. Eringer spoke to Quigley regarding the professor's predicament after running afoul of the 'network'.

11　Dwight D. Eisenhower, Farewell Speech to the American People, 17 January 1961, IV, http://www.h-net.org/~hst306/documents/indust.html.

3) The threat involves 'the power of money'.

4) The threat is that of the accumulation of power by these elites.

Did not Karl Marx state that capitalism would internationalise, and that the internationalisation of the 'modes of production' would have what today is called a 'globalising' effect on society? Did not Marx also state that it is the forces of 'social production' that determine not only the economics, but also the culture, morals and religion of a society? Had Marx not seen this as a necessary part of the *dialectical* process towards Communism? Is it too wide of the mark therefore, even from a Marxian perspective, to state that there is a convergence of outlook between international capitalism and international socialism? But this is dismissed by conformist academia as a right-wing *conspiracist* 'over-simplification'.

Cycles of History

The explanation is indeed far more complex than 'conspiracy theory', and involves the *Zeitgeist* or 'spirit of the age' under which both capitalism and socialism emerged. I allude to this early in *Revolution from Above*, stating that there is nothing 'new' or 'progressive' about current trends, which have been seen many times before over millennia, during analogous epochs of civilisations in decay.[12] Hence, when a budding academic such as Andrew Woods mockingly refers to 'conspiracy theory', he is himself projecting his own simplifications without understanding the historical contexts. Both the thesis and antithesis (capitalism and socialism) that emerged at the same time were born from the same *Zeitgeist*, as reflections of one another. A century ago the seminal philosopher of the Right, Oswald Spengler, who is quoted in *Revolution from Above*,[13] but who is not likely to be taught

---

12 Bolton, *Revolution from Above*, p. 22.

13 Bolton, *Revolution from Above*, Spengler quoted on page 23.

by the present social sciences, wrote of this relationship between the two:

> There is no proletarian, not even a communist, movement that has not op-
> erated in the interests of money, in the directions indicated by money, and
> for the time permitted by money — and that without the idealist amongst
> its leaders having the slightest suspicion of the fact.[14]

So far from attempting to explain social and historical complexities with the 'oversimplification' of 'conspiracy theory', the Right predicates such conspiracies as symptoms rather than causes, which can only prosper when society has reached a cycle of decay that allows money to dominate: *plutocracy*. Plato outlined a similar series of cycles in *The Republic*: Aristocracy, Timocracy (debasement of aristocratic values), Oligarchy, Democracy, and Tyranny.[15]

The social pathogens that are being promoted by plutocracy and the Left are seen as 'progress'. In presenting his critical analysis of 'right-wing conspiracy theory', Andrew Woods neglected to mention, in his ridicule of the notion that capitalist theorists might have their own dialectical outlook, that the source for this hypothesis is Zbigniew Brzezinski. One of the intelligentsia close to the oligarchy, particularly the Rockefeller dynasty, throughout his long career Brzezinski used a dialectical method in explaining the 'progressive' unfolding of history, where 'Marxism represents a further vital and creative stage in the maturing of man's universal vision'.[16]

Certain conspiracy theorists misunderstood Brzezinski's refer-ences to Marxism as indicating that he was a Marxist. This is a typi-cal misunderstanding of how historical dialectics operates. The John Birch Society, for example, in its obituary for Brzezinski, writes:

---

14 Oswald Spengler, *The Decline of the West*, Vol. 2, p. 506.
15 Plato, *The Republic*, Book VIII.
16 Zbigniew Brzezinski, *Between Two Ages*, p. 34, quoted by Bolton, *Revolution from Above*, p. 13.

While pointing out the evils of Communism as practiced in the Soviet Union, Brzezinski showed his fondness for Marxist ideology. In 1970 — seven years before becoming President Jimmy Carter's national security advisor — Brzezinski wrote *Between Two Ages*. The book laid out his plans for bringing about an incremental world government. *Between Two Ages* became the blueprint for the globalist Trilateral Commission, which was founded in 1973 by David Rockefeller with Brzezinski becoming its first director.

In the book, Brzezinski — who had been, by this time, an American citizen for 12 years — wrote:

The social blinders that have made America unaware of its shortcomings have been ripped off, and the painful awareness of American society's lingering inadequacy has been rendered more acute by the intensity and pace of change. In a word, America is undergoing a new revolution, whose distinguishing feature is that it simultaneously maximizes America's potential as it unmasks its obsolescence.

Brzezinski's disdain for America's 'lingering inadequacy' and 'obsolescence' was matched by his high view of the "victory" and "action" of Marxism. He wrote:

That is why Marxism represents a further vital and creative stage in the maturing of man's universal vision. Marxism is simultaneously a victory of the external, active man over the inner, passive man and a victory of reason over belief: it stresses man's capacity to shape his material destiny — finite and defined as man's only reality — and it postulates the absolute capacity of man to truly understand his reality as a point of departure for his active endeavors to shape it. To a greater extent than any previous mode of political thinking, Marxism puts a premium on the systematic and rigorous examination of material reality and on guides to action derived from that examination.[17]

---

17   C. Mitchell Shaw, 'Globalist Zbigniew Brzezinski Dead at 89', *New American*, 27 May 2017; https://www.thenewamerican.com/usnews/foreign-policy/item/26125-globalist-zbigniew-brzezinski-dead-at-89.

In *Revolution from Above* I quote more extensively from Brzezinski's *Between Two Ages*, in hypothesising that there is a capitalist dialectic that operates in mirror image to that of Communist dialectic.[18] My hypothesis is that the globalist intelligentsia, among whom Brzezinski was prominent, saw Marxism as a dialectical phase in globalisation, in a sense paralleling that of Karl Marx, who conversely saw capitalism as a phase in internationalisation, leading to world Communism. Marx saw Communism as the end of history in this dialectical process; globalist intellectual Francis Fukuyama saw liberal-capitalism as 'the end of history'. To the rightist, and Spengler saw this a century ago, capitalism and Communism reflect the same *spirit*; the same *Zeitgeist*. **It is this convergence of dialectic outlook that explains why arch-capitalists would support organisations and ideologies that are supposedly dedicated to the destruction of capitalism.** This makes more sense than assuming that these capitalists are being hoodwinked and manipulated and that Marxists have taken over the funds of oligarchs through guile. It is more plausible that the oligarchy know exactly what they are promoting.

Congressional Investigation

Woods' attempt to trace 'conspiracy theory origins' with which to link *Revolution from Above*, and the 'attack on The New School', is inept. It is an ineptitude born of intellectual arrogance of the type that pervades the leftist intelligentsia:

> Bolton's attack on The New School contributes to a tradition of American conspiracy theorizing that has endured since the mid-twentieth century. Specifically, his work builds on enduring right-wing myths about the Fabian Society and the Frankfurt School. In 1964, the author and preacher John A. Stormer wrote the *conspiracist* classic *None Dare Call It Treason* to warn American citizens that communists had infiltrated churches, the education system, the media, the labor movement, and the medical establishment.

---

18 Bolton, *Revolution from Above*, pp. 9–14.

.... Building on Stormer's allegations, Bolton explains that — in a classic twist of dialectical capitalism — Webb and Shaw secured generous funding from the Rothschild family to establish the London School of Economics in 1895. For the Fabian Society, universities functioned as ostensibly innocuous channels for transmitting collectivist propaganda. Following Webb and Shaw's example, Dewey conspired to convert young American intellectuals to the pernicious doctrine of Fabian Socialism through The New School.[19]

The use of Stormer's *None Dare Call It Treason*, one of only two cited works in Woods' endnotes, is odd. Woods does not identify the 'enduring right-wing myths about the Fabian Society and the Frankfurt School'. It is sufficient to call something a 'right-wing myth' in order to have it dismissed. Woods alludes to Stormer having been a 'preacher' when he wrote *None Dare Call It Conspiracy*. This is incorrect. Stormer became prominent in the Baptist church and education after writing *None Dare Call It Treason*. However, calling Stormer a 'preacher' is enough to raise sneers and smirks among the leftist intelligentsia; to evoke an image of a snake-handling preacher speaking in tongues at a little church in the backwoods of Appalachia.

Of the many sources cited in *Revolution from Above*, and Woods concedes there are a plenitude, *None Dare Call it Treason* is **not** among them. Furthermore, while I had heard of Stormer's book decades ago, it was not until reading Woods' paper that I sought out this supposed source of my ideas. The thesis of *Revolution from Above* is not only different from Stormer's, but in significant ways antithetical.

Stormer's book is an example of the growing feeling during the Cold War that 'Communists' had 'infiltrated' the tax exempt foundations and were using the money in ways antithetical to the wishes of the oligarchs. It is on occasion pointed out that Henry Ford Jnr. resigned as a trustee from the Ford Foundation in December 1976 because he considered the recipients of Foundation largesse too left-wing. However, in this instance Ford Jnr. resigned because he thought the Foundation was over-extending its resources, and suggested cut-backs

---

19   Woods, *A Secret Invasion*.

on the arts, that the staff was too large, that there was not enough support for initiative outside the Foundation programmes, and he regretted that the board was no longer a Ford family affair. When the Reece Congressional Committee on tax exempt foundations criticised the Ford Foundation in 1954 for funding leftist causes, Ford Jnr. stood firmly against Reece and the conservative critics. Nonetheless, the Foundation remained firmly in the hands of Establishment figures, such as John J. McCloy, including those at odds with Ford Jnr.[20]

The thesis of *Revolution from Above*, to the contrary, to quote Professor Quigley, is that 'it must be recognized that the power of these energetic Left-wingers exercised was never their own power or Communist power but ultimately the power of the international financial coterie...'[21] Quigley's opinion that the leftists in the tax exempt foundations were subordinate to the oligarchs accords with the statements made by the Rockefeller Foundation, previously quoted, in regard to the agendas of the Social Science Research Council being set by the Foundation. These matters had previously been examined by the Reece Congressional Committee investigating the Foundations during 1954. The research director for the Congressional Committee, Norman Dodd, commented:

> The broad study which called our attention to the activities of these organizations has revealed not only their support by Foundations but has disclosed a degree of cooperation between them which they have referred to as 'an interlock', thus indicating a concentration of influence and power. By this phrase they indicate they are bound by a common interest rather than a dependency upon a single source for capital funds. It is difficult to study their relationship without confirming this. Likewise, it is difficult to avoid the feeling that their common interest has led them to cooperate closely with one another and that this common interest lies in the planning

---

20 Lally Weymouth, 'Foundation Woes: The Saga of Henry Ford II', *The New York Times*, March 12, 1978.

21 Carroll Quigley, pp. 954–955, quoted in Bolton, *Revolution from Above*, p. 27.

and control of certain aspects of American life through a combination of the Federal Government and education.

This may explain why the Foundations have played such an active role in the promotion of the social sciences, why they have favored so strongly the employment of social scientists by the Federal Government and why they seem to have used their influence to transform education into an instrument for social change.[22]

Dodd saw the purpose of the social sciences being patronised by the Foundations as being that of 'social control' and 'social engineering'.

...For these reasons, it has been difficult for us to dismiss the suspicion that, latent in the minds of many of the social scientists has lain the belief that, given sufficient authority and enough funds, human behavior can be controlled and that this control can be exercised without risk to either ethical principles or spiritual values and that therefore, the solution to all social problems should be entrusted to them. In spite of this dispute within his own ranks, the social scientist is gradually becoming dignified by the title 'Social Engineer'. This title implies that the objective view point of the pure scientist is about to become obsolete in favor of techniques of control. It also suggests that our traditional concept of freedom as the function of natural and constitutional law has already been abandoned by the 'social engineer' and brings to mind our native fear of controls, however well intended.[23]

Left-Wing Red Herring: Lyndon LaRouche

We are told with a blurb from the New School that Woods is working on a book showing the origins of conspiracy theories about Cultural Marxism. The character of Woods' scholarship in researching this book is indicated by his article on the subject appearing in *Commune*, a quarterly journal in the mould of the revolutionary rhetoric of the

---

22 Norman Dodd, 'The Dodd Report to the Special Committee of the House of Representatives to Investigate the Tax Exempt Foundations' (1954).

23 Ibid.

1960s New Left.[24] Here Woods claims to have traced the origins of conspiracy theories about Cultural Marxism to Lyndon LaRouche. Woods states that LaRouche (who had been a leader of the Maoist Progressive Labor Party, before founding the U.S. Labor Party) first wrote about Cultural Marxism in 1974. Woods advances a conspiracy hypothesis of his own about the FBI's COINTELPRO programme aimed at causing internal disruption in radical groups of both Left and Right, wondering whether LaRouche's paranoia about enemy agents might have been fed by the FBI.[25] When writing the *Commune* article, perhaps Woods had not yet found Stormer's *None Dare Call It Treason*, which had been published a decade earlier than the LaRouchean musings?

Woods in weaving his own version of conspiracy theory, contends that opposition to Cultural Marxism is responsible for the mass shootings by Anders Behring Breivik in Norway in 1992, and by Brenton Tarrant in New Zealand in 2019, and that they are traceable to LaRouche. Woods explains:

> Neither Breivik nor Tarrant obtained their irrational and erroneous opinions on Marxism from interwar Nazi propaganda. They absorbed these views from the long-established discourse on 'Cultural Marxism' within the American right, which has been perpetuated by figures such as the New Left apostate David Horowitz, conservative music critic Michael A. Walsh, and paleoconservative politician Pat Buchanan. Even if LaRouche's *EIR*[26] articles from the 1970s remain unread and unacknowledged, his specter haunts this discourse.[27]

Therefore, with the same rationale it can be stated that Woods and those at *Commune* are motivated by the spectres of the psychopathic Mao Zedong, Pol Pot, Bela Kun, Robespierre, and stand on the

---

24 Commune, https://communemag.com/about/.

25 Andrew Woods, 'The American Roots of a Right-Wing Conspiracy', *Commune*, March 20, 2019; https://communemag.com/the-american-roots-of-a-right-wing-conspiracy/.

26 EIR = *Executive Intelligence Review*, a periodical LaRouchean 'conspiracist' report.

27 Andrew Woods, 'The American Roots of a Right-Wing Conspiracy'.

shoulders of 100,000,000 victims of Communism.[28] Whenever there is a *Wahhabi* terrorist act committed in the West, liberals are the first to object to the allegation of any causal relationship between Islam *per se* and terrorism. When it comes to the Right, however, are we supposed to believe that the 'lone-wolf' actions of the likes of Breivik and Tarrant are motivated by the doctrines of Joseph de Maistre, Thomas Carlyle, Anthony Ludovici, Pope Leo XIII, or the Vicomte de Bonald? There is a wide disconnect between Islamophobes such as Breivik and Tarrant, and the traditional Right, which has historically identified with the intransigence of Islam 'against the modern world'.[29]

The Critical Theorist must resort to reductionist banalities and clichés about 'conspiracy theories' being the 'lifeblood of contemporary fascism', thereby discarding any need to explain the historiography of the Right. Instead it serves their agendas to only see Hitler and the KKK. Woods states that 'historical conditions that generated them' need to be investigated, but the Left never bothers to do so. In the climate of hysteria generated against the Right, banality suffices. The concluding sentence indicates that at work is a tactic to achieve support for the Left, if not also as a way to climb the greasy pole of academia for easy accolades, by focusing on an 'extreme Right' or 'fascist' boogeymen: 'Fascism spreads whenever radical leftist politics is sabotaged, silenced, and suppressed. Whereas fascism constructs scapegoats, we must identify the true culprits. The fight against fascism is the first step in the fight for revolution'.[30] To which it might be asked:

1) Where is radical leftist politics being 'sabotaged'? What anti-left conspiracy is involved in this suppression? What leftist academics even of the most extreme type are removed from academia?

---

28 Stephan Courtois et al., *The Black Book of Communism*.

29 For the historical relationship between the Right and traditional Islam, see: Bolton, *Zionism, Islam and the West*, pp. 239–250.

30 Andrew Woods, 'The American Roots…'

When is any of the 'antifa' violent posturing condemned by the mainstream media? The leftist is psychologically obliged to maintain the myth of his role as the 'revolutionary martyr' even when he is an ensconced part of the System. A feeling of persecution paranoia must be maintained by projecting his own position onto the 'Right'.

2) What is this 'Fascist menace' other than a scapegoat for the consequences of culture-pathogens such as multiculturalism and globalisation?

3) Is the purpose of this mythical 'global Fascist conspiracy' that is hyped by pundits, politicians and news media a diversion tactic to obscure the **causes** and **purposes** of social fracture; to delegitimise and demonise criticism of globalist agendas?

Far from the origins of the criticism of Cultural Marxism deriving from Stormer, LaRouche or the 'Right', we need to look elsewhere.

Soviets Condemn Cultural Marxism

Most of the American Right during the Cold War were confused by Establishment anti-Sovietism. They saw Cultural Marxism as a conspiracy headquartered in Moscow, and its funding by oligarchic wealth was the result of Marxist infiltration of the Foundations. They saw the conflict being between Marxism and free enterprise, and many 'American patriots' have never transcended this flawed notion, grounded in the deification of free enterprise and individualism.

The Moscow-aligned Communists were the first to understand the character of Critical Theory or Cultural Marxism. Attempting to replace class struggle with the struggle for an orgasm, Wilhelm Reich[31] was expelled from the German Communist Party. In 1932 Reich's 'sex-economics' doctrine, after being endorsed by a Communist youth conference, was condemned by the party leadership as relegating

---

31 Reich was not a member of the Frankfurt School, despite the ideological convergences.

politics 'down to the level of the gutter'. The party announced in its periodical *Roter Sport* that Reich's pamphlets were contrary to the party's aims for youth education. Reich was accused by the party leadership of wanting to turn the party associations into 'fornication organisations'. The party leaders said that 'there were no orgasm disturbances among the proletariat, only among the bourgeoisie'. The party considered the doctrine as creating a generational conflict.[32] In 1929 Reich visited the USSR but noted that already there was a reversal of the early Bolshevik anti-family policies.[33] Arriving in the USA, he found liberalism more to his liking, 'while "socialist" Russia witnessed reactionary, anti-sexual developments'.[34] Such developments under Stalin were regarded by Trotsky as 'the revolution betrayed', and the reinvigoration of Russian family life and of traditional gender roles was particularly appalling.[35]

When decades later the influence of Cultural Marxism had reached sufficient critical mass to help spark New Left rioting from Chicago to Paris to Prague, so far from this being a Russian plot, Soviet commentators condemned Herbert Marcuse, whose name was being paraded through the streets along with Mao and Marx. Marcuse became the guru of the New Left. Like Wilhelm Reich, Marcuse's theme was that capitalism represses the *libido* of the proletariat.[36]

Soviet journalist Yuri Zhukov[37] wrote in *Pravda* of Marcuse's ideas having infiltrated the youth to 'sow confusion' and divide them from the working class movement, whose vanguard was the Moscow-aligned Communist Party.[38] Zhukov stated that Marcuse was being

---

32   Myron Sharaf, *Fury on Earth*, pp. 169–170.

33   Ibid., p. 142.

34   Ibid., p. 318.

35   Leon Trotsky, *The Revolution Betrayed*, chapter 7.

36   Herbert Marcuse, *Eros and Civilisation* (1955).

37   Zhukov had been foreign affairs editor for *Pravda*, a member of the Foreign Affairs Committee of the Supreme Soviet, and recipient of the Lenin Prize, and the Order of the Red Banner.

38   Yuri Zhukov, 'Werewolves', *Pravda*, May 30, 1968.

promoted by the Western press, 'like a film star'. Marcuse was promulgating generational conflict instead of the fight against capitalism. He had repudiated the need for revolutionary organisation in favour of 'spontaneous revolt'. Zhukov denounced Marcuse for contending that the proletariat has ceased to be revolutionary, and that the revolt must be assumed by others[39] (the disaffected and fractured minorities of 'identity politics'). Zhukov stated that 'bourgeois ideologists' 'brought into play ultraleft anarchist ideas, often echoing those of Mao Tse-tung, in order to cause confusion and disorient ardent but politically inexperienced youths, divide them, and turn those who take the bait into a blind tool of provocations'.[40] Zhukov regarded certain socialists in the German Federal Republic and in Italy as serving the same purposes. These various factions were 'werewolves' using the name of Marx to 'decommunize Marxism'.[41]

Zhukov had excoriated Marcuse ten years earlier; six years prior to Stormer's *None Dare Call It Treason*, and sixteen years prior to LaRouche. Zhukov had in 1958 condemned Marcuse's attack on Soviet society as an effort by Western intellectuals to 'split the progressive forces and set them against one another'.[42]

---

39 Ibid.
40 Ibid.
41 Ibid.
42 Yuri Zhukov, 'Taking Marcuse To The Woodshed', *Atlas*, XVI (Sept., 1958), pp. 33–34.

Psychiatry & Dissent

Although we may not know it, we have, in our day, witnessed the birth of the Therapeutic State. This is perhaps the major implication of psychiatry as an institution of social control.

— Dr Thomas S. Szasz[1]

WHO AND WHAT have the only ability to eliminate the remnants of custom that might lead to 'Fascism' other than the state? Liberal authoritarianism must be imposed to repress the growth of a populist authoritarianism that is contrary to the *brave new world*. This necessitates a coercive bureaucracy of counsellors, social workers, psychiatrists, psychologists, sociologists … In the name of 'freedom' the outcome is the *therapeutic state*, a term coined in 1963 by Thomas Szasz, a notable professor of psychiatry.

Szasz extensively critiqued the uses of 'institutional psychiatry' for political purposes. He saw social scientists such as *Frankfurtian* Erich Fromm as props for the political Establishment, rather than as genuine dissidents. The Soviet intelligentsia discerned the same. Szasz compared the use of psychiatry to the Inquisition, and the finding of witches. In *Manufacture of Madness*, Szasz states that 'institutional psychiatry' provides a ritualistic affirmation for society's 'dominant ethic'. This serves to 'tranquilize' a society that has too many choices because of its plurality; that is 'excessively heterogeneous'. Szasz states

---

1   Thomas S. Szasz, *Law, Liberty, and Psychiatry*, p. 212.

that this serves capitalist and Communist societies 'equally well', 'so long as they all adhere to a "scientific" view of human life' that enables both to define opposition as a mental disorder.[2] As will be shown below, *Frankfurtian* Hebert Marcuse, iconic patron of the New Left, insisted that what is ideologically 'right and wrong' can be empirically proven, and that those doctrines that are 'proven' to be 'wrong' would need to be suppressed for the sake of universal happiness.

Fromm was looking for a 'tranquiliser' in his fear that excessive democracy would lead not to 'spontaneous' freedom but to 'Fascism'. The insecurities that come from excessive freedom might be assuaged by the therapeutic state, albeit resulting from further pervasive intrusions on the individual in the name of suppressing innate 'Fascist' tendencies. This is why the Critical Theorists needed to categorise average White Gentile Americans with an 'F scale', to erect a coercive therapeutic state as a necessary transition to the utopia of universal love and spontaneity. Robespierre, Pol Pot, and Mao purged their populations of those elements regraded as innately reactionary. There has been perpetual warfare for over a century in the name of liberal-democracy and free market capitalism, which alone can provide universal human happiness, once all 'rogue states' are eliminated.

MK-Ultra & the CIA

Szasz was questioning the creation of the therapeutic state when the U.S. Administration was confining dissidents, such as General Edwin Walker[3] and Frederick Seelig,[4] to prison psychiatric wards and asylums. Szasz stated that, 'organized American psychiatry was

2   Thomas Szasz, *The Manufacture of Madness*, p. 59.
3   Szasz advised the defence in the Edwin Walker case. See: 'The Shame of Medicine: The Case of General Edwin Walker', 2009; https://fee.org/articles/the-shame-of-medicine-the-case-of-general-edwin-walker/.
4   Frederick Seelig, *Destroy the Accuser* (1967); https://archive.org/stream/SeeligFrederickDestroyTheAccuser_201610/Seelig_Frederick_-_Destroy_the_accuser_djvu.txt.

becoming overtly political, seeking the existential invalidation and psychiatric destruction of individuals who do not share the psychiatric Establishment's left-liberal "progressive" views'...[5] This was also the time of the CIA's MK-ULTRA project with LSD and other mind control experiments, for which the hippie movement served a purpose. David Price states of the use of social scientists by the CIA in MK-ULTRA:

> A 1963 CIA report describing MK-Ultra projects stressed the interdisciplinary development of the program, as the CIA's Technical Service Division explored use of 'radiation, electro-shock, **various fields of psychology, psychiatry, sociology, and anthropology**, graphology, harassment substances, and paramilitary devices and materials' to control human behavior ...[6]

While the social scientists were often unaware of the CIA connections, the extensive involvement of social scientists with Cold War projects was the result of a convergence of aims and ideologies in regard to the 'control of human behaviour', which had been at the foundation of the social sciences.

'Pathology of Normalcy'

What is regarded as 'normal' in a traditional sense, became pathological, especially after 'Fascism' provided the Establishment with a boogeyman, which, according to Fromm and Adorno, was an endemic condition that required mass therapy by way of social revolution. Fromm referred to the 'pathology of normalcy', writing:

> The 'pathology of normalcy' rarely deteriorates to graver forms of mental illness because society produces the antidote against such deterioration. When pathological processes become socially patterned, they lose their individual character. On the contrary, the sick individual finds himself at home with all other similarly sick individuals. The whole culture is geared to this kind of pathology and arranges the means to give satisfactions which

5   Szasz, 'The Shame of Medicine'.
6   David Price, p. 196. Emphasis added.

fit the pathology. The result is that the average individual does not experience the separateness and isolation the fully schizophrenic person feels. He
feels at ease among those who suffer from the same deformation; in fact,
it is the fully sane person who feels isolated in the insane society — and he
may suffer so much from the incapacity to communicate that it is he who
may become psychotic.[7]

Fromm saw the 'neurotic' as the individual who has not compromised
his individuality for the sake of functionality in society.[8] Hence the
new 'normal' is he who rejects society, because society has itself become abnormal:

> From a standpoint of human values, however, a society could be called
> neurotic in the sense that its members are crippled in the growth of their
> personality. Since the term neurotic is so often used to denote lack of social
> functioning, we would prefer not to speak of a society in terms of its being
> neurotic, but rather in terms of its being adverse to human happiness and
> self-realization.[9]

The way to mental health was to cut the individual from the 'primary
ties' and set him adrift to pursue what in the parlance of the allied
field of *humanistic psychology* becomes *self-actualisation*, regardless
of where that leads, as in the self-actualised examples of the Marquis
de Sade, Charles Manson, and Jim Jones; all paragons of liberalism.
Should the individual become unhinged, the therapeutic state would
be there to offer — or impose — the direction needed to reach the nirvana of 'freedom' and 'happiness'.

To the Freudo-Marxists 'society is sick' and sickness becomes the
norm, so that the genuine healthy individual is looked on by society as
'sick'. It is society that needs changing, to realise that what was normal
is sick, and what is regarded as sick must become the real normal.

---

7   Eric Fromm, *The Anatomy of Human Destructiveness*, p. 356.

8   Fromm, *Fear of Freedom*, p. 120.

9   Ibid., p. 120.

A 'right-wing dissident' remains very much part of a 'lunatic fringe', according to Critical Theory, 'proven' by the 'F scale'. Even Senator Barry Goldwater, the anti-Establishment candidate running against Nelson Rockefeller in the Republican presidential selection, was diagnosed as mentally unfit by a clique of psychiatrists solely due to his conservative views.

Wilhelm Reich's Sexual Reductionism

Twenty years prior to the publication of *The Authoritarian Personality*, Wilhelm Reich, a Freudian-Marxist psychoanalyst in Germany, concluding that the revolution would only occur through a satisfactory orgasm, in what he tried to sell to the Communist Party as 'sex-politics', and 'sex-economics', formulated the theory that Fascism was a result of mass sexual repression by religion, state and family. His studies began in the early 1930s. *The Mass Psychology of Fascism* was first published in Denmark in 1933, and was published in English in 1946. Reich states that excerpts from the book 'were printed in France, America, Czechoslovakia, Scandinavia and other countries, and it was discussed in detailed articles'; it was the Moscow-aligned Communists who avidly rejected the thesis.[10]

Mary Higgins, a trustee of the Wilhelm Reich Infant Trust Fund, summarises Reich's thesis in her foreword to the 1970 edition:

He understands fascism as the expression of the irrational character structure of the average human being whose primary, biological needs and impulses have been suppressed for thousands of years. The social function of this suppression and the crucial role played in it by the authoritarian family and the church are carefully analysed. Reich shows how every form of organized mysticism, including fascism, relies on the unsatisfied orgastic longing of the masses.[11]

---

10   Wilhelm Reich, *The Mass Psychology of Fascism*, Preface (third ed., 1942). This will be examined further in the chapter on Reich's 'Sex-Pol' doctrine.

11   Mary Higgins, in Wilhelm Reich, *The Mass Psychology of Fascism* (1970), Foreword.

By this time Reich, who reached the USA in 1939, where he obtained employment teaching a course at the New School for Social Research, had become antagonistic towards Marxist orthodoxy and was promoting his 'sex-economic-biologic' theory that continued to utilise those aspects of Marxism considered still valid:

> Just as the concept of sexual energy was lost within the psychoanalytic organization only to reappear strong and young in the discovery of the orgone, the concept of the international worker lost its meaning in the practices of Marxist parties only to be resurrected within the framework of sex-economic sociology.[12]

Here we see the primary elements of the Critical Theorist attack on family and religion, and orgasm replacing class struggle in the socialist revolution. Despite the fate of Reich in being jailed in the USA for fraud in 1957 for claiming miraculous cures for his *orgone* energy accumulators, his theories became an integral part of post-Marxist deconstruction.

Reich regarded 'Fascism' as innate to every race and nationality, because it expressed the repression of innate biological drives. Hence, what is required is a universal freedom of the individual from those bonds that restrict orgasm and result in Fascism. Every individual harbours Fascist tendencies, and Fascism as a movement differs from other 'reactionary' forms insofar as it mobilises masses:

> My character-analytic experiences have convinced me that there is not a single individual who does not bear the elements of fascist feeling and thinking in his structure. As a political movement fascism differs from other reactionary parties inasmuch as it is borne and championed by masses of people.[13]

Reich's sex-economic sociology was re-expressed in *The Authoritarian Personality*. Reich had collaborated with Critical Theorists such as

---

12 Reich, ibid.

13 Reich, *The Mass Psychology of Fascism*, 'Preface'.

Erich Fromm, when reaching Berlin from Vienna. The premises are the same, other than Reich's mystical dogma on the cosmic pervasiveness and healing properties of *orgone*. Reich's biographer and colleague Sharaf states of his influence:

> Today, through the efforts of such social analysts as Erich Fromm, Theodor Adorno, and Richard Hofstadter, we have become very familiar with the notion that to understand political movements one must grasp the psychological structure of the people connected with them. But when Reich wrote *The Mass Psychology of Fascism* in 1933 (almost ten years before Fromm's *Escape from Freedom*, and almost twenty years before *The Authoritarian Personality*), his ideas were exceedingly original.[14]

While the Left has been adept at the use of psychoanalysis in undermining reaction to its assault, having become mainstream in academic and state circles, a *psychohistorical* method applied to analysing the Left produces many insights.[15] Reich's vehement attack on the patriarchal family as the seedbed of authoritarianism and 'Fascism', for example, might be traced to his own family background. Sharaf states that Reich's father was ten years older than the mother. Reich regarded his mother as 'very beautiful', although Sharaf states that this is not evident from the extant photo. 'It is clear that he preferred her to his father, a much sterner, more authoritarian person'.[16] Sharaf quotes a 'disguised self-history' by Reich of his 'complex family dynamics' that reveal the root of Reich's obsession with the destruction of the traditional family:

> He [Reich] was brought up very strictly by his father and always had to accomplish more than other children in order to satisfy his father's ambition. From his earliest childhood, he had tenderly clung to his mother who protected him from the daily outbursts of the father. The parental marriage was not happy for the mother suffered horribly from the father's

---

14 Mryon Sharaf, *Fury on Earth*, p. 164.

15 Bolton, *The Psychotic Left*.

16 Mryon Sharaf, *Fury on Earth*, p. 36.

jealousy. Even as a five and six year old he had witnessed hateful scenes of jealousy on the father's part, scenes which even culminated in the father's violence towards the mother. He took the mother's side which is readily understandable since he himself felt under the same whip as the mother and he deeply loved her.[17]

In the same article Reich relates that the father would accuse his wife of being a 'whore'. According to Reich's third wife, Ilse Ollendorff, 'Reich idealised his mother, always citing her cooking as a model that Ilse could not reach'. As a boy on the father's farm in care of peasants, by the time he was four he was sexually aware, due 'in part to his sexual play with his nursemaid'.[18]

Here we have, in a single passage the rationalisation for Reich's generalised projection of his own authoritarian and *Oedipal* childhood onto the entirety of the traditional Western family. Sharaf comments that 'there seems to have been a degree of family tension beyond the "normal" range, stemming from the father's jealous rages and his high expectations for his children'.[19] In another 'self-analysis', which was intended to be heavily disguised, Reich wrote of an affair his mother had with his tutor. Reich relates that as he became aware of the fleeting daily sexual encounters, while his father had an after-lunch nap, he would play 'spy and pursuer', and 'defender', should the father wake up. He thought the motives to be both 'unconscious hatred' against his father or an incestuous titillation toward his mother. Yet Reich also ruminates on his awareness as forever having 'besmirched anew with dirt and muck' his memories of his mother. One evening, as he was heard by mother and tutor outside the bedroom door, he retreated back to his bed, worried that mother and tutor might 'kill' him. However, he returned to the bedroom door night after night; 'the

---

17   Wilhelm Reich, 'Über einen Fall von Durchbruch der Inzestschranke in der Pubertät', *Zeitschrift fur Sexualwissenschaft*, VII, 1920, p. 221; translated by Sharaf, p. 37.

18   Sharaf, p. 39.

19   Ibid., p. 40.

horror disappeared and erotic feelings won the upper hand'. 'And then the thought came to me to plunge into the room, to have intercourse with my mother with the threat that if she didn't I would tell my father. For my part, I went regularly to the chambermaid'. Reich, in the disguised persona of a patient, concluded: 'the father apparently discovered it, and the mother committed suicide by taking poison'. Reich states of his 'patient' that after the suicide, the relationship with his father 'improved', and that he became his father's 'best friend and adviser'.[20] Reich later told others that it was he, as a twelve-year old, who had 'hinted' at the affair to his father, and that he had witnessed her being confronted with this. Reich had been conflicted, and wrote of how his 'patient' 'struggled with two impulses: the desire to tell his father, thereby striking back at the mother and the tutor, on the one hand; and, on the other, the desire to protect his mother from his father's revenge'. The compromise was to 'hint'. 'The results were devastating, and the guilt and remorse he must have felt as a child and a young man can only be imagined. Even into his thirties, Reich would sometimes wake in the night overwhelmed by the thought that he had "killed" his mother'.[21]

The 'sex-economics' reductionism of Reich interpreted Fascist religious-mysticism as 'sadism', in transforming 'the masochistic character of the old patriarchal religion of suffering into a sadistic religion'.[22] Hence, immediately a blow is struck against traditional religion as patriarchal sadism, in an ironic twist of history regarding the origin of the word *sadism*.

---

20 Wilhelm Reich, 'Über einen Fall von Durchbruch', pp. 222–223, cited by Sharaf, pp. 42–43.

21 Sharaf, p. 44.

22 Reich, *Über einen Fall*.

Victimising Dissent

I T IS WELL-KNOWN that psychiatry was used by the Soviet bloc against political dissidents to both undermine their credibility and confine them without trial on the pretext of claiming them to be mentally impaired.[23] As we have seen, the Frankfurt School prepared the way for the use of psychiatry against dissidents in the West with studies such as *The Authoritarian Personality*, and Reich's *Mass Psychology of Fascism*, which ascribed abnormal personality types to conservativism and those values, ethics and morals that had for centuries been regarded as 'normal'. Now, these values were not only abnormal, but intrinsically 'Fascist' and genocidal. Hence, the state has to be eternally vigilant lest in moments of crisis Fascism re-emerges to commit genocide. This repression is undertaken in the name of 'freedom', and is what Herbert Marcuse meant by 'repressive tolerance'.[24]

We see today how far-reaching this repression by liberal states has become in attempts to quell rising tides of national-populism that threaten the 'open borders' demanded by capitalist globalisation.

In the aftermath of Senator Joseph McCarthy, there was a reaction among American elites seeking to purge the Right from society. In the post-McCarthy era, psychiatry became a means of silencing rightist, conservative opponents of the Establishment.

---

23 Sidney Bloch and Peter Reddaway, 'Your Disease Is Dissent', *New Scientist* (July 21, 1977), p. 149.

24 Herbert Marcuse, 'Repressive Tolerance' (1965).

In 1961 the 'Reuther Memorandum' was adopted by the Kennedy Administration as a guideline in purging conservatives from positions of influence, particularly from the military, where it was feared that officers might organise a coup.[25] There was a similar 'memorandum' issued by Senator William Fulbright of the Senate Foreign Relations Committee.[26] The primary target was Major General Edwin Walker, who had initiated a 'citizenship program' in the U.S. Army in Germany, which explained Communism and 'Americanism'. While the U.S. sought to contain the USSR, the purpose was to spread liberal hegemony over the world, not nationalism which, if spread among the military ranks, was seen as a bigger threat than the Soviet Union.

'Siberia Bill'

During this era there was a major effort to establish a large mental health complex in Alaska. This was promoted by Senator Jacob Javits and by the Anti-Defamation League of B'nai B'rith. The American Right was suspicious about what they called the 'Siberia Bill'. The contention was that the Alaska Mental Health Act would be used to kidnap, incarcerate and mentally destroy dissident Americans, in a scenario similar to that of the USSR.

Jewish columnist Milton Friedman [not the economist], writing in *The Canadian Jewish Chronicle*, described the temper of the times:

> An assault on 'Jewish quacks' in President Kennedy's new mental health program has emerged from the extreme Right-wing. The rightists are now seeking to brand psychiatry as subversive.

---

25 Walter and Victor Reuther, 'The Reuther Memorandum to the Attorney General of the United States', (December 19, 1961), http://www.scribd.com/doc/31124491/The-Reuther-Memorandum-Precusor-to-the-Ideological-Organizations-Audit-Project-Created-by-President-John-F-Kennedy-and-Attorney-General-Robert-Kenn.

26 James W. Fulbright, 'Propaganda Activities of Military Personnel Directed at the Public', Congressional Record (2 August 1961), pp. 14433–14439 (Senate).

Attacks on the mental health movement are jeopardizing gains made in public understanding in recent years according to a survey on anti-psychiatric activities throughout the country. The survey was made by Dr. Alfred Auerbach for the American Psychiatric Association. APA's concern at the growing denunciations of mental health as 'atheistic' or 'Communistic' was confirmed by the Association's president Dr. C. H. C. Hardin Branch.

The main targets have been the psychiatrists, psychologists and mental health leaders of the Jewish faith. Note was taken of the recent popularity of a play and film about the life of Dr. Sigmund Freud.

A recent Alaska Mental Health Act established mental hospitals in Alaska. It was previously necessary to send Alaskan patients to Portland, Ore., for treatment. Right-wingers charged that Christian anti-Communists were to be shipped off to Alaska for brainwashing by 'Jew psychiatrists'. They portrayed a sort of American Siberia.[27]

Friedman quoted Senator Thomas H. Kuchel (R., California) about an upsurge in anti-Semitism among the extreme Right, tying in the anti-Communist John Birch Society, which, although eschewing anti-Semitism and racism, was a major bugbear of the U.S. Administration due to its success with grass-roots organising. Javits commended Kuchel 'for rallying the Senate against resurgent Birchism'.[28] It is evident from Friedman that the liberal, left and Jewish partisans were themselves eager to link opposition to the Mental Health Bill to a wider condemnation on the American Right, including comparatively mainline conservatives such as the John Birch Society.

This is confirmed from a liberal academic source of the period. Ralph E. Ellsworth and Sarah M. Harris in a paper on the 'American Right-Wing', which they defined as anything that is 'not Left-wing', stated in a section on the rightist response to 'mental health':

The mental health program is also interpreted as a conspiracy, and often as one aimed directly at the Right Wing. This interpretation is found in the

---

27 Milton Friedman, 'Washington Spotlight', *The Canadian Jewish Chronicle*, 31 May 1963, p. 6.

28 Ibid.

articles by George Todt which were read into the Congressional Record by Senator Barry Goldwater. The Alaskan Mental Hospital Law which was passed in 1956 distressed many conservatives because it appeared to them to create a kind of Siberia to which political prisoners might be sent against their will, and it seemed clear to them that these prisoners would be right wingers. There had already been the classic cases of Lucille Miller… and, of course, most famous of all, Ezra Pound — **all right wingers whose political views unquestionably figured in determining their assignment to mental hospitals.** Lucille Miller, in her paper *The Green Mountain Rifleman*, first called the Right's attention to the incarceration in 1945 of Ezra Pound as a political prisoner at St. Elizabeths Hospital in Washington, D. C.

John Kasper,[29] of the Clinton, Tennessee, litigations, testified before a Senate Committee in 1956 that Pound was not insane, as certified, but was being punished for treason, for which he had never been tried in any court. Psychiatry, Kasper added, was a Jewish invention, and thoroughly un-American. Both Pound and Kasper himself have been defended by the American Civil Liberties Committee, on the ground that their civil liberties have been invaded, and it appears that in Pound's case **the indignation of the Right, if sometimes a little histrionic, is certainly entirely reasonable.**[30]

The American Legion, the U.S. war veterans' organisation, expressed concern that normal American values were being redefined as symptoms of mental illness, as they indeed had been by the Critical Theorists, citing the American Friends Service Committee, a prominent Quaker organisation:

Characteristic of this reaction is the comment of the American Legion writer who quotes the following passage from an *American Friends Service*

---

29   John Kasper, an intellectual publisher, was also a fiery young orator and organiser for the White Citizens Councils that defended segregation in the South. He became one of Pound's protégées while Pound was in St. Elizabeths. See: Dr. Robert S. Griffin, 'The Tale of John Kasper', *The Occidental Observer*, 15 December 2017; https://www.theoccidentalobserver.net/2017/12/15/the-tale-of-john-kasper/.

30   Ralph E. Ellsworth and Sarah M. Harris, *The American Right-Wing, A Report to the Fund for the Republic*, pp. 14–15. Emphasis added.

Committee Bulletin (May, 1952, p. 7): 'What makes a super-patriot a super-patriot? The following paragraphs speculate on the forces within, which drive such men and women. It is an expression of a belief that understanding may enable us to help them. The superpatriots are clearly afraid. Being adults, they must rationalize their fears. They may call it "concern for country." They see a threat to the nation in the U.N. and UNESCO (or whatever) because these groups include strangers — people of different culture, language, religion and race. But their fears, to cause such hysteria, must be related to something far more basic than 'flag' or 'country'.... This is the purest paranoid delusion: 'I have hundreds of lurking, secret enemies!' Explaining away the fancied enemies one by one forever will never relieve the condition for the person who is deluded. A friendly and loving attitude toward each mentally ill person is basic to being helpful. He feels the enemies and invents and seizes upon the person or group to be the enemy, to explain the feeling to himself."[31]

Ellsworth and Harris quote the American Legion as commenting:

The A.F.S.C. implies that 'super-patriots' who refuse to be conditioned (to world understanding) are mentally ill. Presumably such mentally ill people should have the benefit of medical treatment as prescribed by world-minded individuals who are not afflicted with the 'disease' of patriotism.[32]

Compare this to Harry A. Overstreet's statement in *The Great Enterprise* (1952): 'A man, for example, may be angrily against race equality, public housing, the TVA, financial and technical aid to backward countries, organized labor, and the preaching of social rather than salvational religion. ... Such people may appear normal in the sense that they're able to hold a job and otherwise maintain their status as members of society; but they are, we now realize, well along the road toward mental illness'. This passage is quoted by Edith K. Roosevelt in her article, 'Bats in the UN Belfry?' 'What Dr Overstreet describes, of course,' she says, 'is the prototype of millions of conservative people everywhere'. Even more disturbing is her report that Povl Bang-Jensen, who served as Deputy Secretary to the U.N. Special Committee on the Problem of Hungary, and who refused to deliver to the United Nations a list of Hungarian witnesses against Communism,

31   Quoted by Ellsworth and Harris, p. 15.
32   Ibid.

was suspended as an officer of the U.N. and is now spoken of as not 'rational', but as 'aberrant', 'odd', hence inevitably unreliable and incapable of telling the truth and exercising good judgment. Or as Mrs Alice Widener puts it, 'Povl Bang-Jensen stands officially accused, by a U.N. Committee, of conduct that departed markedly from normal and rational standards of behaviour'.[33]

Ellsworth and Harris referred to Walter Reuther as stating that Senator Barry Goldwater, a senior political figure, part Jewish and moderately conservative, was in need of psychiatric examination. 'One learns, too, that Walter Reuther has stated that Senator Barry Goldwater needs a psychiatrist. This, of course, is exactly what Senator Goldwater would expect him to say. It appears that the Alaska Mental Hospital may eventually need its entire land grant after all'.[34]

Goldwater on the Couch

When Goldwater ran for the presidency, having prevailed against Nelson Rockefeller for the Republican nomination, over a thousand psychiatrists declared him 'mentally unfit'. It is indicative of the uselessness of such 'progressives' in genuinely confronting the 'Establishment'. It was also an election that saw the New Left SDS campaigning for Lyndon Johnson rather than have a 'Fascist' such as Goldwater in the White House.[35] Harry Stein of *City Journal* writes of the era:

---

33   Ibid.
34   Ibid.
35   Lance Selfa, *The Democrats: A Critical History*, pp. 223–224. The SDS slogan was 'Half the Way with LBJ'. It is indicative of how easily co-opted even the most ostensibly 'revolutionary' Left can be. Meanwhile, 'Sixty percent of the members of the Business Council, an extremely influential Washington advisory group composed of chief executives of the largest and most important U.S. companies, backed Johnson. And LBJ won the lion's share of the corporate contributions to the presidential candidates'. (p. 224).

At the height of the 1964 race between Arizona's junior senator, Barry Goldwater, and President Lyndon Johnson, the cover headline of *Fact* magazine's September–October issue practically screamed: 1,189 PSYCHIATRISTS SAY GOLDWATER IS PSYCHOLOGICALLY UNFIT TO BE PRESIDENT! Inside, every page was given over to the feature, titled "The Unconscious of a Conservative: A Special Issue on the Mind of Barry Goldwater."[36]

Fact was published by Ralph Ginzburg (found guilty the year previously of violating Federal obscenity laws), publisher of *Eros* magazine,[37] at a time when pornography was being lauded as rebellious, prior to becoming anathema to the Left for 'objectifying women'. Stein continues:

Forgotten today, *Fact* even then was far from a major player on the journalistic scene. It had launched earlier that year and would survive just until 1967. Still, it enjoyed a status among the day's progressive *bien pensants* far beyond what its limited circulation might suggest. ...[38]

The psychiatrists' reaction was classic Critical Theory, and reached its own levels of paranoia reminiscent of what was heard among 'progressives' after Trump's winning the presidential elections:

The issue's introduction set the tone for the 63 pages to follow. Ginzburg described Goldwater as the product of a "sadistic childhood," a "paranoiac" with an "obsessive preoccupation with firearms" who "compulsively must prove his daring and masculinity," adding that "psychoanalysts who find a connection between sadism and an anal character will not be surprised that bathrooms seemed to fascinate Goldwater."[39]

---

36   Harry Stein, 'The Goldwater Takedown', *City Journal*, Autumn 2016; https://www.city-journal.org/html/goldwater-takedown-14787.html.

37   *Eros* was itself ideologically a synthesis of Leftist Freudinanism. This will be considered in the chapter on 'Sexology'.

38   Ibid.

39   Ibid.

Stein states that 'the "psychiatric evaluations' that took up the next 40 pages were in response to a question that *Fact* sent to the nation's psychiatrists from a list supplied by the American Medical Association: "Do you believe Barry Goldwater is psychologically fit to serve as President of the United States?"'

Among the responses[40] a New York psychiatrist stated that she saw in Goldwater 'a strong identification with the authoritarianism of Hitler, if not identification with Hitler himself'. Another stated: 'I believe Goldwater has the same pathological make-up as Hitler, Castro, Stalin and other known schizophrenic leaders'. Paul Fink from Philadelphia responded that like Hitler, Goldwater 'appeals to the unconscious sadism and hostility in the average human being'. G. Templeton, of Glen Cove, New York, warned that '**if Goldwater wins the Presidency, both you and I will be among the first into the concentration camps**'. Stein notes that the Ginzburg feature did real damage, with a notable comment in regard to the source of funding for Ginzburg's advertising campaign for the *Eros* edition in the major press:

> That the entire exercise was ethically dubious was apparent at the time. As longtime Goldwater advisor Stephen Shadegg noted in disgust, "Those who presumed to reach a medical and psychiatric conclusion about Goldwater without ever having seen him or followed any other of the normal procedures required in a patient-physician relationship betrayed themselves as men unfit to practice any profession." **But the feature drew widespread attention via the media coverage that it generated and full-page ads in the nation's leading dailies—Goldwater's people rightly wondered how a modest publication afforded their $100,000 cost—and it undeniably did real damage.**[41]

---

40 Nonetheless, among the respondents, '511 said, "We don't know enough"… 657 said they thought Goldwater fit…' Alan Stone, 'The Psychiatrists' Goldwater Rule in the Trump Era', *Lawfare*, 19 April 2018; https://www.lawfareblog.com/psychiatrists-goldwater-rule-trump-era.

41 Harry Stein. Emphasis added.

Stein states of the Rockefeller campaign against Goldwater:

> Rockefeller made it easy. His reeling campaign's objective, his chief con-
> sultant Stuart Spencer said later, became "to destroy Barry Goldwater as
> a member of the human race." To that end, they set up an unprecedented
> oppo-research operation, rummaging through every corner of Goldwater's
> past and, notes Perlstein, arranging for "friendly reporters to record for
> transcription every word Goldwater said in public..."[42]

With the Cold War at its height, these were highly paranoid times,
but the post-Freudians placed the onus of mass paranoia entirely
at the Right. Stein relates that the paranoia was not a monopoly of
McCarthyism and Birchers, and that it was the paranoia of the Left
that held sway in influential quarters such as the mass media (which
had a decade previously been an important factor in destroying
Joseph McCarthy).

> Why did so transparent a hit job arouse so little indignation among
> Ginzburg's press colleagues? At the time, no sentient observer of the
> campaign would have had to ask. "In your heart, you know he's right," ran
> the Goldwater slogan that fired up his legions of young supporters, but in
> progressive circles, there came the mocking rejoinder: "In your guts, you
> know he's nuts." Ginzburg could not have played more precisely to the lib-
> eral view of conservatism's dark heart; just a month later would appear, to
> subsequent fame, Richard Hofstadter's Harper's essay "The Paranoid Style
> in American Politics," saying many of the same things more politely. Yet
> if conspiracy-obsessed zealots of the Far Right often seemed to live in an
> alternate reality—exemplified by John Birch Society founder Robert Welch
> calling Dwight Eisenhower a Red stooge—so did the innumerable liberals
> who imagined (as Hollywood several times put on film) that superpatriots
> were busily plotting military coups. With the Cold War at its hottest, the
> paranoia ran both ways, and liberals, too, saw in their foes "a perfect model
> of malice," in Hofstadter's phrase. Not only were conservatives wrong; they
> were moral primitives.[43]

---

42 Ibid.
43 Ibid.

Alan Stone, past president of the American Psychiatric Association, and Emeritus Professor of Law and Psychiatry, Harvard University, opined over forty years later, 'It must be said that in the years that followed, it became clear to everyone who knew him that Goldwater was neither mentally ill nor suffering from major psychoses, as America's leading psychiatrists had diagnosed him'.[44] Stone in his review of Bandy Lee's compilation of psychiatric diagnoses of Donald Trump, in comparing this to the compilation of views published in *Eros* on Goldwater, cites one of the respondents, and makes some apt observations:

> One must admit that there were some embarrassingly extreme condemnations of Goldwater. So extreme, in fact that they ought to have raised questions about the professional objectivity or even mental status of some of the psychiatric experts:
>
> I believe Goldwater is grossly psychotic. His statements reveal a serious thinking disorder … He is grandiose, which is suggestive of delusions of grandeur. He is suspicious, suggestive of paranoia. He is impulsive, suggesting that he has poor control over his feelings and that he acts on angry impulses. This alone would make him extremely psychologically unfit to serve as President. A President must not act on impulse! But in addition he consciously wants to destroy the world with atomic bombs. He is mass-murderer at heart and a suicide. He is amoral and immoral. A dangerous lunatic!
>
> Signed: A Board-certified psychiatrist
>
> Stamford, CT
>
> P.S. Any psychiatrist who does not agree with the above is himself psychologically unfit to be a psychiatrist.

This psychiatrist of most liberal disposition, like his or her counterparts featured in the Bandy Lee symposium (see below), and like Marcuse as he expressed it in his essay 'Repressive Tolerance', betrays a deeply authoritarian, paranoid personality projected on to perceived

---

44   Alan Stone, 'The Psychiatrist's Goldwater Rule in the Trump Era'.

heretics. It is the character of a Robespierre or a Beria. It is always latent and waiting to burst forth in times of social decay.

Trump on the Couch

Today we might assume that the use of psychiatry as a political weapon against dissidents in the West has gone. This is especially so since in 1973 the American Psychiatric Association adopted the so-called 'Goldwater Rule',[45] in response to the 1964 smear campaign against Senator Goldwater, which prohibits psychiatrists from offering opinions on someone they have not personally evaluated. However, Harvard emeritus professor Alan Stone, who regards Trump as a 'danger' for reasons other than psychiatric, points out that, 'The American Psychological Association, by contrast to the American Psychiatric Association, for example, has no Goldwater rule. The American Psychoanalytic Association no longer adheres to the rule. Furthermore, the American Psychiatric Association is a voluntary organization which has no authority over psychiatrists who are non-members'.[46]

In 2017 Yale psychiatrist Brandy Lee published the views of 27 psychiatrists on Trump, based on a conference themed 'Duty to Warn', in New Haven on 20 April 2017.[47] Stone writes:

> She discovered that many of her more distinguished colleagues shared her concerns. Several of them compared their situation to that of German

---

45   The 'Goldwater Rule' reads: 'On occasion psychiatrists are asked for an opinion about an individual who is in the light of public attention or who has disclosed information about himself/herself through public media. In such circumstances, a psychiatrist may share with the public his or her expertise about psychiatric issues in general. However, it is unethical for a psychiatrist to offer a professional opinion unless he or she has conducted an examination and has been granted proper authorization for such a statement'. American Psychiatric Association, *Principles of Medical Ethics with Annotations Especially Applicable to Psychiatry*, Section 7.3.

46   Alan Stone, 'The Psychiatrist's Goldwater rule in the Trump Era'.

47   Bandy X. Lee, *The Dangerous Case of Donald Trump*.

psychiatrists during the rise of Hitler who had failed to speak out. Some of her colleagues felt morally compelled not only to speak out, but also to share their professional opinions with President Obama, the leaders of the military, and top Democrats in Congress.

The book rehashes the same opinions that had been used against Goldwater fifty years previously, according to Stone. That is because such commentators have been imbued, whether directly or not, by Critical Theory. This is evident from Stone's description:

> Ironically, many of the book's contributors seemingly avoid reference to the "official" diagnostic categories specified in the current *Diagnostic and Statistical Manual of Psychiatry*—while offering versions of the same derogatory labels as the psychiatrists who "diagnosed" Goldwater in 1964: narcissistic personality, paranoid personality, bipolar disorder, delusional disorder, presenile dementia, and impulsivity. **As their predecessors had done with Goldwater, many contributors to the book also compare Trump to Hitler or mention them in the same paragraph.** The only major difference between the labels attached to these men is that Trump is said to be sociopathic whereas Goldwater was deemed compulsively rigid.[48]

There is also direct allusion to the *Frankfurtian* influence. In an interview about the Bandy Lee symposium, Bill Moyers[49] raises Erich Fromm with psychiatrist Robert Lifton, a contributor to the book:

---

48 Stone, Emphasis added.

49 Journalist, political commentator and Press Secretary for Lyndon Johnson, a president noted for his opportunism and duplicity. During the Kennedy administration Moyers had served as a director of the Peace Corps, which plays an important role in expanding American globalism to the Third World. During the 1964 presidential campaign when Johnson's chief of staff, Walter Jenkins, was caught soliciting a homosexual act at a public toilet, Johnson instructed Moyers to request the FBI to investigate the personal lives of members of the Goldwater campaign, and of those of Johnson's own staff. This veteran champion of the liberal-Left has been a Trustee of the Rockefeller Foundation, sitting along with John D. Rockefeller IV, fellow Bilderberger Vernon Jordan et al. (1975 RF Annual Report), is a member of the premier globalist think tank, the Council on Foreign Relations, and has been on the Steering Committee of the Bilderberg Group, where he can attend secret conclaves with the Rothschilds

Moyers: You mentioned extreme narcissism. I'm sure you knew Erich Fromm.

Lifton: Yes, I did.

Moyers: — one of the founders of humanistic psychology. He was a Holocaust survivor[50] who had a lifelong obsession with the psychology of evil. And he said that he thought "malignant narcissism" was the most severe pathology—"the root of the most vicious destructiveness and inhumanity."[51] Do you think malignant narcissism goes a long way to explain Trump?

Lifton: I do think it goes a long way. In early psychoanalytic thought, narcissism was—and still, of course, is—self-love. The early psychoanalysts used to talk of libido directed at the self. That now feels a little quaint, that kind of language. But it does include the most fierce and self-displaying form of one's individual self. And in this way, it can be dangerous. When you look at Trump, you can really see someone who's destructive to any form of life enhancement in virtually every area. And if that's what Fromm means by malignant narcissism, then it definitely applies.[52]

In 2012 Lifton was awarded an honorary doctorate from the New School.[53]

---

and directors from Goldman Sachs. Bilderberg Group, Steering Committee: https://web.archive.org/web/20140202095633/http://www.bilderbergmeetings.org/former-steering-committee-members.html.

50 That Moyers describes Fromm as a 'Holocaust survivor' might indicate something of his very loose interpretation of facts. Fromm was safely ensconced in the USA throughout the Hitler period.

51 Malignant narcissism is the most persistent trait I found among leftist ideologues and leaders. See: Bolton, *The Psychotic Left*.

52 Bill Moyers' interview with Robert Jay Lifton, 'The Dangerous Case of Donald Trump: Robert Jay Lifton and Bill Moyers on "A Duty to Warn"', Psychiatrist Robert Jay Lifton on the Goldwater Rule: We Have a Duty to Warn if Someone May be Dangerous to Others', *Salon*, 19 September 2017; https://www.salon.com/test/2017/09/19/the-dangerous-case-of-donald-trump-robert-jay-lifton-and-bill-moyers-on-a-duty-to-warn_partner/.

53 New School News, 'The Right Mixture for a New School Commencement', 1 May 2012; https://blogs.newschool.edu/news/2012/05/a-new-school-commencement/#.Wz6GBxJKgWo.

Stone states that in the final chapter, 'He's Got the World in His Hands and his Finger on the Trigger', that 'two psychiatrists urge Congress to appoint a panel of experts to examine the president'. ...[54] This says more about the mentality of such 'professionals' using psychiatry as a political weapon. The 1964 campaign against Goldwater, which inflicted the most damage to his presidential bid, was of precisely that nature: the characterisation of Goldwater as likely to embroil the world in a nuclear holocaust, dramatized by the image of a little girl picking daisies before being radiated. Yet for all the ineptitude, ignorance and backtracking of Trump, who was going to 'drain the [Washington] swamp', purge the state of Goldman Sachs influence, return the USA to an 'America First' foreign policy, 'bring the troops home'; it was Hillary Clinton who campaigned on a policy of confrontation with Russia, as Secretary of State escalated U.S. intervention in the Middle East, and expressed psychotic glee on hearing of the murder of Colonel Qaddafi.[55]

A lesson to be taken from *The Dangerous Case of Donald Trump* is that the *brave new world* envisaged by the social engineers will be able to readily recruit sufficient numbers of functionaries from the social sciences to impose Marcuse's vision of 'repressive tolerance'.

---

54   Alan Stone.

55   Hilary Clinton on CBS News on hearing of the murder of Qaddafi: https://www.youtube.com/watch?v=Fgcd1ghag5Y.

Marginalising Dissidents

THE STAGE HAD been set by President Franklin Roosevelt refer- ring to the 'lunatic fringe' in a 1944 speech.[1] The American Jewish Committee had sponsored *The Authoritarian Personality* to 'prove' that those with hitherto normal values were latent 'Fascists', and society was in need of social engineering. This social engineering is now regarded as more efficacious in eliminating dissident views than targeting individuals for 'treatment'. Dissidents, by which is meant tra- ditional conservatives and rightists, can now be readily marginalised by the mass media, as values that were assumed to be normal until a few decades ago have become stigmatised as regressive, *passé*, pa- triarchal, Fascist, White supremacist, Nazi, sexist, racist, anti-Semitic, homophobic, transphobic, *ad infinitum*. The words induce a Pavlovian reflex.

There is no longer a requirement to crudely incarcerate dissidents in psychiatric institutions in the manner which seemed to have been quite routine for several decades.[2] The way that Senator Joseph McCarthy was portrayed by CIA-sponsored journalists shows that one can be destroyed to the point of death as surely as cyber-bullying can induce a teenager to commit suicide. The same psychological methods are at work through ever greater means of mass communications and mind-manipulations that are far more invasive and enduring than the

---

1   William Safire, *Safire's Political Dictionary*, 'Lunatic Fringe', p. 405.
2   Just how horrendous this process was can be seen from the book by investiga- tive journalist Frederick Seelig on his experiences.

blatant propaganda of 'people's democracies'. If a dissident becomes too problematic, the media is sufficiently influential, and its consumers sufficiently pliant, to demonize the individual to the point where he becomes a pariah.

The method of pathologising traditional values has been refined within the social sciences, and in well-funded think tanks that are organised to study 'the danger of the Right and of populism'. From these the mass media across the world is fed with backgrounders to enable hack-journalists to uniformly generate smears.

The Christchurch (New Zealand) mosque shootings of March 2019 opened up an intensive campaign against the Right and 'populism' that has not abated. The term 'witch-hunt'[3] is precise in describing the campaign.

Since it was discovered that Christchurch mosque shooter Tarrant gave small donations to Martin Sellner of Generation Identity (GI) in Austria over a year previously, and consequently a couple of emails were exchanged in acknowledgement, a witch-hunt has been launched against the 'Far Right' in a cynical use of the Muslim deaths.

In particular, Sellner was targeted because of his articulate and professional manner. It is claimed that Sellner is of such influence that his (GI's) campaign against the *United Nations Compact on Migration* was responsible for several states not signing as the result of what is called 'fake news' and 'lies' about the U.N. document being 'binding'. Whether Sellner was responsible for Israel rejecting the *Compact* on the basis that it interferes with national sovereignty was not stated. The *Compact* is the equivalent of U.N. 'covenants' that have become 'binding' in terms of being legislated as laws and policed by U.N. agencies. The *Compact* provides for such policing to ensure the compliance of signatory states. The purpose is to open borders for the benefit

---

3   'A witch-hunt is an attempt to find and punish a particular group of people who are being blamed for something, often simply because of their opinions and not because they have actually done anything wrong'. *Collins English Dictionary.*

of globalisation and address demographic imbalances in industrialised states through what the U.N. calls 'Replacement Migration'.[4] Accusations about *Identitarians* and others of the Right making false claims are nonsense, as reading the provisions of the *Compact* readily shows. The Right is ridiculed for its so-called 'scare-mongering' and 'false news' (sic) in referring to open borders and mass migration flows into Europe as 'The Great Replacement', but the term is close in both phrasing and meaning to the U.N.'s own term 'Replacement Migration'.[5]

Institute for Strategic Dialogue

A primary question to be asked is the whence of the media's information on the *Identitarian* 'Far Right'. It is the Institute for Strategic Dialogue (ISD). Here we reach 'conspiracy theory'. Indeed, following the 'Far Right' and 'White supremacist' websites, according to the ISD, 'conspiracy theory' websites were most responsible for spreading Sellner's so-called 'lies' on the *U.N. Migration Compact*. It is not plausible, we are assured, that conspiracies among oligarchs exist, in contrast to an 'international Austro-Nazi conspiracy', which is so influential and well-funded as to be determining the policies of major political parties and governments.

Patrick Gower, a New Zealand television current affairs journalist, who was determined to redeem himself after his humiliation in the course of an interview with Canadian 'right-wingers' Stefan Molyneux

---

4   Replacement Migration, 'Is It a Solution to Declining and Ageing Populations?' (Population Division Department of Economic and Social Affairs United Nations Secretariat, 2001); https://www.un.org/en/development/desa/population/publications/ageing/replacement-migration.asp.

5   Bolton, 'United Nations Global Migration Compact: Origins & Aims', *Arktos Journal*, 7 January 2019; https://arktos.com/2019/01/07/united-nations-global-migration/.

and Lauren Southern,[6] used the ISD as his source for smearing the supposed 'Far Right' in New Zealand, stating:

> An investigation by the Institute for Strategic Dialogue, which monitors extremism online, found: 'Far-right and right-wing populist influencers... began spreading large-scale distorted interpretations and misinformation about the UN migration pact'.[7]

What hack journalist is going to investigate the character of the Institute for Strategic Dialogue? According to Gower it is some type of definitive authority, 'monitoring online extremism', and almost sounds official, like a branch of Interpol. The ISD embarked on an international smear campaign against Generation Identity and Sellner. It is pertinent to ask whether this has been undertaken precisely because Sellner and GI upset the proverbial applecart in regard to the *U.N. Migration Compact*; a cause that happens to be a part of the ISD agenda?

Among the major smears against GI and Sellner, the Friedrich-Ebert-Stiftung featured an interview with Jakob Guhl, 'Project Associate at the Institute for Strategic Dialogue (ISD), where he mainly works with the Online Civil Courage Initiative, a project that aims to improve and promote civil society reactions to hate speech and extremism on the Internet'. Guhl claimed in regard to the *U.N. Migration Compact* that,

> While the agreement was barely talked about on social media until mid-September, far-right and right-wing populist influencers 'discovered' the issue in mid-September and began spreading large-scale distorted interpretations and disinformation about the UN migration pact. ... and

---

6   Gower interview with Molyneux and Southern, *Newshub*, 3 August 2018; https://www.youtube.com/watch?reload=9&v=mUR9U6Srj7g.

7   Patrick Gower, 'Exclusive: Police Investigating White Supremacist Death Threats against Winston Peters', *Newshub*, 30 June 2019; https://www.newshub.co.nz/home/new-zealand/2019/06/exclusive-police-investigating-white-supremacists-death-threats-against-winston-peters.html.

far-right representatives such as Martin Sellner played a big role in shap-
ing the discussion about the migration pact online. His 'Stop Migration
Pact' petition was the most shared URL link in our dataset until the end of
October.[8]

Guhl complained that there was insufficient information about the
Compact, until the 'Far Right' discovered it. That the U.N. was negli-
gent in providing information on the *Compact* is surely an indictment
on that body, not on the 'Far Right', which sought to address the information void. It was the 'Far Right' that helped publicise the very scant
information that the U.N. did provide, which enabled one to make an
informed judgement based on the presentation of both sides, which
clearly the U.N. and its allies were unwilling to do.

'The Friedrich-Ebert-Stiftung (FES) is the oldest political foundation in Germany with a rich tradition in social democracy dating back
to its foundation in 1925. The foundation owes its formation and its
mission to the political legacy of its namesake Friedrich Ebert, the
first democratically elected German President'.[9] There is nothing
new about a leftist organisation taking its party-line from a plutocratic
think tank such as the ISD. In good left-wing Social Democratic fashion, the Ebert Foundation promotes NATO, trans-Atlantic free trade,
and generally how to keep Germany subservient to the USA.

A report in the *New Zealand Herald* stated that 'European investigators are digging deeper into possible links between far-right ideologues and the suspected Christchurch mosque gunman, who sent at
least two donations to an anti-Muslim group with branches around
Europe ... "One of the dangers of this ideology is that it creates an im-
minent threat from the outside: a coming war if we don't do anything
about it," said Austrian right-wing extremism researcher Julia Ebner,

---

8   'Too Little, Too Late', Friedrich-Ebert-Stiftung, 7 February 2019; https://www.
    fes.de/en/displacement-migration-integration/article-page-flight-migration-
    integration/too-little-too-late/.

9   Friedrich-Ebert-Stiftung, 'About Us', https://www.fesdc.org/about/friedrich-
    ebert-stiftung/.

with the London-based Institute for Strategic Dialogue. "A violent escalation is part of their ideology."[10] The mass media presents such baseless scare-mongering as 'expertise'. As GI showed in a detailed response to media smears and Establishment repression, there was no violent intent.[11]

A report in *The Washington Post* included the widespread theme that there were 'extensive' links between Sellner and Tarrant, citing Jacob Davey, 'the author of a forthcoming Institute for Strategic Dialogue paper on the subject';[12] meaning, there were three brief emails in regard to Tarrant's small donations. *Post* columnist Anne Applebaum, introducing a Judaeocentric dimension added:

> The obsession with the Jewish financier George Soros, a feature of far-right propaganda everywhere from Hungary to Alabama, is linked to this set of ideas. And when President Trump or Italian Interior Minister Matteo Salvini talk about immigrant 'invasions,' they are nodding and winking to *Identitarianism*, too.[13]

A conspiracy involving 'anti-Semites' is the frequent fare for commentators: *reductio ad Judaeum*. However, Applebaum having mentioned Soros, an examination of those behind ISD renders familiar results. Should there be involvement from Soros, are we supposed to overlook the fact lest it indicates an 'anti-Semitic obsession'?

The 'partners and funders' of the ISD are high-powered globalist corporations. They include: Facebook, Google, Twitter, Jigsaw, M &

---

10   'Probe into Links between Accused Christchurch Gunman and European Far-Right Groups', *Auckland Herald*, 7 April 2019; https://www.nzherald.co.nz/nz/news/article.cfm?c_id=1&objectid=12220026.

11   Generation Identity, https://www.identitaere-bewegung.at/unwahrheiten/.

12   Anne Applebaum, 'How Europe's "Identitarians" are Mainstreaming Racism', *Washington Post*, 17 May 2019; https://www.washingtonpost.com/opinions/global-opinions/how-europes-identitarians-are-mainstreaming-racism/2019/05/17/3c7c9a6e-78da-11e9-b3f5-5673edf2d127_story.html?noredirect=on&utm_term=.2641dfd32252.

13   Anne Applebaum, ibid.

C Saatchi, Microsoft, Love Frankie, Asia Foundation (Rockefeller), Carnegie Corporation NY, Eranda Rothschild Foundation, Gen Next, Open Society Foundations (Soros), Robert Bosch Foundation, Vodafone Foundation.[14]

Love Frankie is a Saatchie-sponsored 'social change' project in Asia. Among those who 'Love Frankie' are the U.S. State Department, USAID, World Bank Group, Facebook, Google, various U.N. agencies, *et al.*[15]

Other partners of the ISD include the U.S. State Department, International Republican Institute, Brookings Institution, Chatham House, the London School of Economics 'Arena' project that targets anti-globalists; Royal United Services Institute, etc.

The ISD is a globalist institution founded to smear and agitate for the suppression of opposition to globalisation. The character of its sponsors makes this clear. They exist to target anti-globalisation as 'fascistic'. That is their terminology:

> We believe it is the task of every generation to challenge such divisive, fascistic movements and to invest in the ongoing edification of open, democratic, and free civic culture, without which there can be no lasting protection of the rights of others, no cohesion and no lasting peace'.[16]

Here again is the doctrine of the Critical Theorists such as Marcuse with his double-think 'repressive tolerance'.

ISD has 'advised 40 governments', reached 120 'strong cities network members', indoctrinated with their globalism 80,000 youths in 'education programmes', presided over 75 reports and policy briefings, and 'trained over 32,000 activists'.[17] 'Activists' is usually a euphemism for psychotics of the antifa variety.

---

14 ISD, 'Partners and Funders', https://www.isdglobal.org/isdapproach/partnerships/.

15 Love Frankie, https://lovefrankie.co/.

16 'About ISD', https://www.isdglobal.org/isdapproach/.

17 ISD, 'Programmes'; https://www.isdglobal.org/programmes/.

Based on our far-right analysis and research we briefed and advised a range of national and regional policy makers, ministries and security and intelligence agencies on the latest trends in online and offline extremism. Our research and analysis featured across major international and national news outlets and informs our engagement with tech firms and civil society.[18]

This is where the governments and media get their smear briefings from, and it should be noted, 'security and intelligence agencies', which might explain the baseless character of the police witch-hunt for elusive 'far rightists' in New Zealand, and the banal questions police pose to those suspected of dissident views.

Among ISD 'partners' are organisations — 'civil society' — that have been involved in 'regime change' and 'colour revolutions', on behalf of the U.S. Government and/or international plutocracy, including: The International Republican Institute, established to promote the USA's version of democracy and culture-pathology worldwide. IRI funders include USAID, The Bush Institute, Freedom House, National Democratic Institute, Solidarity Center of the AFL-CIO, Australian, Canadian and British governments, and many others.[19] IRI states that it influences the formation and policies of political parties around the world.[20] It encourages 'civil society organizations';[21] that is, it establishes subversive organisations in states marked by the USA for 'regime change' of the type that were expelled from Russia and Hungary. It uses 'the digital revolution'[22] that has been a major factor in facilitating 'colour revolutions' across the world. While IRI boasts of its global interference in the internal affairs of states, they have the

---

18   ISD, 'Far-Right', https://www.isdglobal.org/issues/far-right/.

19   IRI, 'Funders', https://www.iri.org/who-we-are/our-partners.

20   IRI, 'Link Political Parties and People'; https://www.iri.org/program/link-political-parties-and-people.

21   IRI, 'Bring Citizens Together'; https://www.iri.org/program/bring-citizens-together.

22   IRI, 'Promote Digital Democracy'; https://www.iri.org/program/promote-digital-democracy.

audacity to moralise via their 'Beacon Project' (founded to suppress alternative views over the internet) that 'IRI is launching a new program aimed at countering the increasing threat of Russian soft power and propaganda.'[23] What is the IRI, other than an agency to purvey the 'soft power and propaganda' of the USA?

Other ISD sponsors, Gen Next, Facebook, and Google, were among the founders of Movements.org, a globalist project aiming to use digital technology to foment 'regime change' in states targeted by globalists. Its original name was Alliance of Youth Movements. Corporate sponsors of Movements.org have included Howcast, Edelman, Music TV, Meetup, Pepsi, CBS News, Mobile Accord, You Tube, MSNBC, National Geographic, Omnicom Group, Access 360 Media. 'Public Partnerships' are Columbia Law School and the U.S. State Department. Representatives at the organisation's summits have come from the Rand Corporation, World Bank, National Democratic Institute, YouTube, Freedom House, et al. Movements.org was particularly active in the 'Arab Spring', where a string of regimes were toppled in quick succession.[24]

ISD initiated its own youth-focused, digital project, similar to Movements.org, YouthCAN (Youth Civil Activism Network).[25]

The ISD is part of a world-wide network of NGOs, so-called 'civil society' that promotes globalisation. The part the ISD plays in this process is to help suppress dissent against globalisation in the name of combatting 'racism', 'xenophobia' and 'Fascism'. Those who dissent from this process must be eliminated by being demonised and delegitimised, and smeared as a prelude to the actual banning of dissidents with the use of terms such as 'hate speech', and 'counter-terrorism'. The result is a form of mass brainwashing concomitant

---

23 IRI, 'Beacon Project'; https://www.iri.org/web-story/beacon-project-shines-light-moscows-meddling.

24 K. R. Bolton, *Revolution from Above*, pp. 235–240.

25 ISD, 'YouthCAN', https://www.isdglobal.org/programmes/grassroots-networks/youth-civil-activism-network-youthcan-2/.

with what Dr. Szasz referred to as the *therapeutic state*. The incessant media campaigns, in conjunction with the entertainment industry, are the liberal state's quieter — and hence more insidious — version of the incessant loud-speaker sloganeering of Mao's China and Jim Jones' Guyana commune. Both versions are intended to impose and maintain conformity.

Cold War Agendas

By the mid-1970s, some 5,000 academics were cooperating with the CIA.

— KATHERINE VERDERY

I N 1964 MARCUSE's *One-Dimensional Man* was published. Douglas Kellner writes: 'In contrast to orthodox Marxism, Marcuse championed non-integrated forces like minorities, outsiders and radical intelligentsia, attempting to nourish oppositional thought through promoting radical thinking and opposition....'[1] As such he can be credited as being the ideological father of 'identity politics'. Kellner writes of Marcuse's influence:

> During the 1960s, Marcuse achieved world renown as 'the guru of the New Left'... his work was often discussed in the mass media. A charismatic teacher, Marcuse's students began to gain influential academic positions and to promote his ideas, making him a major force in US intellectual life. After working for the US Government for almost ten years Marcuse returned to university life. He received a Rockefeller Foundation grant to study Soviet Marxism, lecturing on the topic at Columbia University during 1952–53, and Harvard from 1954–55.[2]

While the leftist social scientists denounced 'American neo-colonialism', their studies were sponsored and used by the CIA and other

---

1   Douglas Kellner (ed.) *Herbert Marcuse, The New Left and the 1960s*, Vol. III, p. 5.

2   Douglas Kellner, 'Marcuse, Herbert', *The American National Biography*.

agencies of U.S. policy in the interests of this 'neo-colonialism'. The USA had its own revolutionary agenda since the democratic-internationalism espoused by President Woodrow Wilson in his 'Fourteen Points' for the post-1918 world. The USA, in presenting itself as the Big Brother of anti-colonialism, could point to its own revolutionary origins in rebelling against an imperial power.

Anti-Soviet Analyses

Marcuse and other Critical Theorists were employed by the OSS during World War II to analyse the USSR and National Socialism.[3] Marcuse's *Soviet Marxism: A Critical Analysis* was published in 1958.[4] *Soviet Marxism* was based on the research he had started in the OSS, and continued at the Russian Studies institutes of Columbia and Harvard universities. The book was partly funded by the Rockefeller Foundation.[5] Marcuse continued in state employment until 1951, as head of the State Department's Central European Bureau. Marcuse, so far from being part of a Soviet conspiracy against the 'free world' was part of the Cold War apparatus against the USSR.

When the New Left mobilized on the streets throughout the world in 1968, the mantra was 'Marx, Mao, Marcuse'. The New Left was spawned in the Cold War as an alternative to Moscow-aligned Communism, which could be manipulated for anti-Soviet purposes. Feminism, chiefly through Gloria Steinem, a CIA asset (recruited by the CIA's Cord Meyer) came from this milieu.[6] The New Left also served the 'Establishment' dialectically: the rampaging extremes of the likes of the Students for a Democratic Society, Black Panthers, Weathermen, and Yippies, made the leftist programmes being promoted by Rockefeller et al. seem moderate, and hence the USA was

---

3   Franz Neumann, Herbert Marcuse, and Otto Kirchheimer, *Secret Reports on Nazi Germany*.

4   Herbert Marcuse, *Soviet Marxism*.

5   Ibid., Acknowledgments.

6   Bolton, *Revolution from Above*, pp. 164–170.

pushed imperceptibly leftward, while the public focus was on the ultra-left riots and Soviet agents.[7]

It is at times claimed that there was a secret collusion between the USA and the USSR to create a world state. Often the aims of the USA and USSR converged, such as the push by both for European decolonisation. Even the Shah of Iran, puzzled by the treachery of his U.S. 'ally', asked Nelson Rockefeller whether he thought there was a covert U.S.-Soviet alliance to rule the world.[8] However, the Cold War was no ruse. The aim of establishing a world government after World War II via the United Nations Organisation was stymied by the USSR. While the USA sought to establish the U.N. General Assembly as a world parliament, where votes could be controlled with money and aid, in a democratic-plutocratic manner, the USSR insisted that authority must be vested in the Security Council, any one of whose members could veto any decision. Hence, the prospect of a world government was quashed before it started, thanks to the USSR. Secondly, the USA's *Baruch Plan* for the 'internationalisation of nuclear energy' under the U.N. Atomic Energy Commission, was also rejected by the USSR, which regarded this as another means of securing U.S. control.[9] American patriots for decades condemned the UNO as a Kremlin plot. Rather, the intransigence of the USSR was the sole factor in postponing a 'new world order'.

While Stalin had closed down the Comintern in 1943, having long considered it a nest of traitors,[10] Washington and New York started another *Comintern* in the aftermath of the World War, when the USSR had repudiated its wartime alliance and rejected globalist manoeuvres.

---

7   Ibid., pp. 144–200.

8   Mohammad Reza Pahlavi, p. 185.

9   For the origins of the Cold War see: Bolton, *Stalin: The Enduring Legacy*, pp. 125–136. The background is confirmed by Soviet foreign minister Gromyko in his memoirs: *Andrei Gromyko, Memories*, pp. 138–140 (Baruch Plan); p. 116 (U.N. Security Council veto).

10   Bolton, *Stalin: The Enduring Legacy*, pp. 6–9.

The CIA established a front during 1949–1950 with Foundation funding, particularly from Ford and Rockefeller. This was the Congress for Cultural Freedom (CCF). The purpose was to steer the intelligentsia and artistic *avantgarde* to social democracy and away from Soviet influence. The president was the eminent socialist intellectual Sidney Hook, who had helped John Dewey set up the 'Dewey Commission' in 1938 to protest the Stalinist accusations against Leon Trotsky. The CCF included an array of liberals, Fabians, social democrats, Mensheviks, Trotskyites; socialists disaffected by the turn of events in the USSR,[11] as described in Marcuse's *Soviet Marxism*, and Trotsky's *Revolution Betrayed*.[12] The CCF had been preceded by the American Committee for Cultural Freedom, founded by Dewey and Hook in 1939, in opposition to both Nazism and Stalinism.[13] Dewey joined the CCF.[14] While the U.S. State Department, CCF and Rockefeller Foundation sponsored jazz and Abstract Expressionism to showcase the cultural wonders of democracy under U.S. auspices, the USSR condemned 'rootless cosmopolitanism' and bourgeoisie decadence, in favour of 'socialist realism'.[15] This was what has been called the 'Cultural Cold War'.

In 1948 Horkheimer was funded by the Rockefeller Foundation to return to Frankfurt University for a month to investigate the possibilities of bringing the Institute of Social Research back to the university while he took up a guest professorship. Officially he was returning to Germany to assist with the 're-education' process.[16] When Adorno returned to the re-established Frankfurt Institute in Germany he wrote

11   Bolton, ibid., pp. 33–38; *Revolution from Above*, pp. 138–141. Frances Stonor Saunders, The Cultural Cold War, passim.

12   Leon Trotsky, *Revolution Betrayed* (1937).

13   'Origins of the Congress for Cultural Freedom 1949–50', CIA, https://www.cia.gov/library/center-for-the-study-of-intelligence/csi-publications/csi-studies/studies/95unclass/Warner.html.

14   Saunders, p. 92.

15   Bolton, *Revolution from Above*, pp. 141–143.

16   Ibid., Rolf Wiggershaus, p. 307.

for *Der Monat*, a mouthpiece for the CIA's Congress for Cultural Freedom, although Horkheimer did not share the same willingness to serve the USA's Cold War agendas as other Critical Theorists.[17]

The re-establishment of the Institute at Frankfurt was funded by grants totalling 430,000 DM given by U.S. High Commissioner John McCloy in 1950,[18] indicating the importance of the Institute in the USA's 're-education' of Germany, and hence as part of Cold War strategy.

Although the CCF had been outed as a CIA front and folded in 1979, and was replaced by the National Endowment for Democracy in 1983, with a similar neo-Trotskyite and social democratic background,[19] the CCF offensive had been effective. In 1985 the CIA assessed the attitude of the New Left intelligentsia in France, stating that the prevalent anti-Soviet attitude 'will make it difficult for anyone to mobilize significant opposition to U.S. policies'.[20] The 'confidential' CIA report states that the leftist intelligentsia started departing from the Communist Party and from Moscow alignment after the 'traumatic events of May 1968', when New Left student riots spread to Paris and almost toppled the USA's bugbear, Charles de Gaulle. The French Communist Party had repudiated the New Left revolt as bourgeois and anarchist. The French leftist intelligentsia had rejected the USSR as authoritarian.[21] In France it was the *structuralist* anthropology of Foucault and Claude-Levi Strauss that played a key role. The CIA report alludes to the influence of *structuralism* on scholarship in France and elsewhere in Western Europe.[22] The report comments that anti-Americanism among the intelligentsia was not only out of vogue,

---

17 Ibid., p. 406.

18 Ibid., p. 434.

19 Bolton, *Revolution from Above*, pp. 218–221.

20 'France: Defection of the Leftist Intellectuals: A Research Paper', Directorate of Intelligence, Central Intelligence Agency, December 1985, v.

21 Ibid., p. 5.

22 Ibid., p. 6.

but that 'finding virtues in America — even identifying good things about U.S. Government policies — is looked upon as an indication of discerning judgment'.[23]

Contrary to Andrew Woods' claims, criticism of Critical Theory did not start with John Stormer or Lyndon LaRouche, but with the German Communist Party, and was continued by the USSR. However, one might think that the most likely place to trace the U.S. origins of 'conspiracy theory' in regard to the social sciences would be the congressional investigations into the funding of education and the social sciences by the Foundations. Again, it was widely assumed that the Foundations had been taken over by Soviet agents and were financing pro-Soviet Russian propaganda. To the contrary, the investigations showed that the Foundations, while funding left-liberal ideologies, were an integral part of the Cold War offensive against the USSR, in tandem with the Congress for Cultural Freedom, Gloria Steinem's 'feminism'; and the National Student Association (NSA),[24] the precursor of the New Left.

Foundation Funds

Charles Dollard,[25] president of the Carnegie Corporation was questioned during the Cox Committee congressional investigations into the Foundations in 1952. What some Congressmen expected to find was that the Carnegie Corporation was dispensing funds to

23 Ibid., p. 11.

24 For a critique of the CIA use of Steinem and of the NSA see the memoirs of the New Left eminence Tom Hayden, *Reunion*. Hayden states that the NSA was formed in the first years of the Cold War, and 'was funded primarily by the CIA and State Department', for the purpose of combatting Soviet influence among youth abroad. (p. 36). He stated that Gloria Steinem was a CIA asset from the start, working for the USA at the World Youth Festivals to counter Soviet influence. (p. 37).

25 Dollard was an educationist, who was also a member of the omnipresent globalist think tank the Council on Foreign Relations, and a director of the Rand Corporation, the 'research and development' defence contractor that began amidst the Cold War, and branched into social policy.

educational institutions to study Russia with a pro-Soviet perspective. What they were funding was what Gunnar Myrdal described as the 'American Creed', free market capitalism and liberalism. Hence, when Dollard was asked whether *Das Kapital* was among 'great books' being sponsored into university libraries by Carnegie, he replied that it was Adam Smith's *Wealth of Nations* that was the primary text being promoted.[26]

Dollard was questioned on the funding for Russian studies institutes at universities, as there was a widespread perception that the Foundations were promoting appeasement with the USSR, and even treason. Carnegie funded programmes at universities to study the Far East, British colonies, Latin America. However, the largest funding went to Russian studies, giving rise to suspicion. American patriots had made faulty assumptions about the character of the 'international network' that Quigley had described as controlled by Wall Street, not the Kremlin, but operating in a like manner to the Communists, and hence often mistaken as a 'Communist conspiracy'.

Dollard stated that the largest programme funded by Carnegie was the Russian Research Center at Harvard University, 'which we helped to get underway in 1948'. Other grants were made to Columbia University, Dartmouth College, and a network of Pennsylvania colleges. Dollard was asked to elaborate on the Russian studies programmes, being told that this was the 'sore spot' among many who thought that there was too much focus on Russian studies, with the assumption that this was a pro-Soviet project. Dollard answered by quoting from his 1949 annual report that up until the aftermath of World War II the only rival powers the USA had dealings with were from Western Europe. Now the USSR was the contending superpower, and Americans knew very little about the Russians. 'Without such understanding our best efforts either to create a stable world or

---

26 'Tax Exempt Foundations, Hearings Before the Select Committee to Investigate Tax Exempt Foundations & Comparable Organizations before the House of Representatives', Washington D.C. (1952), Dollard testimony, p. 333.

to defend our own freedom may be futile… If you are going to combat an enemy intelligently and aggressively, you have to know all you can about him'.[27]

The Center at Harvard served a double purpose of researching all aspects of Russia, and of training graduates in Russian language, sociology, economics, politics, and psychology. At Columbia, the Russian Institute focused on training rather than research.[28] When Dollard stated that 'one of the essential ways we fight the Russians is to know more about them',[29] it seems a reasonable conclusion that the purpose was to train a core of Cold Warriors, CIA operatives and analysts.

Dollard was questioned on whether Carnegie had sponsored anything that would undermine the 'traditional American way of life', which was described by the General Counsel Harold Keele as synonymous with 'the capitalistic system'. Dollard gave an unequivocal 'no'. Dollard cited the National Planning Council, representing labour, business, government and industry, which asked Carnegie to sponsor a study on the impact of American corporations overseas, and the ways capitalism could be introduced to the decolonised Third World states.[30]

Russell Leffingwell, chairman of the Carnegie Board of Trustees, whose background was in Wall Street at J. P. Morgan, describing himself to the committee as ideologically a 'free trader',[31] reiterated the testimony of Dollard in stating the great 'dreadful threat' posed by the USSR.[32] Leffingwell stated that the funding of the social sciences by Carnegie established a more balanced relationship in the funding of academia at a time when the physical sciences received funding from government and business. The need was for research into psychology,

---

27 Dollard p. 344.

28 p. 345.

29 Ibid., p. 346.

30 Ibid., pp. 354–355.

31 R. Leffingwell, p. 375.

32 Ibid., p. 373.

anthropology, political economy and sociology, which became the responsibility of the Foundations. **Leffingwell explained that the Foundations could provide funding where government was best left out, because of the controversial political nature of the studies**.[33]

What the Carnegie and other Foundations were funding was not Soviet subversion but American liberal subversion, and since that included the destruction of traditional attitudes, there was widespread confusion with 'Communism'.

Role of Social Sciences

That the social sciences, such as those described by Dollard, were used by Cold War agencies was documented in 2016 by David Price.[34] As seen from the 1952 testimony of Dollard and Leffingwell, there would have been no ideological or ethical objection to the use of Carnegie-sponsored social science programmes by the CIA and others.

Clyde Kluckhohn at Harvard, the recipient of the largest amount of Carnegie largesse, was a primary figure in the 'dual use' of anthropology for Cold War agendas. Commenting on Price's research, Katherine Verdery writes,

> By the mid-1970s, some 5,000 academics were cooperating with the CIA. CIA agents were put on the funding boards of foundations and CIA officers joined university communities under aliases, until exposés of covert operations in the late 1960s caused Congress to begin limiting the CIA's activities.[35]

Through the Asia Foundation, the CIA created 'part of a widespread pattern linking hundreds of anthropologists and other regional specialists with Cold War intelligence agencies'.[36] Verdery, travelling

33 Ibid., p. 376.
34 David Price, *Cold War Anthropology*.
35 Katherine Verdery, 'The CIA is Not a Trope', *Hau: Journal of Ethnographic Theory* (2016), Vol. 6, No. 2, p. 447.
36 Price, p. 193.

to Romania with funding from IREX (International Research and Exchanges Board), set up 'to facilitate scholarly exchange between the United States and the Soviet bloc', discovered that the funding came from the Ford Foundation, the State Department's Bureau of Education and Cultural Affairs, the National Endowment for the Humanities, the Social Science Research Council, and the American Council of Learned Societies. Soviet authorities regarded IREX-sponsored scholars as CIA agents.[37] Verdery considers that she and other scholars working in the Soviet bloc unwittingly served the Cold War agenda. But many social scientists, starting with those who worked for the OSS [in which we might recall the employment by Marcuse and other Critical Theorists], regarded the fight against the USSR as a 'just war'.[38]

In 1951 Bryce Wood, executive associate of the Social Science Research Council, wrote to Allen Dulles, director of the CIA, urging the Agency's use of the Council's plan, 'A Project for Training Area Specialists'.[39] Lt. Colonel Matthew Baird, CIA Director of Training, wrote to the CIA Deputy Director (Plans) recommending the project manual for implementation for pre-employment training and recruitment for the CIA 'and certain other government agencies'. The project was suggested as a 'one shot' effort to build up 1000 area specialists by 1954, but Baird recommended it as a permanent programme. The aim was to recruit university students into the CIA and the State and Defense Departments prior to graduation.[40] In a memorandum from the assistant director, the Bureau of the Budget, it was recommended that in implementing the project a close working relationship with the Social Sciences Research Council and with the American Council of Learned Societies was required, and a meeting was held with

---

37   Verdery, p. 449.

38   Ibid., p. 450.

39   Bryce Wood, letter to Allen Dulles, 1 February 1951.

40   Matthew Baird, CIA Memorandum, 19 February 1951.

representatives from these associations on 19 March 1951.[41] The ensu-
ing meeting discussed the prior funding by the Foundations for training specialists at universities, but federal funding was now required to
expand the programmes, for both selecting and training undergradu-
ates and for training existing personnel.[42]

Where anthropologists were of particular use to American foreign policy was in their work with those peoples who were being
de-colonialised. The former colonies were up for grabs by the USA
and the USSR, as both sought to present themselves as the leaders of
anti-colonialism. David Price states of this:

> The United States' postwar global political stance shifted American orien-
> tations toward the peoples anthropologists studied. As the United States
> and the Soviet Union competed for the hearts, minds, debts, and arms
> contracts of the world's nonaligned nations, there were tangible uses for the
> forms of intangible knowledge that anthropologists brought home from
> the remote areas where they worked; whether their work involved esoteric
> symbolic studies or **radical Marxist analysis**, the CIA saw prospects of
> useful knowledge.[43]

Note that Price alludes to the use of leftist social scientists. In historical context this was a time when there was such hatred among the
Left for the USSR under Stalin that Natalia Sedova, Trotsky's widow,
resigned from the Fourth International, declaring the USSR, not the
USA, to be the main obstacle to 'world revolution'.[44] The Marxist and
liberal intelligentsia flocked to the Congress for Cultural Freedom to

---

41 Memorandum from the assistant director, Bureau of the Budget, to Lt. General
    Beddell Smith, and Matthew, 16 March 1951.

42 CIA Director of Training to all CIA Assistant Directors, 'Summary of
    Discussion on the Social Sciences Research Council Project for Training Area
    Specialists', https://archive.org/details/CIA-RDP55-00001A000100050023-6/
    mode/1up.

43 David Price, p. 27. Emphasis added.

44 Natalia Sedova Trotsky, 'Resignation from the Fourth International', 9 May
    1951; https://www.marxists.org/archive/sedova-natalia/1951/05/09.htm.

fight the Russians in a culture-war, while leftist social scientists served U.S. Cold War programmes.

The director of the Russian Research Center at Harvard, Clyde Kluckhohn, recruited fellow academics for the CIA.[45] David Price refers to 'the work of Kluckhohn, [Margaret] Mead, [Ruth] Benedict, or others whose research aligned with the interests of the CIA or the Pentagon'.[46]

Price states of Ruth Benedict that in 1946 she 'launched a cross-cultural anthropological seminar at Columbia University to teach the war time techniques developed by the Office of War Information to study enemy cultures. Benedict's students were enthralled with this approach, and Benedict's $100,000 Office of Naval Research (ONR) grant empowered Columbia University's Research in Contemporary Cultures (RCC) project to fund a large group of students and senior scholars'. Mead was co-director of the RCC group studying Russia.[47]

> There was a flurry of activity after Benedict announced the receipt of the ONR grant, as Mead and Benedict recruited junior and senior scholars to build a prototype interdisciplinary project to expand techniques pioneered at OWI, OSS, and other intelligence agencies. Mead wrote that they re-cruited "the gifted people who had somehow managed in war time but who did not fit into the peacetime mold—the aberrant, the unsystematic, the people with work habits too irregular ever to hold regular jobs".[48]

Additional funding was obtained from the RAND Corporation.[49] Mead regarded her group of bohemians organised along idealised so-cialist lines as the heirs of her mentor Franz Boas, founder of cultural anthropology, and despite her own supposed disquiet, she worked assiduously for the Cold War agenda:

---

45   David Price, p. 160.

46   Ibid., p. 359.

47   Ibid., p. 100.

48   Ibid., p. 100.

49   Ibid., p. 101.

Mead thought of this project as the spiritual descendent of a Boasian seminar yet, unlike in Boas's seminars, participants focused not on eso-teric features of language, culture, or mythos as a tool for understanding the psychic unity of humankind but on cultural features for ends linked to Cold War contexts. This shift enticed some anthropologists to refocus their intellectual depth of field from one of theoretical abstractions to a plane of interest aligned with the growing militarized state.[50]

Given what Derek Freeman was to contend about Mead's seminal research on Samoa, it is of interest that Price comments that Mead's *Soviet Attitudes Toward Authority* (1951), published by RAND, sim-plistically characterized Soviet national character with references to 'authoritarianism and political police'. ...[51] In 1956 Mead assisted with the recruiting of social scientists for the CIA's MK-ULTRA experi-ments in mind control and brainwashing by turning over the mailing list of the Institute for Intercultural Studies (IFIS) to MK-ULTRA's di-rector Harold Wolff. At IFIS, Mead worked with Brookings Institution pollster and social psychologist Donald Michael on the 'Man in Space' project which examined American attitudes towards U.S. and Soviet space programmes.[52]

The role of the anthropologist was to understand the character of the societies that were to be brought under the orbit of the USA through aid and assistance programmes. These programmes oper-ated under the Foreign Operations Administration (FOA). Price states that, 'The FOA needed people with anthropological skill sets to help implement these assistance programs, and anthropologists

---

50 David Price, p. 101. The research project had been suggested to the RAND Corporation in 1948 by Ruth Benedict, when she was directing research for the Office of Naval Research at Columbia University Research in Contemporary Cultures. Dr. Nathan Leites, from RAND, co-ordinated the research team under Mead for the study. Meade, *Soviet Attitudes Toward Authority* (RAND Corporation, 1951), p. 9, n. 1. The team is listed on pp. 11–12.

51 David Price, p. 101.

52 Ibid., p. 102.

contributed to FOA projects in India and the Philippines.[53] USAID, founded in 1961, is the culmination of these Cold War programmes. These aid programmes began during World War II with the founding of the Institute of Inter-American Affairs (1942–55) which 'was overseen by Nelson Rockefeller, one of the world's richest men, who at times mixed his own long-term financial interests with the interests of the institute.'[54]

In 1966, USAID and the Rockefellers' Asia Society established the Southeast Asia Development Advisory Group, which recruited anthropologists to study that region. The role of the Asia Society was pivotal in shaping the agendas:

> The relationships between SEADAG, the Asia Society, and USAID blurred institutional boundaries in ways that bypassed normal peer review processes and connected university scholars with the needs of state. An overview of SEADAG activities in the late 1960s reported that 'the Asia Society initiated an AID-funded program of research grants through SEADAG, and recommended to AID, after a large number of proposals from various sources had been screened by appropriate seminars and then by a Screening Committee of eminent scholars from outside the SEADAG organization's structure—according to criteria for valuation established by the Executive Committee. …[55]

> This community of scholars linked public (USAID) and private (Rockefeller's Asia Society) groups interested in Southeast Asian research that could inform American policies in Asia. Some scholars applying for these funds met at meetings sponsored by USAID or the Asia Society, where participants learned which research topics were being funded. …[56]

That the Asia Society is a Rockefeller family think tank is readily determined. The Society was founded by John D. Rockefeller III in

---

53   Ibid., p. 114.

54   Ibid., p. 116.

55   Ibid.p. 127.

56   Ibid., p. 128.

1956.[57] What these anthropologists studied about cultures, societies and peoples, enabled globalisation to proceed, with much of this involving Rockefeller enterprises, continuing to the present.

The Non-Communist Manifesto: Rostow's Dialectics

When Harry S. Truman stated in his inaugural speech that his administration would embark on a four-point programme for world reconstruction, the fourth point was to 'embark on a bold new program for making the benefits of our scientific advances and industrial progress available for the improvement and growth of underdeveloped areas'. Responding to this, the American Anthropological Association established the Committee on Anthropology & Point IV.[58] This was chaired by Gordon Wiley, who authored a manual on anthropology for Foreign Service personnel to assist in working in foreign cultures.[59]

In 1960, senior foreign policy adviser Walt Rostow wrote a doctrinal treatise for strategic U.S. aid, *Stages of Economic Growth: A Non-Communist Manifesto*, sponsored by the Center for International Studies, and funded by the CIA, and Ford and Rockefeller Foundations. Rostow developed a historical model by which developing states would achieve a capitalist economy through stages; 'an evolutionary progression for underdeveloped nations, culminating in their achievement of a lifestyle of high mass consumption'.[60] Of the social sciences, Price states of this dialectical approach:

> Cold War anthropologists and other social scientists often worked as foot soldiers, interacting with local populations, solving logistical problems, or getting "local buy-in" for development projects. Yet many of these programs were of the type later excoriated by John Perkins in *Confessions of an Economic Hitman* (2004) as undertakings that delivered minimal goods

---

57   'About Asia Society', https://asiasociety.org/about.

58   David Price, p. 116.

59   Ibid., p. 117.

60   Ibid., p. 119.

or services and established debts that were used to manipulate domestic policies in client states.[61]

This was a dialectical process for capitalism and U.S. foreign policy, to the extent that Rostow refers to *The Communist Manifesto* in the title of his treatise, *Stages of Economic Growth: A Non-Communist Manifesto,* to underscore the purpose as being a dialectical antithesis. At this time the strategies and doctrines of today's globalisation were being established. Price comments:

> Many development anthropologists have been uncomfortable acknowledg-ing Rostow's ideological end goal for world development, instead preferring visions of Third World self-sufficiency that ignore development programs' legacies of debt and their failures to live up to envisioned outcomes.[62]

Marxist and liberal cultural anthropologists were swept along in this globalist programme to supplant European colonialism with U.S. finance-capitalism by self-persuasion that what they were doing was opening every corner of the Earth up to 'progress'. If these Marxists and liberals had not been imbued with the same *progressive-positivist* world-view as capitalism, they would have rejected even the notion of such 'progress'. But this 'progress' is based on the late Western eco-nomic model, and it was lauded by Marx for the internationalising impact it would have over the world. The anti-globalisation of the Left is worthless because it is not a transcendent opposition, but a mirror image. It means breaking down traditional customs, cultures, bonds and myths, so that everyone on Earth can become a consumer in the 'global village'. Price describes the process:

> Modernization theory provided a philosophical justification for hundreds of development projects in which anthropologists played supportive roles on the ground. This work seldom required anthropologists to critically evaluate the successes or failures of their projects: they simply needed to

---

61   Ibid.,, p. 120.

62   Ibid., p. 121.

complete assigned work in a well-funded bureaucratic process of institutional self-replicating reification. **Some applied anthropologists found themselves serving as cheerleaders of progress, or working as apologists for the failures of the Green Revolution, facilitating evacuations of indigenous peoples in the way of hydraulic projects, acting as brokers for overpriced irrigation or technology transfer projects, or advising the World Bank, International Monetary Fund, or major corporations interested in "developing" new markets and sources of (or dumping ground for) goods in the Third World. ...**[63]

If one accepts that there is a capitalist dialectic at work, it becomes understandable how readily Marxist and liberal social scientists are drawn into the process.

While much of the social science research funded by SEADAG was linked to development projects designed to bring stabilizing counterinsurgency ends (for example, anthropologist Jasper Ingersoll's work on the Nam Pong Project in northeast Thailand), SEADAG also funded more critical progressive or radical work, including that of antiwar critics. By funding a range of political work, SEADAG exemplified the broad Cold War funding strategy successfully used by public and private organizations to generate knowledge, even extremely critical knowledge.[64]

There were ample funds aligned with strategic interests coming from private foundations and governmental agencies for anthropological work ranging from classroom language study to field-work research projects. These funds financed a theoretically and geographically broad range of research activities, with the work of conservatives, conformists, liberals, progressives, Marxists, Maoists, and other radicals (during the late 1960s and the 1970s) financed by public and private sources.[65]

As Price comments, there were those who objected to this seeming paradox of funding leftist academics. Price writes of a dialectical process at work, concluding with an allusion to the training of 'area

63 Ibid., p. 135. Emphasis added.
64 Ibid., p. 130.
65 Ibid., p. 351.

specialists', as a partnership between the state military-intelligence apparatus, academe, and the social science associations:

> Government and foundation funding programs spread their resources broadly. While much of the research funded in the postwar 1940s and throughout the 1950s aligned well with the needs and ideologies of the American Cold War state, **in the 1960s and 1970s radical voices used these funds to generate their own critiques.** The links between Cold War funds and outcomes were often not just nonlinear; **at times they were oppositional, as scholars like Andre Gunder Frank and June Nash financed their graduate work, leading to powerful radical critiques, with funds from military-linked projects.** While such unintended consequences had real significance in the development of American anthropology, **these outcomes do not argue against payoffs for the national security state's gambit—which still produced knowledge of use to national priorities and helped train generations of younger scholars, including some who would work within these governmental systems.** Regardless of the analytical or political orientation of a particular work, anthropological writings informed a **larger intellectual zeitgeist** and supported the training of a broad universe of area specialists outside the discipline.[66]

In this process, the anthropologists and other social scientists have played a vanguard role, opening up every hill and river tribe to globalisation. As Price states, a convergence of interests was possible between leftist social scientists and Cold War agencies because of 'a larger intellectual *zeitgeist*'.

---

66   Ibid., p. 351. Emphasis added.

Deconstructing the 'Primary Ties'

No nation can give itself liberty if it is not already free, for human influence extends only as far as existing rights have developed.

— Joseph de Maistre

THIS CONVERGENCE of aims between the Left and oligarchy continues in regard to the deconstruction of race, family, and gender, all of which must become 'fluid' 'social constructs' to expand globalisation.

Where Marxism attacks the family on economic grounds as a 'bourgeois institution', the Critical Theorists and post-Freudians condemn the traditional 'patriarchal marriage and patriarchal family'[67] as the home of bourgeois sexual repression, and *ipso facto* of authoritarianism, leading to Fascism,[68] as Wilhelm Reich stated it. According to the Critical Theorists, the exploitive system of capitalism rests upon sexual repression in the patriarchal family. From the revolutionary viewpoint, Reich states that 'sexual inhibition alters the structure of the economically suppressed individual in such a manner that he thinks, feels and acts against his own material interests'.[69] The family is the 'central reactionary germ cell' of the authoritarian state: 'Since authoritarian society reproduces itself in the structure of the mass

---

67 Wilhelm Reich, *The Mass Psychology of Fascism*, p. 24.

68 Ibid.

69 Ibid., p. 26.

individual by means of the authoritarian family, it follows that political reaction must defend the authoritarian family as the basis of the state, of culture and of civilization'.[70] Reich's biographer Myron Sharaf wrote, 'Reich also anticipated many recent social developments'.[71]

The Frankfurt Institute's Erich Fromm proclaimed the emergence of the sovereign individual 'liberated' from the *primary ties*. However, this 'freedom' presented a problem that he and other Critical Theorists sought to resolve: The individual, cut off from the security and sense of place provided by traditional societies, which Fromm called 'pre-individualistic', so far from creating the freedom for what humanistic psychologists call 'self-actualisation', results in loss of meaning. Fromm, in preparing the ground for deconstruction, wrote of modern man and the new society that he and others were preparing ideologically:

> This isolation is unbearable and the alternatives he is confronted with are either to escape from the burden of this freedom into new dependencies and submission, or to advance to the full realization of positive freedom which is based upon the uniqueness and individuality of man.[72]

Fromm and his colleagues were refugees from Hitlerism. The Critical Theorists were bothered by the hard-wired preferences for individuals to desire security more so than freedom, and would sooner turn to authoritarianism. Fromm et al. saw that Fascism sought to return man to his pre-modernist, pre-industrial state of organic community, where the individual finds meaning in duty to the greater whole. Such bonds were regarded by Fromm et al. as 'tyranny'. The central question was,

> that man, the more he gains freedom in the sense of emerging from the original oneness with man and nature and the more he becomes an 'individual', has no choice but to unite himself with the world in the spontaneity

---

70   Ibid., p. 88.

71   Ibid., p. 4.

72   Erich Fromm, *The Fear of Freedom* (1942), Foreword, IX. Also named *Escape from Freedom* (1941).

of love and productive work or else to seek a kind of security by such ties with the world as destroy his freedom and the integrity of his individual self.[73]

The Critical Theorists, having arisen from the chaotic milieu of the Weimar Republic, presaged the New Left and what is today called 'identity politics'. During the Weimar epoch, they witnessed how the masses turned to Hitler rather than enduring democratic chaos, and authoritarian states emerged throughout Europe and further afield.

Organic bonds (*primary ties*) would be deconstructed as historically *passé* and the resulting alienated individuals and minorities would be reconstructed with new identities while simultaneously allowing the individual to pursue self-actualisation through 'spontaneity' and 'love for humanity', as Fromm put it. Once these 'progressive' beings are liberated from the bonds of tradition, they will build 'democracy' under the guardianship of a technocratic and intellectual elite, where democratic debate would not be confused by the intrusion of contrary opinions. The road to self-actualisation, according to Fromm, was unity with the world 'in the spontaneity of love and productive work'; a nebulous nirvana. 'Productive work' is not 'spontaneous' at any level, no matter how primitive the society. Even hunter-gatherers require organisation. However, this *brave new world*, as Aldous Huxley saw it in its inevitable dystopian reality, became the aim of the New Left in their narcotised stupor of 'love and spontaneity', interrupted by Charles Manson and Jim Jones.

---

73 Fromm (1942), ibid., p. 18.

Organic 'Freedom' vs Rootless 'Freedom'

To be 'free' in the traditional sense means to dwell in peace (*Friede* = peace), at a place, free from harm and danger, suitable for dwelling.[74] Dwelling is 'the basic character of Being',[75] which is an uncovering of what one is. Martin Heidegger predicated freedom on place and Being. While the Critical Theorists and humanistic psychologists sought 'self-actualisation' in the destruction of 'primary ties', for Heidegger 'freedom now reveals itself as letting beings be',[76] whereby freedom is not a capricious inclination towards one direction or another,[77] but requires a memory of what the essence of things are. Heidegger contrasted this with the modernist impulsion to conceal the nature of Being by forgetfulness, where 'historical-man is left to his own resources', taking his own standards while 'forgetting being as a whole', continually supplying himself with 'new standards, yet without considering either the ground for taking up standards or the essence of what gives the standard'.[78] This forgetfulness is a 'constant erring'.[79] Modernism demands forgetfulness as the path to 'self-actualisation', and the destruction of all that binds; firstly of the family, which implies continuity and stability, then the 'forgetting' of all traditions. Since these traditions and *primary ties* bind the individual to a sense of place and of roots, they are regarded by Critical Theory as repressing individual freedom and spontaneity. There is an abyss between security and total freedom, which few want to traverse. When pushed towards this unbound freedom, the individual, according to Critical Theory, prefers to resort to authoritarianism, such as Fascism. This process is what Fromm called an 'escape from freedom'.

---

74 Martin Heidegger, 'Building Dwelling Thinking', in *Martin Heidegger: Basic Writings*.

75 Ibid.

76 Martin Heidegger, 'The Essence of Truth: (4) The Essence of Freedom', ibid.

77 Ibid.

78 Ibid., '(6) Untruth as Concealing'.

79 Ibid., '(7) Untruth as Errancy'.

Martin Heidegger, the philosopher who taught Marcuse and others who went left, countered that this detached individualism is an escape from meaning and belonging. After 1945, Heidegger was blacklisted by democracy as ideologically suspect. The problems of alienation and lack of meaning in industrial society that Fromm sought to address, the danger of modern man wanting to 'escape from freedom' and from his 'awareness and conception of himself as an independent and separate being',[80] were addressed by Heidegger. He considered modern, industrialised, urbanised man to be *enframed*, to have been engulfed by an outlook that prevents the revealing of who he is. This *enframing* has existed prior to industrial society, but technology and industry block the path to Being.

For Fromm, '[t]here is only one possible, productive solution for the relationship of individualized man with the world: his active solidarity with all men and his spontaneous activity, love and work, which **unite him again with the world, not by primary ties but as a free and independent individual....**'[81]

Fromm adapted the dialectical approach to history from Marx, but rather than *class,* the historical process had been one of widening individualism from the time of the Reformation. Many sought 'escape from freedom', and the insecurity individual freedom entails, by embracing the paternal authority of Fascism, which had once been provided by the Church and the feudal order. Here Fromm writes of 'modern history' (sic). Like Marx and other social theorists, typical of the 19th century and after, he sees humanity marching in a 'progressive', lineal ascent from 'primitive to modern'. While the Critical Theorists claim to have rejected *positivism*, whose most famous exponent, Auguste Comte, coined the word *sociology*, they were within the same historical school. From the time of the Reformation, which was the birth of the West's 'modern' epoch, Fromm sees the start of the process where the individual becomes aware of himself and detached

---

80 Fromm (1942), p. 19.
81 Erich Fromm, *Escape From Freedom*, p. 36. Emphasis added.

from communal ties, as a child matures to become detached from biological dependence on the mother.[82] The mission of the 'modern' epoch is to continue the process of cutting the individual from the organic identity that existed prior to the Reformation, where the individual found meaning in guild, village, family, and Church, craft and land. It is during this pre-Reformation epoch that could be found the organic 'freedom' referred to by Heidegger in its primordial meaning.

According to Fromm, this organic sense of purpose is a primitive trait that needs replacing by the 'modern': that is the meaning of modernist 'freedom' according to the Critical Theorists and other *positivists*, whether socialist or capitalist. This is the ego-driven 'freedom' that became the battle cry of the 1960s New Left : the 'freedom' that has fractured society from the time of the Reformation, heralding the individualism of the bourgeois and the rise of the oligarchy. For Fromm, **dialectically** this was a necessary part of the historical process:

> To the degree to which the individual, figuratively speaking, has not yet completely severed the umbilical cord which fastens him to the outside world, he lacks freedom; but these ties give him security and a feeling of belonging and of being rooted somewhere. I wish to call these ties that exist before the process of individuation has resulted in the complete emergence of an individual, '**primary ties**'.[83]

Organic Community vs Contractual Society

Here Fromm introduces his concept of *primary ties*. This is the most important concept, because it is here that Fromm and the Critical Theorists sought to deconstruct Western civilisation. Fromm explicitly calls these *primary ties* '**organic**', and that is an essential factor in rightist analysis: the foundations of traditional society, and the traditional view of history are *organic*; it is the *organic* that the Right

---

82 Ibid., p. 20.

83 Ibid. Emphasis added.

seeks to restore. The 'progressive' aims to obliterate the organic community (*Gemeinschaft* in sociological terms), and fracture the *primary ties* that bond that community.

Fromm saw in the child a temporary phase from which to be liberated and in which self-actualisation would progress beyond the *primary ties*. He states of these *primary ties* that they are the barrier to the next stage in human 'evolution'.

> They are organic in the sense that they are a part of normal human development; they imply a lack of individuality, but they also give security and orientation to the individual. They are the ties that connect the child with its mother, the member of a primitive community with his clan and nature, or the medieval man with the Church and his social caste. Once the stage of complete individuation is reached and the individual is free from these primary ties, he is confronted with a new task: to orient and root himself in the world and to find security in other ways than those which were characteristic of his preindividualistic existence. Freedom then has a different meaning.[84]

Fromm's doctrine of liberation from anything of duration, giving the individual total freedom to deconstruct and reconstruct himself without restraint, seeded today's doctrine of the fluidity of everything, where gender, race and family are social constructs. Nothing need bind, nothing need endure, nothing need be anchored by tradition, custom, law, religion or morality. This is the dichotomy of *Gemeinschaft* and *Gesellschaft*, sociological terms coined in the late 19th century to distinguish the traditional pre-capitalist organic community from the rise of the contractual society.

The Right revolts against the modernist notion that nations and states are formed by declarations, constitutions, and legal contracts between citizens, such as formed the USA on the basis of a written Constitution; the French Republic on the basis of the 'Declaration on the Rights of Man & the Citizen', and the present notion that a world order can be formed on the basis of the United Nations Charter, U.N.

---

84 Ibid.

Declaration on Human Rights, United Nations Declaration on the Rights of Indigenous Peoples, and multiple other haughty pronouncements. Such contractual projects are designed to reconstruct the individual as a 'citizen' of a liberal state and more latterly as a 'citizen of the world', based on agreed legal rights; the 18th century doctrine of the 'social contract' and of the 'general will' formulated by Rousseau. This is what Fromm described as a 'different meaning of freedom', and as finding 'security in other ways than those which were characteristic of his preindividualistic existence'.

Comparison of Gemeinschaft and Gesellschaft

GEMEINSCHAFT RELATIONSHIPS	GESELLSCHAFT RELATIONSHIPS
Personal	Impersonal
Informal	Formal and contractual
Intimate and familiar	Task-specific
Traditional	Utilitarian
Sentimental	Realistic
Emphasis on ascribed statuses	Emphasis on achieved statuses
Less tolerance to deviance	Greater tolerance to deviance
Holistic relationships	Segmental (partial) relationships
Long duration	Transient and fragmented
Relatively limited social change	Very evident social change
Predominance of informal social control	Greater formal social control
We-feeling	They-feeling
Typifies rural life	Typifies urban life

For the Right then, a constitution forming a state is organic, and it is unwritten. It is firstly an *ethos* rooted in tradition. Whatever changes are made are the result of **growth**, not upheaval. An organic constitution which maintains the health and guides the limits of growth of the *Gemeinschaft* is not a proclamation of rules agreed by majority vote and announced by a parliamentary assembly of lawyers like a commercial contract. Hence, the Comte Joseph de Maistre, in the aftermath of the epochally destructive Jacobin Revolution in his country, defined the growth of the organic ('natural') constitution:

> No constitution arises from deliberation. The rights of the people are never written, except as simple restatements of previous, unwritten rights. ... Although written laws are merely the declarations of pre-existing laws, it is far from true that all these laws can be written. ... The more of it one puts into writing, the weaker the institution becomes. ... No nation can give itself liberty if it is not already free, for human influence extends only as far as existing rights have developed. ... There never existed a free nation which did not have seeds of liberty as old as itself in its natural constitution. ... Nor has any nation ever successfully attempted to develop, by its fundamental written laws, rights other than those which existed in its natural constitution. ... One of the greatest errors of a century which professed them all was to believe that a political constitution could be created and written *a priori*, whereas reason and experience unite in proving that a constitution is a divine work and that precisely the most fundamental and essentially constitutional of a nation's laws could not possibly be written. ...

> Promises, contracts, and oaths are mere words. It is as easy to break this trifling bond as to make it. Without the doctrine of a Divine Legislator, all moral obligation becomes illusory. Power on one side, weakness on the other: this constitutes all the bonds of human societies.

> The codifiers of Roman law unpretentiously inserted a remarkable fragment of Greek jurisprudence in the first chapter of their collection. Among the laws which govern us, it says, some are written and others are not. Nothing could be more simple and yet more profound. ...[85]

In the comparative chart (above) on *Gemeinschaft* and *Gesellschaft* can be seen the differences in outlook between the traditional and the modernist, where the modernist is contractual, utilitarian, transient, fragmented, held together by means of 'formal social controls'. *Gemeinschaft* means freedom of group association, upheld by custom and tradition; *Gesellschaft* means the individual beholden to a

---

85 Joseph de Maistre (1809).

theoretical social contract in the name of 'liberty', formerly upheld by the guillotine and firing squad, and now by the technocratic methods of social control. One means *Right,* the other means *Left.*

Individuation

While Fromm refers to *individuation,* the concept was explained in a contrary manner by Carl Jung, founder of analytical psychology. Jungian *individuation* proceeds from what is inborn, rather than being cut off. Again it is an *organic* approach. *Individuation* is 'inherited possibilities', Jung wrote. Where for the Critical Theorists self-actualisation requires revolt, both individually against one's family and collectively against 'society', Jung countered that *individuation* is a process that unfolds organically. The primary ties, far from suppressing individual growth, provide the sustenance: 'Insofar as this process [*individuation*], as a rule, runs its course unconsciously as it has from time immemorial, it means no more than that the acorn becomes an oak, the calf a cow, and the child an adult'.[86] It is a conception that accords with Heidegger's unfolding of 'Being'; 'to let be'.

A few **consciously** strive for *individuation* in the sense of Nietzsche's *sublimation* of instincts, or *psychisation* as Jung called it, but for most it is an organic unfolding of life; one does not need to be in existential crisis against one's parents or homeland. 'Individuation is just ordinary life and what you are made conscious of', said Jung.[87] Jung wrote of this innate creativity:

It is in my view a great mistake to suppose that the psyche of a new-born child is a *tabula rasa* in the sense that there is absolutely nothing in it. In so far as the child is born with a differentiated brain that is predetermined by heredity and therefore individualized, it meets sensory stimuli coming from outside not with any aptitudes, but with specific ones, and this necessarily results in a particular, individual choice and pattern of apperception. These aptitudes can be shown to be inherited instincts and preformed

86 Carl Jung, 'Answer to Job', *Collected Works* (2010), Vol. 11, para. 755.
87 Carl Jung, *Letters,* Vol. 1, p. 442.

patterns, the latter being the *a priori* and formal conditions of apperception that are based on instinct. Their presence gives the world of the child
and the dreamer its anthropomorphic stamp. They are the archetypes,
which direct all fantasy activity into its appointed paths and in this way
produce, in the fantasy-images of children's dreams as well as in the delusions of schizophrenia, astonishing mythological parallels such as can also
be found, though in lesser degree, in the dreams of normal persons and
neurotics. It is not, therefore, a question of inherited ideas but of inherited
possibilities of ideas.[88]

Where Fromm saw the 'primary ties' as the continuation of an infantile dependency of the individual, Jung saw in the infant the presence
of all the instincts and experiences of his ancestors over millennia,
from where potentialities arise. This is not something from which
to be dissociated, but to be integrated into the total personality; the
process of *individuation* in the Jungian sense. Here is the difference
between Jung's *individuation*, and that of the Critical Theorists. The
first means *integration*, the second means *fracture*. The meaning of
Critical Theory is to facture: the individual and society in the name of
an unbound freedom. Of the beginnings of this *individuating* process
from childhood, Jung stated:

Childhood is important not only because various warpings of instinct have
their origin there, but because this is the time when, terrifying or encouraging, those far-seeing dreams and images appear before the soul of the
child, shaping his whole destiny, as well as those retrospective intuitions
which reach back far beyond the range of childhood experience into the
life of our ancestors.[89]

This is what the modernist zealots for the autonomous individual seek
to break in the name of 'freedom' and 'self-actualisation', according
to their preconceptions of such abstractions, 'blinded' by what Jung
called 'the garish conceits of enlightenment'.[90] Jung warned that in

---

88 Carl Jung, *Collected Works* (2000), Vol. 9, para. 136.

89 Ibid., Vol. 8, para. 98.

90 Ibid., Vol. 8, para. 528.

breaking the bonds and instincts conveyed through untold generations, '**Disalliance with the unconscious is synonymous with loss of
instinct and rootlessness**'.[91]

The Individual and 'Collective Norms'

The progressive states that *individuation*, or 'self-actualisation', as the
fad became known in humanistic psychology, can only be gained by
breaking 'free' from ties that restrict the ego. Jung to the contrary,
said that *individuation* must flower from one's primordial rootedness: 'Individuation is only possible with people, through people. You
must realise that you are a link in a chain, that you are not an electron
suspended somewhere in space or aimlessly drifting through the cosmos'.[92] The path to *individuation*, to authentic self-actualisation, to the
uncovering of one's Being, is through a consciousness of the self as
part of something greater. Where Fromm and the 'progressives' can
see only restriction, Jung sees potential: 'Individuation is not that you
become an ego—you would then become an individualist. You know,
an individualist is a man who did not succeed in individuating; he
is a philosophically distilled egotist'.[93] *Individuation* is not 'individu-
alisation', 'but a conscious realisation of everything the existence of an
individual implies: his needs, his tasks, his duties, his responsibilities,
etc.'[94] 'Individuation does not isolate, it connects'.[95]

While Fromm talked of the detached individual somehow recom-
bining with the entirety of humanity through a new social consciousness, Jung did not proceed from the notion that the individual must be
first detached from bonds, but rather that he grows out of such bonds:
'You see as the individual is not just a single, separate being, but by his
very existence presupposes a collective relationship, it follows that the

---

91   Ibid., Vol. 77, para. 195.
92   Carl Jung, *Nietzsche's Zarathustra: Notes of the Seminar*, Vol. II, Part I, p. 103.
93   Carl Jung, *The Psychology of Kundalini Yoga*, p. 39.
94   Carl Jung, *Letters*, Vol. 1, pp. 503–505.
95   Ibid.

process of individuation must lead to more intense relationships and not to isolation'.[96] Jung refers to the necessity of identification with 'collective norms' as a prerequisite for *individuation*: 'Before [*individuation*] can be taken as a goal, the educational aim of adaptation to the necessary minimum of collective norms must first be attained. If a plant is to unfold its specific nature to the full, it must first be able to grow in the soil in which it is planted'.[97]

The Danger of 'Freedom'

The Critical Theorists advocate a process of 'deconstruction'[98] that must proceed before the world can be reconstituted. But Fromm warns that it is a dangerous course because 'freedom' can only be gained by cutting loose from all that is familiar and by leaping into an abyss where self-destruction rather than utopia might await. In particular, the Critical Theorists fear that individuals might choose *en masse* the 'security' of Fascism (said to be the authority of the father-figure) rather than a rootless 'freedom'. Yet if one reaches the other side, what awaits in a world of unbounded universal freedom is to live 'spontaneously'.

> There is only one possible, productive solution for the relationship of in-
> dividualized man with the world: his active solidarity with all men and his

---

96 Carl Jung, *Collected Works*, Vol. 6; para. 758.

97 Carl Jung, Definitions, ibid., para. 761.

98 *Deconstruction* is a method of criticism where a text, law, idea or institution etc., is analysed for internal contradictions. The term was coined during the late 1960s by the French-Jewish philosopher Jacques Derrida. Its relationship to Critical Theory and post-Marxism — or what Derrida called 'deconstructed Marxism' — might be discerned with Derrida's comment that deconstruction is the 'problematisation of the foundation of law, morality and politics.' Jacques Derrida, 'Force of Law: The Mystical Foundation of Authority' in Cornell et al. (eds.), *Deconstruction and the Possibility of Justice* (Routledge, 1992), p. 8. Perpetual deconstruction is another method of bringing about a fluidity of all meaning, and is essentially the destruction of anything of duration; custom, tradition, faith, religion and institutions that arise therefrom.

spontaneous activity, love and work, which unite him again with the world, not by primary ties but as a free and independent individual. However, if the economic, social and political conditions on which the whole process of human individuation depends, do not offer a basis for the realization of individuality in the sense just mentioned, while at the same time people have lost those ties which gave them security, this lag makes freedom an unbearable burden. It then becomes identical with doubt, with a kind of life which lacks meaning and direction. Powerful tendencies arise to escape from this kind of freedom into submission or some kind of relationship to man and the world which promises relief from uncertainty, even if it deprives the individual of his freedom.[99]

Fromm is warning that 'freedom' can only be had if society is revolutionised by destroying the 'primary ties'. A falling into the abyss can result in madness, which Wilhelm Reich sought to examine in *The Mass Psychology of Fascism*, and Horkheimer, Adorno et al., sought to measure in *The Authoritarian Personality*. Fromm and his colleagues stated that if the aspirant fails and madness ensues, it is the fault of society. The masses are therefore prone to flee from freedom, and return to what is ordered and secure, which for Critical Theorists is the meaning of 'Fascism'. Yet for Jung, *individuation* is to be had in a manner that is precisely the contrary of that of the post-Marxists, where the *primary ties* so far from restraining *individuation* are the organic and timeless predicates from which *individuation* grows.

---

99   Erich Fromm, *Escape from Freedom*, pp. 30–31.

Mother, Child, Fascism

ROMM ALLUDES TO the child increasingly seeking independence from the mother as part of the education process, until the mother is considered 'a hostile and dangerous person'. This 'antagonism' sharpens the distinction between the 'I' and the 'thou'.

> This process entails a number of frustrations and prohibitions, which change the role of the mother into that of a person with different aims which conflict with the child's wishes, and often into that of a hostile and dangerous person. This antagonism, which is one part of the educational process though by no means the whole, is an important factor in sharpening the distinction between the 'I' and the 'thou'.[1]

The antagonism towards the mother, the father, and the traditional family, becomes a matter of political ideology, in which the family as the incubator of 'Fascism' has to be eliminated. Through the surveys of Americans published as *The Authoritarian Personality*, Max Horkheimer, Theodor Adorno and their team sought to 'prove' that the more one maintains a love of parents, the more one possesses an authoritarian personality and scores high on an 'F [Fascism] scale'.[2]

---

1   Fromm, ibid., p. 21.
2   M. Horkheimer (ed.), T. W. Adorno et al., *The Authoritarian Personality* (American Jewish Committee, 1950), passim. How ironic, but not unique, that an organisation dedicated to the preservation of Jewish ethnic identity sponsored such a study. Only white Christian Americans seem to have been the subjects of the surveys. This follows a theme from the beginning of psychoanalysis. The B'nai B'rith Lodge in Vienna delighted in hearing Freud lecture

The Authoritarian Personality states of the family, comparing it to other hierarchical and authoritarian elements of society: 'The conception of the ideal family situation for the child is similar: un-critical obedience to the father and elders, pressures directed unilaterally from above to below, prohibition of spontaneity and emphasis on conformity to externally imposed values'.[3] Even in 1950, Horkheimer, editor of *The Authoritarian Personality*, referring to the psychiatry of Freud, stated that there had been a social revolution in the relationship between parents and children:

> The **permeation of the social consciousness at large** with the scientifically acquired experience that the events of early childhood are of prime importance for the happiness and work-potential of the adult has brought about a revolution in the relation between parents and children which would have been deemed impossible a hundred years ago.[4]

The primary factor in the surveys of *The Authoritarian Personality* was the relationship of the respondent to the family:

> Family Figures: Personal Aspects. After the inquiry into the sociological aspects of the family background, the personal conception of the family figures by the subject was recorded. The subject's conception of the parent figures could reveal, among other things, whether the picture was dominated by the authoritarian aspects of the parent-child relationship **or by a more democratic type of relationship**. In this connection the attention of the interviewer was further focused on the ability of the subject to appraise his parents objectively — whether on the more critical or on the more loving side — as contrasted with an inclination to put the parents on a very high plane, exaggerating their strength and virtuousness.[5]

> The power-relationship between the parents, the domination of the subject's family by the father or by the mother, and their relative dominance

---

on the neuroses of Western civilisation, according to Jewish historian Howard Sachar, pp. 400–401.

3   Horkheimer, Adorno et al., *The Authoritarian Personality*, p. 150.

4   Max Horkheimer, ibid. Preface, X. (Emphasis added).

5   Ibid., p. 313. Emphasis added.

in specific areas of life also seemed of importance for our problem. The sources within the family of satisfactions and tensions in general were also explored.[6]

It is notable that the primary factor in the New Left 'rebellion' was a revolt against parents, and against the state as a substitute parental authority figure. Like Fromm and Reich, the Critical Theorists working on *The Authoritarian Personality* are unequivocal in stating that 'rebellion' against traditional society is healthy, and that continuing adherence to such traditions ranks one high on the 'F scale' of latent 'Fascism'. Of the relationship with the father, Adorno *et al.* stated:

> The inquiry regarding early memories, wishes, fears, dreams, and so forth had the purpose of getting material which stood out for the subject in connection with his childhood and seemed relevant as a basis for inference. Among the underlying questions, the structure of the emotional attachment to the parents seemed of paramount importance. Here we were specifically interested in the parents as objects of cathexis as well as of identification. In the case of a man, it was important to learn whether there was at any time an explicit rebellion against the father, and against what sort of father, or whether there was only passive submission. The assumption behind this question, later proved correct, was that **the pattern developed in the relationship to the father tends to be transferred to other authorities and thus becomes crucial in forming social and political beliefs in men.** In this connection it is of importance to know not only about rebellion against the father but also how far such rebellion is conscious and accepted as such. Rebellion against, or submission to, the father is only one part of the picture. **Another part deals with the question of identification, or the lack of identification, with the father, and thus with the masculine role in general.**[7]

Interestingly, a study has found that there is a difference in relationship with the father between those on the Far Left, and those who are ethnic-nationalist separatists. Leftists have a dysfunctional relationship

6   Ibid., p. 314.
7   Ibid., p. 315. Emphasis added.

with the father, while ethnic separatists see their rebellion as being in honour of the father; symbolic of one's forefathers. Unlike those of the extreme Left, the ethnic-separatist nationalists were found to be well-adjusted within their communities and with family support.[8]

On the relationship with the mother, the Critical Theorists wrote:

> The establishment of masculinity in the boy is, of course, also closely connected with the boy's attitude toward the mother. To what degree was there love for the mother and to what degree identification with the mother? Was such an identification, in its turn, sublimated and accepted by the ego, or was it rejected on the conscious level because the mother symbolized not only something 'admirable' but at the same time something weak and therefore contemptible? How did the boy defend himself against the rejected and feared passivity? A compensatory display of 'toughness' and ruthlessness is, according to findings from the F scale, correlated with antidemocratic social and political beliefs.[9]

Yet such motives were found not among 'Fascists' but among New Leftists two decades later. The relationship, especially of the Jewish radical to his mother, was a significant factor in his 'rebellion'. Jewish psychohistorians Stanley Rothman and S. R. Lichter, in their surveys, found the nerdy Jewish kid was trying to prove his masculinity to a mother who had, he felt, emasculated him,[10] while non-Jewish New Leftists were rebelling against both parents.[11]

Another interpretation of youth revolt is 'immature personality disorder', where the demand is for instant gratification. This does not only describe the widespread mentality of youngsters, but also the widespread mentality of the modern world in general. As Fromm stated, the doctrines of the Critical Theorists have 'permeated the

---

8   J. M. Post, 'Notes on a Psychodynamic Theory of Terrorist Behavior', in *Terrorism: An International Journal*, Vol. 7, no. 3, 1984, p. 243.

9   Horkheimer, Adorno et al., *The Authoritarian Personality*, pp. 315–316.

10 Stanley Rothman, 'Group Fantasies and Jewish Radicalism: A Psychodynamic Interpretation', *The Journal of Psychohistory*, Fall 1978, pp. 211–240.

11 Stanley Rothman and S. R. Lichter, *Roots of Radicalism*, p. 227.

social consciousness', but they have also *reinforced* a hedonistic, banal and egotistical world-view that comes to the fore in the degenerative epoch of a civilisation.

Where instant gratification is not had, it is regarded not just by youngsters but by ostensible adults as 'repression'. As children, they had cried 'it's not fair', 'I want...' In Critical Theory it is called 'spontaneous creativity', and in 'identity politics' denial of instant gratification becomes part of a narrative of *underprivilege.*

Children as Consumers

Constant 'need' serves an essential part of the economic process of capitalism. Novelty rather than duration ensures consumer demand, which like everything else is rapidly fluid. While Marcuse, Fromm et al. intended to critique industrialism and consumerism, and point the way to 'self-actualisation', their deconstruction of the organic, the durable, and the traditional could only result in a world of continual flux, which would benefit the capitalist mode of mass production based on 'planned obsolescence', whether in music or automobiles. This process explains why there can be a convergence between the Left and the oligarchy; why the New School and the London School of Economics & Political Science, founded as socialist institutions, have always received oligarchic funding. Horkheimer, Adorno et al. continued:

> Since the way in which the parents transmit social values to the child, and the punishment and rewards with which they reinforce them, are decisive for the establishment of the superego, we are led from highly personal problems back to problems of social conscience. The effects are mirrored in interpersonal relationships, on a smaller scale in one's private life and on a larger scale in one's public function as a citizen. A person with a mature, integrated, and internalized conscience will certainly take a different stand on moral and social issues than a person with an underdeveloped, defective or overpunitive superego, or a person who still, as in childhood, clings to a

set of rules and values only as they are reinforced by an external authority, be it public opinion or be it a leader.[12]

Fromm had previously written that 'Fascist' tendencies would persist so long as the incipient 'Fascism' of the parents in the traditional family remained. It sounds very 'modern' as the attack on the family has accelerated. Fromm wrote of the 'suppressive' character of the family: 'It is the thwarting of expansiveness, the breaking of the attempt to assert himself, the hostility radiating from parents — in short, the atmosphere of suppression — which create in the child the feeling of powerlessness and the hostility springing from it'.[13] What the Critical Theorists here referred to as mature and immature outlooks inverses reality.

Ironically, the Institute for Social Research, which relocated back to Frankfurt after World War II, and at which Adorno was director, was not immune from the student riots of the 1960s: 'As early as 1964 he [Adorno] sued two students from the Student Aktion group for producing a satirical poster that used quotations from his work without his permission...' From then on, the student nihilists regarded Adorno not as a venerable Marxist philosopher but as an obstacle to student radicalisation. For his part Adorno stated to Marcuse that 'the student movement in its current form is heading towards the technocratization of the university that it claims it wants to prevent'. He regarded the New Left as reverting to a 'pre-Oedipal' state of development with its use of violence, and saw it as 'Left fascism'. Adorno feared that the infantile student nihilists, as he regarded them, would destroy the 'tradition' of radicalism and any chance of a genuinely progressive movement. 'Things came to a head in the first six months of 1969', not long prior to Adorno's death. At the end of January, members of the German Socialist Student Alliance occupied the Institute. Adorno had the police remove 76 of them. In April the faction invaded Adorno's

---

12   Horkheimer, Adorno et al., *The Authoritarian Personality*, p. 317.
13   Fromm (1942), p. 21.

lecture, three female students bared their breasts at him, while leaf-
lets were distributed saying that 'Adorno as institution is dead' (sic).
'Plunged into depression by his various battles against the students
Adorno died of a heart attack while on holiday in Switzerland in
August.'[14]

Adorno had faced the nihilism he had helped to create, saw it in
practice as serving the System it claimed to oppose, and was overwhelmed by it.

Wilhelm Reich's 'sex-politics' and 'sex-economy'[15] pre-empted *The
Authoritarian Personality* in describing the repression of the release of
orgone energy (primordial sexual energy) as the basis of psychological,
sociological and political disorders. This starts with childhood sexual
repression.

When Reich established the groundwork for the deconstruction
of traditional morals, taboos, and family bonds, he was projecting
his own *Oedipal* struggle onto the entirety of Western civilisation. If
we compare the previously cited self-analysis by Reich of his childhood relations with his parents, we see that what continued to fester
in Reich's mind throughout his life formed the basis of generalised
psychoanalytic principl es about society.

> ... childhood sexuality, of which what is most crucial in the child-parent
> relationship ('the Oedipus complex') is a part, is usually repressed out of
> fear of punishment for sexual acts and thoughts (basically a 'fear of castra-
> tion'); the child's sexual activity is blocked and extinguished from memory.
> Thus, while repression of childhood sexuality withdraws it from the influ-
> ence of consciousness, it does not weaken its force. On the contrary, the
> repression intensifies it and enables it to manifest itself in various patho-
> logical disturbances of the mind. As there is hardly an exception to this

---

14 Philip Bounds, 'Just Say No: Herbert Marcuse and the Politics of Negationism',
    in David Berry (ed.), *Revisiting the Frankfurt School*, pp. 58–61.
15 See the chapter 'Wilhelm Reich's "Sex-Pol"'.

rule among 'civilized man', Freud could say that he had all of humanity as his patient.[16]

The *Oedipal* struggle within the family replaced the Marxist class struggle and the laws of social production as the foundation on which the institutions of Western society were based. Where Marx had seen economics, religion, family, morals, laws, as arising from the laws of production, Reich and the Critical Theorists saw the *Oedipal* struggle. Fascism was something other than only the 'last line of defence of capitalism'; it was a mass revolt of sexually inhibited bourgeoisie, Reich writing that,

> man's moral code was derived from the educational measures used by the parents and parental surrogates in earliest childhood. At bottom, those educational measures opposed to childhood sexuality are most effective. The conflict that originally takes place between the child's desires and the parent's suppression of these desires later becomes the conflict between instinct and morality within the person. In adults the moral code, which itself is unconscious, operates against the comprehension of the laws of sexuality and of unconscious psychic life; it supports sexual repression ('sexual resistance') and accounts for the widespread resistance to the 'uncovering' of childhood sexuality. Through their very existence, each one of these discoveries [by Freud] constitutes a severe blow to **reactionary moral philosophy and especially to religious metaphysics, both of which uphold eternal moral values, conceive of the world as being under the rulership of an objective 'power', and deny childhood sexuality, in addition to confining sexuality to the function of procreation.**[17]

Here the groundwork has been prepared for promising new avenues of left-wing agitation: that of child sexual liberation. If the inhibition of childhood sexuality is a primary cause of mass psychosis and exploitation, *ipso facto*, according to this premise, the age of consent is a dangerously inhibitive bourgeois law, propped up by religion and

---

16   W. Reich, *The Mass Psychology of Fascism*, Ch. 'Family Ties and Nationalistic Feelings'.

17   Ibid.

custom. Indeed, Danny — 'The Red' — Cohn-Bendit, leader of the 1968 New Left Paris student revolt that almost brought down the de Gaulle government, and now co-president of the Federation of Green Parties in the European Parliament, alluded in his 1975 book *The Big Madness*, to the 'erotic flirting' that took place with five-year old girls when he was working at an 'anti-authoritarian kindergarten' in Germany. Danny had been placed in a difficult position because he was unable to deny that 'children have a sexuality'.[18]

The sexualisation of children has proceeded from commercial interests that aim to integrate children at the earliest possible age into the consumer process, analogous to the way that women were integrated into the production process in the name of 'freedom'. Bernays brought women the 'freedom' to consume tobacco behind the banner of 'emancipation'. The Marquis de Sade, when urging the overthrow of all morals restraints, to expand his own opportunities for perversion, did so behind the façade of universal 'liberty', in the name of 'philosophy'. The sexology of Alfred Kinsey is of the same order and purpose. Critical Theory has provided the rationalisation for this process.

If children need 'liberating' from the patriarchal family, then that implies what is today considered most important: their independence as consumers. 'Child identity' is consistent with 'identity politics', where identities can be created to order. There can be multiple identities within the pre-adult context, including that of babies, toddlers, tweenies, teenagers; analogous to the ever-expanding 'genders' that now exceed several dozen categories. Referring to the way women now control 85% of household expenditure, the sociology of marketing notes that 'Kid Power' (sic) has arisen from 'fewer children per family', full-time working or single parents needing assistance from children, 'aggressive, child-aimed marketing', and 'media-wise kids'. In particular, there is an 'age compression': 'kids getting older younger' (KGOY), where 'children are more mature psychologically due to their

---

18   Bolton, *The Psychotic Left*, pp. 214–215.

increased independence and spending-power'. 'That is why marketers target nine-year-olds with apparel and accessories once considered appropriate only for teens'.[19]

Would the opportunities opened for marketing to children have been possible without the 'age compression' that saw a paradigm shift in morals with the '68 Generation', which had emanated from social sciences sponsored by the oligarchy? For academia it is an example of unintended consequences, resulting from a will to deconstruct in the name of 'progress'. **Undermining parental authority was the prerequisite for establishing the child as a sovereign individual, and hence as a consumer.**

'Patriarchal Repression'

Reich, who fell out with Freud and was expelled from the Psychoanalytic Association,[20] considered that orthodox Freudianism had stopped short of reaching the necessary revolutionary conclusions to deconstruct and reshape society. This was also the outlook and purpose of Critical Theory, to translate Freudian psychoanalysis into a revolutionary doctrine.

> However, these [Freud's] discoveries could not exercise a significant influence because the psychoanalytic sociology that was based on them retarded most of what they had given in the way of progressive and revolutionary impetus.[21]

Reich claimed that the authoritarian patriarchal society was a comparatively late historical development. Here Reich associates sexual repression with patriarchal class interests. Again it is notable that marriage, family, and religion are the foundations of this class exploitation. The Church functions as a 'sex-political organization', whose

---

19   Geoffrey P. Lantos, *Consumer Behavior in Action*, p. 262.

20   Sharaf, pp. 160–191.

21   W. Reich, *The Mass Psychology of Fascism*, Ch. 'Family Ties and Nationalistic Feelings'.

motive is sex-negation, the aim of which is to eliminate the small degree of happiness for humanity that is based on sexual gratification. Again we see the spectre of de Sade. It is an extraordinarily reduction- ist doctrine, devoid of historical understanding as to the character of religion, myth and the formation of social structures.[22] For Reich and the post-Freudians, history is propelled by whether the orgasm is expressed or repressed.

> It was not until relatively late, with the establishment of an authoritarian patriarchy and the beginning of the division of the classes, that suppression of sexuality begins to make its appearance. It is at this stage that sexual interests in general begin to enter the service of a minority's interest in material profit; in the patriarchal marriage and family this state of affairs assumes a solid organizational form. With the restriction and suppression of sexuality, the nature of human feeling changes; a sex-negating religion comes into being and gradually develops its own sex-political organization, the church with all its predecessors, the aim of which is nothing other than the eradication of man's sexual desires and consequently of what little hap- piness there is on earth. There is good reason for all this when seen from the perspective of the now-thriving exploitation of human labour.[23]

The patriarchal family is the authoritarian state in microcosm, where repression begins in the form of orgasmic inhibition and taboos. That taboos are by definition inhibitive and form a complex matrix starting from the most primitive societies does not negate a dogma that arose during the 18th century epoch of the West's so-called 'Enlightenment' which began the process of substituting faith and tradition for very absurd assumptions. One of these assumptions was the doctrine of the 'noble savage', which became the basis of the liberal critique of Western Civilisation, in the belief that the 'noble savage', untainted by

---

22 For an overview of traditionalist historicism see: Bolton, *The Decline & Fall of Civilisations*. Also: Oswald Spengler, *The Decline of the West*; Julius Evola, *Revolt Against the Modern World*; G. Vico, *The New Science*; Mircea Eliade, *The Sacred and the Profane*.

23 Reich, *The Mass Psychology of Fascism*, Ch. 'The Social Function of Sexual Repression'.

civilisation with its laws, church, property, and morals, lives in perfect freedom, equality, and happiness.

> To comprehend the relation between sexual suppression and human ex-
> ploitation, it is necessary to get an insight into the basic social institution in
> which the economic and sex-economic situation of patriarchal authoritar-
> ian society are interwoven. Without the inclusion of this institution, it is
> not possible to understand the sexual economy and the ideological process
> of a patriarchal society. The psychoanalysis of men and women of all ages,
> all countries, and every social class shows that: The interlacing of the socio-
> economic structure with the sexual structure of society and the structural
> reproduction of society take place in the first four or five years and in the
> authoritarian family. The church only continues this function later. **Thus,
> the authoritarian state gains an enormous interest in the authoritarian
> family: it becomes the factory in which the state's structure and ideol-
> ogy are moulded.**[24]

Reich's claim and that of the Critical Theorists that the authoritarian family is integral in forming the authoritarian state is a *non-sequitur*. It is notable that the first target of the authoritarian state is the family, for the very reason that the family is a social bond that is a hindrance to the pervasive power of the authoritarian state. Strong, self-reliant families, working their own plots of land, exist where state tyranny wishes to intrude. It is precisely outside and against the family where there is erected the 'factory in which the state's structure and ideology are moulded'. Under both plutocracy and Communism, the 'factory' is literal, as the production processes of such societies aim to replace the family. Hence, the early Soviet Union sought to replace the parental bond with the factory crèche and the communal factory kitchen so that the productivity of the parents, especially that of women, would no longer be interrupted by family duties. This was what the early Bolsheviks called freedom, and what is lauded by feminists as 'libera-tion' from the home.

---

24   Ibid. Emphasis added.

What one sees here is the projection of Reich's own *Oedipal* child-hood: repressed incestuous complexes projected onto the entirety of Western society and made into a doctrine that was mainstreamed decades later with the publication of *The Authoritarian Personality*.

> We have found the social institution in which the sexual and the economic interests of the authoritarian system converge. Now we have to ask how this convergence takes place and how it operates. Needless to say, the analysis of the typical character structure of reactionary man (the worker included) can yield an answer only if one is at all conscious of the necessity of posing such a question. The moral inhibition of the child's natural sexuality, the last stage of which is the severe impairment of the child's genital sexuality, makes the child afraid, shy, fearful of authority, obedient, 'good', and 'docile' in the authoritarian sense of the words. It has a crippling effect on man's rebellious forces because every vital life-impulse is now burdened with severe fear; and since sex is a forbidden subject, thought in general and man's critical faculty also become inhibited. In short, morality's aim is to produce acquiescent subjects who, despite distress and humiliation, are adjusted to the authoritarian order. Thus, the family is the authoritarian state in miniature, to which the child must learn to adapt himself as a preparation for the general social adjustment required of him later. Man's authoritarian structure — this must be clearly established — is basically produced by the embedding of sexual inhibitions and fear in the living substance of sexual impulses.[25]

Reich emphasises that the family is the incubator of authoritarianism or 'Fascism'. Here the wife is the subject of sexual repression, culminating in voting for a Fascist party or, if we update this, for Donald Trump.

> We will readily grasp why sex-economy views **the family as the most important source for the reproduction of the authoritarian social system** when we consider the situation of the average conservative worker's wife. Economically she is just as distressed as a liberated working woman, is subject to the same economic situation, but she votes for the Fascist party; if we further clarify the actual difference between the sexual ideology of the

---

25 Ibid.

average liberated woman and that of the average reactionary woman, then we recognize the decisive importance of sexual structure. Her anti-sexual, moral inhibitions prevent the conservative woman from gaining a consciousness of her social situation and bind her just as firmly to the church as they make her fear 'sexual Bolshevism'. The result is conservatism, fear of freedom, in a word, reactionary thinking.[26]

Here Reich describes **his** father, **his** family, **his** upbringing, which ended in tragedy:

For one thing, the political and economic position of the father is reflected in his patriarchal relationship to the remainder of the family. In the figure of the father the authoritarian state has its representative in every family, so that the family becomes its most important instrument of power.

The authoritarian position of the father reflects his political role and discloses the relation of the family to the authoritarian state. Within the family the father holds the same position that his boss holds towards him in the production process. And he reproduces his subservient attitude towards authority in his children, particularly in his sons. Lower middle-class man's passive and servile attitude towards the fuhrer-figure issues from these conditions.[27]

Louis Althusser, the leading French Communist philosopher, whose incorporation of Freud into his '*Structuralist Marxism*' aligned him to Critical Theory, has a profound influence on the social sciences, despite becoming totally psychotic and murdering his wife-mother-figure. Althusser suffered *Oedipal* complexes as severe as Reich's.[28] Like Reich and the Critical Theorists, he generalised and projected this *Oedipal* 'struggle' onto society. For Althusser also the family is a structure where obedience to the System is seeded. The family is one of what he called the 'Ideological State Apparatuses' (ISA), and a unit of production. Althusser wrote that, 'The family obviously has

---

26   Ibid.

27   Ibid., 'Family Ties and Nationalistic Feelings'.

28   Bolton, *The Psychotic Left*, pp. 114–123.

other "functions" than that of an ISA. It intervenes in the reproduction of labour power. In different modes of production it is the unit of production and/or the unit of consumption'. The family is among a series of institutions that induce and maintain the authority of capitalism, Althusser writing: ... 'Thus Schools and Churches use suitable methods of punishment, expulsion, selection, etc., to "discipline" not only their shepherds, but also their flocks. The same is true of the Family....'[29]

The aim is not to abolish these institutions but to take them over: 'To my knowledge, no class can hold State power over a long period without at the same time exercising its hegemony over and in the State Ideological Apparatuses'. For Althusser the predominant ISA in capitalist society is the 'School/Family couple', having replaced the pre-capitalist 'Church/Family couple':[30]

> It takes children from every class at infant-school age, and then for years, the years in which the child is most 'vulnerable', squeezed between the Family State Apparatus and the Educational State Apparatus, it drums into them, whether it uses new or old methods, a certain amount of 'know-how' wrapped in the ruling ideology.[31]

> In fact, the Church has been replaced today in its role as the dominant Ideological State Apparatus by the School. It is coupled with the Family just as the Church was once coupled with the Family. We can now claim that the unprecedentedly deep crisis which is now shaking the education system of so many States across the globe,[32] often in conjunction with a crisis (already proclaimed in the *Communist Manifesto*) shaking the family system, takes on a political meaning, given that the School (and the School/Family couple) constitutes the dominant Ideological State Apparatus, the Apparatus playing a determinant part in the reproduction of the relations

---

29 Louis Althusser (1971), note 8.

30 Ibid., 'Ideology and Ideological State Apparatuses'.

31 Ibid.

32 A reference to the New Left student riots of the late 1960s.

of production of a mode of production threatened in its existence by the world class struggle.[33]

Fromm stated that what requires eliminating are those social and moral restrictions that interfere with 'individuation'. This is 'growth':

> If every step in the direction of separation and individuation were matched by corresponding growth of the self, the development of the child would be harmonious. This does not occur, however. While the process of individuation takes place automatically, the growth of the self is hampered for a number of individual and social reasons. The lag between these two trends results in an unbearable feeling of isolation and powerlessness, and this in its turn leads to psychic mechanisms, which later on are described as mechanisms of escape.[34]

Other factors in determining the measure of freedom were the evolutionary overcoming of hereditary instincts. Fully *human* society is to be measured by the extent to which instinct has been eliminated.

> Human existence begins when the lack of fixation of action by instincts exceeds a certain point; when the adaptation to nature loses its coercive character; when the way to act is no longer fixed by hereditarily given mechanisms. In other words, human existence and freedom are from the beginning inseparable. Freedom is here used not in its positive sense of 'freedom to' but in its negative sense of 'freedom from', namely freedom from instinctual determination of his actions.[35]

Jung wrote of those social theorists who attempt to destroy the genuine character of Being in the name of a rootless 'freedom' that,

> The danger that faces us today is that the whole of reality will be replaced by words. This accounts for that terrible lack of instinct in modern man, particularly the city-dweller. He lacks all contact with life and the breath of nature. He knows a rabbit or a cow only from the illustrated paper, the

---

33   Louis Althusser, 'Ideology and Ideological State Apparatuses'.

34   Fromm (1942), p. 26.

35   Ibid.

dictionary, or the movies, and thinks he knows what it is really like — and is then amazed that cowsheds 'smell', because the dictionary didn't say so.[36]

The *primary ties* that must be eliminated are stubborn in their removal. As Fromm laments, when these *primary ties* are eliminated, the instinct is for new organic bonds to be formed, in an ongoing 'escape from freedom'. The perpetual resistance to 'freedom' tends to be answered by the ideologues who demand that man be 'free' against his 'instinct', with the use of the hangman's rope, axe, guillotine, firing squad, and concentration camp, where the outcome is often 'to be free or die', in the name of 'no Pope here'; 'liberty, equality, fraternity'; 'all power to the Soviets'; 'fight Fascism'; 'end racism'... Marcuse admitted that this free society could only be maintained by the repression of dissent.[37]

In the natural course of human social and organic development, the family came into existence as the most fundamental organic bonding unit that linked individuals to each other, promoted orderly cooperation, and ensured the survival of the tribe. Anthropologist Roger Pearson[38] wrote of this:

> It is generally accepted that human social organization evolved from pair-bonding. Pair-bonding led to the emergence of families, and beyond families, kinship ties that formed a basis for the regulation of behavior in larger societies, and to a lesser extent in the much larger societies which we know as nations. The family was fundamental to the emergence of more complex social institutions, and while the family as an institution has always been a pillar of a healthy society in all its forms, ancient and modern, it has proved a defense for the individual against the overweaning power of the modern political state.[39]

---

36 Carl Jung, *Collected Works*, Vol. 10, p. 882.

37 Hebert Marcuse, 'Repressive Tolerance'.

38 Roger Pearson, Autobiographical outline: https://www.professor-roger-pearson.com/.

39 Roger Pearson, 'The Misuse of the Term "Nation State"', *The Mankind. Quarterly*, Volume 44, Numbers 3 & 4, pp. 403–408, Fall/Winter, 2008.

While even familial love is regarded as harbouring 'Fascist' tendencies by the progressive social engineers, the ethologist Konrad Lorenz pointed out a factor at variance with that of these social scientists. In regard to 'natural rank', which the progressives aim to eliminate so that other forms of hierarchy might be substituted, Lorenz said that 'without such a rank order, not even the most natural form of human love that normally united members of a family can develop; thousands of children have become unhappy neurotics because of the well-known "nonfrustration" upbringing'. ... a child in a group without rank order finds itself in a thoroughly unnatural situation'. Since the instinct for rank is repressed, the child tyrannizes over his parents and finds itself in a group leader role, 'a position in which he cannot possibly feel satisfied'. Without a "stronger" superior he feels frustrated in a hostile world, for non-frustration children are never popular. 'When in understandable irritation, such a child provokes his parents, "begging for a smack", it does not meet the instinctively expected and subconsciously hoped-for counteraggression, but comes up against the padded wall of calm, pseudorational phrases'. 'Nobody ever identifies with a slavish weakling' or allows such a person to convey 'behaviour norms' or 'cultural values' to him.[40] In Lorenz's view most adolescents are lacking a 'father figure'. Now we can state that it is more than adolescents who lack a 'father figure'. Toddlers have their rights, and what this really leads to is their 'rights as consumers', where the attitudes of toddlers, as much as any other age group, are shaped by advertising, fashion, and the entertainment industry.

---

40 Konrad Lorenz, *Civilized Man's Eight Deadly Sins*, p. 72.

Lessons from Samoa: Margaret Mead

It would be desirable to mitigate, at least in some slight measure, the strong role which parents play in children's lives, and so eliminate one of the most powerful accidental factors in the choices of any individual life.

— Margaret Mead

CULTURAL ANTHROPOLOGY developed parallel to Critical Theory. The father of cultural anthropology, Franz Boas, headed the Anthropology Department at Columbia University during 1899–1942.

Boas trained the first generation of cultural anthropologists, who undertook their own 'march through the institutions' of anthropology departments and ethnological museums. Among his early protégés was Alexander Goldenweiser. He took his Ph.D. under the supervision of Boas in 1910. Goldenweiser lectured at the New School for Social Research, where he taught another budding eminence in cultural anthropology, Ruth Benedict, who wrote her doctoral dissertation under Boas' supervision. She became an extreme proponent of the notion that Man was from birth a creature of the culture into which he was born.[1]

Boas sought to separate anthropology from biology, and again in parallel with Critical Theory aimed to detach the individual from the

---

1   D. Freeman (1984), pp. 56–57.

bonds of tradition. Dr. Derek Freeman comments on Boas' intellectual origins:

> As a youth he had been shocked when one of his fellow students had 'declared his belief in the authority of tradition and his conviction that one had not the right to doubt what the past had transmitted to us'. Such implicit belief in the authority of tradition was foreign to Boas' mind. In 1888, in discussing the aims of ethnology, he emphasized how important it is 'to observe the fight of individuals against tribal customs' and to see 'how far the strong individual is able to free himself from the fetters of condition'. ... In his anthropological credo ... he recorded that he had been stimulated to action in his own life by cultural conditions that ran counter to his ideals, and confessed that his whole outlook upon social life had been 'determined by the question: How can we recognize the shackles that tradition had laid upon us'. He added that once these shackles had been recognized, we are able to break them.[2]

Among Boas' students who became a seminal influence in anthropology was Margaret Mead. She studied under Boas when Ruth Benedict was his teaching assistant, to whom she became particularly close.[3]

Boasian anthropology had been of specific interest to the Frankfurt School. Mead, as 'the best known figure' of the Boasians, had been introduced to the Frankfurtians at Columbia by Erich Fromm during the 1930s. She wrote for their journal, *Zeitschrift für Sozialforschung* ('Studies in Philosophy and Social Science'). She was brought into the study of anti-Semitism commissioned by the American Jewish Committee (AJC),[4] undertaken by Horkheimer, Adorno et al. *The Authoritarian Personality* became one of the *Studies in Prejudice* volumes sponsored by the AJC.[5]

---

2   Franz Boas, 'An Anthropologist's Credo', 'The Aims of Ethnology', quoted by D. Freeman (1984), pp. 23–24.

3   Ibid., p. 57.

4   Rolf Wiggershaus, pp. 357–358.

5   Ibid., p. 408.

In 1925, Boas sent Mead on what he regarded as a particularly important mission to American Samoa to undertake what she described as a special inquiry into 'the relative strength of biological puberty and cultural pattern' among girls.[6] This was at a time of great debate about the sexual mores of American youth. The Mead study was intended to prove that, like the 18th century notion of the noble savage, Samoan society was free of the civilised West's sexual travails and the Samoans lived in a happy idyll. The result was *The Coming of Age in Samoa*, which became a seminal text in anthropology. Her conclusion was:

> It is proved that adolescence is not necessarily a specially difficult period in a girl's life — and proved it is if we can find any society in which that is so — then what accounts for the presence of storm and stress in American adolescents? First, we may say quite simply that there must be something in the two civilizations to account for the difference. If the same process takes a different form in the two different environments, we cannot take any explanations in terms of the process, for that is the same in both cases.[7]

The subtitle of the book shows the intent: 'A psychological study of primitive youth for Western civilisation'. The lesson to be had was for the West to give free reign to the sexual impulse; the same theme as that of Marcuse, Fromm, Reich, Kinsey, de Sade et al. Boas, writing the introduction, referred to the same themes as that of the Critical Theorists and Kinseyans: the results of Mead's 'painstaking research confirm the suspicion long held by anthropologists, that much of what we ascribe to human nature is no more than a reaction to the restraints put upon us by our civilisation'.[8]

Mead laid out the intent of her study: to show that what was assumed to be human nature and inevitable was the 'result of civilisation' that is not necessarily present in other societies, and that the individual reacts to the 'social conditions' into which he is born. Mead

---

6   Derek Freeman, p. 61.

7   Margaret Mead, (1973), p. 197.

8   Boas in Mead, *Coming of Age in Samoa*, xv.

alluded to the common ground between Boasian anthropology and Behaviourism. For both it is a question of 'malleable humanity',[9] and the 'plasticity of human beings'.[10] The possibilities of social engineering and hence of social control become apparent.

Mead explained that primitive societies are most suitable for anthropological study because 'a trained student can master the fundamental structure of a primitive society in a few months'.[11] It was for Mead 'an uncomplex, uniform culture', and hence studying only fifty girls in three small neighbouring villages enabled her to 'generalise' her findings.[12] It is the arrogance typical of liberals whose assumption is that their ideology is applicable to the world, and will bring 'progress' and 'human rights' to the 'primitive', while they project their own 'supremacism' onto those who, in the tradition of de Maistre, reject the doctrine that there are any universal laws.

Mead was funded by a grant from the National Research Council,[13] the conduit of funds from Rockefeller. She had 'proven' the assumptions of 17th and 18th century novelists and poets who dreamed of a primitive utopia among far-off Indians and Africans, living in happiness and equality because of the lack of restraints.

Yet what we see already within a few pages is that Samoan society is based on the patriarchal family, where the father as head of the household is the first to eat.[14] Age brings authority. Girls are ignored until married.[15] Admonitions and punishments of toddlers by older children are constant, and a part of socialisation.[16] Etiquette between

---

9   Mead, *Coming of Age in Samoa*, p. 4.

10   Ibid., p. 5.

11   Ibid., p. 8.

12   Ibid., p. 11.

13   Ibid., vii.

14   Ibid., p. 18.

15   Ibid., p. 21.

16   Ibid., p. 25.

boys and girls is strict.[17] Virginity is expected until after marriage, particularly for the daughters of chiefs.[18] A girl's marriageability is based on her reputation for performing 'domestic tasks'. The boy is expected to be an adept fisherman, builder or boatman,[19] and there is much competition for status.[20] From adolescence, the boys are part of a disciplined village group (*Aumaga*) supervised by chiefs.[21] Local government is by the assembly of headmen (*Fono*), who have individually proven their status by example.[22] The status of a woman is dependent on her husband.[23]

It seems that what Mead wanted to see in Samoan society did not exist even by her own account. However, she concludes by drawing lessons for American adolescents, in contrast to the 'easy going Samoan, who is not hurried or harshly punished'. Love, hate, jealousy and revenge quickly pass. Mead discerns a quality among Samoans she regarded as commendable:

> From the first months of its life, when the child is handed carelessly from one woman's hands to another's, the lesson is learned of not caring for one person greatly, not setting high hopes on any one relationship. ... Samoa is kind to those who have learned the lesson of not caring, and hard upon those few individuals who have failed to learn it.[24]

What Mead claimed to have learned from Samoans is the desirability of lacking depth of feeling and attachment. It is little wonder that Samoans asked Freeman to repudiate Mead's claims. However, if familial attachments and sense of duty are so superficial in a natural

---

17 Ibid., p. 44.
18 Ibid., p. 99.
19 Ibid., p. 33.
20 Ibid., p. 191.
21 Ibid., p. 34.
22 Ibid.
23 Ibid., p. 78.
24 Ibid., p. 199.

society unburdened by the restraints and demands of civilisation, we are again presented with the post-Freudian aim for the destruction of traditional customs, ethics, morals and laws in the name of 'freedom' and 'happiness'. Yet in Mead's own account it is difficult to discern the reality of her conclusions. Rather, Samoa has all the aspects of what one would expect in a traditional society: hierarchy, taboos, patriarchal families, many children, strongly delineated gender roles, and disparities in social status based on achievement. Mead failed to find the egalitarian paradise expected from her by Boas, but attempted to obfuscate what she did find.

Nonetheless, Ruth Benedict regarded Mead as having proved that 'enormously variable social determinants ... fashion our human nature', and that mankind is 'unbelievably flexible'.[25] The victory of social determinism had been assisted with the previous rise of *Behaviourism*, alluded to by Mead in her introduction, and the coalescing of the social sciences under Rockefeller auspices, which had already embraced this reductionist approach. As Charles Merriam had said from the viewpoint of sociology, human nature was in fact not 'nature' but an ever-fluid response to tradition, that could be changed at will by the new social sciences. That is what Mead set out to prove for her mentor Boas.

In reality, Mead's account of the primitive idyll had no more reality than John Dryden's poem over 250 years previously:

I am as free as nature first made man,
Ere the base laws of servitude began,
When wild in woods the noble savage ran.[26]

It took decades before Mead was thoroughly debunked by an actual authority on Samoa, although Boasian anthropology remains established as a dogma in academia, impervious to evidence since it

25 R. Benedict, 'Nature and Nurture', *The Nation*, No. 118 (1924); quoted by Freeman, p. 81.

26 John Dryden, *The Conquest of Granada* (1672).

serves political agendas. Freeman, for his part, received opprobrium from social scientists committed to the Boasian dogma, and ridicule for having supposedly presented himself to the public as a 'heretic'.[27] Unlike Mead, who remained a stranger to Samoan society during her brief stay, Freeman, Professor of Anthropology at Australian National University, worked for six years in Samoa. He was the Foundation Professor of Anthropology and the Academic Pro-Chancellor of the University of Samoa, and an honorary Samoan chief. His book *Margaret Mead and Samoa* was written at the plea of tertiary-educated Samoans who were appalled at Mead's description of their society, while others regarded Mead's depiction of their 'simple life' as insulting. Mead thought it took a few months to understand a simple society such as Samoa, devoid of the complexities of European civilisation. Freeman states that it is evident she 'greatly underestimated the culture, society, history and psychology of the people among whom she was to study adolescence'. Samoan society is as complex as any other. It seems extraordinary that this underestimation of Samoan society is the premise of a cabal of anthropologists who sought to eliminate 'racism' and 'prejudice'. As Freeman showed, Samoan society is rent with violence, and studies show this has been the case since pre-colonial times. Physical punishment of children has been the norm, rape is 'unusually common' and among the highest rates in the world. The Samoan temperament is volatile. Submissiveness and obedience towards the chiefly caste are the basis of the traditional social order, maintained by punishment.[28]

Freeman was not alone in his criticism of Mead. Other criticisms came from social scientists, although also critical of what they considered Freeman's 'racism' in his taking a sociobiological approach. In a symposium critiquing Mead, Peter Worsley, an Australian

---

27 James E. Côté, et al., 'The Mead-Freeman Controversy in Review', *Journal of Youth and Adolescence*, Vol. 29, No. 5, 2000; https://www.academia.edu/27125304/The_Mead_Freeman_Controversy_in_Review.

28 Freeman, p. 274.

anthropologist and sociologist of leftist persuasion wrote, 'Critical evaluation of Margaret Mead's work is long overdue, particularly in the United States, where I have frequently found it difficult to engage in discussion about Mead, since the slightest breath of criticism commonly evokes a passionate — and to my mind quite uncritical — defense of the entire corpus of her very uneven writings and of her life-career'.[29] In a 1957 review article, 'Margaret Mead: Science or Science-Fiction?', Worsley had referred to the 'impressionistic and often dubious nature of the evidence' in her books for popular consumption.[30] Worsley alluded to the 'uncritical adulation' of Mead, citing a 1983 symposium in the *American Anthropologist*, lambasting Freeman's critique, which Worsley stated was not a repudiation of Freeman's careful evidence, but a denunciation of his 'theoretical orientation'.[31] John Waiko, former director of the New Guinea Institute of Social & Economic Research, having observed Mead in New Guinea, criticised her for similar reasons: New Guineans had been dismayed by the way 'she had inaccurately depicted their culture', and she had been dismissive of those who challenged her.[32]

Again it was the traditional family being deconstructed. Among Mead's conclusions were that: '... It is very possible that there are aspects of the life of the young child in Samoa which equip it particularly well for passing through life without nervous instability'.[33] Such is the casual existence that Mead thought she saw, while nonetheless writing much to the contrary, that she stated those measured as mentally retarded in the West would live without notice in Samoa, and

---

29 Peter Worsley in Lenora Forestel and Angela Gilliam (eds.), *Confronting the Margaret Mead Legacy*, ix.

30 Ibid., x.

31 Ibid., xii.

32 John Waiko, 'Culture, Identity, Commitment', in *Confronting the Margaret Mead Legacy*, p. 245.

33 Mead, *Coming of Age*, p. 208.

that 'Samoan civilisation' would never reach the artistic sublimity of the West.

Mead claimed she found that the carefree existence of the Samoan child recedes only to the extent that there is any parental authority imposed. The lesson, in the chapter 'Our [the West's] Educational Problems' is that it is the parent bond that needs eliminating. Only then will it be possible to reach the happy existence of a society that Mead had opined cannot distinguish between normal and subnormal intelligence and is incapable of producing great art.

> With this hypothesis in mind it is worthwhile to consider in more detail which parts of the young child's special environment are most strikingly different from ours. Most of these center about the family situation, the environment which impinges earliest and most intensely upon the child's consciousness. The organisation of the Samoan household eliminates at one stroke, in almost all cases, many of the special situations which are believed to be productive of undesirable emotional sets. ... but in the few cases where Samoan family life does approximate ours, the special attitudes incident to order of birth and to close affectional ties with the parent tend to develop.[34]

To Mead, the Samoan family was devoid of patriarchal (or matriarchal) authority. They would presumably score low on the 'F' Scale if measuring for Samoan Fascism. Conversely, there is a **collective authority**, which Mead regards as superior to the parental pair bond. It is strongly hierarchical. Are we to conclude that Mead believed parental authority is the root of all evil in the West, as do the Critical Theorists, but that a strongly hierarchical society taking the place of parental authority is preferable? It hardly seems to accord with the ideal of the carefree individual self-actualising without restraint. It does accord, however, with the construction of a centralised regime replacing the authority of parents and the independence of the household.

---

34 Ibid., p. 208.

The close relationship between parent and child, which has such a decisive influence upon so many in our civilisation, that **submission to the parent or defiance of the parent may become the dominating pattern of a life-time, is not found in Samoa**. Children reared in households where there are half a dozen adult women to care for them and dry their tears, and half a dozen adult males, all of whom represent constituted authority, do not distinguish their parents as sharply as our children do. … Instead of learning as its first lesson that here is a kind mother whose special and principal care is for its welfare, and a father whose authority is to be deferred to, the Samoan baby learns that its world is composed of **a hierarchy of male and female adults**, all of whom can be depended upon and **must be deferred to**.[35]

In the context of an industrial society, whose **economic** structure is more complex than that of Samoa, what replaces the mother-father-child bond, and the authority of two parents whose authority 'must be deferred to'? In pre-Stalin Bolshevik Russia, the authority was assumed by the factory crèche, and factory communal kitchens and canteens replaced the family hearth; for women the 'drudgery' of household work and child-rearing was replaced by the exciting possibilities of factory labour on equal terms with the men.

Mead referred to 'casual sex relations' that 'carry no onus of strong attachment, that the marriage of convenience dictated by economic and social considerations is easily born and casually broken without strong emotion'.[36] Might we assume that Samoan chiefs during the 18th century had acquired a copy of de Sade's *Philosophy in the Bedroom* and used it as the foundation of Samoan society? For the increasingly concentrated capitalist society, the situation in regard to marriage, family and parental bonds, has increasingly become 'bolshevised', except it is done in the name of 'free enterprise' instead of 'socialism', a development particularly noted by the ex-leftist scholar Christopher Lasch.

---

35   Ibid., pp. 209–210. Emphasis added.
36   Ibid., p. 210.

Mead observed that children are

> schooled not by an individual but by an army of individuals into general conformity upon which the personality of their parents has a very light effect. ... It is possible that where our own culture is so charged with choice, **it would be desirable to mitigate, at least in some slight measure, the strong role which parents play in children's lives, and so eliminate one of the most powerful accidental factors in the choices of any individual life.**[37]

Might we here be getting to the reason why Mead was sponsored by Rockefeller in her field work, why her books are heavily promoted for popular consumption, and why she and other Boasians have remained dominant in anthropology, with anathema placed on those scholars who dissent? The only way of imposing and maintaining 'general conformity' is by 'mitigating the role parents play in children's lives'. For industrial societies that means the child is shaped not by parents but by an army of functionaries, industrial psychologists, social workers, advertising and public relations agencies, and programmes in industry to ensure conformity to the corporation's ethos of profit maximisation in an 'inclusive economy'. Where there was once the commissar, there is today the corporate 'human relations officer'.

Role in Revival of Freudianism

Following World War I, Freudianism, which had been in vogue among the *avantgarde* and those who saw its use in promoting 'sexual freedom', took a back seat in favour of other psychobiological theories. Margaret Mead, as the most energetic of Boas's protégés in publishing popular accounts on her anthropological studies,

> probably did as much as anyone in the U.S. to keep the left-Freudian critique of *libidinal* repression in modern civilization percolating on the cultural backburner during those years. Consistently throughout her career Mead used her forays into participant/observation to construct

---

37   Ibid., p. 214. Emphasis added.

a comparative anthropological model of human cultures as unique, syncretic, and dynamic manifestations of a universal tendency to create meaning and community, grounded in a rejection of racist theories as scientifically and ethically invalid, and deeply rooted in a Freudian-based conviction that private social interactions and customs, particularly those surrounding sexuality, are particularly useful for understanding larger social formations.[38]

Although the radical exponents of 'free love', such as Margaret Sanger's colleague, the anarchist Emma Goldman, had been suppressed by law, Mead and Ruth Benedict, both of 'old American stock', unlike many of the prior radicals, were better placed to continue 'that older agenda' of the left-radicals and their bourgeois liberal allies, 'thanks in part to the vacuum created by the purges'. They 'undertook leadership in advancing the now-internalized libertarian agenda of that old alliance'.[39]

> *Coming of Age in Samoa* presents a clear example of how that work carried out by Mead helped lead the newly emerging field of cultural anthropology in this direction, and in fact would be incomprehensible to an audience not already well-versed in the outlines of the Freudian worldview.[40]

Leading American psychoanalyst A. A. Brill, in a promotional blurb for *Coming of Age in Samoa* (1963 edition) stated that 'Mead produced nothing short of a thoroughgoing corroboration, through practical demonstration, of the psychosexual theories promulgated by Freud and his pupils'.[41] Mead had ostensibly shown that Samoa was free of neuroses and the stresses of puberty because of the supposed libertine existence of the mythic noble savage. Again, one might wonder whether Mead, like Wilhelm Reich, Althusser, Kinsey, was projecting her own personality onto a whole society, as a means of normalising her own traits. Charles Williams opines that this might account for

---

38   Charles F. Williams, p. 58.

39   Ibid., p. 59.

40   Ibid.

41   Cited by Charles F. Williams, p. 61.

the polemical nature of *Coming of Age in Samoa*, with its recommendations that Western societies draw lessons from 'primitive societies'. Mead claimed that 'normal group standards' included casual and common lesbian encounters, albeit not of enduring character.

> This of course points, at least to a westerner, to an obvious and central underlying motivation for the polemical tone of the book: her own personal history of attending all-women's colleges with strong traditions of homosocial crushes and her intermittent adult experience of homosexual love, including her well-known affair with Ruth Benedict.[42]

It is Mead's *Coming of Age in Samoa* that 'most clearly demonstrates how a psychoanalytically informed free love rhetoric was carried forward by White liberals in the wake of the post World War I purges of radicals from politics and clinical psychoanalytic practices alike'. The books of Mead's and Benedict's were intended 'to facilitate a transformation, or at least a significant adjustment in the neo-Freudian sense of the term, in U.S. modern culture'.[43]

---

42 Ibid., p. 67.
43 Ibid., p. 76.

Perennial Character of Primary Ties

Morality is not imposed from outside; we have it in ourselves from the start — not the law, but our moral nature without which the collective life of human society would be impossible.

— JUNG

CARL JUNG STATED that man is by no means above instinct, nor past eras of history; that they are layered upon his unconscious and are ignored or repressed at peril. Jung sought not the elimination of instinct, but a balance. That was his concept of *individuation*; the integration of the self as a total being. Instincts are part of the unconscious along with archetypes, and these manifest as myths and religion in the collective unconscious of a people, as they do among individuals. They are essential for the psychic well-being of the individual and the group. They manifest as the *primary ties* that the Critical Theorists sought to eliminate as a primitive and childish barrier to the 'progress' of mankind towards the fully autonomous self.

Jung said of the 'laws man created' that they reflect an innate imperative that is necessary to manifest, not eliminate. The creative expression of these instincts Jung called *psychisation*; Friedrich Nietzsche's *sublimation*. This will-to-order is the foundation of creativity; not, as Fromm et al. insisted, a suppression of it. For Wilhelm Reich, therefore, the way to self-actualisation is the unrestrained orgasm, while the post-Freudians agree in stating that the basic drives must be given free reign; as supposedly 'free' as the 'noble savage' of 18th century poetic imagination, or the 'free love' of the 1960s generation, or of Mead's perception of Samoan adolescents.

Jung & Nietzsche

For Nietzsche, one of the most misunderstood and misinterpreted of philosophers, whose ideas were appropriated and skewered by Critical Theorists, despite his abhorrence for all things socialist, 'a sexual impulse, for example could be channelled into a creative spiritual activity, instead of being fulfilled directly. Similarly the barbarian desire to torture his foe can be sublimated into the desire to defeat one's rival, say, in the Olympic contests...'[1] Critical Theorists elaborated on Nietzsche's *will-to-power* as a precursor to the *self-actualisation* of humanistic psychology that became a fad during the 1960s, and found its infantile expression in the New Left, and most stridently in Charles Manson's 'Family'. Hence, Christine Swanton considers that '[s]everal key areas are at the heart of will-to-power as a *developmental* theory', 'developed by psychologists such as Fromm... In a way reminiscent of Nietzsche, Erich Fromm distinguished between "life furthering syndrome" and "life thwarting syndrome". ... As with Nietzsche, for Fromm alienation from self is destructive of life affirmation'...[2] Nietzsche thus becomes, along with Fromm, Marcuse, and the hapless Adorno, the philosophical father of hippies, yippies, yuppies, and group-therapy patients. Swanton alludes to Fromm, stating that the regression to primal cruelty is 'the unbearable frustration caused by social constraints'... 'custom, respect, self-control'... 'and the need for freedom from them'.[3] If we suppose that Nietzsche's *self-overcoming* means, like Fromm, Reich, and Marcuse, the rejection of restraint, custom and self-control, to become another type of 'developmental theory', then the profundity of this philosopher is reduced

---

1   Walter Kaufmann, p. 214.

2   Christine Swanton, p. 140.

3   Ibid., p. 142.

to the banality of the modern epoch. While Nietzsche distinguished between 'slave morality', and 'master morality', this is not defined by a hedonistic and petty rejection of morals and restraint in the quest for the inane 'self-actualisation' of pop therapy, but as the quest for *higher man* as a prelude to the far-off *overman*. That is as far removed as one can get from the indulgent hippie *nirvana* of post-Freudian 'freedom'. Nietzsche's regard for the Hindu *Code of Manu*, 'a natural law of the first rank, over which no arbitrary fiat, no "modern idea"',[4] for example, indicates that he was not on a mission to liberate man from restraint but to herald the return of a hard morality on the self. Nietzsche's *will-to-power*, as Swanton herself states, is antithetical to the free reign of the 'pleasure principle', yet this is the premise of the post-Freudians. To such 'modern ideas' Nietzsche countered in writing of the *Code of Manu*,

> The most intelligent men, like the strongest, find their happiness where others would find only disaster: in the labyrinth, in being hard with themselves and with others, in effort; their delight is in self-mastery; in them asceticism becomes second nature, a necessity, an instinct.[5]

As for Nietzsche's regard for those who would reduce man to inanity in the name of 'freedom' from restraint: 'Whom do I hate most heartily among the rabbles of today? The rabble of Socialists. ...'.[6]

To such notions of man 'freeing' himself from the organic bonds that had been the substance of his being since times immemorial, Jung answered:

> Moral law is nothing other than an outward manifestation of man's innate urge to dominate and control himself. This impulse to domestication and civilization is lost in the dim, unfathomable depths of man's evolutionary

---

4   Nietzsche, *The Antichrist*, Section 57.
5   Ibid.
6   Ibid.

history and can never be conceived as the consequence of laws imposed from without, Man himself, obeying his instincts, created his laws.[7]

Morality was not brought down on tables of stone from Sinai and imposed on the people, but is a function of the human soul, as old as humanity itself. Morality is not imposed from outside; we have it in ourselves from the start — not the law, but our moral nature without which the collective life of human society would be impossible.[8]

This innate 'moral nature' is the basis of the unfolding of one's being individually and collectively. Laws are a manifestation of it, not its origin. The Left seeks to replace this innate 'moral nature', which to them is only the reflection of the laws of social production.

Spirituality is also an innate imperative that the Freudians and Marxians consider as superstition and magic. Jung wrote of this, and indicated his Nietzschean influence:

The spiritual principle does not, strictly speaking, conflict with instinct as such but only with blind instinctuality, which really amounts to an unjustified preponderance of the instinctual nature over the spiritual. The spiritual appears in the psyche also as an instinct, indeed as a real passion, a 'consuming fire', as Nietzsche once expressed it. It is not derived from any other instinct, as the psychologists of instinct would have us believe, but is a principle *siti generis*, a specific and necessary form of instinctual power.[9]

The myth of the 'noble savage', unspoiled by civilisation, is an ideal that had inspired the dreams of the salon intelligentsia since the Age of the Enlightenment. On the basis of an imagined natural innocence, utopians believe they can recreate man in that primal image that has never actually existed, and that man can be 'free' and 'spontaneous'. Although the hippies came close to the ideal in wallowing in their own filth and disease, Jung had no such illusions:

---

7   Carl Jung, *Collected Works*, Vol. 4, para. 486.

8   Ibid., Vol. 7, para. 30.

9   Ibid., Vol. 8, para. 108.

Man living in the state of nature is in no sense merely 'natural' like an animal, but sees, believes, fears, worships things whose meaning is not at all discoverable from the conditions of his natural environment. Their underlying meaning leads us in fact far away from all that is natural, obvious, and easily intelligible, and quite often contrasts most sharply with the natural instincts.[10]

Myth, and what Jung called the 'religious instinct', is an essential part of the development of man and the expression of his place in the universe; not 'the opiate of the masses', a weapon of the ruling class to maintain a servile population, or a childish superstition that is holding the individual back from unbounded spontaneous creativity. All peoples throughout all of history have had an inner impulsion to create religion and a conception of the Godhead; 'the strongest inner compulsion, which can only be explained by the irrational force of instinct'. 'One could almost say that if all the world's traditions were cut off at a single blow, the whole of mythology and the whole history of religion would start all over again with the next generation'.[11] Rationalism is a severing of the primordial well-spring of thinking, art and religion. Jung stated that, 'My whole endeavour has been to show that myth is something very real because it connects us with the instinctive bases of our existence'.[12]

Instinct is not an isolated thing, nor can it be isolated in practice. It always brings in its train archetypal contents of a spiritual nature, which are at once its foundation and its limitation. In other words, an instinct is always and inevitably coupled with something like a philosophy of life, however archaic, unclear, and hazy this may be. Instinct stimulates thought, and if a man does not think of his own free will, then you get compulsive thinking, for the two poles of the psyche, the physiological and the mental, are

---

10   Ibid., Vol. 8, para. 98.
11   Ibid., Vol. 4, para. 30.
12   Carl Jung, *Letters*, Vol. II, p. 468.

indissolubly connected. For this reason instinct cannot be freed without freeing the mind, just as mind divorced from instinct is condemned to futility.[13]

The scholar of mythology, Joseph Campbell, discussed the difference in outlooks between Jung and Freud, the Freudian outlook also being that of the Critical Theorists. For Freud, myths are public dreams, and dreams are private myths. 'Both, in his opinion, are symptomatic of repression of infantile incest wishes, the only essential difference between a religion and neurosis being that the former is more public. ... Civilisation itself in fact is a pathological surrogate for unconscious infantile disappointments. And thus Freud ... judged the world of myth, magic and religion negatively, as errors to be refuted, surpassed, and supplanted finally be science.'[14]

With Freud the Critical Theorists are able to deconstruct and fracture 'civilisation' in ways more far-reaching than the class struggle of Marxism. They strike at the very root of man's being, which is far more than simply the economic relations of Marxism. Jung had 'an altogether different approach', wrote Campbell, with myth and religion serving 'positive, life-affirming ends'. Myths, when properly read, writes Campbell in reference to Jung, are the means by which the individual might reconnect with one's 'inward forces', when obscured by mundane routine. Myths are the wisdom of millennia. 'Thus, they have not been, and cannot be, displaced by the findings of science...'[15] This was not a call for Western man, however, to regress into primal atavisms, as *individuation* requires balance:

> However, there is a danger here as well; namely, of being drawn by one's dreams and inherited myths away from the world of modern consciousness, fixed in patterns of archaic feeling and thought inappropriate to contemporary life. What is required, states Jung therefore, is a dialogue,

13   Carl Jung, Collected Works, Vol. 16, para. 185.
14   Joseph Campbell (1961).
15   Ibid.

not a fixture at either pole; a dialogue by way of symbolic forms put forth
from the unconscious mind and recognized by the conscious in continuous
interaction.[16]

Even in the subtle methods of the modern world, where secularism is
promoted and religion disdained, the great yearning arises for a myth
that can replace the gods that have been killed; albeit distorted into a
fascination especially for the myths and religions of cultures **not** of
one's own. Jung warned of the injurious character of fetishizing the
foreign, writing that because of the primordial differentiation among
races psychologically, 'we cannot transplant the spirit of a foreign race
in globo into our own mentality without sensible injury to the latter, a
fact which does not deter those of feeble instinct from attempting to
do so'.[17]

In a repudiation of the notion of a *universal humanity* other than
at the most primal level of existence, and the modernist dogma that
races can adopt wholesale the lessons and outlooks of others, Jung
stated:

> We are in reality unable to borrow or absorb anything from outside, from
> the world, or from history. What is essential to us can only grow out of
> ourselves. When the white man is true to his instincts, he reacts defensively
> against any advice that one might give him. What he has already swallowed
> he is forced to reject again as if it were a foreign body, for his blood refuses
> to assimilate anything sprung from foreign soil.[18]

This is an unequivocal statement warning of multiculturalism and
notions of 'cultural enrichment', by the conscious or unconscious, voluntary or imposed, adoption of what might be called 'foreign bodies'
into the culture-organism.

Where the Freudo-Marxian sees repression of individual 'freedom'
and the blocking of the road to 'self-actualisation', the organic thinker

---

16 Ibid.
17 Jung, *Collected Works*, op. cit., Vol. 7, p. 149, n. 8.
18 Ibid., Vol. 7, para. 31.

sees perennial foundations for all that **truly** self-actualises. Fromm, in aiming to sever these 'ties' sought to create new ones. Where is the anchorage in such a severance? One must return for any type of polity to the 18th century idea of individuals in contractual agreement to form a 'society', which is indeed the premise of our present-day notions of 'civil society'. How one 'contracts out' of such a civil society, which has now become universal, is another matter as witnessed by the Jacobin 'Reign of Terror' in France or the destruction of so-called 'rogue states' by the U.N.O. and NATO. Rousseau, in formulating the doctrine of the 'social contract', predicated it on the abstraction of the 'general will', which, once established, could not be discarded by the individual 'citizen'.

Jung perceived that the West's modern epoch had been centuries in the making. Culture epochs do not arise as sudden and clearly delineated eras, any more than an individual's old age, middle age and youth can be precisely demarcated; but there are signs. Jung saw that these modern doctrines had arisen in prior centuries, and pointed to the 'Age of Reason', and to 'American psychologists' as a product of this epoch: 'Most of your [American] psychologists, as it looks to me, are still in the 18th century inasmuch as they believe that the human psyche is *tabula rasa* at birth, while all somewhat differentiated animals are born with specific instincts'.[19]

> The citizen's instinct of self-preservation should be safeguarded at all costs, for, once a man is cut off from the nourishing roots of instinct, he becomes the shuttlecock of every wind that blows. He is then no better than a sick animal, demoralized and degenerate, and nothing short of a catastrophe can bring him back to health.[20]

Cutting off from 'the nourishing roots of instinct' is precisely the aim of modernist doctrines. What are these 'nourishing roots' if not the 'primary ties' condemned as repressive by the Critical Theorists', and

---

19   Carl Jung, *Letters*, Vol. II, p. 150.
20   Carl Jung, *Collected Works*, Vol. 10, para. 413.

scoring high on the 'F scale'? Further: 'As no animal is born without its instinctual patterns, there is no reason whatever to believe that man should be born without his specific forms of physiological and psychological reactions'.[21] But for Fromm et al., what one is 'born with' is something that is to be eliminated as a burden.

For the Critical Theorists, once the 'primary ties' were broken, they could never be restored; the danger was that man would not choose this 'freedom' to become 'spontaneous' through 'love' but would run back to the paternal-like security of authority.

Fromm denounced Jung as a 'reactionary'. Defence of the 'primary ties' showed 'Jung's lack of commitment to authenticity', according to Fromm, with Jung's 'blend of outmoded superstition, indeterminate heathen idol worship, and vague talk about God, and with the allegation that he is building a bridge between religion and psychology...'[22]

---

21   Carl Jung, *Letters*, Vol. II, p. 152.
22   Fromm cited by Frank McLynn, *Carl Gustav Jung: A Biography*, p. 434.

Dialectics of Critical Theory

A university must not be an end in itself; it must be an institution responsive to the needs of society, a powerful force in social and economic development, engaging in the kinds of teaching and research required for the transition from traditional to modern ways of life.

— The Rockefeller Foundation, 1968

CRITICAL THEORY took from Marx the dialectical method. Social development was based on historical laws in which opposites clash, and out of the conflict a synthesis emerges, proceeded by a new clash of opposites: the equation of *thesis + antithesis = synthesis...*, also expressed as the thesis containing the seeds of its own destruction. This is the lineal, 'progressive' 'march of history'. Marx believed *messianically* that out of the clash of bourgeoisie and proletarian would emerge a socialist and finally a Communist world society, and thereafter history would be completed; there would not be a further dialectic. Why world Communism should be the culmination of history does not seem to have been explained by Marx, but rests on notions typical of the English *Zeitgeist* under which he wrote. Likewise, the liberal-capitalist theorist Professor Francis Fukuyama stated that once liberal-democratic-capitalism had been established throughout the world, that would be what he literally called 'the end of history'.[1] Nineteenth century Darwinian scientists considered their century the

---

1   Francis Fukuyama (1992).

culmination of all history, and the Great Exhibition (1851) was held in London to prove it. The future was industry and science, and the vision remains the same today.

The Critical Theorists applied the Marxian dialect to the psychoanalysis of Freud and saw this 'progressive' 'march of history' in psychological terms. Like Marx, the Critical Theorists stated that capitalism was an essential phase of this dialectic because capitalism, and the Reformation and Renaissance eras that preceded it, ushered in new concepts of freedom by undermining the traditional social order. Fromm wrote of capitalism in this psycho-social dialectic, in similar terms to Marx's comments on capitalism in regard to class struggle:

> Any critical evaluation of the effect which the industrial system had on this kind of inner freedom must start with the full understanding of the **enormous progress which capitalism has meant for the development of human personality**. As a matter of fact, any critical appraisal of modern society which neglects this side of the picture must prove to be rooted in an irrational romanticism and is suspect of criticizing capitalism, not for the sake of progress, but for the sake of the destruction of the most important achievements of man in modern history.[2]

Here Fromm condemns those who do not view capitalism as an essential part of the process in the 'development of human personality' as propounding 'irrational romanticism'. Marx condemned it as '*reactionism*'. The Right is shown to be the only doctrine that genuinely opposes capitalism, seeing it not as a step in the 'development of the human personality', but as a regression. It is no wonder that the Left can align so readily with the oligarchy in attacking the Right. Fromm continues:

> What Protestantism had started to do in freeing man spiritually, capitalism continued to do mentally, socially, and politically. Economic freedom was the basis of this development, the middle class was its champion. The individual was no longer bound by a fixed social system, based on tradition

---

2   Erich Fromm (1942), p. 92.

and with a comparatively small margin for personal advancement beyond the traditional limits. He was allowed and expected to succeed in personal economic gains as far as his diligence, intelligence, courage, thrift, or luck would lead him. His was the chance of success, his was the risk to lose and to be one of those killed or wounded in the fierce economic battle in which each one fought against everybody else. Under the feudal system the limits of his life expansion had been laid out before he was born; but under the capitalistic system the individual, particularly the member of the middle class, had a chance — in spite of many limitations — to succeed on the basis of his own merits and actions. He saw a goal before his eyes towards which he could strive and which he often had a good chance to attain. He learned to rely on himself; to make responsible decisions, to give up both sooth-ing and terrifying superstitions, Man became increasingly free from the bondage of nature; he mastered natural forces to a degree unheard and un-dreamed of in previous history. Men became equal; differences of caste and religion, which once had been natural boundaries blocking the unification of the human race, disappeared, and men learned to recognize each other as human beings. The world became increasingly free from mystifying elements; man began to see himself objectively and with fewer and fewer illusions. Politically freedom grew too. On the strength of its economic po-sition the rising middle class could conquer political power and the newly won political power created increased possibilities for economic progress.[3]

Fromm stated that the oligarchic and bourgeoisie revolutions in the name of 'the people' had continued the process that had started with the Renaissance and Reformation and continued with, 'The great revolutions in England [Cromwell] and France [Jacobinism] and the fight for American independence [which] are the milestones marking this development.'[4]

For the Critical Theorists, the next stage of the psycho-sociologi-cal-historical dialectic must be to correct the alienation resulting from the breaking of the 'primary ties' by inventing new forms of iden-tity. The way to the utopia of self-actualisation requires a revolution. Capitalism had freed man from his organic bonds, *Gemeinschaft* has

---

3   Erich Fromm (1942), p. 92.

4   Ibid., p. 92.

been replaced by contractual civil society. All that is left is commodity, and none more so than the commodification of one's work, whereas in the medieval epoch there was God-ordained craft as a social function. Fromm explained:

> The attitude towards work has the quality of instrumentality; in contrast to a medieval artisan the modern manufacturer is not primarily interested in what he produces; he produces essentially in order to make a profit from his capital investment, and what he produces depends essentially on the market which promises that the investment of capital in a certain branch will prove to be profitable. Not only the economic, but also the personal relations between men have this character of alienation; instead of relations between human beings, they assume the character of relations between things. But perhaps the most important and the most devastating instance of this spirit of instrumentality and alienation is the individual's relationship to his own self. Man does not only sell commodities, he sells himself and feels himself to be a commodity. The manual labourer sells his physical energy; the business man, the physician, the clerical employee, sell their 'personality'. They have to have a 'personality' if they are to sell their products or services.[5]

Here the traditional-Right is in agreement, as it is with a similar assessment by Marx. But where Marx condemned the *reactionists* who sought a return to the Gothic ethos, and the Critical Theorists have their 'F scale', the traditional-Rightist questions the wisdom of rejecting the past in order to cross an abyss towards a future whose only selling point is in the name of a self-defined 'progress'. Fromm refers to the philosophers of the Age of Enlightenment and the Industrial Revolution as heralds of the future, where the self is the total meaning of existence, obscenely grouping Nietzsche with Diderot, Rousseau, and Marx along the way. Like Marx, Fromm condemns the 'reactionaries' for wanting to restore what capitalism has destroyed.

---

5   Ibid., p. 103.

The philosophers of the period of the French Revolution, and in the nineteenth century, Feuerbach, Marx, Stirner, and Nietzsche, have again in an uncompromising way expressed the idea that the individual should not be subject to any purposes external to his own growth or happiness. The reactionary philosophers of the same century, however, explicitly postulated the subordination of the individual under spiritual and secular authority. The second half of the nineteenth century and the beginning of the twentieth show the trend for human freedom in its positive sense at its peak. Not only did the middle class participate in it, but also the working class became an active and free agent, fighting for its own economic aims and at the same time for the broader aims of humanity.[6]

Fromm, in alluding to the 'working class' as being part of the same revolutionary process as the bourgeoisie, also unwittingly indicates what Spengler more clearly saw, that 'there is no proletarian, not even a communist, movement that has not operated in the interest of money'.[7] The socialist response to capitalism was its mirror image and not its transcendence. What has occurred instead of what was supposedly, according to Fromm, the great promise of individual 'freedom' occurring during the 19th century, is the rise of an oligarchy.[8] The critical faculties of modern man are also being dulled by advertising, laments Fromm,[9] while here also advertising and the very notion of mercantile competition was shameful to the Gothic mind. But any talk of a restoration of the Gothic ethos is anathema to Marx and Fromm.

The task rather is one of continuing the revolution to secure 'human happiness and self-realization' in a process that was started by Luther, Henry VIII, Calvin, and continued by Cromwell, Robespierre, Franklin, Marx, and Freud. Man cannot 'go back' to the traditional life from which he was severed; he can try to 'escape' the insecurity of his

6   Ibid., p. 106.

7   Oswald Spengler, *The Decline of the West*, Vol. II, p. 402.

8   Fromm, *Fear of Freedom*, p. 106.

9   Ibid., p. 110.

'freedom' by turning to authoritarianism, but his self-realised future lies in a new-found 'spontaneity'.[10]

'Love' is the means by which the alienation of the spontaneous individual can find new relationships, but not 'love' in the sense of any renunciation of sacrifice of oneself for another. But 'love' also would result in the repression of spontaneity, as it is sacrifice to someone beyond oneself, unless the Critical Theorists refer to what might euphemistically be termed 'self-love'? Since there must be *polarity* in 'love', this is 'love' of a nebulous, universal kind, which 'springs from the need of overcoming separateness', leading to 'oneness — and yet that individuality is not eliminated'.[11] This is not familial love but the 'love' of everything in general and nothing in particular. Charles Manson's doped-up acolyte Susan Atkins stated the same philosophy to her probation officer: 'Love is everything; everything is nothing'.[12] Atkins articulated the entire Freudo-Marxian dialectic in six words, where it took Fromm, Marcuse, Adorno, Horkheimer, et al., a mountain of paper. The individual, by cutting the 'primary ties' to family, heritage, faith, and homeland, instead gets new meaning from this nebulous commitment to 'humanity'; an obliteration into a universal earthly nirvana.

> If the individual realizes his self by spontaneous activity and thus relates himself to the world, he ceases to be an isolated atom; he and the world become part of one structuralized whole; he has his rightful place, and thereby his doubt concerning himself and the meaning of life disappears.[13]

Man's 'aloneness' is thus 'dissolved', as the 'individual embraces the world'. This new way of self-actualising means rejection of property, and 'mental qualities like emotions or thoughts', which only hinder the individual's pursuit of self-actualisation.

---

10   Ibid., p. 121.

11   Ibid., p. 225.

12   Tom O'Neill, p. 278.

13   Ibid., p. 226.

Positive freedom also implies the principle that there is no higher power
than this unique individual self, that man is the center and purpose of his
life; that the growth and realization of man's individuality is an end that
can never be subordinated to purposes which are supposed to have greater
dignity.[14]

To subject oneself to a 'higher power' implies 'Fascism', yet one of
the few practical measures, albeit vague, that Fromm advocates is a
'planned economy',[15] which he identifies as 'democratic socialism'.
However, Fromm sees the danger in this also, so that 'planning from
the top is blended with active participation from below',[16] lest this
ends up like the USSR; the socialist dream turned sour. It might be
wondered how 'creative spontaneity' would work within a 'planned
economy' if the individual's notion of 'love of work' did not enable
production schedules to be met? Is this when 'rational authority'
would be justified, 'with active participation from below', enforced say
with a bullet to the head, or a cut in rations from the factory canteen?

What matters is the activity, not the result, writes Fromm. By
so doing, activity ceases to become a commodity, and happiness is
achieved not by striving for a goal but by experiencing what is in the
present.[17] Just how one 'plans' an economy like that is again perplex-
ing. That is not to say there should not be 'ideals', just that the 'ideals'[18] should not go beyond self-actualization, and must remain at one
with the world. Here might be discerned the premises of the various
dictums that marked the 1960s youth revolt: to 'live in the now', by becoming part of a 'new relatedness to the world', through spontaneity.[19]

If the whole premise seems too nebulous and contradictory to
grasp, Fromm has an explanation: 'We may not always know what

---

14 Ibid., p. 228.
15 Ibid., p. 235.
16 Ibid., p. 236.
17 Ibid., p. 226.
18 Ibid., p. 229.
19 Ibid., p. 226.

serves this end…' However, he assures us that the great question is one that can be answered not metaphysically, but by empirical science; Freudo-Marxian science.[20] This science has proven that any 'ideal' that is outside the individual, is not an 'ideal' but a 'pathology'.[21] Whatever uncertainties there are in Fromm's treatise, he returns and concludes with the central target of the Critical Theorists, the family, whose influence on the child must be circumvented by the educational system:

> … Freud has shown that the early experiences of the child have a decisive influence upon the formation of its character structure. If this is true, how then can we understand that the child, who — at least in our culture — has little contact with the life of society, is moulded by it? The answer is not only that the parents — aside from certain individual variations — apply the educational patterns of the society they live in, but also that in their own personalities they represent the social character of their society or class. They transmit to the child what we may call the psychological atmosphere or the spirit of a society just by being as they are — namely representatives of this very spirit. The family thus may be considered to be the psychological agent of society.[22]

Althusser arrived at the same conclusion, as did Reich and Horkheimer: the family is the primary incubator of social order and social morality, which must be eliminated for the next stage of human evolution to proceed. Fromm stated of the parental relationship that,

> if hostility develops and is repressed, and if at the same time his father or mother offers affection or care under the condition of surrender, such a constellation leads to an attitude in which active mastery is given up and all his energies are turned in the direction of an outside source from which the fulfilment of all wishes will eventually come. This attitude assumes such a passionate character because it is the only way in which such a person can attempt to realize his wishes.[23]

---

20   Ibid., p. 229.

21   Ibid., p. 230.

22   Ibid., pp. 246–247.

23   Ibid., p. 250.

Yet how is the family to be reshaped — as urged by Althusser — or eliminated, unless it is under the imposition of an 'outside source'?

Fromm's Bastards

Where was all of this leading? In place of the redundant class conflict, what emerged during the 1960s was the conflict of multiple identities, starting with disaffected Blacks and with privileged youth alienated from 'authoritarian' parents. These 'rebels' were following the scenario prepared decades previously. Well-funded studies legitimised doctrines that permeated society from the academy.

Fromm saw the student tumult at his university, Columbia, in 1968 as the birth of the revolution for which he and his colleagues had prepared since their days in Weimar Germany. Speaking as an honoured guest to the 'counter-commencement ceremony' at Columbia University,[24] which had been organised as a protest against the administration by the Students for a Restructured University,[25] Fromm stated that the student protest was 'a revolution of life' 'in a society of zombies', and that 'anyone who does not lose his mind does not have a mind to lose'.[26]

It had been Columbia University where the Frankfurt Institute exiles had gained their initial academic employment, and where Franz Boas had previously inaugurated his school of cultural anthropology.

Rebellion against parents was healthy and would usher in Fromm's utopia of 'spontaneity in love and work'. Youngsters, aligned with Blacks, were the wave of the future, and would redeem the inherent racism and 'White privilege' of their parents.

Could it be that Fromm was projecting his own dysfunctional parental relationships, as had Althusser and Reich? There was much

---

24 'Commencement to Be Held Amidst Protest', *Columbia Daily Spectator*, Vol. CXII, no. 120, 3 June 1968.

25 The SRU was funded by the Ford Foundation and other sources. See: Jerry Avorn et al., (1968), p. 283.

26 Cited by Dan Berger (2005), p. 65.

about the New Left that was a temper tantrum against parents, to the extent of demanding matricide and patricide.[27] In 1912, Fromm's father Naphtali employed Oswald Sussman in his wine business. Sussman lived in the Fromm household, introduced Erich to the writings of Marx and Engels, and became Erich's father figure. Erich said of Sussman that he was the first adult to take a real interest in him as an individual.[28] Of his father, Erich stated that he was 'very neurotic' and 'obsessive'. Erich stated he 'suffered under the influence of a pathologically anxious father who overwhelmed me with his anxiety, at the same time not giving me any guidelines and having no positive influence on my education'.[29] The Fromm marriage was not happy, and Erich described his father as distant and his mother as overprotective.[30]

In 1923, Fromm opened a psychiatric clinic with Freudian analyst Frieda Reichmann to treat specifically Jewish patients by making them aware of their Jewish tradition and identity.[31] Fromm had been raised in an Orthodox household and had immersed himself in Talmudic studies as a youth. It is notable that while he was zealous in his mission to detach Gentile individuals from tradition, this did not apply to Jewish individuals, whose anxieties could be treated by a reattachment to their heritage; that is, a reattachment to *primary ties*.

Jewish Factor

This Jewish factor is significant and has been commented on by Jewish scholars. Yet when a Gentile scholar, Dr. Kevin MacDonald, an extensively experienced psychologist from California State University (Long Beach), examined Jewish involvement in Critical Theory and

---

27   See: Bolton, *The Psychotic Left*, pp. 148–189.

28   Lawrence J. Friedman, p. 8.

29   Rainer Funk, p. 17.

30   Daniel Burston, p. 8.

31   Lawrence J. Friedman, p. 20.

other subversive movements as a survival mechanism,[32] he was vilified as an 'anti-Semite' and his conclusions and sources were brought into question with the standard *ad hominem* and straw man arguments.[33] Carl Jung underwent similar smears when he broke with Freud. Jack Jacobs, a notable Jewish scholar,[34] states in the first paragraph of his book on Jews and the Frankfurt School that,

> The history of the Frankfurt School cannot be fully told without examining the relationships of Critical Theorists to their Jewish family backgrounds. Jewish matters had significant effects on key figures in the Frankfurt School, including Max Horkheimer, Theodor W. Adorno, Erich Fromm, Leo Löwenthal, and Herbert Marcuse. At some points their Jewish family backgrounds clarify their paths[35]...

Jacobs states that those who were 'in whole or in part' of Jewish background formed the 'overwhelming majority' of the Institute for Social Research during the Weimar era. The number of non-Jews was 'rather small', and one, Paul Massing, felt that being non-Jewish prevented his full acceptance by the Institute's 'inner circle'. This was a matter of 'elective affinity'[36] between the Jewish leftist intelligentsia; a psychosociological factor, although apologists for Critical Theory retort with accusations of *conspiracism* when such matters are cited by non-Jewish researchers. In regard to Fromm, for example, Jacobs regards

---

32   Kevin MacDonald, *A People That Shall Dwell Alone: Judaism As a Group Evolutionary Strategy, With Diaspora Peoples*, (Praeger 1994); *Separation and Its Discontents: Toward an Evolutionary Theory of Anti-Semitism*, (Praeger 1998); *The Culture of Critique: An Evolutionary Analysis of Jewish Involvement in Twentieth-Century Intellectual and Political Movements*, (Praeger 1998).

33   Nathan Cofnas, 'Is Kevin MacDonald's Theory of Judaism "Plausible"? A Response to Dutton (2018)', *Evolutionary Psychological Science*, Vol. 5, (2019) pp. 143–150; https://doi.org/10.1007/s40806-018-0162-8.

34   Jack Jacobs: professor of political science at John Jay College, and the Graduate Center, City University of New York; Fulbright Scholar at Tel Aviv University (1996–1997); Fulbright Scholar at Vilnius Yiddish Institute (2009).

35   Jack Jacobs, i.

36   Ibid., p. 3.

his Orthodox background as significant in shaping his outlook, and that he 'was active in Zionist organizations'. In 1919 he co-founded the Frankfurt Society for Jewish Adult Education.[37] He diligently studied the encyclopaedic *Talmud*, the Jewish religious and legal code, during the mid-1920s.[38] Long after leaving Judaism, in 1966 Fromm was still crediting his Jewish religious background, stating of his Jewish teachers that 'at no point has the continuity between their teaching and my own view been interrupted'.[39]

Jacobs contends that although many of the Jews who founded the Institute, like Jewish socialists generally, later abandoned Judaism and Zionism, 'it remains true that they all travelled to it down recognizably Jewish roots'.[40] Horkheimer's ambiguity towards the state of Israel was predicated on a Jewish critique; of the state being a 'graven image'.[41] The attitudes of Löwenthal and Marcuse were also ambiguous, and both accepted invitations to speak in Israel.[42] The problem was that Israel as a state contradicted the global *messianism* of Judaism, the mission of diaspora Israel as a cosmopolitan, not a nationalist, people; what Löwenthal referred to as the 'prophetic-messianic message' that was obscured by Zionism. In 1982 Löwenthal wrote of the 'utopian-messianic motif', 'deeply rooted in Jewish metaphysics and mysticism' as 'playing a significant role' for Critical Theorists, such as Marcuse, Horkheimer and himself,[43] while Fromm became antagonistic towards the Israeli state.[44]

Of the New School for Social Research in New York, Val Vinokur, Associate Professor of Literary Studies at the New School, writes:

---

37   Ibid., pp. 33–34.

38   Ibid., p. 36.

39   Jacobs citing Fromm (*Ye Shall be as Gods*, p. 166), pp. 36–37.

40   Jack Jacobs, p. 42.

41   Horkheimer interview with *Der Spiegel*, (1970), Jacobs, p. 142.

42   Jacobs, p. 142.

43   Löwenthal cited by Jacobs, pp. 146–147.

44   Jacobs, p. 148.

So what's so Jewish about The New School? Well, it depends on what you mean by 'Jewish.' … Rutkoff and Scott's *History of The New School for Social Research* asserts a direct link between the school's origins in philosophical pragmatism one hundred years ago and the entry of Jews into the American academy, noting that during its first two decades, 'half of the regular lecturers at The New School were Jewish,' and that this was before the Graduate Faculty was established in 1933 to rescue the 'largely Jewish' European scholars fleeing from the Nazis. Rutkoff and Scott also observe that The New School 'acted as a rallying point for Jewish activities,' with Horace Kallen actively supporting the efforts of American Zionists while his colleague Morris Cohen, who had opposed Kallen's Zionism in the twenties as 'contrary to secular philosophy,' nonetheless established the Conference on Jewish Relations at The New School in 1933, to 'help educate the public on the international threat of anti-Semitism.'[45]

Vinokur refers to Horace Kallen as being the father of 'cultural pluralism' and this as being the forerunner of 'identity politics'.

Kallen's cultural pluralism turned into what many now call campus identity politics or social justice and civic engagement, reflecting an ideological shift away from the sovereignty of the nation state and the individual in favor of social groups. In other words, the 'Jewish history of The New School' eventually merged into the long history of post-war American universities.[46]

Marcuse & the New Left

It was Herbert Marcuse who defined the 'New Left' in 1967, and called for the necessity of student organisations to unite across the world. This they had long been doing under the leadership of the National Student Association, with CIA sponsorship, as part of a Cold War

45 Val Vinokur, 'What's so "Jewish" about The New School? Inventing a Parable of Pluralism', *Public Seminar*, 7 February 2019; https://publicseminar.org/2019/02/whats-so-jewish-about-the-new-school/.

46 Ibid.

agenda to thwart Soviet influence among youth.[47] However, it was with the founding of the Students for a Democratic Society (SDS) as the 'student department' of the League for Industrial Democracy, a Fabian organisation featuring John Dewey, that the New Left came into its own. The founding document of the SDS, *The Port Huron Statement*, was imbued with Critical Theory. The SDS demands were analogous to those of the 'Establishment' they professed to oppose:

- Global industrialisation led by the USA;

- Opposition to Senator Barry Goldwater, the rebel contender for the Republican Party presidential nomination against Nelson Rockefeller;

- Hatred of the 'Dixiecrats' (Southern Democrats), the last line of defence against the intrusion of the Northern oligarchy into the South;

- Extension of United Nations authority in the name of 'disarmament', which had been advocated by the USA as the 'Baruch Plan', and had been rejected by the USSR as creating a *de facto* world government;

- Zealous proselytizing of American liberal-democracy across the world; the reinvigoration of Woodrow Wilson's 'Fourteen Points' manifesto of post-1918 democratic-internationalism, which has become the moral façade for U.S. global hegemony.

Hayden explained in *The Port Huron Statement*:

> It will involve the simultaneous creation of international rulemaking and enforcement machinery beginning under the United Nations, and the gradual transfer of sovereignties — such as national armies and national determination of 'international' law — to such machinery.[48]

---

47 See: Louis Menand, 'A Friend of the Devil', *The New Yorker*, 23 March 2015; https://www.newyorker.com/magazine/2015/03/23/a-friend-of-the-devil.

48 Tom Hayden et al., *The Port Huron Statement*, 'What is Needed? (2)'.

Many Americans are prone to think of the industrialization of the newly developed countries as a modern form of American *noblesse*, undertaken sacrificially for the benefit of others. On the contrary, the task of world industrialization, of eliminating the disparity between have and have-not nations, is as important as any issue facing America.[49]

If respect for democracy is to be international, then the significance of democracy must emanate from American shores, not from the 'soft sell' of the United States Information Agency.[50]

Whatever the intentions of the SDS, and there is much that is commendable in *The Port Huron Statement* in critiquing capitalism and the influence of the corporations, what was lacking was a transcendence of capitalism, which had caused Christopher Lasch to reject the Left as irrelevant as a genuine alternative. For all its revolutionary rhetoric, Vietcong flags, clenched fists, and street and campus riots, the SDS did not look beyond 'reforming' the Democratic Party. In terms that would become familiar as 'identity politics', Hayden wrote in *The Port Huron Statement* of this liberalisation of the Democrats: 'An imperative task for these publicly disinherited groups, then, is to demand a Democratic Party responsible to their interests'.[51]

Marcuse saw the 1960s as the time to create a strategy of tension across the world. The New Left was 'post-Marxist' rather than 'Marxist', and was influenced by Maoism, Third World revolutionary movements, and 'neo-anarchism'.[52] Marcuse defined the Left in something other than the old class terms, and here the notion of *identity politics* emerges:

---

49   Ibid., 'The Industrialization of the World'.

50   Ibid. (5). One such emanation of democracy from the USA was the Peace Corps, an idea that had been promoted, and perhaps initiated, by Hayden (*Reunion*, xviii).

51   Tom Hayden et al., *The Port Huron Statement*, 'Alternatives to Helplessness (5)'.

52   Herbert Marcuse, 'The Problem of Violence and the Radical Opposition, Psychoanalyse und Politik'; lecture delivered at the Free University of West Berlin, July 1967; https://www.marxists.org/reference/archive/marcuse/works/1967/violence.htm.

The New Left itself cannot be defined in terms of class, consisting as it does
of intellectuals, of groups from the civil rights movement, and of youth
groups, especially the most radical elements of youth, including those who
at first glance do not appear political at all, namely the hippies, to whom I
shall return later.[53]

Marcuse stated that the revolution would not be made by the proletariat, who were being co-opted by the System, but by disaffected and
alienated elements. Ironically, it was the 'youth revolt' and other 'alienated elements' that were co-opted by the System, and it was precisely
the proletariat that had not shown itself amenable to Establishment
manipulation.[54]

In 1964, Marcuse published his *One-Dimensional Man* as the credo
of a new type of revolution that would mobilise disaffected ethnics,
women, and youth — the harbinger of *identity politics* — with grants
from the Rockefeller Foundation, the Rockefeller-spawned Social
Science Research Council, the Louis M. Rabinowitz Foundation,
a Marxist fund; and the American Council of Learned Societies,[55]
which was also under Rockefeller influence.[56]

Of this book, David Kellner states: 'In contrast to orthodox
Marxism, Marcuse championed non-integrated forces like minorities,
outsiders and radical intelligentsia, attempting to nourish oppositional thought through promoting radical thinking and opposition...'
The tactic is infiltration, Marcuse counselling, 'working against the
established institutions while working in them'.[57] Kellner, in his introduction to the second edition, wrote that *One-Dimensional Man*:

53 Herbert Marcuse, 'The Problem of Violence...', ibid.

54 As indicated, for example, by the condemnation of the 1968 student revolt in
    France by the French Communist Party, which saw the movement as a bour-
    geois phenomenon, and the antagonism that existed between Danny Cohn-
    Bendit and the 'Stalinist' working class leadership.

55 Herbert Marcuse, *One-Dimensional Man*, Acknowledgments.

56 Raymond Fosdick, pp. 264–265.

57 Herbert Marcuse, *Counterrevolution and Revolt*, p. 55.

... was one of the most important books of the 1960s. First published in 1964, it was immediately recognized as a significant critical diagnosis of the present age and was soon taken up by the emergent New Left as a damning indictment of contemporary Western societies, capitalist and communist. Conceived and written in the 1950s and early 1960s, the book reflects the stifling conformity of the era and provides a powerful critique of new modes of domination and social control. Yet it also expresses the hopes of a radical philosopher that human freedom and happiness could be greatly expanded beyond the one-dimensional thought and behavior prevalent in the established society. ...'[58]

One-Dimensional Man was touted as a new ideology of revolt against an industrial system that had co-opted the proletariat through consumerism and rendered them impotent as the class agent of revolution. Marcuse's critique of industrialism is, from the attitude of the dissident Right, correct in many respects. The book could be part of a rightist intellectual corpus if one discards the concluding chapter, which derails genuine revolt or what Marcuse called the 'great refusal'. Like other Critical Theorists and going back to Marx and Engels, while the analyses had merit, the premises of resistance are so flawed as to become useless. Max Horkheimer realised the inanity of the student pseudo-revolt when confronted with Marcuse's ideological offspring at the Frankfurt Institute. Horkheimer assessed the New Left revolt as 'having no theory, merely a blind commitment to action. Most of the leaders, he claimed, would adjust quite readily to a totalitarian order'. He no longer believed in the prospects of a revolution.[59] While it was Marcuse whose name was chanted in the streets together with Marx and Mao, Horkheimer and the Frankfurt School had worked for decades to prepare the ground for this revolt and when it transpired, it was too puerile to present a genuine challenge to the System.

Why would the Critical Theorists and others of the Left have been so assiduously supported for decades by the oligarchy if they

---

58   David Kellner in Marcuse, *One-Dimensional Man*, xi.
59   Peter Stirk, p. 180.

had presented an actual challenge to the 'Establishment'? The Critical Theorists had not been sufficiently critical.

The merit of Marcuse's critique traces back to his having been taught by Martin Heidegger in Germany in the 1920s and 1930s and, like Heidegger, 'sees technological rationality colonizing everyday life, robbing individuals of freedom and individuality by imposing technological imperatives, rules, and structures upon their thought and behavior'.[60] Marcuse necessarily parted company, being Jewish and Marxist, from Heidegger, when the latter saw possibilities in the National Socialist regime for modern man to recover a sense of place and purpose, where the old values of land, family and home seemed to be resurgent. *One-Dimensional Man* received 'laudatory' (Kellner) reviews from the Establishment at a time when Marcuse was identified as the 'guru' of the New Left rioters. One must ask why. Kellner, in writing of its reception, states that

> … It was reviewed in most major intellectual journals, many national magazines and newspapers, and many specialized academic journals in a wide variety of fields. The text was read as a classical study of contemporary trends of the current society in the same league with the works of C. Wright Mills, Daniel Bell, John Galbraith, and other critics of contemporary American society.[61]

What then was the interest the Establishment had in Marcuse's doctrine? The answer might be found in the concluding chapter. Justified by the *dialectical* method, the aim is **economic centralisation** in the name of individual 'freedom'. While the economic structure is to be concentrated, the individual is to be detached from any of those 'primary ties' that Critical Theory states restricts individual 'freedom'. It seems that the detachment of the individual from any type of organic group association is the means by which potential resistance would become impossible. By this process, the individual ceases to have an

---

60   David Kellner in Marcuse, xiv.
61   David Kellner in Marcuse, ibid, xxxvi.

identity beyond being part of the centralised economic process in the name of efficiency and just distribution:

> Here, **technological rationality**, stripped of its exploitative features, is the sole standard and guide in planning and developing the available resources for all. **Self-determination in the production and distribution of vital goods and services would be wasteful.** The job is a technical one, and as a truly technical job, it makes for the reduction of physical and mental toil. In this realm, **centralized control is rational** if it establishes the preconditions for meaningful self-determination. The latter can then become effective in its own realm—in the decisions which involve the production and distribution of the economic surplus, and in the individual existence. In any case, the combination of **centralized authority** and direct democracy is subject to infinite variations, according to the degree of development. **Self-determination will be real to the extent to which the masses have been dissolved into individuals liberated from all propaganda, indoctrination, and manipulation, capable of knowing and comprehending the facts and of evaluating the alternatives.** In other words, society would be rational and free to the extent to which it is organized, sustained and reproduced by an essentially new historical Subject.[62]

It is what Orwell called *double-think*. Engels also said that the ultimate aim was the 'withering away' of the state:

> The first act by virtue of which the State really constitutes itself the **representative of the whole of society**—the taking possession of the means of production in the name of society—this is, at the same time, its last independent act as a State. State interference in social relations becomes, in one domain after another, superfluous and then dies out of itself; the government of persons is replaced by the **administration of things, and by the conduct of processes of production.** The State is not 'abolished.' It withers away.[63]

Both Marcuse and Engels were stating that absolute freedom is predicated on the centralisation of production, which becomes a

---

62   Marcuse, *One-Dimensional Man*, p. 256. Emphasis added.
63   F. Engels, *Socialism: Utopian and Scientific*, p. 76.

technocratic problem. Marcuse renders his 'great refusal' against the pervasiveness of industrial-technological society redundant by stating that the answer in precisely that: technocracy. This path to self-actualisation, which was the purpose of Critical Theory, is rendered as nothing other than a technocratic question. He wrote unequivocally of this:

> The goal of authentic self-determination by the individuals depends on effective social control over the production and distribution of the necessities (in terms of the achieved level of culture, material and intellectual).[64]

When Marcuse refers to the 'masses' being dissolved into 'individuals', he is seeking the obliteration of any type of group association, accelerating a process that has been taking place since the Jacobins banned the guilds in the name of 'liberty' and free commerce. Like Marx, rather than calling for resistance to this process of capitalism, Marcuse sees it as part of the dialectic of progress. However, as Critical Theory makes clear, the 'mass' that is to be abolished is constituted of the 'primary ties' of family, church, village, craft, homeland, ethnos. What remains of identity is attachment to the production process. What else is left? Who controls that? Technocrats and social engineers.

Increased Production: Meaning of Life

For Marxism, attachment to the production process is the means of accomplishing self-actualisation. Georg Lukács, a founding-father of so-called 'Western Marxism', among whom are counted the Frankfurt Institute, stated clearly that Marxist 'morality' is based on raising production and 'labour discipline'.

> The point at which individual and class interests converge is in fact characterized by increased production, a rise in productivity and a corresponding strengthening of labour discipline. Without these things the proletariat cannot survive, without them the class hegemony of the

---

64 Marcuse, *One-Dimensional Man*, p. 255.

proletariat disappears — without them (even if we disregard the disastrous consequences entailed in such a dislocation of the class for all proletarians), no single person can develop fully, not even as an individual. For it is clear that those aspects of the power of the proletariat which are most oppressive and whose immediate consequences every proletarian feels most keenly — namely, shortage of goods and high prices — are a direct result of slackening labour discipline and declining productivity. To effect a remedy for this state of affairs and thereby raise the level of the individuals concerned, the causes of such phenomena must be removed.[65]

Here we are told that true individual freedom is to be had through 'labour discipline' to ensure increasing production, and thereby eliminate shortages and high prices. Marcuse was stating the same in regard to the key to individual freedom being to harness production. Economics becomes the determinant of life under this 'socialism' as it does under both bourgeoisie and oligarchic forms of capitalism. An intelligentsia claiming to resist capitalism with a 'great refusal' or a revolution are doing nothing of the kind when their 'revolutionary morality' is based on 'labour discipline' as the means of increasing production as the supposed panacea for social, moral, and economic well-being. No wonder that the 'Establishment' lauded and funded these theorists. 'Work harder' is precisely the formula sought by free market capitalists in periods of stagnation.

In the name of economic efficiency and productivity, of 'technological rationality' — a familiar outlook among capitalist economists — as Marcuse called it, the destruction of the 'primary ties' is demanded behind the façade of 'individual freedom', concomitant with the refrain, 'work harder' for your own freedom and welfare. The Gothic epoch of Western high culture regarded such *economism* as godless and morally crass. That was the era of real socialism.

---

65 Georg Lukács, 'The Role of Morality in Communist Production' (1919), in R. Livingstone (ed.), *Georg Lukács: Political Writings.*

New Conceptions of Family Bonding

Marcuse saw revolutionary potential in the hippies. They were the ful-filment of Fromm's 'creative spontaneity' and 'love' of humanity, who could reach the revolutionary nirvana at an accelerated pace via LSD. They were what can be achieved when family bonds are deconstruct-ed, and new bonds formed amidst narcotic stupor, indiscriminate sex, and the free reign of all atavistic impulses.

New Left spokesman Jerry Rubin, head of the Yippies, reminisced about a 'psychic therapy session' in which participants sought libera-tion from 'childhood deprivation', taking on matricidal proportions:

> I started shouting at my mother for the specific messages she gave me. 'Thanks, mommy. You white-skinned, no-good sexless asshole cap-toothed cancerous venom of a snake who destroyed me from birth .... I have your self-righteous right-wrong should-should not programming... with that stupid JUDGE inside me that I got from you. I don't see people as they are, but as they fit my standards, my self-righteous beliefs .... Oh, it is so liberating for me to tell the truth. MOMMY I AM GLAD THAT YOU DIED. IF YOU HAD NOT DIED OF CANCER, I WOULD HAVE HAD TO KILL YOU... You taught me to compete and compare, to fear and outdo. I became a ferocious achievement-oriented, compulsive obsessive live-in-my-head asshole... Well, fuck you Mommy, fuck you in the ass with a red hot poker.[66]

Self-Actualising with Charles Manson

Charles Manson played out the premises of Critical Theory in the quest for self-actualisation perhaps more intensely than anyone. That the 'Manson Family' was part of the CIA's MK-ULTRA social engineering experiments is indicated by the 'hands-off' approach the police[67] were instructed to follow in regard to the petty crimes of Manson and his followers, and by the association between the 'Family'

---

66   Jerry Rubin, *Growing (Up) At 37*, pp. 140–142.
67   Tom O'Neill, pp. 154–160.

and the CIA-connected Haight-Ashbury Free Medical Clinic, which dispensed LSD to hippies.[68]

Manson had a 'special hatred for women as mothers', according to his acolyte Tex Watson.[69] Manson maintained his 'Family' through the deconstruction of the primary ties of each member, by the use of 'love, sex, and drugs'. Orgies were enacted under Manson's direction. Inhibitions were broken down by Manson, forcing his followers to submit to 'unconventional sexual practices', invoking 'pop psychology', and using LSD to 'negate the ego'.[70] The 'programming' of one's parents had to be purged.[71] Hollywood talent scout and stuntman Gregg Jakobson was particularly admired by Manson and the 'Family', writes Manson biographer O'Neill:

> As an orphan, Jakobson held a special place in the Family's mythology. Manson loathed the influence of parents, and Jakobson, despite his adopted family, was held up as a parentless icon. 'They used to call me an angel', Jakobson told me, 'because I came into the world without parents'.[72]

Members of the Manson Family were prohibited from contacting their own families. Manson gave his followers new names in order to completely break them free[73] from their 'primary ties'. As Manson's followers fell increasingly under his spell, he stated that they were being freed from the 'straight world', where people were programmed like computers. We might recall how Fromm commended the dissident students at Columbia University for their breaking free of a zombified society, by up-ending traditional perceptions of normality.

---

68 Ibid., pp. 304–340.
69 Ibid., pp. 28–29.
70 Ibid., p. 308.
71 Ibid., p. 38.
72 Ibid., p. 136.
73 Ibid., p. 39.

In August 1969, the Family embarked on the famous Tate-LaBianca murders. A couple of female Manson Family members, who remained free, toting guns and knives, called for an undefined 'revolution', and the New Left took them seriously. In 1969 at a 'war council' of the Weather Underground led by Bernadine Dohrn, today an esteemed academic, she introduced a three-fingered salute to the Weathermen in honour of the fork that was said to have been used to repeatedly stab the pregnant Sharon Tate. Dohrn declared: 'Offing those pigs with their own forks and knives, and then eating a meal in the same room, far out! The Weathermen dig Charles Manson!' Weathermen at the 'war council' shouted that 'all white babies are pigs', (hence the *offing* of Tate's foetus was no more aberrant than the legal abortions that are part of the new 'normal'). The adulation was widespread. Jerry Rubin and fellow New Left leader Phil Ochs visited Manson in jail. New Left journal *Tuesday's Child* featured a crucified Manson on its cover during his trial, and proclaimed him 'man of the year'.[74]

The Manson murders are often claimed to have ended the hippie epoch by exposing its psychotic underside. Haight-Ashbury became a centre not of 'peace and love', but of homicides, disease, aborted foetuses and a mass of drugged-up imbeciles wallowing in their own excrement. Was it really a failure in terms of shifting the USA, and hence the rest of the Western world, leftward? The riots from Chicago to Prague, drugs, Manson murders, and student strikes, served as a warning if changes were not forthcoming. The social sciences lavishly funded by Rockefeller, Ford, Carnegie and others, provided the academic rationalisation for assuring the 'majority', looking in askance, that the troubles could be handled if reforms were instituted. What a generation previously would have been regarded as psychotic, now seemed moderate in comparison to Manson, the Weathermen, the Days of Rage, Yippies, hippies, and calls to 'bring the war home'. Martin Luther King and the NAACP became the mainstream answer

---

74   Bolton, *The Psychotic Left*, pp. 175–177.

to ghetto riots and the Black Panthers; the government's Peace Corps superseded the SDS, and what was once regarded as 'revolutionary' and nihilistic is today seen as 'centrist' and even 'conservative'.

Spawning the New Left

Certain things cannot be said, certain ideas cannot be expressed, certain policies cannot be proposed, certain behavior cannot be permitted...

— Marcuse

WHILE MARCUSE wrote of the 'great refusal' towards the 'Establishment' among the young and the intelligentsia, particularly in regard to the Vietnam War, to what extent can such sentiments be regarded as a genuine 'refusal' against the oligarchy? The assumption, in this instance, that the Vietnam War was propelled by the war-profiteers of the Establishment, against which the New Left was resisting, is a myth. The war was causing major dislocations in the U.S. economy. Writing on the economic consequences of the war for the USA, a report in *The New York Times* describes the deficit reaching $23 billion in 1968. '... But, more than that, the war tended to sour the climate of international monetary negotiation, and it certainly did not help financial psychology. ...'[1] On 16 October 1969, brokers and executives joined with the New Left to march through Wall Street demanding the end of the war.[2]

---

1 Edwin L. Dale Jr., 'What Vietnam Did to the American Economy', *The New York Times*, 28 January 1973.

2 'Bankers Join Forces with Hippies and Folk Singers against the Vietnam War', *The Guardian*, 16 October 1969, reproduced 16 October 2012; https://www.theguardian.com/theguardian/2012/oct/16/wall-st-bankers-against-vietnam-war-1969-archive.

Marcuse stated that the primary elements in this youth mobilisation were two polarities, the ghetto *underprivileged* and the *privileged*, who, through their education and resources, can analyse the situation better than any White proletarian. This elite have a high state of consciousness that can escape 'social control', whereas the White proletariat and middle class did not have revolutionary potential. Tom Hayden had said the same in 1962 in the founding manifesto of the New Left:

> First, the university is located in a permanent position of social influence. Its educational function makes it indispensable and automatically makes it a crucial institution in the formation of social attitudes. Second, in an unbelievably complicated world, it is the central institution for organizing, evaluating, and transmitting knowledge. Third, the extent to which academic resources presently are used to buttress immoral social practice is revealed, first, by the extent to which defense contracts make the universities engineers of the arms race. **Too, the use of modern social science as a manipulative tool reveals itself in the 'human relations' consultants to the modern corporation, who introduce trivial sops to give laborers feelings of 'participation' or 'belonging', while actually deluding them in order to further exploit their labor. And, of course, the use of motivational research is already infamous as a manipulative aspect of American politics. But these social uses of the universities' resources also demonstrate the unchangeable reliance by men of power on the men and storehouses of knowledge: this makes the university functionally tied to society in new ways, revealing new potentialities, new levers for change.** Fourth, the university is the only mainstream institution that is open to participation by individuals of nearly any viewpoint.[3]

Hayden understood the role of the social sciences as a 'manipulative tool' of the oligarchy. Hayden imagined that 'men of power' rely on universities', without mentioning the reliance of the institutions on the endowments by these 'men of power', and the ways by which even 'radicals' such as the Critical Theorists were utilised by the oligarchy as

---

3   Hayden, *The Port Huron Statement*, 'The University and Social Change'. Emphasis added.

the 'new levers for change', according to the courses steered by oligarchical funding. It is precisely because academia is 'a crucial institution
in the formation of social attitudes', and has 'a permanent position of
social influence', as Hayden put it, that the oligarchy has ensured their
compliance.

In 1968, the year of the worldwide New Left student riots, in which
the SDS took a pivotal role, the Rockefeller Foundation gave its outlook on universities in the same terms as Hayden:

> A university must not be an end in itself; it must be an institution re-
> sponsive to the needs of society, a powerful force in social and economic
> development, engaging in the kinds of teaching and research required **for
> the transition from traditional to modern ways of life**.[4]

**'Transition from traditional to modern ways of life' for the purpos-
es of 'social and economic development' is the raison d'etre for the
oligarchic endowments to academia and the social sciences. This
is where the changes to subvert tradition start. It is here that we
might discern the convergence between the oligarchy and the Left.
The method is 'transition', Fabian-style, gradual, and presented as
a moderate and even as a 'conservative' alternative to the riotous
behaviour of the burgeoning Black Power movement and the New
Left.**

The year of student revolt saw the Rockefeller Foundation overtly
utilising the same rhetoric of the New Left in regard to 'participatory
democracy' and the 'politicisation' of the arts as a means of social
change:

> The new viewpoint looks at 'culture' not as a commodity but as a condi-
> tion, that is, a situation where changing needs indicate social and artistic
> changes. In this sense, participatory democracy is related to participatory
> theatre and visual art; technology influences art forms; interculturization
> affects arts and philosophy; and the civil rights movement leads to new
> political, economic, and artistic positions. The **politicization of the arts**

---

4   The Rockefeller Foundation Annual Report, 1968, p. 60.

represents a conviction of more and more people that the arts play a vital role in the establishment and debate of the most essential values of our society.[5]

On the pretext of repudiating the commodification of the arts, the oligarchy was supporting the transition of the arts into a means of social engineering and social control, candidly referring to 'politicization', which is stated to include:

- *Technification* of art-forms, which in detaching the arts from tradition has ensured its *commodification*;

- *Participatory democracy* in the arts, which in practical terms has meant detachment from tradition, and commodification by catering to the mass denominator, hence creating and enlarging fluid markets;

- *Interculturization* as a means of creating a nebulous cosmopolitan international art, again more apt for mass worldwide commercialisation.

The educated class cited by Hayden and Marcuse is most susceptible to indoctrination by the Establishment's education system. In 1954, when grant-making by the tax-exempt foundations came under congressional scrutiny, the research director of the Reece Committee, Norman Dodd, reported that the Foundations since the 1930s had brought a revolution to the education system:

> ... [G]rants had been made by Foundations (chiefly by Carnegie and Rockefeller) which were used to further this purpose by:
>
> Directing education in the United States toward an international viewpoint and discrediting the traditions to which it [formerly] had been dedicated.
>
> Training individuals and servicing agencies to render advice to the Executive branch of the Federal Government.

---

5   Ibid., p. 92.

Decreasing the dependency of education upon the resources of the local community and freeing it from many of the natural safeguards inherent in this American tradition.

Changing both school and college curricula to the point where they sometimes denied the principles underlying the American way of life.

Financing experiments designed to determine the most effective means by which education could be pressed into service of a political nature.[6]

Hayden stated that the new vanguard role of the revolution would be assumed by students, Blacks, and Third World peoples. This was the precursor of today's *identity politics,* which Marcuse had ideologically formulated as the revolt of *outsiders* who would replace the proletariat as the agents of revolution.

In the United States the underprivileged are constituted in particular by national and racial minorities, which of course are mainly unorganized politically and often antagonistic among themselves (for example there are considerable conflicts in the large cities between Blacks and Puerto Ricans). **They are mostly groups that do not occupy a decisive place in the productive process and for this reason cannot be considered potentially revolutionary forces from the viewpoint of Marxian theory — at least not without allies.**[7]

Let us deconstruct Marcuse's statement:

The oligarchy had even by the late 1960s long been funding Black and ethnic minorities. It is exactly because they did not 'occupy a decisive place in the productive process' that the oligarchs sought their full integration — as with women — into what is today called an 'inclusive economy'. As a representative example, in 1967, the year that Marcuse made this statement, the Rockefeller Foundation records that its focus was on integrating the Blacks into the economic process, with 'grants for the development of Negro leadership in public service and business; for the easier and more effective transition of the Negro into the

6   Norman Dodd (1954), p. 7.
7   Herbert Marcuse, 'The Problem of Violence...' Emphasis added.

world outside the ghetto; and for legal and educational assistance to the underprivileged, particularly in the South'.[8] Such funding co-opted and channelled Black discontent and bought-off Black leaders, directing them away from separatism and self-help, towards the integrated economy. Among the primary organisations utilised by the oligarchy for these purposes has long been the National Urban League. The Rockefeller Foundation reported its work with the organisation in 1967 aimed at creating a leadership that could organise the Black community according to the requirements of corporate capital:

> An attempt both to increase the number of leaders and improve the quality of leadership in the ghettos was reflected in a three-year grant renewal for the National Urban League's Leadership Development Program. The change in the Program's direction was significant. **Whereas the intent of the original Program had been to draw on upper- and middle-class Negroes, the effort is now aimed increasingly at development of neighborhood leaders and local civic leaders.**[9]

What the Rockefeller Foundation is implying is clear: upper and middle-class Blacks had been co-opted into the economic system, and it was now time to proceed with the rest, who could be channelled by the use of 'civil rights' rhetoric.

> In its first 18 months of operation, some 950 Negroes participated in programs organized by the Urban League in ten cities. Of this number, 200 persons are now listed as members of community boards, welfare councils, and other public and private agencies. The Foundation underscores the importance of this program, which seeks out **grass-roots leaders whose responsibility to the community welfare will be reflected upwards, while they reflect their guidance down.**[10]

---

8   The Rockefeller Foundation Annual Report (1967), 'Towards Opportunity for All', p. 146.

9   Ibid. Emphasis added.

10   Ibid. Emphasis added.

The Rockefeller Foundation was scouting for potential trouble-makers who could be bought off with positions on boards, councils and agencies, assuring that change would be in the direction of their sponsors. Their 'responsibility to the community welfare will be reflected upwards, while they reflect their guidance down', so that the changes that take place within the Black communities would be determined from the top down, not at grass-roots levels, despite the rhetoric. The iconic 'radical' Saul Alinksy, with his Industrial Areas Foundation, helped this process by smashing European ethnic neighbourhoods, pushing non-white integration in the name of 'human rights'. This guru of rebellion was funded by the Rockefeller Foundation, and eulogised as a hero.[11] It is one of a multitude of examples of how the pseudo-revolt of the 1960s was funded and channelled by the oligarchy to scare the masses into 'change' for the sake of peace and order. **It was the dialectic of creating the problem and offering the solution**.

'Materialization and Quantification of Values'

Addressing the issues of the Cold War, Marcuse advocated peaceful economic competition between the USA and the Soviet bloc, 'on a global scale and through global institutions'. Marcuse explains:

This pacification would mean the emergence of a **genuine world economy**—the demise of the nation state, the national interest, national business together with their international alliances. And this is precisely the possibility against which the present world is mobilized.

The fateful interdependence of the only two 'sovereign' social systems in the contemporary world is expressive of the fact that the conflict between progress and politics, between man and his masters has become total. When capitalism meets the challenge of communism, it meets its own capabilities: spectacular development of all productive forces after the subordination of the private interests in profitability which arrest such development. When communism meets the challenge of capitalism, it too meets its own capabilities: spectacular comforts, liberties, and alleviation of the burden

---

11 Saul David Alinsky [Eulogy], *RF Illustrated*, Vol. I, No. 1, October 1972, p. 3.

of life. Both systems have these capabilities distorted beyond recognition and, in both cases, the reason is in the last analysis the same — the struggle against a form of life which would dissolve the basis for domination.[12]

While Marcuse seems to be critiquing 'capitalism' and 'communism', what he is calling for is a **synthesis** leading to a 'genuine world economy' 'through global institutions'. It should not be misunderstood that Marcuse's call for the 'demise of national business' is antithetical to the aims of those who sponsored him. What he is proposing is the agenda of global capitalism. What the globalist oligarchy requires are fundamental changes in capitalism, and they have long backed 'radicals' for this objective. **They are not involved in 'national business'** but in globalisation, and have funded the 'global institutions' referred to by Marcuse to facilitate a world social, political and economic order. Like Marcuse, their aim is a 'genuine world economy'. This can only be achieved by breaking down the same 'primary ties' that the Left condemns: a confluence of aims.

After stating much that is laudable about the dehumanising impact of technology, betraying vestiges of his old teacher Heidegger, it transpires that it is not the overthrow — the 'Great Refusal' as he calls his 'rebellion' — of techno-industrial domination that Marcuse urges. Rather, the new order 'depends on the continued existence of the technical base itself'.

I have stressed that this does not mean the revival of 'values,' spiritual or other, which are to supplement the scientific and technological transformation of man and nature. On the contrary, the historical achievement of science and technology has rendered possible the translation of values into technical tasks — the materialization of values. Consequently, what is at stake is the redefinition of values in technical terms, as elements in the technological process. The new ends, as technical ends, would then operate in the project and in the construction of the machinery, and not only in its utilization. Moreover, the new ends might assert themselves even in the construction of scientific hypotheses — in pure scientific theory.

12   H. Marcuse, *One-Dimensional Man*, p. 58.

From the quantification of secondary qualities, **science would proceed to the quantification of values.**[13]

Hence, for all the rhetoric and sophistry about the dehumanising impact of technology, the ultimate aim is not a transcendence of technocratic-industrial-late-capitalism, but its global ascendance, until it defines *universal values.*

In Marcuse's call for the **'materialization of values and quantification of values', we have the crux of the whole struggle between the forces of Matter whether capitalist or socialist, and the rear-guard of Tradition; what truly defines the dichotomy of 'Left' and 'Right', beyond the muddled terminology of journalists and academics.**

To emphasise the soulless character of his doctrine, Marcuse cites a footnote assuring readers that such questions remain solely technical and cannot be considered as 'ethical and sometimes religious'.[14] It transpires to be the hubristic mastery over Nature, the transformation of 'values into needs' and of 'final causes into technical possibilities'. The earthly paradise is finally reached: 'the free development of needs on the basis of satisfaction'; the ultimate condition of Man being a 'pacified existence'.[15] Yet Marcuse warns against making a 'fetish' of technology, but relies on a 'collective effort' of 'free individuals'. Should these contradictions seem to lack coherence, they can be rationalised through *dialectically.*[16]

Tyranny Means 'Freedom'

It has been heard from Marxist theorists: the withering away of the state and the unfolding of 'true Communism' after the transition phase of socialism, where the laws of social production will usher in a utopia of total freedom. Marcuse's utopia of 'pacified existence', however, has

---

13   Ibid., p. 236. Emphasis added.
14   Ibid.
15   Ibid., p. 239.
16   Ibid., p. 240.

its own transitional phase that, like the path to Communism via socialism, requires repression. Pol Pot tried to rush the process. Marcuse
is explicit in his 1965 essay 'Repressive Tolerance'. He condemns the
toleration of ideas that are contrary to his ideology:

> The active, official tolerance granted to the Right as well as to the Left, to
> movements of aggression as well as to movements of peace, to the party of
> hate as well as to that of humanity. I call this non-partisan tolerance 'ab-
> stract' or 'pure' inasmuch as it refrains from taking sides — but in doing so
> it actually protects the already established machinery of discrimination....
>
> ...However, this tolerance cannot be indiscriminate and equal with respect
> to the contents of expression, neither in word nor in deed; it cannot protect
> false words and wrong deeds which demonstrate that they contradict and
> counteract the possibilities of liberation. Such indiscriminate tolerance is
> justified in harmless debates, in conversation, in academic discussion; it
> is indispensable in the scientific enterprise, in private religion. But society
> cannot be indiscriminate where the pacification of existence, where free-
> dom and happiness themselves are at stake: here, **certain things cannot
> be said, certain ideas cannot be expressed, certain policies cannot be
> proposed, certain behavior cannot be permitted without making toler-
> ance an instrument for the continuation of servitude.**[17]

By demonising others, Marcuse enables the Left to declare in the
interests of 'peace and humanity' that the repression of opposition is
necessary. It is heard in the histrionics of antifa et al.: 'No free speech
for fascists', including scholars, whose leftist colleagues are just as avid
in seeing such heretics purged from academia.

Hence, when today we see liberals and leftists committing acts of
violence against dissidents in the name of 'peace and freedom', they are
being consistent according to their dialectic. One can more than suspect that what Marcuse is proposing is a dictatorship of technocrats,
who eliminate any threats to 'freedom and happiness' in the manner
by which Robespierre and his committee upheld 'public safety' in the
name of the 'Declaration of the Rights of the Man and the Citizen'.

---

17   Marcuse, 'Repressive Tolerance' (1965). Emphasis added.

In his 1968 addendum, Marcuse elaborates on how this technocratic 'elite' would operate, citing John Stuart Mill that, 'In any case, John Stuart Mill, not exactly an enemy of liberal and representative government, was not so allergic to the political leadership of the intelligentsia as the contemporary guardians of semi-democracy are. Mill believed that "individual mental superiority" justifies "reckoning one person's opinion as equivalent to more than one"'.[18] But then Marcuse assures readers that this would not be necessary if his version of 'democracy' is established through revolution.

What would be unavoidable is the establishment of what Orwell called in *1984* the 'Ministry of Truth', with censors and enforcers maintaining Marcuse's formulae for 'freedom':

- Certain things cannot be said,

- Certain ideas cannot be expressed,

- Certain policies cannot be proposed,

- Certain behaviour cannot be permitted.

Again, turning to Orwell's' dystopia, Marcuse uses *doublespeak*. The term 'Repressive Tolerance' is itself outlandishly one of *doublespeak*; almost a spoof of itself, 'like peaceful violence'.

This revolution would be made by **'minorities intolerant, militantly intolerant'** against the 'majority', for the latter's true happiness.[19] Here we see the stirrings of today's *identity politics*.

Marcuse claimed that an objective criterion can be established to determine what should be tolerated and what should be repressed:

...Moreover, in endlessly dragging debates over the media, the stupid opinion is treated with the same respect as the intelligent one, the misinformed may talk as long as the informed, and propaganda rides along with education, truth with falsehood. This pure toleration of sense and nonsense is

18   Ibid, (1968 addendum).
19   Ibid.

justified by the democratic argument that nobody, neither group nor individual, is in possession of the truth and capable of defining what is right and
wrong, good and bad. Therefore, all contesting opinions must be submitted
to 'the people' for its deliberation and choice. But I have already suggested
that the democratic argument implies a necessary condition, namely, that
the people must be capable of deliberating and choosing on the basis of
knowledge, that they must have access to authentic information, and that,
on this basis, their evaluation must be the result of autonomous thought.[20]

Marcuse betrays himself as a bigot and a fanatic. The Left has followed
in those footsteps from the days of the Jacobins' guillotine. Once a
body of guardians — technocrats and social scientists — defines
'what is right and wrong, good and bad', on the basis of 'science', and
disregarding outmoded traditions and morality, only then would
'the people' be asked for their 'democratic deliberation', without the
encumbrance of contrary opinions. Dissent would be suppressed by a
bureaucracy of censors on the grounds that such opinions are 'stupid'.
Should anyone dissent from the 'democratic' consensus, they would
at the most charitable be classed as in need of therapy. The process of
finding 'truth' on the presumption of dogma and upholding it through
repression is a reformulation of Rousseau's 'general will' that inspired
Jacobinism and its 'Reign of Terror' in the name of 'human rights', and
later the 'Red Terror'.

Marcuse updated his essay in 1968, at the time of the riots, stating
that extremism is justified in the most tolerant democracies, because
the opinions of the majority are not legitimately formed. Hence only
the New Left is the custodian of what is right: 'this means that the
majority is no longer justified in claiming the democratic title of the
best guardian of the common interest'.[21] At the time Marcuse was
writing, the 'best guardian of the common interest' was represented
by the rampaging, screaming, bomb-throwing lunatics of the Weather

20 Ibid.
21 Ibid.

Underground and the Yippies. Marcuse continued that the repression would be against the 'Right'.

> ... Given this situation, I suggested in 'Repressive Tolerance' the practice of discriminating tolerance in an inverse direction, as a means of shifting the balance between Right and Left by restraining the liberty of the Right, thus counteracting the pervasive inequality of freedom (unequal opportunity of access to the means of democratic persuasion) and strengthening the oppressed against the oppressor. Tolerance would be restricted with respect to movements of a demonstrably aggressive or destructive character (destructive of the prospects for peace, justice, and freedom for all). Such discrimination would also be applied to movements opposing the extension of social legislation to the poor, weak, disabled.[22]

Marcuse's definition of the 'Right' is a straw-man. The Critical Theorists had defined anyone maintaining what were still normal views on family and morality as scoring high on a 'Fascist Scale and in need of therapy.

When Julius Evola's book *Revolt Against the Modern World* (1934) was republished in 1969 and received notice amidst the 'student revolt', he was at times called the 'Marcuse of the Right'. Evola pointed out that, unlike the Left, his was a 'truly radical "no"' to the 'system', as he examined the roots of modern existence in ways that the Left could not. 'Neither Marcuse nor any of the "protestors" have done the same: for they have neither the ability nor courage to do so'. 'In particular, I think that the "sociology" of Marcuse should be completely rejected: it only tends towards a sort of gross form of Freudianism... likewise, the ideal society Marcuse envisages once all this "dissent" has led to the end of the so-called "system" is as squalid and insipid as can be'.[23]

---

22 Ibid.

23 Evola interview with *Playmen* 2 (February 1970), appended in Julius Evola, *The Path of Cinnabar*, pp. 256–257.

Lasch Dissents

D R. CHRISTOPHER LASCH, as one of America's most respected leftist intellectuals, caused much anguish among the intelligentsia when he realised that the Left had become irrelevant as an opposition to capitalism. Moreover, he saw a commonality between the Left, capitalism and what had become 'false-conservatism': they are united in their repudiation of tradition, the organic community, and the family around which these are premised. They all have a reductionist outlook based on economics. Lasch stated of feminism:

> A feminist movement that respected the achievements of women in the past would not disparage housework, motherhood or unpaid civic and neighborly services. It would not make a paycheck the only symbol of accomplishment. ... It would insist that people need self-respecting honorable callings, not glamorous careers that carry high salaries but take them away from their families.[1]

Lasch wrote of the arts that '[c]onstant experimentation' 'has resulted in so much confusion about standards that the only surviving standard of excellence is novelty and shock value, which in a jaded time often resides in a work's sheer banality and ugliness'. He wrote of the pseudo-radical character of leftist critics, stating that while 'cultural radicalism' 'poses as a revolutionary threat to the status quo, in reality it confines its criticism to values already obsolete and to patterns

---

1   C. Lasch, *Women and the Common Life* (1979).

of American capitalism that have long ago been superseded.' He described 'Left-wing social critics' as 'essentially conformist'.[2]

To Lasch, the 'elites' that control the economic, political, cultural and social foundations of the USA were inaugurating a social order on the ruins of tradition, including especially the ruins of the family. He said of these 'elites':

> Even liberal individuals require the character forming discipline of the neighborhood, the family, the school, and the church, all of which (not just the family) have been weakened by the encroachments of the market. The market notoriously tends to universalize itself. It does not easily coexist with institutions that operate according to principles antithetical to itself: schools and universities, newspapers and magazines, charities, families. Sooner or later the market tends to absorb them all. It puts an almost irresistible pressure on every activity to justify itself in the only terms it recognizes: to become a business proposition, to pay its own way, to show black ink on the bottom line. It turns news into entertainment, scholarship into professional careerism, social work into the scientific management of poverty. Inexorably it remodels every institution in its own image.[3]

Lasch far surpassed his Freudo-Marxian intellectual origins, critiqued what was being called the 'Right' especially in the USA for its defence of free enterprise as the bedrock of 'American tradition', while unable to recognise the intrinsically subversive character of capitalism. Along with actual rightist philosophers, such as Julius Evola[4] and Oswald Spengler,[5] Lasch pointed out that capitalism is the most morally, socially and culturally subversive of doctrines. In a critique perceptively

---

2   C. Lasch, *The Culture of Narcissism: American Life in an Age of Diminishing Expectations*, chapter V.

3   Lasch, *Revolt of the Elites and the Betrayal of Democracy*.

4   Julius Evola, *Men Among the Ruins*. Here Evola writes in genuinely anti-capitalist manner: 'Nothing is more evident than that modern capitalism is just as subversive as Marxism. The materialistic view of life on which both systems are based is identical...' (p. 166).

5   'Prussianism and Socialism' (1919) in Oswald Spengler, *Prussian Socialism and Other Essays*.

describing the failings of the American 'Right' of the time, Lasch first
stated of the Left:

> Progressive rhetoric has the effect of concealing social crisis and moral
> breakdown by presenting them 'dialectically' as the birth pangs of a new
> order. The left dismisses talk about the collapse of family life and talks
> instead about the emergence of 'alternative life-styles' and the growing new
> diversity of family types. Betty Friedan expresses the enlightened consen-
> sus when she says that Americans have to reject the 'obsolete image of the
> family;' to 'acknowledge the diversity of the families people live in now;'
> and to understand that a family, after all, in the words of the American
> Home Economics Association, consists simply of 'two or more persons
> who share values and goals, and have commitments to one another over
> time.' This anaemic, euphemistic definition of the family reminds us of the
> validity of George Orwell's contention that it is a sure sign of trouble when
> things can no longer be called by their right names and described in plain,
> forthright speech. The plain fact of the matter — and this is borne out by
> the very statistics cited to prove the expanding array of 'lifestyles' from
> which people can now choose — is that most of these alternative arrange-
> ments, so-called, arise out of the ruins of marriages, not as an improve-
> ment of old fashioned marriage. 'Blended' or 'reconstituted' families result
> from divorce, as do 'single-parent families': As for the other 'alternative'
> forms of the family, so highly touted by liberals — single 'families,' gay
> 'marriages,' and so on — it makes no sense to consider them as families and
> would still make no sense if they were important statistically, as they are
> not. They may be perfectly legitimate living arrangements, but they are ar-
> rangements chosen by people who prefer not to live in families at all, with
> all the unavoidable constraints that families place on individual freedom.
> The attempt to redefine the family as a purely voluntary arrangement (one
> among many 'alternative' living arrangements) grows out of the modern
> delusion that people can keep all their options open all the time, avoiding
> any constraints or demands as long as they don't make any demands of
> their own or 'impose their own values' on others. The left's redefinition of
> the family encourages the illusion that it is possible to avoid the 'trap' of
> involuntary association and to *enjoy* its advantages at the same time.[6]

---

6   C. Lasch, 'What's Wrong with the Right?', *Tikkun*, No. 1, 1987, pp. 23–29;
    https://web.archive.org/web/20040317084407/http://thor.clark.edu/sengland/

What Lasch critiques is the doctrine from whence he started, Cultural Theory, with its call for liberation from the constraints of the 'primary ties' of family, home, church, and state. Unlike other renegades from the Left, such as Irving Kristol,[7] many ex-Trotskyites, who formed the misnamed *neoconservative*[8] movement, Lasch did not latch on to the 'free market', but rather saw this as antithetical to tradition. In critiquing the pro-capitalist and equally progressivist outlook of the American pseudo-Right, Lasch cited a book by Rita Kramer on the family:

> But if the family issue illustrates characteristic weaknesses of American liberalism, which have been effectively exploited by the right, it also illustrates why the right-wing defense of 'traditional values' proves equally unsatisfactory. Consider Rita Kramer's book, *In Defense of the Family*. Although this book contains much good sense about childrearing, its explanation of the plight of the family is completely inadequate. Kramer blames the plight of the family on interfering experts, on liberal intellectuals pushing their own permissive morality as scientific truth, on the mass media, and on the bureaucratic welfare state. She exonerates industrial capitalism, 'which gets a bum rap on this issue,' and she becomes absolutely lyrical whenever she touches on the subject of industrial technology. She speaks scornfully of those who want to 'throw out all the machines and go back to pre-industrial ways of arranging our lives.' She insists that we can resist the 'numbing and all-pervasive media' and still enjoy the 'undeniable blessings of technology.' Her position seems to be that the nuclear family is so far

---

previous%20features/a_dialogue_with_christopher_lasc.htm.

7   Kristol started his political journey as an anti-Soviet Trotskyite, and became the 'godfather of neoconservativism'. He was a director of the CIA Cold War front, the American Committee for Cultural Freedom, and was awarded the Presidential Medal of Freedom. Barry Gewen, 'Irving Kristol, Godfather of Modern Conservatism, Dies at 89', *The New York Times*, September 18,   2009;   https://www.nytimes.com/2009/09/19/us/politics/19kristol.html?pagewanted=all.

8   Misnamed because it is neither 'new' nor 'conservative', but free market libertarianism, having its origins in 19th century English Whig-liberalism, not conservativism. This is why Lasch went looking for 'genuine conservativism' in the USA, but could not find it.

superior to any other form of childrearing that its persistence can be taken for granted—if only the experts would go away and leave it alone.

…It is the logic of consumerism that undermines the values of loyalty and permanence and promotes a different set of values that is destructive of family life — and much else besides. Kramer argues that the old bourgeois virtues should be given a long, hard look before we discard them in the name either of greater self-fulfillment or greater altruism. But these values are being discarded precisely because they no longer serve the needs of a system of production based on advanced technology, unskilled labor, and mass consumption.

The therapeutic ethic, which has replaced the 19th century utilitarian ethic, does not serve the 'class interest' of professionals alone, as Daniel Moynihan and other critics of the 'new class' have argued; it serves the needs of advanced capitalism as a whole. Moynihan points out that by emphasizing impulse rather than calculation as the determinant of human conduct, and by holding society responsible for the problems confronting individuals, a government-oriented professional class has attempted to create a demand for its own services. Professionals, he observes, have a vested interest in discontent, because discontented people turn to professional devices for relief. But the same principle underlies modern capitalism in general, which continually tries to create new demands and new discontents that can be assuaged only by the consumption of commodities. Professional self-aggrandizement grew up side by side with the advertising industry and the whole machinery of demand-creation. **The same historical development that turned the citizen into a client transformed the worker from a producer into a consumer. Thus the medical and psychiatric assault on the family as a technologically backward sector of society went hand in hand with the advertising industry's drive to convince people that store-bought goods are superior to homemade goods.**[9]

The right insists that the 'new class' controls the mass media and uses this control to wage a 'class struggle' against business, as Irving Kristol puts it. Since the mass media are financed by advertising revenues, however, it is hard to take this contention seriously. It is advertising and the logic of consumerism, not anti-capitalist ideology that governs the depiction of reality in the mass media. Conservatives complain that television mocks

9   Emphasis added.

free enterprise and presents businessmen as 'greedy, malevolent, and corrupt,' like J. R. Ewing. To see anti-capitalist propaganda in a program like *Dallas,* however, requires a suspension not merely of critical judgment but of ordinary faculties of observation. Images of luxury, romance, and excitement dominate such programs, as they dominate the advertisements that surround and engulf them. *Dallas* is itself an advertisement for the good life, like almost everything on television—that is, for the good life conceived as endless novelty, change, and excitement, as the titillation of the senses by every available stimulant, as unlimited possibility. 'Make it new' is the message not just of modern art but of modern consumerism, of which modern art, indeed—even when it claims to side with the social revolution—is largely a mirror image. We are all revolutionaries now, addicts of change. The modern capitalist economy rests on the techniques of mass production pioneered by Henry Ford but also, no less solidly, on the principle of planned obsolescence introduced by Alfred E. Sloane when he instituted the annual model change. Relentless 'improvement' of the product and upgrading of consumer tastes are the heart of mass merchandising, and these imperatives are built into the mass media at every level. Even the reporting of news has to be understood not as propaganda for any particular ideology, liberal or conservative, but as propaganda for commodities, for the replacement of things by commodities, use values by exchange values, and events by images. The very concept of news celebrates newness. The value of news, like that of any other commodity, consists primarily of its novelty, only secondarily of its informational value. ...

Conservatives sense a link between television and drugs, but they do not grasp the nature of this connection any more than they grasp the important fact about news: that it represents another form of advertising, not liberal propaganda. Propaganda in the ordinary sense of the term plays a less and less important part in a consumer society, where people greet all official pronouncements with suspicion. Mass media themselves contribute to the prevailing skepticism; one of their main effects is to undermine trust in authority, devalue heroism and charismatic leadership, and reduce everything to the same dimensions. The effect of the mass media is not to elicit belief but to maintain the apparatus of addiction. Drugs are merely the most obvious form of addiction in our society. It is true that drug addiction is one of the things that undermines 'traditional values,' but the need for drugs—that is, for commodities that alleviate boredom and satisfy the socially stimulated desire for novelty and excitement—grows out of the very nature of a consumerist economy.[10]

Lasch points out what has been known to dissident rightists for generations, but which escapes the understanding of the proponents of 'classical economics', the lauding of the individual over the organic community, the basis of which is the family. Lasch observed:

> The intellectual debility of contemporary conservatism is indicated by its silence on all these important matters. Neoclassical economics takes no account of the importance of advertising. It extols the 'sovereign consumer' and insists that advertising cannot force consumers to buy anything they don't already want to buy. This argument misses the point. The point isn't that advertising manipulates the consumer or directly influences consumer choices. The point is that it makes the consumer an addict, unable to live without increasingly sizeable doses of externally provided stimulation and excitement. Conservatives argue that television erodes the capacity for sustained attention in children. They complain that young people now expect education, for example, to be easy and exciting. This argument is correct as far as it goes. Here again, however, conservatives incorrectly attribute these artificially excited expectations to liberal propaganda—in this case, to theories of permissive childrearing and 'creative pedagogy'. They ignore the deeper source of the expectations that undermine education, destroy the child's curiosity, and encourage passivity. Ideologies, however appealing and powerful, cannot shape the whole structure of perceptions and conduct unless they are embedded in daily experiences that appear to confirm them. In our society, daily experience teaches the individual to want and need a never-ending supply of new toys and drugs. A defense of 'free enterprise' hardly supplies a corrective to these expectations.
>
> Conservatives conceive the capitalist economy as it was in the time of Adam Smith, when property was still distributed fairly widely, businesses were individually owned, and commodities still retained something of the character of useful objects. Their notion of free enterprise takes no account of the forces that have transformed capitalism from within: the rise of the corporation, the bureaucratization of business, the increasing

---

10   C. Lasch, 'What's wrong with the Right?'

insignificance of private property, and the shift from a work ethic to a consumption ethic. Insofar as conservatives take any note of these developments at all, they attribute them solely to government interference and regulation. **They deplore bureaucracy but see only its public face, missing the prevalence of bureaucracy in the private sector. They betray no acquaintance with the rich historical scholarship which shows that the expansion of the public sector came about, in part, in response to pressure from the corporations themselves.**[11]

Lasch pointed out the fundamental error of American 'conservatism' in assuming the same ideological position of the Left in regard to industrial progress:

> Conservatives assume that deregulation and a return to the free market will solve everything, promoting a revival of the work ethic and a resurgence of 'traditional values.' Not only do they provide an inadequate explanation of the destruction of those values but they unwittingly side with the social forces that have contributed to their destruction, for example in their advocacy of unlimited growth. **The poverty of contemporary conservatism reveals itself most fully in this championship of economic growth, the underlying premise of the consumer culture, the by-products of which conservatives deplore.** A vital conservatism would identify itself with the demand for limits not only on economic growth but on the conquest of space, the technological conquest of the environment, and the human ambition to acquire godlike powers over nature. A vital conservatism would see in the environmental movement the quintessential conservative cause, since environmentalism opposes reckless innovation and makes conservation the central order of business. Instead of taking environmentalism away from the left, however, conservatives condemn it as a counsel of doom. 'Free enterprisers,' says Pines, 'insist that the economy can indeed expand and as it does so, *all* society's members can increase their wealth.' **One of the cardinal tenets of liberalism, the limitlessness of economic growth, now undergirds the so-called conservatism that presents itself as a corrective and alternative to liberalism.**[12]

---

11   Ibid. Emphasis added.
12   Ibid. Emphasis added.

Lasch looked for a real conservatism in the USA and could not find it. He saw the 'rugged individualism' championed by 'conservatives' as antithetical to actual tradition, exalting a rootless 'freedom'; 'the values of the man on the make, in flight from his ancestors, from the family clan, from everything that ties him down and limits his freedom of movement. What is traditional about the rejection of tradition, continuity, and rootedness? A conservatism that sides with the forces of restless mobility is a false conservatism'.[13]

This pseudo-conservatism had encroached on the development of actual conservatism, which had historically repudiated capitalism and free trade for the reasons Lasch was suggesting. In Britain, Thomas Carlyle, part of the genuine conservative tradition, had condemned capitalism at the start of the modern, industrial epoch, at the time Marx was still just a radical liberal. Carlyle wrote in 1843:

> True, it must be owned, we for the present, with our Mammon-Gospel, have come to strange conclusions. We call it a Society; and go about professing openly the totalest separation, isolation. Our life is not a mutual helpfulness; but rather, cloaked under due laws-of-war, named 'fair competition' and so forth, it is a mutual hostility. We have profoundly forgotten everywhere that *Cash-payment* is not the sole relation of human beings; we think, nothing doubting, that it absolves and liquidates all engagements of man. 'My starving workers?' answers the rich Mill-owner: 'Did not I hire them fairly in the market? Did I not pay them, to the last sixpence, the sum covenanted for? What have I to do with them more?'—Verily Mammon-worship is a melancholy creed. ...[14]

> One thing I do know: Never, on this Earth, was the relation of man to man long carried on by Cash-payment alone. If, at any time, a philosophy of Laissez-faire, Competition and Supply-and-demand, start up as the exponent of human relations, expect that it will soon end.[15]

---

13 Ibid.

14 Thomas Carlyle, (1843) Book III, Chapter II: 'Gospel of Mammonism'.

15 Ibid., Book III, Chapter X: 'Plugston of Undershot'.

Carlyle saw that free trade capitalism would not enable the 'English Nation' to be maintained as an organic community. The *cash nexus* would not provide a bond of kinship, but of fracture, competition and distrust. Both Marx and the Free Traders saw this as 'progress'. Carlyle foretold the coming of the rootless merchant class, committed to profit beyond borders, which Marx later (1848) lauded as an 'internationalising' process. Carlyle using organic metaphors of tree roots to emphasise the literal rootedness of the human being in his traditional life, saw the merchant as being confronted by the promise of wealth further afield and becoming a 'Universal Being', which a century and a half later the economic journalist G. Pascal Zachary was lauding as the 'Global Me'.[16] Carlyle, on the contrary, saw the coming *homo globicus* as 'apelike' and devoid of spirit.

> O unwise mortals that forever change and shift, and say, Yonder, not Here! Wealth richer than both the Indies lies everywhere for man, if he will endure. Not his oaks only and his fruit-trees, his very heart roots itself wherever he will abide;—roots itself, draws nourishment from the deep fountains of Universal Being! Vagrant Sam-Slicks, who rove over the Earth doing 'strokes of trade', what wealth have they? Horseloads, shiploads of white or yellow metal: in very sooth, what are these? Slick rests nowhere, he is homeless. He can build stone or marble houses; but to continue in them is denied him. The wealth of a man is the number of things which he loves and blesses, which he is loved and blessed by! The herdsman in his poor clay shealing, where his very cow and dog are friends to him, and not a cataract but carries memories for him, and not a mountain-top but nods old recognition: his life, all encircled as in blessed mother's arms, is it poorer than Slick's with the ass-loads of yellow metal on his back? Unhappy Slick! Alas, there has so much grown nomadic, apelike, with us: so much will have, with whatever pain, repugnance and 'impossibility', to alter itself, to fix itself again,—in some wise way, in any not delirious way![17]

---

16   G. Pascal Zachary (2000).

17   Thomas Carlyle, Book IV, Chapter V: 'Permanence'.

It is the fundamental difference in cultural, moral, and spiritual outlook that separates the dissident Right from the common elements
of the Left and capitalism, as Evola pointed out. Carlyle categorised
this dichotomy with the words *Permanent* and *Temporary*. One of the
defining elements of the genuine Right is that of *Permanence*, of the
meaning of perpetuity, through family lineage and personal property.
These are organic, 'primary ties', that the Left and capitalism both demand must be deconstructed in favour of 'liberty' — meaning without
attachment and perpetuity. Carlyle described this 'liberty' that was
even then threatening the foundations of civilisation:

> Permanent not Temporary:—you do not hire the mere red-coated fighter
> by the day, but by the score of years! Permanence, persistence is the first
> condition of all fruitfulness in the ways of men. The 'tendency to persevere,'
> to persist in spite of hindrances, discouragements and 'impossibilities:' it is
> this that in all things distinguishes the strong soul from the weak; the civi-
> lised burgher from the nomadic savage,—the Species Man from the Genus
> Ape! The Nomad has his very house set on wheels; the Nomad, and in a still
> higher degree the Ape, are all for 'liberty;' the privilege to flit continually is
> indispensable for them. Alas, in how many ways, does our humour, in this
> swift-rolling self-abrading Time, shew itself nomadic, apelike; mournful
> enough to him that looks on it with eyes! This humour will have to abate;
> it is the first element of all fertility in human things, that such 'liberty' of
> apes and nomads do by freewill or constraint abridge itself, give place to
> a better. The civilised man lives not in wheeled houses. He builds stone
> castles, plants lands, makes lifelong marriage-contracts;—has long-dated
> hundred-fold possessions, not to be valued in the money-market; has pedi-
> grees, libraries, law-codes; has memories and hopes, even for this Earth,
> that reach over thousands of years. Life-long marriage-contracts: how
> much preferable were year-long or month-long—to the nomad or ape![18]

This English liberalism had by Lasch's time become the dominant
trend in American 'conservativism', and hence he failed to find genuine conservatism. Hence, Lasch questioned whether the Left-Right

---

18   Ibid., Chapter V: 'Permanence'.

dichotomy remained relevant. The Left did not challenge capitalism, and never really had. In particular, Lasch contended that what was being called 'conservatism' in the USA (and other Anglophone countries, epitomised by Reaganism in the USA and Thatcherism in Britain) was 'false'. This pseudo-conservatism did not defend traditions, but upheld industrialism and capitalism, and like the Left, accepted the 'progressive' or 'positivist' approach to history. Modern 'false conservatism', as Lasch called it, failed to uphold the pre-capitalist tradition, and instead defended the bourgeoisie, capitalism and industrialism, in the sacred name of 'progress'. Lasch stated of the false dichotomy:

> The hope of a new politics does not lie in formulating a left-wing reply to the right; it lies in rejecting conventional political categories and redefining the terms of political debate. The idea of a 'left' has outlived its historical time and needs to be decently buried, along with **the false conservatism that merely clothes an older liberal tradition in conservative rhetoric.** The old labels have no meaning anymore. They can only confuse debate instead of clarifying it. They are products of an earlier era, the age of steam and steel, and are wholly inadequate to the age of electronics, totalitarianism, and mass culture. Let us say good-bye to these old friends, fondly but firmly, and look elsewhere for guidance and moral support.[19]

The Left Reacts

Among the first from the Left to react to Lasch's heresy was Dr. Lillian Rubin,[20] Professor of Sociology at the University of California, Berkeley, who responded with *ad hominem* quips comparing Lasch's views to that of 'Moral Majority' preacher Jerry Falwell, and President

---

19   C. Lasch, 'What's Wrong with the Right?' Emphasis added.

20   Rubin, an eminent feminist academic had, as an adolescent, been denied the opportunity to attend college because her mother told her to get a job to support her brother's education. Her mother had the traditional Jewish outlook, which, using psychoanalysis, we might see as resulting in Rubin's feminism, being a projection of her upbringing onto society. Rubin did not graduate until adulthood.

Ronald Reagan, and accusing Lasch of giving the debate on social issues over to 'the meanest and most reactionary forces in our land'. Using the straw man argument she accused Lasch of not understanding the impact of the Industrial Revolution on family life, which is precisely what he *did* understand, Rubin stating: 'And the issue of family instability that plagues us today has, in one way or another, been with us at least since the Industrial Revolution, so effectively split work from family life and family members from each other. ... Yet Lasch, the historian, manages to write as if he knows nothing of all this'.[21]

Rubin objected to Lasch's identifying feminism as a reflection of the System: '... The family may be under threat from economic pressures, he concedes, but the real threat comes from a feminist ideology; which, in his words, "devalues motherhood, equates personal development with participation in the labor market, and defines freedom as individual freedom of choice, freedom from binding commitments."'[22]

Rubin lauds the role of feminism in opening the labour market up to women, unable to understand that this is a primary example of how the Left and capitalism converge. An expanding labour market is a common ground for the Left and capitalism, and Lasch refers to the need for industrial crèches, so that the drudgery of raising children and administering a home will not interfere with women as fully integrated units of the capitalist production process.

Lasch responded to Rubin's attack with gusto: 'These stale polemics, full of moral outrage and theoretical hot air, inadvertently show why the Left has no future. ...'[23] Lasch stated that the Left had adopted an elitist position, contemptuous of the common people. He stated that the Left had abandoned 'the fiction of democracy and to

---

21 Lillian Rubin, pp. 89–91;

22 Ibid.

23 C. Lasch, 'Why the Left Has No Future', *Tikkun*, ibid., pp. 92–97;

lead the people to the promised land against their own judgment and inclinations'.[24] With the rejection of leftist doctrine by the masses,

> the American Left has had to choose, in effect, between two equally futile and self-defeating strategies: either to wait hopelessly for the revolution, while fulminating against 'capitalism,' or to try to gain its objectives by out-flanking public opinion, giving up the hope of creating a popular constituency for social reform, and relying instead on the courts, the mass media, and the administrative bureaucracy. As militant outsiders or bureaucratic insiders, radicals have succeeded only in laying the basis of a conservative movement that has managed to present itself, infuriatingly, as a form of cultural populism, even though its own program, especially its economic program, seeks only to perpetuate the existing distribution of wealth and power—indeed, to reverse most of the democratic gains actually achieved over the last five decades.[25]

Lasch pointed to a process that had long been taking place within the Left, that of estrangement from the masses, with the realisation that the masses are instinctually conservative. He pointed to the common outlook between the Left and liberal-capitalism. He stated that both looked to the contractual rights of the individual rather than the pre-capitalist spontaneity of group association, stating that conservativism was derailed by adopting the liberal economic model.

> The whole tendency of modern society, of modern liberalism in particular, consigns family life (by any reasonable definition of family life) to the realm of 'nostalgia.' Note that I don't blame the instability of family life on feminism. Since feminism is an expression of well-founded grievances, and since the economic and ideological assault on the foundations of family life antedated the emergence of a feminist movement, it would be foolish to blame feminism for the collapse of the family. But it is equally foolish to pretend that feminism is compatible with the family. **Feminism is itself an outgrowth of liberalism, among other things, and it shares liberalism's belief in individual rights, contractual relations, and the primacy of**

---

24 Ibid.
25 Ibid.

justice, all of which make it impossible to understand the nature or the value of spontaneous cooperation.[26]

Lasch described a 'cultural civil war,'[27] now commonly called 'Cultural Marxism', which estranged the masses from the Left. The ultimate aim of it was described by Lasch in regard to the modernist conception of the 'family':

> A 'family policy' designed to shift this responsibility to the state is no solution at all. Nor is it a 'radical' solution. It would merely ratify the pattern of **bureaucratic individualism that already exists, in which the state takes over the nurturing functions formerly associated with parenthood and leaves people free to enjoy themselves as consumers.**[28]

This is the 'soft dictatorship' described by Huxley in *Brave New World*. The process that had been tried in the earliest phase of Bolshevik Russia, but proceeds more thoroughly and permanently under liberal-capitalism.

---

26 Ibid. Emphasis added.
27 Ibid.
28 Ibid. Emphasis added.

Sexology

CHARLES MERRIAM, the 'dean' of the U.S. social sciences, made a sales pitch for funding a unified approach to the social sciences as a means of social engineering and control. This appealed to the oligarchy. Merriam saw immense possibilities in directing human evolution. The control of sexual relationships and of reproduction and child-rearing plays a primary role in how humans can be organised to fit into economic processes.

The National Research Council Committee for Research in Problems of Sex (CRPS), founded in 1921, pioneered *sexology*. CRPS was originally funded by the Bureau of Social Hygiene. The latter was founded by John D. Rockefeller Jr. to study numerous social problems, including those of sexuality and birth control, operating from 1913 to 1940. Paul Warburg, scion of the international banking family, was among the funders.[1] Funding of CRPS was assumed by the Natural Sciences Division of the Rockefeller Foundation from 1931. It was here that the sciences of reproduction and sexology were defined.[2] With Rockefeller funding, there was a major shift from biological research to social research. 'This culminated in the 1940s with the NRC/CRPS providing extensive sponsorship for Alfred Kinsey's pathbreaking research on human sexuality.'[3]

---

1   Adele E. Clarke, p. 94.

2   Ibid., pp. 90–91.

3   Ibid., p. 93.

In 1936, Earl Zinn, executive secretary of CRPS, left to take up a position with the Yale University Institute of Human Relations. The institute was funded with $4.5 million from the Rockefeller Foundation for
its first decade (1929–1939), with the purpose of 'integrating scientific
knowledge of human behaviour, with rational control of behaviour as
the ultimate goal'.[4] The concept of 'social medicine' had been introduced from Europe as a method of 'human engineering';[5] the premise
being that medicine would not only look at the individual's physical
health, but at man's 'entire social and economic environment'.[6]

Social medicine had arisen when 'Radical clinicians like Jules
Guérin in revolutionary Paris in 1848 and Rudolf Virchow in Prussia
believed that medicine should adopt a new social scientific profile
along with a consciousness of social responsibility and play a political role in the emergent modern state'.[7] Developments in France
and Prussia influenced the formation of the National Association
for Social Science in Britain in 1856, which included physicians. The
intentions were noble and have contributed immeasurably to human
welfare in considering the impact of social and economic conditions
on the causes of ill-health. The problems start, depending on one's
perspective, when such projects are co-opted and re-directed by the
oligarchy, whose system of economics cause the problems that they
subsequently claim to be trying to solve. Moreover, the turn of events
reflected the materialistic *Zeitgeist* of the time, where society was seen
as a 'mechanistic model', a 'physical machine', 'redefining life, labour
and language in terms of the functional discourse of scientific rationality in a modern capitalist society'.[8]

Yale's University Health Service became 'a laboratory for psychological, sociological, and economic studies of patients conducted

---

4   Ibid., p. 105.
5   Arthur J. Viseltear, p. 872.
6   Ibid., p. 875.
7   Dorothy Porter, p. 4.
8   Ibid., p. 7.

by students and experts of law, medicine, and sociology'. Data was analysed by a team of 'sociologists, psychologists, psychiatrists, economists, and biologists on the Institute staff'.[9]

The aim was to determine what readjustments needed to be made between the individual and the environment.[10] The oft-cited ideal of the institute was 'human happiness';[11] an elusive ideal that remains the basis of political and religious utopias, generally culminating in the guillotine of the Jacobins, the firing squads of the Bolsheviks, and the Kool-Aid of Jim Jones. When asked by a wealthy Yale alumnus, the Institute's director Milton Winternitz attempted a definition of 'happiness' as 'the degree to which the psychophysical organism becomes adapted to its environment...'.[12]

Largely thanks to the Rockefeller Foundation, an initial $7.5 million was raised to establish the Institute.[13] The ideology of the Institute continues to influence, for example, Yale's Institution for Social and Policy Studies,[14] presently headed by Jacob S. Hacker, a board member of The American Prospect, The American Century Foundation, and the Economic Policy Institute; liberal-progressive think tanks.[15]

9   Arthur J. Viseltear p. 875.

10 'Yale Proposed to Study Man', *The Human Welfare Group, New Haven Connecticut* (1929), pp. 12–13; cited by Arthur J. Viseltear, p. 876.

11 Arthur J. Viseltear, p. 882. The phrase was a feature of the Institute's pamphlets and the speeches of its faculty.

12 Milton C. Winternitz to Henry H. Covell, 9 January 1930, cited by Arthur J. Viseltear, p. 882.

13 Arthur J. Viseltear, p. 878.

14 Ibid., p. 885.

15 Jacob S. Hacker, https://isps.yale.edu/team/jacob-s-hacker.

Alfred Kinsey

Dr. Kinsey ridiculed 'socially approved patterns of sexual behaviour', calling them 'rationalizations', while usually referring to socially condemned
forms of sexual behavior as 'normal' or 'normal in the human animal'.

— Rene A. Wormser

A LFRED KINSEY is the most widely known founder of sexology in
the USA. Kinsey's surveys into sexual habits provide the data for
revolutionary agendas. Dr. John Bancroft, when director of the Kinsey
Institute, championed 'sexual nonconformity' as a 'vehicle for dissent'.[1]

Kinsey began his studies in sex in 1938 at Indiana University. Of
18,000 individual case studies in sexual behaviour, Kinsey personally interviewed 7,983. By 1941, Kinsey's research was being funded by
the Rockefeller Foundation through the National Research Council
(NRC). By 1947, the Committee for Research on Problems of Sex
had given Kinsey and his team $40,000. That year Kinsey estab-
lished the Institute for Sex Research at Indiana University.[2] In 1946,
the Rockefeller Foundation granted $14,000 for Kinsey's research
library. Rockefeller Foundation funding continued until 1954, when
Congressman Reece started his hearings into the Foundations.

---

1   Bolton, *Revolution from Above*, p. 114. (The Kinsey website is no longer as
    forthcoming as previously). See also: http://stopthekinseyinstitute.org/kinsey-
    brief/.
2   Kinsey Institute, 'A Brief History', https://kinseyinstitute.org/about/history/
    alfred-kinsey.php.

According to a statement filed with the Reece Committee, the Rockefeller Foundation granted $414,000 to Kinsey over the period 1941–49.

The Reece Committee was formed originally with the specific purpose of investigating the funding of Kinsey. Representative Reece stated: 'The Congress has been asked to investigate the financial backers of the institute that turned out the Kinsey sex report last August'.[3] The Kinsey Institute states that 'The Rockefeller Foundation's Board of Directors, under pressure from Reece's committee, withdrew financial support for Dr. Kinsey's research'.[4] Kinsey had been name-dropping the Rockefeller Foundation as a sales-pitch for his work. Kinsey's biographer James H. Jones writes that '[f]rom the Foundation's viewpoint ... Kinsey was out of line. As a rule the Foundation shunned publicity regarding its awards'. This was particularly so in regard to grants 'that in any way could be considered controversial'. Funding sexology through the National Research Council had enabled the Foundation to 'remain safely in the shadows'. Kinsey's statements were exposing the Foundation's role in 'social policy'.[5]

However, after the Reece Committee concluded, funding for Kinsey resumed. The Institute states:

> President Wells then approached the Trustees of Indiana University to ask for continued support of the Institute for Sex Research, which they granted. Since then the Institute has received funding from various private and public sources, including the National Institutes of Health (NIMH, NICHD, NIDA), Rockefeller Foundation, Ford Foundation, Eli Lilly & Co., and Indiana University.[6]

---

3   'What Really Happened to Funding for Sex Research?', The Kinsey Institute for Research in Sex, Gender and Reproduction, http://74.125.155.132/ search?q=cache:D-Db_DNVADAJ:www.kinseyinstitute.org/about/Movie-facts.html.

4   Ibid.

5   James H. Jones, p. 445.

6   Ibid.

The Rockefeller Foundation continues to fund the Kinsey Institute, and a myriad of fellowships and research centers have arisen with Foundation funding for the purpose. The Sexuality Research Assessment Project of the Social Science Research Council was funded by the Ford Foundation,[7] Gund Foundation, Robert Wood Johnson Foundation, Henry J. Kaiser Family Foundation, MacArthur Foundation, and Rockefeller Foundation, according to a statement by the Kinsey Institute.[8] The Sexuality Research Fellowship Program, started in 1996 under the National Sexuality Resource Center, is funded by the Ford Foundation for the purposes of awarding grants to researchers in the field.[9]

In 1948 and 1953, Kinsey's seminal studies, *Sexual Behavior in the Human Male* and *Sexual Behavior in the Female,* respectively, were published. With the publication of *Sexual Behavior in the Male,* Kinsey and his co-authors acknowledged the Rockefeller Foundation as having 'contributed a major portion of the cost of the program over the past six years', the funds having been administered by the Committee for Research on Problems of Sex, which 'encouraged and advised on many aspects of the project'.[10]

While Kinsey's study produced indignation sufficient to prompt Congressman Reece, among the last of the traditional Taft conservative Republicans, to investigate the tax-exempt Foundations directly after the congressional hearings of the Cox Committee, on which he had served, and which were inconclusive, the assumption is now cultivated that Kinsey was battling against Establishment repression

---

7 'From 1996 to 2005, the Ford Foundation supported the Sexuality Research Fellowship Program'; Ford Foundation, www.fordfound.org/pdfs/grants/RFP_SRHR.pdf.

8 The Kinsey Institute, http://74.125.155.132/search?q=cache:pk7iw9arflAJ:www.kinseyinstitute.org/resources/sexrealn.html.

9 SSRC Sexuality Research Fellowship Program, http://74.125.155.132/search?q=cache:oOtSW1bHTLYJ:nsrc.sfsu.edu/press_release/ssrc_sexuality_research_fellowship_program_ (Accessed on January 17, 2010).

10 Kinsey et al. (1949), vii.

and mass prejudice. Such alleged victimhood obscures the powerful backing Kinsey received. *The Washington Post*, which had also gone after Senator Joseph McCarthy, a newspaper particularly close to the Establishment, editorially attacked the Reece Committee as 'incompetent', 'stupidly wasteful', and intended to intimidate.[11] Investigation into Kinsey, the original *raison d'etre* of the Reece Committee, was stymied when Congressman Wayne Hays[12] threatened to halt all hearings unless the Kinsey inquiries were dropped. Rene Wormser, legal counsel to Reece, relates what happened:

> Several lines of inquiry enraged Mr. Hays particularly. One, which disclosed his reluctance to permit freedom of inquiry, was a proposed study of the Kinsey reports. It was undoubtedly reported to him by Miss Lonergan that Dr. Ettinger had dug up some significant material about foundation support of the Kinsey projects. This brought Mr. Hays to a steaming rage, and he asked to see our entire Kinsey file. It was produced for him, and he angrily declared to Mr. Dodd that we were to go no further with this particular investigation, contending that every member of Congress would be against our doing so. Neither Mr. Dodd nor I could see any reason why Dr. Kinsey's foundation-supported projects should not bear as much scrutiny as any other foundation operation. But Mr. Hays then introduced another element into the situation. Our appropriation for 1954 had, at the time, not yet been approved, and Mr. Hays stated emphatically to Mr. Dodd that he would oppose any further appropriation to our Committee unless the Kinsey investigation were dropped. His unreasoning opposition to any study of these projects was so great that he threatened to fight against the appropriation on the floor of the House.
>
> As we were already fearful that an appropriation might not come through, and our work would be frustrated, Mr. Dodd concluded that Mr. Hays must be appeased. He suggested, therefore, that Mr. Hays take the entire Kinsey file and lock it in his personal safe so that he would know the material could not be used without the express consent of the Committee. This

---

11   James H. Jones, p. 725.

12   Ironically, Hays' long career as the Congressman for Ohio was ended in 1976 by a sex scandal involving a congressional clerk.

Mr. Hays did: the file remained in his safe throughout the hearings. For all I know, he may still have it.

The Kinsey reports did, in the course of the open hearings, become part of the Committee evidence through the testimony of Professor Hobbs, who used them as apt examples of "scientism," but the valuable material in our Kinsey file never saw the light of day.[13]

Valuable information was however gained from the testimony of A. H. Hobbs, Assistant Professor of Sociology at the University of Pennsylvania. He described himself as the 'oldest assistant professor east of the Rockies', because he had, in the words of Wormser, 'been told in no uncertain terms by his superiors there that he has no hope of rising in the hierarchy. Why? Because he is a dissident'.[14] Wormser explained that the actual dissidents were those who resisted Foundation-backed social control research in the name of social science, while attention was only given to portraying leftists as martyrs:

The treatment of Professor Hobbs at the University of Pennsylvania is a black mark upon the record of that great institution. It is an outstanding example of suppression of academic freedom. Yet, as far as I know, none of the 'liberals' who cry out so loudly that freedom is being suppressed whenever a Communist professor is discharged have entered even the mildest protest against the persecution of Professor Hobbs, whose only sin has been to have an independent mind and the strength of character to use it.

Behind the persecution of Professor Hobbs, and accountable for it, lies the fact that the foundation-supported 'concentration of power' has been angered by his independence of mind and his frank criticism. He has been a strong critic of many of the methods used in contemporary social-science research, methods which the foundation complex has fostered.[15]

In his testimony before Reece, Hobbs stated on Kinsey's research:

---

13   Rene A. Wormser, p. 351.
14   Ibid., p. 87.
15   Ibid.

Dr. Kinsey ridiculed 'socially approved patterns of sexual behaviour', calling them 'rationalizations', while usually referring to socially condemned forms of sexual behavior as 'normal' or 'normal in the human animal'. This presentation, said Professor Hobbs, 'could give the impression, and it gave the impression to a number of reviewers, that things which conform to the socially approved codes of sexual conduct are rationalizations, not quite right, while things which deviate from it, such as homosexuality, are normal, in a sense right'. Professor Hobbs stressed the fact that such pseudoscientific presentations could seriously affect public morality. Here is part of his testimony:

'For an illustration, in connection with the question of heterosexuality compared with homosexuality, Kinsey in the first volume[16] has this statement: "It is only because society demands that there be a particular choice in the matter (of heterosexuality or homosexuality) and does not so often dictate one's choice of food or clothing." He puts it in [these] terms, it is just a custom which society demands. In the second volume[17] it is stressed, for example, that we object to adult molesters of children primarily because we have become conditioned against such adult molesters of children, and that the children who are molested become emotionally upset, primarily because of the old-fashioned attitudes of their parents about such practices, and the parents (the implication is) are the ones who do the real damage by making a fuss about it if a child is molested. Because the molester, and here I quote from Kinsey, "may have contributed favorably to their later sociosexual development." That is, a molester of children may have actually, Kinsey contends, not only not harmed them, but may have contributed favorably to their later sociosexual development. ...'[18]

Other commentators, having the attention of a mass audience through courtesy of the mass media, were enthused by Kinsey's striking at the roots of traditional America. Howard A. Rusk, noted as the founder of rehabilitation medicine, and medical columnist for *The New York Times*, reviewing *Sexual Behavior in the Male* commented that

---

16   Kinsey, *Sexual Behavior in the Human Male*.

17   Kinsey, *Sexual Behavior in the Human Female*.

18   Wormser, p. 105.

for every individual or group that opposed the study, hundreds cooperated, ranging from Harvard and Columbia Universities to the Kansas State police and the Salvation Army's Home for Unwed Mothers. The auspices of the National Research Council, and the financial underwriting of the Rockefeller Foundation, bespeak the scientific solidarity of the project.

These facts are presented with scientific objectivity, and without moralizing — but they provide the knowledge with which we can rebuild our concepts with tolerance and understanding. ... After the initial impact, when time permits sober reflection and analysis the end results should be healthy. They should bring about a better understanding of some of our emotional problems, and the bases for some of our psychiatric concepts. ... These studies are sincere, objective and determined explorations of a field manifestly important to education, medicine, government and the integrity of human conduct generally. They have demanded from Dr. Kinsey and his colleagues very unusual tenacity of purpose, tolerance, analytical competence, social skills and real courage.[19]

Rusk also saw the revolutionary character of the study in helping to reshape 'legal and moral concepts' as a 'yardstick' in analysing social problems, and a means of creating the ideal 'world citizen':

The findings of Dr. Kinsey's report provide us with the material for sober thought, and a new basis for the personal understanding of our individual sex problems. It presents facts that indicate the necessity to review some of our legal and moral concepts. It gives new therapeutic tools to the psychiatrist and the practicing physician. It offers a yardstick that will give invaluable aid in the study of our complex social problems. It offers data that would promote tolerance and understanding and make us better 'world citizens'.[20]

The post-Freudian assumption had been accepted that an international social revolution might be enacted through *sexual determinism*. Rusk stated the study was 'manifestly important to education, medicine, government and the integrity of human conduct generally'.

19   Howard A. Rusk.

20   Ibid.

Albert Deutsch, award-winning author and journalist noted for his writing on public health issues, wrote a *Harper's* feature on the impending publication of *Sexual Behavior in the Human Male*, that '[a]ge-old ideas about sex embedded in our legal and moral codes are revealed as myths and delusions under the searchlight of this important investigation. ... So startling are the revelations, so contrary to what civilized man has been taught for generations, that they would be unbelievable but for the impressive weight of scientific agencies backing the survey'. Like Rusk, Deutsch assumed credibility was assured by the backing Kinsey had from the National Research Council, the University of Indiana, and the Rockefeller Foundation's Medical Science Division.[21]

Among the 'shattering blows' that the study would deliver, '[s]ex attitudes and habits start in infancy', confirming the view of Freud. 'Sex life, in fact begins virtually at birth'. Four- and five-month-olds were cited as examples. De Sade would have been buoyed.

Deutsch found in the Kinsey study that there are no sex patterns but a myriad of forms based on 'social differences'. The sex habits of the child of a labourer and of a businessman among White Americans diverged more widely than those of widely separated races. Hence there is no 'normal' 'common pattern sexual behavior' among Americans, but there is widespread conformity within social groups. Kinsey claimed that sex habits are based far more on social than on psychological or biological factors; that sexual **habits have a class basis**.[22] 'Lower level females' are able to attain orgasm more often than 'upper level females', and the 'lower level' male does not have to work at it as diligently as the 'upper level' male.[23] Upper class males are also more attentive of female breasts than the working class.[24] The upper

---

21   Albert Deutsch.

22   Kinsey et al., *Sexual Behavior in the Human Male*, p. 329.

23   Ibid., p. 367.

24   Ibid., p. 371.

class male is also more inclined to masturbate.[25] When it comes to homosexuality, however, one approaches class solidarity, with its acceptance particularly in the 'lowest' and the 'highest' classes.[26] At least a third of the American male population have homosexual tendencies to some degree.[27] Kinsey claimed that he could predict the future occupation and hence social class of an adolescent by observing his sex history. 'This set of facts has tremendous significance for the future of marriage, parenthood and education', wrote Deutsch.[28] **The study therefore seeded the notion that to accord with the science of sexology, 'marriage, parenthood and education' need reforming**.

Terms such as 'unnatural' and 'abnormal' for sexual behaviour did not have scientific validity. Deutsch quotes Kinsey as stating, 'the publicly-pretended code of morals, our social organization, our marriage customs, our sex laws, and some of our educational and religious concepts are based upon an assumption that individuals are much alike sexually'. Reiterating a class basis, Kinsey stated that the laws regarding sexual behaviour are written, interpreted and enforced by 'people in the upper educational and social levels'. Among Kinsey's findings are that one-third of adolescent males had homosexual experiences, and 'about 17% of the farm boys had sexual relations' with animals, with 'about as many more' having relations without carrying through to climax.[29] The 'mean age for the first homosexual contact is about 9.21 years'.[30] The average age of the beginning of 'heterosexual play is about 8 years'.[31]

It seems from this that what is required according to the Kinsey surveys is the changing of the laws and the moral attitude regarding

25　Ibid., p. 375.

26　Ibid., p. 383.

27　Ibid., p. 665.

28　Albert Deutsch.

29　Kinsey et al, *Sexual Behavior in the Human Male*, p. 459.

30　Ibid., p. 168.

31　Ibid., p. 173.

bestiality and child-sex. If this is the case, then perhaps it is because Western civilisation, headed by the USA, has become so debased that it is on its way out, as in the analogous epochs of other civilisations? By the time of Augustus, Rome had become so broken that buggery, abortion, infanticide, child-desertion, and sterile sex were the norms. According to Tacitus, despite state efforts, 'childlessness prevailed'. Children were looked on as a hindrance to pleasure.[32] The same process that unfolded in Rome two millennia ago is today called 'progress'.

As with the *Oedipal* struggle of seminal post-Freudians such as Reich, who felt himself guilty for his mother's suicide, and the 'structural Marxist' Louis Althusser, who murdered his mother-figure wife; there was a deep personal motivation for Kinsey's drive to deconstruct traditional normality. Kinsey remarks in the study: 'Normal and abnormal, one sometimes suspects, are terms which a particular author employs with reference to his own position on that curve'.[33] Kinsey biographer James H. Jones writes:

> … Why had Kinsey cared so passionately and worked so hard all those years? The answer lies in his private life, in the fearful things he had kept hidden from the world. Kinsey was a man with secrets, a man whose stupendous guilt had combined with his puritan work ethic to produce his spring-coil vitality. Beginning with childhood, Kinsey had lived with two shameful secrets: he was both a homosexual and a masochist. He had not asked to be either, and he had spent his life deeply conflicted on both accounts. Yet Kinsey understood firsthand how difficult it was to change, and he knew better than to expect sympathy or understanding from society. In order to help himself, he would have to help others. Thus, his messianic crusade to reform the world that oppressed him.

> Flowers. As objects of beauty, they are supposed to make people happy, but they made Alfred Charles Kinsey sad. Not all flowers, to be sure. Only those that had grown in his family's tiny yard in Hoboken, New Jersey, where he spent the first ten years of his life. 'He disliked Hoboken and everything connected with it', Clara Kinsey, his wife, later told an interviewer,

---

32   Bolton, *The Decline and Fall of Civilisations*, pp. 205–211.

33   Kinsey et al., *Sexual Behavior in the Human Male*, p. 199.

'even the flowers that grew in the garden they had in their small backyard'. As an adult, Kinsey became an ardent gardener, but he would not permit marigolds, zinnias, or wisteria in his yard — the flowers his parents had grown in Hoboken. While his reaction was truly visceral, it was not the flowers he loathed but the childhood memories they triggered. Not that he dwelled on these years, for Kinsey believed that bad memories should be suppressed. As an adult, he advised young people 'to learn the art of weighing down unprofitable things in our thoughts'. Referring specifically to unwanted memories, Kinsey added, 'We may not be responsible for the birds (memories) that fly over our heads but we can keep them from roosting in our hair'.

After he gained world fame as a sex researcher, Kinsey received numerous inquiries about his past. People wanted to know his birthday, where he had been born, the names of his ancestors, whether he was married and had children, and even intimate details about his sex history. For a man who had become a celebrity by invading other people's privacy, he guarded his own with cool determination.[34]

Raised in a puritanical Methodist family, we find the familiar tale of an authoritarian father, who 'admonished far better than he nurtured'.

For his oldest child, then, there was no escaping religion. Week after week, month after month, and year after year, Kinsey sat with his family listening to sermons designed to shape his moral view of life as an unending struggle between Good and Evil. Much of what he heard was mean-spirited, hate-filled, and fearful, calculated to produce feelings of dependence and submission rather than love and trust. This was especially true of the sermons that were designed to frighten people into confessing their sins and joining the church.

Kinsey heard many stories that chronicled God's wrath, but for its sheer power to terrorize young minds, none could match that staple of fundamentalist theology — the Judgment Day, the moment of reckoning when every man, woman, and child, living or dead, had to stand before the throne of God and hear His verdict. On that most terrifying of days, the Book of Life would be opened and mankind would be divided into saints

34 James H. Jones, pp. 4–5.

and sinners. Verily, this would be the day of truth, a time of fear and trepidation. When it was over, the righteous would be raised to heaven, the wicked banished to hell. As they ruminated over mankind's fate, however, ministers did not tarry over the blissful paradise awaiting the righteous; they described with flinty severity the horrors in store for those wretched souls who had been weighed and found wanting.[35]

Kinsey was running from the judgement of God-the-Father. In order to escape his own self-destructive childhood guilt, he was impelled to obliterate the 'sins' for which he was judging himself by reconstructing them as the new normal. Therefore, mankind could not be divided for judgement according to what was written in the Book of Life. That had been torn up and incinerated, and God-the-Father had been dethroned. Marx could not have done a better job, given the impact of Kinsey.

Role of the Kinseyan Sexual Dialectics

For all this, John Bancroft, Director of the Kinsey Institute (1995–2004), objected to the manner by which the 'religious Right' portrayed Kinsey as subversive and revolutionary. He also expressed concern at the way the 'religious Right' (sic), which he stated (ironically) is 'well-funded', campaigned to discredit Kinsey and the Institute. Yet in the same lecture commemorating the fiftieth anniversary of the Institute, Bancroft made some significant revelations as to the continuing funding of the Institute's programmes, and expressed views on the impact of Kinsey that are indeed 'revolutionary'.[36] Drawing on Kinsey, he outlined a *sexual dialectic*, which he specifically terms as *dialectical process* as the basis of revolt:

---

35   Ibid., p. 14.

36   John Bancroft M.D., 'Social Changes: Fiftieth Anniversary Lecture on the Kinsey Institute Today', 24 October 1997, at the Indiana University Fine Arts Auditorium, in conjunction with the opening of the Institute's 50th Anniversary Exhibition, *The Art of Desire: Erotic Treasures from the Kinsey Institute*. http://www.kinseyinstitute.org/about/jb-50lecture.html.

As the prevailing sexual morality, by definition, demands conformity, so sexual non-conformity becomes a vehicle for dissent. And as human societies have become more complex, so have mechanisms of social dissent played a crucial role, often through a socially disturbing dialectical process, in the evolution of each society. ...[37]

Bancroft traced the rise of feminism, from the 1960s milieu of the New Left, back to this sexual dialectic, seeing in particular encouraging developments in Catholic societies where the sexual dialectic is making progress in swaying women away from tradition and towards demands for abortion. Bancroft sees the destruction of the traditional family and gender bonds — 'patriarchal society' — as the single most important factor in social evolution:

> Such changes were clearly instrumental in the impressive revival of feminist movements from the 1960s on, and in the 1980s onward, we see political consciousness spreading beyond educated, middle class women to women in general. **For example, the revolt among traditionally faithful women in Roman Catholic countries against unpopular doctrines such as the restrictions on divorce and abortion.** This growing demand by women to improve their rights and to have control over their reproductive lives is now strong worldwide, but still with a fair way to go. The entrenched power structures of patriarchies will not respond readily. Yet I would venture to suggest that no single factor is more important for the further development and improvement of human society than the fundamental issue of establishing the proper relationship between men and women.[38]

While Bancroft stated that 'the revolt among traditionally faithful women in Roman Catholic countries against unpopular doctrines such as the restrictions on divorce and abortion' is a revolutionary act of the utmost significance, it is also an area where the oligarchy has focused its funding. To Catholic states we can add Muslim states and Orthodox Christian Russia, where feminism and 'gender fluidity' are primary means of subverting states targeted for 'regime change'.

---

37 Ibid., 'Social Changes'.
38 Ibid. Emphasis added.

Bancroft acclaimed the rise of the 'youth sub-culture' beginning in the 1960s, again reflecting a sexual dialectic that turned revolutionary, disrupted the bonds of parent and child, and destroyed the traditional authority and respect for parents, from which emerged 'generational struggle' that replaced the previous 'class struggle' of the Old Left. From this youth alienation emerged the New Left based on drugs, sex and music, which all became lucrative commodities, about which Bancroft is aware. Bancroft lauded this as 'social liberation', yet he also described it as creating a 'youth culture' that has a 'major commercial impact'. Bancroft noted the international character of this commercial youth culture as crossing traditional cultural barriers. It can be quite readily seen that this revolutionary sexual dialectic created youth as a new consuming class, as well as forming another front for the assault on tradition:

> …And if we see many of these changes as reflecting a crisis in the relations between the sexes, even more dramatic and revolutionary was the rise of a powerful youth culture, reflecting a profound change in the relations between the generations. We have youth as a self-conscious group, stretching from puberty to the middle twenties, with puberty itself being several years earlier than had been the case in earlier generations. In the 1960s, the political impact of this youth culture was a force to be reckoned with.

> **This new autonomy of youth as a separate social stratum reverberated with the golden years of capitalism, and the increasing earning potential of many young people, to produce a youth culture with major commercial impact**. Music and fashion were perhaps its most commercial manifestations. And the autonomy of this youth culture, and its distancing from the conventions of adulthood, was **all the more dramatic because of the international nature of this movement. The music, the dress, the political ideals crossed long established cultural and language barriers with extraordinary ease,** aided by the miracles of modern information technology, themselves very much the domain of the young.

> The personal liberation of the young from the constraints of their elders became mobilized into social liberation. And inevitably, the most obvious vehicles for liberation were sex and drugs. The rejection of conventional

constraints as part of this youth culture became expressed in an openness to the pursuit of sexual pleasure which probably had no parallel, at least in recent history. The historian, Eric Hobsbawm, has described this cultural revolution as 'the triumph of the individual over society'.[39]

'The rejection of conventional constraints of their elders' and 'the triumph of the individual over society' are precisely what Fromm meant by the elimination of the 'primary ties' as the necessary prelude to self-actualisation. It is notable that Bancroft associated 'cultural revolution' with international commerce, with 'globalisation' requiring the elimination of 'long established cultural and language barriers'.

In relation to this new youth culture of sex, drugs and music, one is reminded of Huxley's *Brave New World* where servitude is accepted in blissful ignorance.[40] In many ways, Huxley is more prescient than Orwell; and his *Brave New World* is centred largely on control mechanisms which are very similar to the sexology of the post-Freudians. Huxley could discern the emergence of a post-Freudian-Marxian synthesis that would be a useful means of social control. In *Brave New World,* Huxley writes of the attitude towards family induced by what he calls the 'World Controllers':

> Our Freud has been the first to reveal the appalling dangers of family life. The world was full of fathers — was therefore full of misery; full of mothers — therefore of every kind of perversion from sadism to chastity, full of brothers, sisters, uncles, aunts — full of madness and suicide.[41]

A 'Controller' states: 'Mother, monogamy, romance. High spurts the fountain; fierce and foamy the wild jet. The urge has but a single outlet. My love, my baby. No wonder those poor pre-moderns were mad and wicked and miserable.'[42] In Huxley's dystopia, where the individual has reached the bliss of obliteration in a collective nirvana, a narcotic,

---

39 John Bancroft M.D., 'Social Changes'. Emphasis added.
40 Aldous Huxley, *Brave New World.*
41 Ibid., p. 52.
42 Ibid., pp. 53–54.

which Huxley calls 'soma', combined with ritualised, sterile sex, keeps the masses in contended servitude.

Aldous Huxley's *Brave New World* is close to the ideology that his brother Julian Huxley, a notable Darwinian biologist, advocated for the world in his role as founding director-general of UNESCO.[43]

Bancroft continued:

> There will be no simple solution; but in searching for solutions we need to understand better the impact of these huge social changes before we can hope to influence their consequences. **And maybe the key will lie in this shift from the family and community to the individual.** How can we instil the sense of responsibility about sexual behaviour in the individual, which was previously defined and reinforced by the family and community? This, I believe, is particularly germane to our approach to the sexuality of the adolescent.[44]

The aims of Kinseyan sexology and of Critical Theory are the same.

The Rockefeller Foundation, in assessing the role of Kinsey, and taking credit for funding him, commented: 'Ultimately, the work transformed American society by challenging American perceptions and attitudes toward sex'.[45]

Judge Morris Ploscowe, an advocate for criminal law reform, premised his arguments on Kinsey, writing:

> [E]nforcement of the prohibitions of sex legislation [are a] failure, our sex crime legislation is completely out of touch with the realities of [life]. [T]he law attempts to forbid an activity which responds to a wide human need.... [N]o bar association, law school journal, or lawyers' committee can consider laws... on sexual matters without reference to the Kinsey study.

---

43 Julian Huxley's UNESCO doctrine is examined below.

44 Bancroft, 'Search for Solutions to Sexuality-Related Problems in Society Today'.

45 'Kinsey Reports', The Rockefeller Foundation; https://rockfound.rockarch.org/kinsey-reports. Emphasis added.

Kinsey's first volume ended an era.... [It is] the single greatest contribution of science to the ... law in my lifetime....[46]

Ploscowe became lead author of the law reform committee established by the American Law Institute (ALI) in collaboration with the American Bar Association, issuing a paper on criminal law reform known as the *American Law Institute's (ALI's) Model Penal Code (MPC) of 1955.* The ALI task force submitted a recommendation to the ALI Council in 1953–54. The recommendations called for the repeal of laws or lessening of penalties against 52 sex crimes.[47] Ploscowe had worked with the Columbia University Criminological Survey and went to Europe in 1931 as a fellow of the Social Science Research Council.[48]

Kinsey served as the scientific consultant for state commissions revising sex laws, such as the revision of sex laws in Illinois, New Jersey, New York, Delaware, Wyoming, and Oregon. States law journals cite the reliance on the Kinsey reports to advocate 'legalizing prostitution (Maine, 1976); harmlessness of boy prostitution (Duke University, 1960); lightening sex crime penalties (Ohio, 1959); legalizing homosexuality (South Dakota, 1968); the need for "beneficent concern for pedophiles" (Georgia, 1969); and for general sex law revisions (Oklahoma, 1970). The journals commonly cited the "fact" that 95% of males are sex offenders (Oregon, 1972); that young children are seducers (Missouri, 1973, Tennessee, 1965); and that judicial bias is the cause of "severe condemnation of sex offenders" (Pennsylvania, 1952).[49]

---

46 Ploscowe, cited by Philippa Davies & Shirley Richards, p. 14; http://www.drjudithreisman.com/archives/JM_20161210_Richards-Davies.pdf.

47 Philippa Davies & Shirley Richards, p. 14.

48 William M. Freeman, 'Ex-Magistrate Ploscowe Dies; Criminal-Law Expert Was 71', *The New York Times*, 22 September 1975.

49 American Legislative Exchange Council (ALEC), 'Restoring Legal Protections for Women and Children: A Historical Analysis of the States Criminal Codes', 2004, p. 10; cited by Shirley Richards and Philippa Davies, p. 14.

On the basis of the Kinsey reports there are still two primary issues that are yet to be resolved: the legalisation of paedophilia with toddlers, or perhaps younger, and of bestiality, both of which are, according to Kinsey, widespread, at least among Americans, apparently.

Wilhelm Reich's 'Sex-Pol'

... The most serious attempt to develop the critical social theory implicit in Freud was made in Wilhelm Reich's earlier writings. In his *Der Einbruch der Sexualmoral* (1931), Reich oriented psychoanalysis on the relation between the social and instinctual structures. ...

— HERBERT MARCUSE

W ILHELM REICH'S colleague and biographer Myron Sharaf states, 'Reich also anticipated many recent social developments'.[1] Reich was another of the post-Freudian Marxists who arose from the moral chaos of post-war Germany, although not part of the Frankfurt School. He sought to create a revolutionary organisation to propagate his views within Marxism.

During the late 1920s, Reich began what he called the 'sex-pol'[2] movement in Vienna. The aim was to use sexual issues 'within the framework of the larger revolutionary movement'. Towards this, Reich, then in Germany and a member of the Communist Party, initiated the formation of a Communist front, the German Association for Proletarian Sex-Politics (GAPSP), of which he was a director.[3] The programme Reich presented to GAPSP included aims that are now mainstream, including: free distribution of contraceptives, 'massive

---

1   Myran Sharaf, p. 4.
2   Ibid., pp. 129–144.
3   Ibid., p. 162.

propaganda for birth control', 'abolition of laws against abortion', 'provisions for free abortions at public clinics', 'abolition of any legal distinctions between the married and the unmarried', 'freedom of divorce', training of teachers and social workers as advocates of sex education, and 'treatment rather than punishment for sexual offenses'.[4]

Despite rivalry from Dr. Magnus Hirschfeld's World League for Sexual Reform, many German sexologists supported GAPSP, with representatives from eight organisations, representing 20,000 members, attending the first congress held in Düsseldorf in 1931. Shortly after, GAPSP had attained 40,000 members.[5]

However, Reich's 'sex pol' caused alarm within the Communist Party. This came to a head in 1932 when Reich addressed a youth conference in Dresden that issued a resolution 'strongly endorsing adolescent sexuality within the framework of the revolutionary movement'.[6] The Communist Party leaders disowned the resolution, stating that it would drag politics 'down to the level of the gutter'. Reich was accused by the party leaders of wanting to make 'fornication organizations out of our associations'.[7] Although Reich had a great deal of support within the party, the leadership prevailed against him in 1933, and he was expelled from the party.

Reich described his doctrine in *The Mass Psychology of Fascism*, which he had been preparing since before the war, and which found a ready audience during the war:

> Suppression of the natural sexuality in the child, particularly of its genital sexuality, makes the child apprehensive, shy, obedient, afraid of authority, good and adjusted in the authoritarian sense; it paralyzes the rebellious forces because any rebellion is laden with anxiety; it produces, by inhibiting sexual curiosity and sexual thinking in the child, a general inhibition of thinking and of critical faculties. In brief, the goal of sexual suppression is

---

4   Ibid., pp. 162–163.

5   Ibid., pp. 162–163.

6   Ibid., p. 169.

7   Wilhelm Reich, *The Mass Psychology of Fascism*, p. 25.

that of producing an individual who is adjusted to the authoritarian order and who will submit to it in spite of all misery and degradation. At first the child has to submit to the structure of the authoritarian miniature state, the family; this makes it capable of later subordination to the general authoritarian system. The formation of the authoritarian structure takes place through the anchoring of sexual inhibition and anxiety.[8]

The preliminary theories of Reich on 'sex economics' in *The Mass Psychology of Fascism* formed the basis of the later studies and conclusions of Adorno et al. in *The Authoritarian Personality*.

Reich considered Marxian economic reductionism too 'vulgar'. He said his theory of 'sex-economics is a method of research which developed over many years through the application of functionalism to human sex life and which has arrived at a series of new findings'.[9] It was Freud who had added to the insights of Marx with the discovery that man is 'governed by psychological processes which are unconscious'.[10] It is the sexual factor that is the critical element:

The second great discovery was that even the small child develops a lively sexuality, that, in other words, *sexuality* and *procreation* are not the same thing, and *sexual* and *genital* are not synonymous. The analysis of the psychological processes showed, furthermore, that sexuality, or, rather, its energy, the *libido,* which derives from bodily sources, is the central motor of psychic life. Biological factors and social conditions converge in psychic life.[11]

The third great discovery was the fact that infantile sexuality—which includes the most essential part of the child-parent relationship, the 'Oedipus complex' — is usually repressed because of fear of punishment for sexual thoughts and actions (basically, 'castration anxiety'). As a result, infantile sexuality becomes excluded from activity and disappears from conscious memory. The repression of infantile sexuality removes it from conscious

---

8   Ibid., p. 25.

9   Ibid., p. 20.

10   Ibid., p. 21.

11   Ibid.

control. This does not, however, deprive it of its strength; on the contrary, it intensifies it and thus enables it to manifest itself in various psychic disturbances. As this repression of infantile sexuality is the rule in 'civilized man,' Freud could rightly state that all humanity was his patient.[12]

The fourth important discovery was that human morality, far from being of supernatural origin, results from the suppressive measures of early infantile education, particularly those directed against sexuality. The original conflict between infantile desires and parental prohibitions lives on as an *internal* conflict between instinct and morals. The moral forces in the adult, which are themselves unconscious, act against the recognition of the laws of sexuality and of unconscious psychic life; they support sexual repression ('sex resistance') and explain the resistance of the world to the discovery of infantile sexuality.[13]

Hence, sexology takes on a revolutionary political rationale, with 'all humanity' as the patient, to be liberated from the repression of parents, tradition, religion, and civilisation. As with the Critical Theorists, Reich's insistence on the need to give the instinctual drives free reign was contrary to Freud's view that civilisation develops from the *sublimation* of the primal instincts.

Reich strikes at the family as the core, fundamental institution of authoritarian structures, and specifically 'patriarchal marriage and patriarchal family'.[14] From this springs repressive forms of religion and their church institutions, providing the sociological reason for the exploitation of work.[15] Hence the whole exploitive system of capitalism rests upon sexual repression starting in the patriarchal family. From the revolutionary viewpoint, '[s]exual inhibition alters the structure of the economically suppressed individual in such a manner that he thinks, feels and acts against his own material interests'.[16] The family

---

12   Ibid., p. 22.
13   Ibid.
14   Ibid., p. 24.
15   Ibid.
16   Ibid., p. 26.

is the 'central reactionary germ cell' of the authoritarian state: 'Since authoritarian society reproduces itself in the structure of the mass individual by means of the authoritarian family, it follows that political reaction must defend the authoritarian family as the basis "of the state, of culture and of civilization."'[17]

Where Bolshevism fell short in Russia was its failure to complete the sexual revolution, Reich's dictum being: 'No freedom program has any chance of success without an alteration of human sexual structure'.[18]

By 1942, writing the 'preface' to the third edition of *The Mass Psychology of Fascism*, Reich pointed out that although the book was written at a time when he was working with Communists and other Marxists and liberals, and utilised the terminology of Marxism for his 'sex-economics' theory, he now considered Marxism *passé*; albeit not rejecting Marxism *per se* but advocating a post-Marxist position. The post-Marxism that was now seen by Reich as championing the necessary synthesis was called 'work democracy' in Scandinavia, which retained 'the best and still valid sociological findings of Marxism'.[19] The sexual struggle had surpassed the class struggle, and psychoanalysis had become the post-Marxian revolutionary doctrine.[20]

By that time Reich had been decisively rejected by the Stalinists, and the USSR had repudiated the original Bolshevik measures in regard to the family and sexuality that Reich had lauded. He describes the resistance he received from the orthodox Marxists and Communists:

> I shall never forget the 'Red professor' from Moscow who was ordered to attend one of the lectures in Vienna in 1928, to advocate the 'party line' against me. Among other things, this professor declared that 'the Oedipus complex was all nonsense', such a thing did not exist. Fourteen years later

17 Ibid., p. 88.

18 Ibid., p. 213.

19 Ibid., xx.

20 Ibid., Preface (1942 ed.), xvi.

his Russian comrades bled to death under the tanks of the fuehrer-enslaved German machine-men.

One should certainly have expected parties claiming to fight for human freedom to be more than happy about the effects of my political and psychological work. As the archives of our Institute convincingly show, the exact opposite was the case. The greater the social effects of our work on mass psychology, the harsher were the countermeasures adopted by the party politicians. As early as 1929–30, Austrian Social Democrats barred the doors of their cultural organizations to the lecturers from our organization. In 1932, notwithstanding the strong protest of their members, the socialist as well as communist organizations prohibited the distribution of the publications of the 'Publishers for Sexual Politics', which was located in Berlin. I myself was warned that I would be shot as soon as the Marxists came to power in Germany. That same year the communist organizations in Germany closed the doors of their assembly halls to physicians advocating sex-economy. This too was done against the will of the organizations' members. I was expelled from both organizations on grounds that I had introduced sexology into sociology, and shown how it affects the formation of human structure. In the years between 1934 and 1937 it was always Communist party functionaries who warned fascist circles in Europe about the 'hazard' of sex-economy. This can be documentarily proven. Sex-economic publications were turned back at the Soviet Russian border, as were the throngs of refugees who were trying to save themselves from German fascism. There is no valid argument in justification of this.[21]

Leon Trotsky made the same criticism particularly regarding the revival of the family under Stalin, where previously there had been factory crèches and communal kitchens intended to replace the parent-child bond.[22] 'The valid argument in justification' was Stalin's rejection of the Bolshevik urge toward *Thanatos*, to use a Freudian term.[23]

Despite Reich's zealous pseudo-science regarding the healing properties of 'orgone energy', and his arrest by the federal government

---

21   Ibid.

22   Leon Trotsky, *The Revolution Betrayed*, Ch. VII.

23   Bolton, *Stalin: The Enduring Legacy*, passim.

for fraud in regard to the latter, he had a notable influence even in the medical profession, as his bizarre opinions and perceived 'martyrdom' appealed to the banal type of rebellion that was beginning to emerge. Psychoanalyst and neo-Marxist theorist Joel Kovel wrote that in the 1960s many medical students turned to Reichian 'orgonomy' and that reading Reich's *Function of the Orgasm* was a rite of passage. For these Reichians, 'society was regarded at most as an impediment to the full expression of the life force, or orgone'.[24]

---

24 Joel Kovel, 'From Reich to Marcuse', in Sohnya Sayres (ed.), p. 258.

Identity Politics

DOUGLAS MURRAY, author, journalist and associate editor of *The Spectator*, a 'gay'[1] conservative, traces the origins of *identity politics* in his informative book *The Madness of Crowds*. Murray cites the 'post-Marxists' Ernesto Laclau and Chantal Mouffe as providing one of the earliest foundations for *identity politics*.[2] Murray refers to their 1985 book *Hegemony and Socialist Strategy* where they wrote of the challenges to socialism by 'the emergence of new contradictions'. Orthodox Marxism being 'centred on the class struggle' and 'the contradictions of capitalism' had to be reappraised. Issues emerged that were not based on class struggle: 'women, national, racial and sexual minorities'.[3] Laclau and Mouffe had written in a preliminary article in 1981 that the enemy could no longer be defined by classical Marxist concepts on class; this had been superseded by power relationships that involve sexism, patriarchy and racism.[4]

Mouffe and the late Laclau are notable 'post-Marxists'. Their article for *Marxism Today* contained the primary elements of *identity politics*:

> Socialist political struggle takes place today on a terrain which has been profoundly transformed by the emergence of new contradictions, with

---

1   Murray delineates between being 'gay' and being 'queer' as one of numerous rivalries between the identities within 'identity politics'.

2   Douglas Murray, p. 55,

3   Ibid., p. 56, citing Laclau and Mouffe.

4   Cited by Murray, p. 57.

which the traditional discourse of Marxism, centered on the class strug-gle and the analysis of the economic contradictions of capitalism, has had great difficulties in coming to terms. To what extent has it become neces-sary to modify the notion of class struggle, in order to be able to deal with the new political subjects — women, national, racial and sexual minorities, anti-nuclear and anti-institutional movements etc — of a clearly anti-capitalist character, but whose identity is not constructed around specific 'class interests'?[5]

Gramscianism

The analysis is *neo-Gramscian*, after the Italian Communist Party theorist Antonio Gramsci, who has had a major influence on post-Marxist thinking, and underlines the purpose of *identity politics* as being that of cultural hegemony: 'The emergence of new contradic-tions in advanced capitalism requires that socialist forces develop the concept of hegemony even further than its formulation in Gramsci, in order to bring out all its theoretical and political effects.'[6] With a convoluted rhetorical flurry, such as only Marxist theorists can truly master, one of the more cogent paragraphs explains the *Gramscian* dialectic:

> It is Gramsci who elaborates this new conception of hegemony, drawing out all the potentialities present in Leninism. With Gramsci, in fact, hegemony is no longer conceived of as mere political leadership exercised over pre-constituted subjects, but as **'political, intellectual and moral leadership'** **through which new political subjects are to be created**. These subjects will express a national popular collective will resulting from the articula-tion by the working class of a **series of democratic popular demands cor-responding to contradictions which are not strictly class ones**.[7]

---

5   Ernesto Laclau and Chantal Mouffe, 'Socialist Strategy — Where Next?', *Marxism Today*, January 1981, pp. 17–22.

6   Ibid., p. 1.

7   Ibid., p. 4. Emphasis added.

Where the value of *Gramscianism* lays is in its multidirectional, metapolitical approach to undermining the System:

> This brings us to the notion of the *war of position*, a key concept in socialist strategy according to Gramsci and one which implies what one might term a **multidimensional conception of political radicalisation**. A conception of this kind goes against the traditional Marxist outlook — including Leninism — which was unidimensional insofar as it considered the political process and the revolutionary struggle as revolving around a single point: the seizure of power. Power was conceived of as a substance, having a source and a specific location within social relations — in the extreme case, as a building: the Winter Palace.[8] The Gramscian concept of war of position implies a rupture with such a conception, a rupture which finds its theoretical source in the notion of integral state. **For if the articulations of the social whole are political articulations, there is no level of society where power and forms of resistance are not exercised. Since these articulations do not come from a single and necessary source, there can be no absolute and essential location of power, but rather a multiplicity of dimensions and struggles, whose unity — or separation — are constantly being re-defined.**[9]

Here we see the strategic purpose of *identity politics* — a multidirectional undermining of the 'integral state'; the social community.[10] It is the means by which society is fractured by subverting and attacking

---

8   Reference to the attack on the Winter Palace during the 1917 Russian Revolution.

9   Ernesto Laclau and Chantal Mouffe, 'Socialist Strategy....', p. 20. Emphasis added.

10 Although capitalism can hardly be called an 'integral state' at any stage, its very existence on the ruins of the traditional hierarchical order means the transition from social community (*Gemeinschaft*) to civil society (*Gesellschaft*); from a community bound by ethos (expressed as the 'primary ties') to a collection of individuals bound contractually. Mouffe and Laclau seem to recognise this difference when they next use the term 'civil society' rather than referring again to the 'integral state'. It is because the state under capitalism is not 'integral' that revolt must be directed at many levels. The Communist revolutions in China and Russia occurred before those states had transitioned to bourgeois capitalism.

it at various levels, not just economically, as hitherto, but socially, culturally, intellectually, and morally. For this purpose, not only are the normal constituent parts of a society, such as class, age, gender and race, fractured, but even these fractures are divided as a social cancer on the *body politic*. Mouffe and Laclau refer to the constant re-definition and multiplication of 'struggles' and their role in 'separation' and 'unity' within the 'social whole'. This continual social fracturing is no less revolutionary than the Leninist conception of revolt against the central authority of the state. The aim is to destroy the social organism at all levels, as cancer destroys at a cellular level.

> **The achievement of socialism, therefore, does not arise from an absolute moment represented by a radical break consisting of the seizure of power.** It must instead be the result of a **series of partial ruptures through which the ensemble of relations of forces existing in a society will be transformed.** What is traditionally known as the seizure of power, that is, control over the state apparatuses, is in fact only one — albeit one of the most important — of the **many ruptures** in this process of transformation. It is, therefore, an error to present the *war of position* strategy as implying a reformist or social democratic position, opposed to another which would be revolutionary. The defence of a democratic socialism, then, has nothing to do with a necessary 'peaceful road' or a slow accumulation of reforms. What it refers to is a novel conception of the radicalisation and the politicisation of **social struggles**, one which **enlarges the field of confrontation and struggle to the whole of civil society.**

Proletariat Reductant as Revolutionary Factor

Laclau and Mouffe trace the change of direction of the Left towards *Gramcianism* at the rise of the New Left. It is here that the student movement, through the formation of the Students for a Democratic Society, aligned with the Black civil rights movement. Here we see the first two elements of *identity politics* emerge: age and race, to which feminism was added.[11] Laclau and Mouffe refer to 1968, the year of the worldwide New Left student riots as the start of 'new contradictions'.

> In fact, the antagonisms that became prominent in the late 1960s, and were to expand and acquire a dynamic of their own in the following decade, exhibit new and specific characteristics. These **new political subjects: women, students, young people, racial, sexual and regional minorities**, as well as the various anti-institutional and ecological struggles, not only **cannot be located at the level of relations of production** (though this is not in itself absolutely new, Gramsci and Togliatti[12] having already understood the importance of contradictions other than 'class' ones); on top of this, they **define their objectives in a radically different way**. Their enemy is defined **not by its function of exploitation, but by wielding a certain power**. And this power, too, does **not derive from a place in the relations of production**, but is the outcome of the form of **social organisation characteristic of the present society**. This society is indeed capitalist, but this is not its only characteristic; it is **sexist and patriarchal as well, not to mention racist**.[13]

The question arises as to why it is the oligarchy that has been encouraging and funding these constituent parts that today form the components of identity politics. What the post-Marxists call 'capitalism' is the remnant of middle class commerce that remains connected to the nation. To global capitalism, the phase of capitalism that Marx predicted as becoming international,[14] this smaller scale, nationally-based commerce is *passé*. What Marx saw as the bourgeoisie being 'its own gravedigger' through the revolutionary character of industrial expansion, has not seen 'the inevitable victory of the proletariat'[15] but a post-bourgeois class of capitalist, which has rendered the old

---

11   For an account of the rise of the New Left, along with Black civil rights and feminism see: Tom Hayden, *Reunion: A Memoir*.

12   Italian Communist Party leader.

13   Ernesto Laclau and Chantal Mouffe, 'Socialist Strategy…', p. 21. Emphasis added.

14   Karl Marx, *The Communist Manifesto*, 'Bourgeois and Proletarians'.

15   Ibid., p. 60.

proletariat as redundant as the old middle class. Marx came near to the reality when he stated that

> the lower middle class, the small manufacturer, the shopkeeper, the artisan, the peasant, all these fight against the bourgeoisie, to save from extinction their existence as fractions of the middle class. They are therefore not revolutionary but conservative. Nay, more they are reactionary, for they try to roll back the wheel of history. If by chance they are revolutionary, they are so only in view of their impending transfer to the proletariat, they thus defend not their present, but their future interests, they desert their own standpoint to place themselves at that of the proletariat'.[16]

Marx wrote that the remnants of the lower middle class were an impediment to the next phase of capitalism, that their resistance is 'reactionary'. This lower middle class would be destroyed or *proletarianised*. The destruction of this lower middle class remnant is sought by both the post-Marxist Left and the globalist elite. It is notable that the Critical Theorists regard the lower middle class as the fossilised remnant of the patriarchy and the authoritarian family. While the working class did not have sufficient inner resolve to resist, according to Fromm, 'the lower middle class has been an important factor in the rise of Nazism'.[17] For Wilhelm Reich, 'the National Socialist movement relied upon the broad layers of the so-called middle, i.e., the millions of private and public officials, middle-class merchants and owners and middle-class farmers. From the point of view of its social basis, National Socialism was a lower middle-class movement, and this was the case wherever it appeared, whether in Italy, Hungary, Argentina or Norway'.[18]

---

16   Ibid., p. 57.

17   Erich Fromm, *The Fear of Freedom*, 'Mechanisms of Escape', p. 159.

18   W. Reich, *The Mass Psychology of Fascism*, 'On the Mass Psychology of the Lower Middle Class'. The assumptions about the class basis of Fascism are incorrect. The membership of the Italian Fascist party in November 1921, about a year before the assumption to government, included 24.3% farmworkers, and 15.4% urban workers, at a time when urban workers constituted a minority of the

The *identity politics* discussed by Laclau and Mouffe in *Marxism Today* in 1981, and explicated as a book in 1985, emerged two decades previously from the Critical Theorists. Even prior to Marcuse, from the start of the Frankfurt Institute in Weimar Germany, the premises of the New Left and *identity politics* had been formulated.

Professor Howard J. Wiarda traces the term *identity politics* to the 1960s. He states that black, women's, gay and lesbian groups all claim 'original authorship'. During the 1960s and 1970s, there emerged in the USA and Europe large-scale movements, including black power, students, feminists, Greens, gays, sundry indigenous movements, and in the Third World women, indigenes, and peasants. 'Each group *identified* with its own individual cause'. In the 1990s, the word was used to 'apply to a broader array of interest groups', 'entered mainstream political discourse', and became the primary focus of the Left.[19]

Wiarda's placing the 1960s as the seminal year seems correct. We can be specific in tracing the origins to Marcuse, who referred to the coming of a 'New Left' when describing the identities referred to by Wiarda. It seems odd that Laclau and Mouffe make no reference to Marcuse in their 1981 article.

---

population. Manufacturers constituted 2.8% of the membership. R. De Felice, *Mussolini il fascista*, Vol. I, p. 6. In Germany, a 1935 census of party members showed that approximately 30% were manual workers, and 20% white-collar employees. Richard Overy, p. 233. In 1936, ex-Communist Party leader Jacques Doriot's *Parti Populaire Francaise* had a comparatively large membership of 100,000, 'many of whom were working class'. Anthony Adamthwaite, p. 167.

19   Howard J. Wiarda, p. 150.

Role of Marcuse

In *One-Dimensional Man,* Marcuse sought to extend the dialectical conflict to include 'the persecuted colored races, the inmates of prisons and mental institutions'.[20] In a 1967 lecture, the year prior to the world-wide New Left riots, Marcuse stated:

> But in the global framework the underprivileged who must bear the entire weight of the system really are the mass basis of the national liberation struggle against neo-colonialism in the third world and against colonialism in the United States. Here, too, there is no effective association between national and racial minorities in the metropoles of capitalist society and the masses in the neo-colonial world who are already engaged in struggle against this society. **These masses can perhaps now be considered the new proletariat and as such they are today a real danger for the world system of capitalism.** To what extent the working class in Europe can still or again be counted among these groups of underprivileged is a problem that we must discuss separately; I cannot do so in the framework of what I have to say here today, but I should like to point out a fundamental distinction. What we can say of the American working class is that in their great majority the workers are integrated into the system and do not want a radical transformation, we probably cannot or not yet say that of the European working class.[21]

What Marcuse, as with Hayden in *The Port Huron Statement,* was advocating was the mobilisation of anti-colonial forces among the Third World and ethnic minorities in the West. With the destruction of the old empires after the exhaustion of Europe following two world wars, it was the USA that was in a position to fill the void with its own neo-colonialism. Organisations such as the Peace Corps and USAID went

---

20   H. Marcuse, *One-Dimensional Man,* pp. 56–57.
     The latter idea found expression in Germany with the Socialist Patients' Collective, where the insane and their psychiatrists joined in socialist struggle against a society whose normality was said to be the real sickness. (See: Bolton, *The Psychotic Left,* pp. 224–234). The doctrine was a logical extension of Critical Theory, and was endorsed by an array of social scientists.

21   Herbert Marcuse, 'The Problem of Violence and the Radical Opposition' (1967).

in with their 'soft-sell' neo-colonialism of development aid, as part of
a global industrialisation process. As we have seen, an important role
was played by anthropologists and other social scientists in providing academic data on those societies that were to receive the blessings
of U.S. state and corporate largesse and loans from the international
banking system, in return for compliance and integration into the
world economy. The African-American Institute was established to
train a leadership cadre for post-colonial Africa, meaning 'neo-coloni-
al' Africa behind the façade of decolonisation and 'liberation'. Founded
in 1953 and mainly funded by the CIA,[22] the Rockefeller Foundation
started funding the AAI in 1972.[23] The Rockefeller Brothers Fund had
been supporting the AAI programme for sponsoring Africans to U.S.
universities since 1961,[24] where a pro-American generation could be
trained to assume control after the scuttling of the European colonies.

'The national liberation struggle against neo-colonialism in
the Third World' was generally the vanguard of Wall Street. The
Rockefeller, Ford and Carnegie Foundations, which had taken control
of the education systems of Africa and Asia even prior to the scuttling
of the European empires, had been preparing for decolonisation for
decades. The USA was ideally placed to posture as the big brother of
'national liberation', having been born from revolt against the British
Empire. The reasoning behind the 'considerable funding' by Ford,
Carnegie and Rockefeller 'for the expansion of educational institutions
in Africa, Asia, and [Latin] America' was that educational and cultural
funding was an important aspect of foreign policy. This was examined
by Philip Coombs (who had come from the Ford Foundation-created
Fund for the Advancement of Education in 1961 to become Kennedy's

---

22 Edward H. Berman, *The Ideology of Philanthropy* (Albany: State University of
    New York Press, 1983), p. 131.
23 The Rockefeller Foundation Annual Report (1972), pp. 71, 137.
24 Rockefeller Brothers Fund, 'African-American Institute 1961'; http://75.rbf.
    org/#!trigger=african-american-institute.

Assistant Secretary of State for Educational and Cultural Affairs) in his 1964 book *The Fourth Dimension of Foreign Policy*.[25]

Marcuse pre-empted Laclau and Moueffe by twenty years in stating that the working class was not going to become the agent for revolutionary change, and that disaffected elements that could not be integrated fully into Western society had to assume the role. These elements were the perpetual *outsiders,* as well as those who could be fractured from society: Blacks, Latinos, and even, as Marcuse and others of the Left advocated, lunatics and criminals, and contrived identities based on gender (feminism, homosexuals) and age (students, Yippies, hippies, drop-outs, and addicts in *Oedipal* revolt).

> But the struggle for the solution has outgrown the traditional forms. The totalitarian tendencies of the one-dimensional society render the traditional ways and means of protest ineffective—perhaps even dangerous because they preserve the illusion of popular sovereignty. This illusion contains some truth: 'the people,' previously the ferment of social change, have 'moved up' to become the ferment of social cohesion. Here rather than in the redistribution of wealth and equalization of classes is the new stratification characteristic of advanced industrial society. However, underneath the conservative popular base is the **substratum of the outcasts and outsiders, the exploited and persecuted of other races and other colors, the unemployed and the unemployable**. They exist outside the democratic process; their life is the most immediate and the most real need for ending intolerable conditions and institutions.[26]

Marcuse saw in conventionally non-political social outcasts the potential for disruption. Their mere existence is disruption: hence they are 'revolutionary even if their consciousness is not'; they are an 'elementary force'. This is the element that Marx called the *lumpenproletariat*. Unlike Marx, Marcuse saw their use, as it manifests in periods of social breakdown as random violence, vandalism, and looting. A particularly extreme example of this was the widespread rioting in

25   Edward H. Berman, p. 12.
26   Marcuse, *One-Dimensional Man*, pp. 260–261. Emphasis added.

Britain in 2011 after police shot the drug dealer Mark Duggan, who was then glorified by the Left,[27] reminiscent of the 1960s 'Days of Rage' in Chicago, and the rioting and looting that periodically spills over from U.S. ghetto districts. The Left seeks to politicise such sociopathy. Marcuse wrote:

> **Thus their opposition is revolutionary even if their consciousness is not.** Their opposition hits the system from without and is therefore not deflected by the system; it is an elementary force which violates the rules of the game and, in doing so, reveals it as a rigged game. When they get together and go out into the streets, without arms, without protection, in order to ask for the most primitive civil rights, they know that they face dogs, stones, and bombs, jail, concentration camps, even death. Their force is behind every political demonstration for the victims of law and order. The fact that they start refusing to play the game may be the fact which marks the beginning of the end of a period. Nothing indicates that it will be a good end. **The economic and technical capabilities of the established societies are sufficiently vast to allow for adjustments and concessions to the underdog**, and their armed forces sufficiently trained and equipped to take care of emergency situations. However, **the spectre is there again, inside and outside the frontiers of the advanced societies.**[28]

Marcuse imagined a nihilistic revolution that could not be 'deflected'. He alluded to a contradiction, however, in stating that 'the economic and technical capabilities of the established societies are sufficiently vast to allow for adjustments and concessions...' So far from the up-heavals resulting in the displacement of the actual power structure in late capitalist societies, comparatively radical changes could be justified to ward off the threat of total social breakdown. These changes are enacted in the name of 'human rights' and 'equality'.

Marcuse approaches the reality of the dialectic: '... But the chance is that, in this period, **the historical extremes may meet again: the most advanced consciousness of humanity, and its most exploited**

---

27 Bolton, *The Psychotic Left*, pp. 236–239.

28 Marcuse, *One-Dimensional Man*, Emphasis added.

force. ...'[29] Those who constitute this 'most advanced consciousness of humanity' are identified by Marcuse in the preface to the 1966 edition of *Eros and Civilization*. Reiterating that the working class had become *passé* as a revolutionary force, in obliterating the vestiges of the lower middle class he stated that the revolutionary role would be assumed by the technocratic bourgeoisie, along with youth:

> To the degree to which organized labor operates in defense of the status quo, and to the degree to which the share of labor in the material process of production declines, *intellectual* skills and capabilities become social and political factors. Today, the organized refusal to cooperate of the **scientists, mathematicians, technicians, industrial psychologists and public opinion pollsters** may well accomplish what a strike, even a large-scale strike, can no longer accomplish but once accomplished, namely, the beginning of the reversal, the preparation of the ground for political action. That the idea appears utterly unrealistic does not reduce the political responsibility involved in the position and **function of the intellectual** in contemporary industrial society. **The intellectual refusal may find support in another catalyst, the instinctual refusal among the youth in protest.** It is their lives which are at stake, and if not their lives, their mental health and their capacity to function as unmutilated humans. ...[30]

The functionaries of the *brave new world* will be drawn from industrial psychologists and public opinion pollsters among others, riotous youth in alliance with social outcasts having provided the tension from below to justify the imposition of a *revolution from above*. One might wonder what type of utopia Marcuse envisaged that drew its functionaries from 'scientists, mathematicians, technicians, industrial psychologists and public opinion pollsters', having also stated that in such a society dissident opinions would be suppressed in the name of 'repressive tolerance'. It is a technocratic, elitist society of the type social scientists have been advocating since the days of the Rockefeller sponsorship of Charles Merriam.

---

29   Ibid. Emphasis added.

30   Marcuse, *Eros and Civilization*, 'Political Preface'. Emphasis added.

Reconstructing Genders

It is my contention that this threat of revolutionary change in our sexual mores and customs has been ushered in by a singular act of considerable consequence: the removal of homosexuality from the category of aberrancy by the American Psychiatric Association.

— DR. CHARLES SOCARIDES

THE LEFT TOOK A LONG time to find that it had a 'gay' agenda. Karl Marx and Friedrich Engels had ridiculed the acceptance of homosexuality. Writing to Marx, Engels referred to a network of pederasts among politicians, and in so doing widened the disgust to include sodomites in general:

The *Urning*[1] you sent me is a very curious thing. These are extremely un-natural revelations. The paederasts are beginning to count themselves, and discover that they are a power in the state. Only organisation was lacking, but according to this source it apparently already exists in secret. And since they have such important men in all the old parties and even in the new ones, from Rosing to Schweitzer, they cannot fail to triumph. *Guerre aux cons, paix aux trous-de-cul* [2] will now be the slogan. It is a bit of luck that we, personally, are too old to have to fear that, when this party wins, we shall have to pay physical tribute to the victors. But the younger generation! Incidentally it is only in Germany that a fellow like this can possibly come forward, convert this smut into a theory, and offer the

---

1   *Urning*, a 19th century German term for homosexual.
2   'War with the cunts, peace with the arse-holes'.

invitation: *introite*[3] etc. Unfortunately, he has not yet got up the courage to acknowledge publicly that he is 'that way', and must still operate *coram publico* 'from the front', if not 'going in from the front' as he once said by mistake. But just wait until the new North German Penal Code recognises the *droits du cul*[4] then he will operate quite differently. Then things will go badly enough for poor frontside people like us, with our childish penchant for females.[5]

While commenting on the importance of women in a revolutionary movement Marx made a quip that would today be regarded by feminists as the 'objectification of women', and if *Herr Doktor* had been teaching at a university, he would certainly have been subjected to feminist histrionics and termination of employment:

> Everyone who knows anything of history also knows that great social revolutions are impossible without the feminine ferment. Social progress may be measured precisely by the social position of the fair sex (plain ones included).[6]

Had Marx been confronted with transgender and a multitude of other derivatives, he would have found the whole idea amusing, but perhaps with not so much mirth had he seen them taking over the 'workers' movement' until few of the proletariat remained. However, the *raison d'etre* of Critical Theory had become the revision of Marxism and its synthesis with a revision of Freudianism to arrive at a new revolutionary theory.

Freud was ambivalent towards homosexuality, but did consider it to be a maladjustment to childhood circumstances, caused by 'an arrest in sexual development', which should not, however, be a source

---

3   Enter.

4   'Rights of the arse-hole'.

5   Engels to Marx, 22 June 1869; *Marx & Engels Collected Works, Letters 1868–70*, Volume 43, pp. 295–296; http://www.koorosh-modaresi.com/MarxEngels/V43.pdf.

6   Marx to Ludwig Kugelmann, 12 December 1868, *Marx & Engels Collected Works*, p. 185.

of distress or shame.[7] Freud regarded homosexuality as a 'perversion', insofar as it was outside the norm of sexual behaviour, the norm being predicated on the drive to reproduce. Freud's views would be today considered 'reactionary' and 'authoritarian' and are not the type to be cited by the apologists of 'homosexuality' as part of a fluid range of sexual experience, such as Kinsey concluded. Freud wrote from a moral perspective:

> What are known as the perverse forms of intercourse ... in which other parts of the body take over the role of the genitals, have undoubtedly increased in social importance. These activities cannot, however, be regarded as being as harmless as analogous extensions [of the sexual drive] in love relationships. They are ethically objectionable, for they degrade the relationships of love between two human beings from a serious matter to a convenient game, attended by no risk and no spiritual participation.[8]

It is notable that over a hundred years ago Freud was referring to homosexuality as an issue that had 'increased in social importance', that from a social viewpoint homosexuality is not 'harmless', and that it degrades the relationships 'from a serious matter to a convenient game'. This casual sexuality is what the Critical Theorists, along with sexologists such as Kinsey and anthropologists such as Mead, were trying to popularise against what they regarded as the repressive strictures of Western society. Tracing the root of homosexuality from within the family, Feud wrote that,

> In all our male homosexual cases the subjects had had a very intense erotic attachment to a female person, as a rule their mother. ... This attachment was evoked or encouraged by too much tenderness on the part of the mother herself, and further reinforced by the small part played by the

---

7   Freud, Letter to an American Mother, 22 December 1949; 'Historical Notes: A Letter from Freud', in: *The American Journal of Psychiatry*, Vol. 107, No. 10, April 1951, pp. 786–78.

8   Freud, 'Civilized Sexual Morality and Modern Nervous Illness', in J. Strachey (ed., trans.), *The Standard Edition of the Complete Psychological Works of Sigmund Freud*, Vol. 9, pp. 26–27.

father during their childhood. Indeed, it almost seems as though the presence of a strong father would ensure that the son made the correct decision in his choice of object, namely someone of the opposite sex.[9]

It is notable that Freud's conclusions are antithetical to those of the Critical Theorists insofar as he states that the patriarchal family is the type conducive to normality.

Freud considered that there was a narcissistic component in homosexuality. Given that the modern epoch is focused on the individual as an isolated being urged to deconstruct and reconstruct the self on the basis of a fad, a whim, or a trend, such sexual-narcissism amounts to perhaps the ultimate expression of self-obsession. Freud wrote of the narcissistic component:

> We have discovered, especially clearly in people whose libidinal development has suffered some disturbance, such as perverts and homosexuals, that in their later choice of love-objects they have taken as a model not their mother but their own selves. They are plainly seeking themselves as a love-object, and are exhibiting a type of object-choice which must be termed 'narcissistic'. In this observation we have the strongest of the reasons which have led us to adopt the hypothesis of narcissism.[10]

The groundwork for 'gender fluidity' had been prepared with theories on *sexual variations* by a new generation of psychiatrists and anthropologists, particularly in the aftermath of World War I. Margaret Mead had described casual and temporary homosexual relations among adolescents in Samoa, calling this 'play' and a matter of indifference to Samoans.[11] Indeed, as we have seen, Mead, who had a

---

9   Freud, 'Leonardo da Vinci and a Memory of His Childhood', in J. Strachey (ed., trans.), *The Standard Edition of the Complete Psychological Works of Sigmund Freud* (London: Hogarth Press, 1932 [1910]), (Original work published in 1910), Vol. 11, p. 99.

10   Freud, 'On Narcissism: An Introduction', in J. Strachey (ed., trans.), *The Standard Edition of the Complete Psychological Works of Sigmund Freud* (London: Hogarth Press, 1957 [1914]) Vol. 14, p. 88.

11   Mead, *The Coming of Age in Samoa*, pp. 149, 223.

relationship with her mentor Ruth Benedict, recommended the West adopt a casual attitude towards family and marriage devoid of deep feeling, claiming this is the lesson to be had from 'primitive society', and would avoid neurosis.

Marcuse wrote of the 'fusion of political rebellion and sexual-moral rebellion which is an important factor in the opposition in America'.[12] While 'gender fluidity' has become a recent fad, this was premised in 1948 by 'The Kinsey Scale', a survey undertaken by Alfred Kinsey's sexology institute. At that time, however, there was only a scale that ran from exclusively heterosexual (0) through to exclusively homosexual (6).[13]

Magnus Hirschfeld: Father of Transvestism and Transgenderism

'Gender reassignment' was pioneered by Dr. Magnus Hirschfeld, himself homosexual, whose sexology emerged, like Wilhelm Reich's, in the moral, social and economic collapse of Germany following World War I. Weimar Germany became the centre for social experimentation. 'Sexual science' had its antecedents in the Scientific Humanitarian Committee founded in 1897,[14] and the Institute for Sexual Science founded in 1919. Both organisations were headed by Hirschfeld, who edited *The Year-Book for Sexual Intermediate Stages*. Hirschfeld organised the First Congress of Sexual Reform in 1921, from which emerged the World League for Sexual Reform.[15]

Initially Hirschfeld considered homosexuals as the 'third sex'. However, he developed the theory of *sexual intermediaries*, which held that there are many naturally occurring sexual variations, including hermaphroditism, homosexuality, and transvestism. Hirschfeld is

---

12   Marcuse, 'The Problem of Violence...'

13   Kinsey et al., *Sexual Behavior in the Human Male*, p. 638.

14   The first advocacy group for homosexuals.

15   Magnus-Hirschfeld-Gesellschaft, http://me.in-berlin.de/~magnus/institut/en/reform/reform_02.html.

regarded as having coined *transvestite*. He published a book entitled *The Transvestites* in 1910.

The first complete male-to-female sexual reassignment operation was undertaken in 1931 on Hirschfeld's recommendation, by two of his co-workers at the institute, Dr. Levy-Lenz, and Dr. Felix Abraham. The patient, Rudolph Richter, adopting the female first name Dora, had been castrated at his request in 1922, and lived and worked at Hirschfeld's institute for more than 10 years as a housemaid.[16]

Hirschfeld was a 'socialist'[17] but he and Wilhelm Reich were in opposition. Reich was not as 'liberal' as Hirschfeld, in that Reich did not consider all forms of sexuality equally valid. Among the three founders of the Hirschfeld Institute was Arthur Kronfeld, also described as a 'socialist', a psychiatrist and psychotherapist, who with his wife committed suicide in the USSR in 1941[18] (perhaps encouraged to do so by the Soviet authorities?).

Despite Reich's rejection by the party, Hirschfeld had important support from Willi Münzenberg, a millionaire newspaper, book and magazine publisher and influential Communist.[19] Münzenberg joined the Communist Party in 1919, was elected to the Central Committee in 1924, served as a Communist Deputy in the Reichstag, as General Secretary of the Comintern Front, Workers' International Relief, and was a pivotal influence in the League Against Imperialism. The Hirschfeld Institute states that Münzenberg was 'an influential

---

16 Magnus-Hirschfeld-Gesellschaft, 'Rudolph Richter', https://www.hirschfeld.in-berlin.de/institut/en/personen/pers_34.html.

17 Magnus-Hirschfeld-Gesellschaft, 'Founders of the Institute: Magnus Hirschfeld', https://www.hirschfeld.in-berlin.de/institut/en/personen/pers_01.html.

18 Magnus-Hirschfeld-Gesellschaft, 'Founders of the Institute: Arthur Kronfeld', https://www.hirschfeld.in-berlin.de/institut/en/personen/pers_02.html.

19 Münzenberg was closely associated with Olof Aschberg, founder of the Nye Banken, Stockholm, who had wide connections with international finance. He facilitated funds for the Bolsheviks and other Marxist causes. Aschberg's townhouse in Paris was used by Münzenberg for meetings with Communist operatives. Sean McMeekin, pp. 135, 138, 296, 297, 301.

proprietor and publisher of several newspapers ... for which institute staff members wrote articles. He thus gave them access to the
Left-wing press'. Münzenberg lived with his wife Babette Gross at
Hirschfeld's Institute, where his flat was used for secret meetings of
the Comintern.[20]

Hirschfeld's books today have familiar themes: *The Homosexual
Question as Judged by Our Contemporaries*; *What Ought the Public
Know about the Third Sex*; *Sexual Transitions*; *The Erotic Impulse to
Wear Other Dress*; *The Homosexuality of Man and Woman*; *Sexology*;
A History of the Morals of the World War. With the rise of Hitler in
1933, Hirschfeld found ready fame outside Germany. His books were
published in the USA, France, and England in 1935.

Hirschfeld is widely honoured, and has a notable influence on
transgender politics. In 2011, the German government, through
the Ministry of Justice, established the Federal Foundation Magnus
Hirschfeld (*Bundesstiftung Magnus Hirschfeld*; BMH). The objectives
are

> to promote educational and research projects and to counter social dis-
> crimination against lesbians, gays, bisexuals, transsexuals, transgenders,
> intersexuals and queers (abbreviation: LGBTTIQ) in Germany. The
> Foundation wants to promote the acceptance of people with a non-hetero-
> sexual orientation in society as a whole; the same applies to people who do
> not define themselves exclusively as men or women.[21]

The Foundation states that it 'builds on the legacy of Dr. Magnus
Hirschfeld's Institute for Sexual Science networking [for] joint research activities with scientists and universities in Germany and
abroad'. The purpose of the Foundation is to integrate gender fluidity

---

20 Magnus-Hirschfeld-Gesellschaft, 'Willi Münzenberg', https://www.hirschfeld.
    in-berlin.de/institut/en/personen/pers_40.html.
    In 1936, Münzenberg was expelled from the Communist Party for his criticism
    of Stalinism and the Soviet purges of the old Bolsheviks.
21 Federal Foundation Magnus Hirschfeld, 'Objectives', https://mh-stiftung.de/
    ueber-die-stiftung/.

into the economy and society by social engineering techniques to promote 'the beneficial nature of recognizing diversity for economic, political, social and cultural contexts. ...'[22]

The Establishment with its corporate sponsors is attempting to construct a broad front combining transgenderism with ethnic, social, generational and religious discontent; called *'intersectionality'*. This is the united front of a 'New Left' that Marcuse urged in the 1960s, again being cultivated by the 'Establishment'. The Foundation states of this:

> *Intersectionality* Research into the interaction of identity-generating categories like especially gender / gender identity, sexual orientation, social, ethnic and religious affiliation, age and disability and the processes of stereotyping and **ideological fading in and out of such** categories.[23]

The aim is stated as promoting 'identity-generating' mechanisms. Thus the individual can be deconstructed and reconstructed, premised on what the Foundation terms the 'ideological fading in and out of such categories'. You are enabled to 'ideologically fade in and out' of your gender, race, nationality, and perhaps best of all, presumably your age and disability. Perhaps this means that additional to gender reassignment, race reassignment via hair and skin re-colouring will be enabled, plus age reassignment through more convincing methods of Botox, and disability by means of organ and robotic limb transplants, as part of the process of *transhumanism*. With dual gender and race reassignments, White males could end self-guilt regarding both patriarchy and 'White privilege'.

You can be precisely what you want to be at any given time, or more probably what you are told you want to be by human relations 'mediators' and 'facilitators', psychiatrists, counsellors; media, advertising, and entertainment industries. There can be no sense of permanence and duration, but rather a perpetual state of fluidity. In the name of 'identity', any type of *organic identity* is destroyed, until

---

22   Ibid.

23   Ibid. Emphasis added.

everyone becomes as nebulous as to slot into an amorphous mass 'humanity' according to the requirements of social engineering and social control.

The indoctrination programme formulated by the Hirschfeld Foundation includes youth, teachers, 'opinion leaders', social workers, inducted into the universal cult through training seminars, 'mediation of best practise models', 'school education projects', and the 'diversity departments' of companies and professional associations. The Foundation outlines its outreach:

> Encouraging media coverage of the Foundation's work, production or commissioning of its own media (e.g. new media, live streams), communication of the results of the Foundation's work through funding and publication of monographs, anthologies, manuals, overviews, art projects — especially regarding funded educational work and educational networking, research and science networking, of knowledge about the situation of LGBTTI mainly since the middle of the nineteen hundreds to the present day, joint events with universities, educational and research institutions, joint events with companies and associations (e.g. LGBTTI company networks, diversity departments, training managers), promoting access to archives and the results of educational work, science and research, promotion and curation of exhibitions, actions with partners, e.g. in schools, universities, adult education institutions, companies, associations, scientific and social networks and discussion forums, information and education campaigns, and memorial days...[24]

The heralding of Hirschfeld as the proud father of the 'gay' movement is enabled by the obsessional self-guilt of Germans in regard to the Third Reich. The Hirschfeld Institute was closed down shortly after the assumption of the National Socialists to government, and Hirschfeld's

---

24 'Grundzüge des Forschungs- und Bildungsprogramms einschließlich der Grundzüge der Vergabe der Stiftungsmittel für Forschungsaufträge und Bildungsarbeit der Bundesstiftung Magnus Hirschfeld' (Basics of the research and education program including the fundamentals of the allocation of foundation funds for research contracts and educational work, Federal Foundation Magnus Hirschfeld, Board of Trustees, Berlin, 27 February 2012), p. 6.

books were among those consigned to the symbolic bonfires. Like the Critical Theorists, Hirschfeld gained recognition outside Germany after 1933. His anti-Nazi credentials as Jewish, socialist and homosexual place him in a pantheon of post-war sainthood.

In the USA, the medical operations and promotion of transgenderism were continued by Dr. Harry Benjamin, who had studied at the Hirschfeld Institute.[25] Among Benjamin's associates in the USA were Alfred Kinsey, and the 'family planning' pioneer Margaret Sanger.

In 1957, Benjamin co-founded the Society for the Scientific Study of Sexuality. In 1966, he published *The Transsexual Phenomenon*, based on his work with clients. He argued for the differentiation between transsexuals, transvestites and homosexuals. In *The Transsexual Phenomenon*, Benjamin also challenged the dominant view that transsexuality could be treated psychologically, stating that this repressed rather than eliminated the drive. Benjamin advocated that transsexuals be given surgery and hormones for the sex they wished to become; the now dominant belief that there is a separation between body and mind that results in transsexuality. During the 1970s, Benjamin formed what became the Harry Benjamin International Gender Dysphoria Association (HBIGDA), composed of therapists and psychologists. In 2007 HBIGDA became the World Professional Association for Transgender Health (WPATH).[26]

Hirschfeld is today honoured by Establishment-sponsored events. Germany officially designated 2018–2019 the years to commemorate Hirschfeld, 2018 being the 150th anniversary of his birth, and 2019 the 100th anniversary of the founding of the Institute of Sexual Science. On 12 July 2018 a postage stamp was issued in his honour.

---

25   Farah Naz Khan, 'A History of Transgender Health Care', *Scientific American*, 16 November 2016, https://blogs.scientificamerican.com/guest-blog/a-history-of-transgender-health-care/.

26   Charles W. Socarides, 'Sexual Politics and Scientific Logic: The Issue of Homosexuality', *The Journal of Psychohistory*, Vol. 19, No. 3, Winter 1992; http://www.geocities.ws/kidhistory/homopolo.htm.

House of World Cultures: Cold War Origins

The House of World Cultures (*Haus der Kulturen der Welt*; HKW) stands on part of the former site of Hirschfeld's institute, a factor that the HKW emphasises. The HKW focus is on cultural globalisation, drawing on *intersectionality* to connect its aims to those of Hirschfeld. HKW has named a room in his honour, and,

> HKW also makes Hirschfeld's geographical and historical heritage visible in its projects by taking up various activist ideas and approaches of the sexologist. In its program, HKW campaigns for the visibility of different lifeworlds and draws attention to marginalization processes. In addition, HKW aims to offer a platform for partner events dealing with queer and non-normative lifeworlds, such as the international LGBTIQ conference. Since 1992, HKW has also tackled the debate[27] over Hirschfeld's scientific heritage and the history of the sexual sciences.[28]

HKW, in addition to showcasing the grandeur of 'non-European' arts, confronts Europe's colonial past. Loss of control and the alienation being caused by elements of globalisation, such a digitalisation, is resulting in support for 'neo-nationalist parties', which HKW states must be thwarted by 'solidarity' with groups and individuals. 'New forms of resistance and alternative models of thought and life are needed. HKW would like to contribute to them.'[29]

HKW is part of what is a familiar theme. It aims to initiate 'new forms of resistance' against the ill-effects of globalisation, yet exists to promote the globalisations of culture, and moreover to play an active part in opposing those movements that truly are trying to offer new forms of resistance to globalisation; what it terms the 'neo-nationalist parties'. What is significant is that the origins of the HKW — as with

---

27 Hirschfeld's support for eugenics — widespread among the Left at the time — becomes problematic for the present-day Left.

28 HKW, 'Magnus Hirschfeld and HKW', https://www.hkw.de/en/hkw/geschichte/ort_geschichte/magnus_hirschfeld.php.

29 HKW, 'HKW is Turning 30', https://www.hkw.de/en/hkw/geschichte/bernd_scherer_zum_30_jubilaeum.php.

much else we have been considering—has its origins as part of U.S. Cold War strategy:

> The square was destroyed during the Second World War. In 1957, **at the height of the Cold War, the Congress Hall** was erected near to the Reichstag. **The building was a present from the US government to the City of Berlin. As a venue for international encounters, the Congress Hall was designed as a symbol of 'freedom' in the 'island city' of Berlin.**[30]

The intention was to serve as a propaganda icon against the Soviet bloc, the aim being to showcase the artistic wonders that are possible under American liberal democracy. This is openly stated:

> In 1955, Hugh Stubbins started work on a design for a building that would soon become a remarkable landmark in the cityscape of post-war Berlin. Stubbins, who had been Gropius's assistant at Harvard before the Second World War, was familiar with Germany. Wanting to make a statement on that conflict between the systems commonly referred to the Cold War, Stubbins planned a building with a hall to hold cultural events and congresses. It was intended to serve as a symbol and beacon of freedom with its message reaching the East too. The former Zeltenplatz square was chosen as the site. To ensure its contours would be clearly seen from 'Communist-ruled' East Berlin, the Congress Hall was erected on an artificial mound.[31]

The architect Stubbins designed a modernist building consciously intended to confront 'socialist realism'. According to Stubbins, speaking at the opening, to which he paid particular tribute to Mrs. Eleanor Dulles (sister of John Foster Dulles, Secretary of State; and Allen Dulles, CIA Director) of the U.S. State Department, 'This hall is dedicated to one of the great freedoms—the freedom of expression. Its form was inspired by an attempt to express that great purpose. In this sense, the form is a symbol'.[32]

---

30 HKW, 'The Site and Its History', https://www.hkw.de/en/hkw/geschichte/ort_geschichte/ort.php.

31 HKW, 'Architecture', https://www.hkw.de/en/hkw/gebauede/gebaeude.php.

32 Ibid.

Gate-Crashing the APA

The watershed moment for the deconstruction of the male-female pair-bond came in 1973 when homosexuality was declassified as a disease by the American Psychiatric Association (APA). Until then, homosexuality had been classified by the APA as a 'sociopathic personality disturbance'. The change of classification was ideologically driven. A particularly cogent description of the process of declassification was given by the widely experienced and acclaimed psychiatrist Charles W. Socarides.[33] He wrote of the 'revolutionary changes' this decision had brought to multiple factors:

> A significant portion of society today is of the belief that homosexuality is a normal form of sexual behavior different from but equal to that of heterosexuality. Many religious leaders, public officials, educators, social and mental health agencies, including those at the highest level of government, departments of psychiatry, psychology, and mental health clinics, have been taken in by a widespread sexual egalitarianism, by accusations of being 'undemocratic' or 'prejudiced' if they do not accept certain scientific assertions thrust upon them, as if deprived of all intellectual capacity to judge and reason. It is my contention in this paper that this threat of revolutionary change in our sexual mores and customs has been ushered in by a singular act of considerable consequence: the removal of homosexuality from the category of aberrancy by the American Psychiatric Association.[34]

---

33 Socarides was Clinical Professor of Psychiatry at the Albert Einstein College of Medicine, New York; taught at Columbia University and the State University of New York Downstate Medical Center, co-founder in 1992 of National Association for Research and Therapy of Homosexuality; which is dishonestly portrayed as practising 'conversion therapy' (see the unbalanced Wikipedia entry for the association: https://en.wikipedia.org/wiki/National_Association_ for_Research_&_Therapy_of_Homosexuality).   Awards: Distinguished Psychoanalyst (Association of Psychoanalytic Psychologists); Sigmund Freud Lectureship Award (New York Center for Psychoanalytic Training); Physicians Recognition Award (American Medical Association); Sigmund Freud Award (American Society of Psychoanalytic Physicians).

34 Charles W. Socarides, 'Sexual Politics and Scientific Logic: The Issue of Homosexuality'.

Socarides provided the historical background, referring to a 1963 enquiry into homosexuality by the Committee on Public Health of the New York Academy of Medicine. The committee in its 1964 report reaffirmed the then scientific consensus that 'homosexuality is indeed an illness', warning that 'some homosexuals have gone beyond the plane of defensiveness and now argue that deviancy is a "desirable, noble, preferable way of life"'. Socarides urged an enquiry into the treatment of homosexuality, and this resulted in a Task Force of the National Institute for Mental Health issuing a report in 1969. However, this had been stacked with those who had been biased in favour of normalising homosexuality, including Paul Gebhard, co-author of the second Kinsey report, *Sexual Behavior in the Human Female*; and Dr. John Money, of Johns Hopkins University, 'an early proponent of transsexual surgery'. The Task Force report neglected to provide an opinion on homosexuality being 'arrested psychosexual development', hence lending tacit approval to its normalisation.

At this time, homosexual agitation began to intrude on scientific conferences: 'Meanwhile, militant political homosexual groups continued to disrupt a number of scientific programs both at the national and local level in which findings as to the psychopathology of homosexuality, its origins, symptomatology, course, and treatment, were going to be discussed. ...' Psychiatrists who maintained the traditional opinion came under attack in the APA journal *Psychiatric News*, and a campaign of threats of violence emerged. In 1972, Socarides succeeded in having the New York County District Branch of the American Psychiatric Association establish a task force on homosexuality comprised entirely of psychiatrists, drawn from the 'major medical centers of New York City'. After two years of deliberation, the task force 'attempted to submit its report on homosexuality to the Executive Council of the New York City District Branch of the APA. However, the report was 'not acceptable', so the task force published the report in 1974, without recognition by the APA New York Executive.

In mid-1973, Vice President Judd Marmor of the APA and John Spiegel, President of the APA, and other psychiatrists met with the Gay Activist Alliance, the Mattachine Society and its female ancillary, the Daughters of Bilities, and the Nomenclature Committee of the American Psychiatric Association at Columbia University, New York City, to discuss the deletion of 'homosexuality' from the diagnostic nomenclature.[35]

The meeting with Marmor and Spiegel was fruitful: in November 1973, a cocktail party was held at the Washington D.C. APA headquarters celebrating the revised definition of homosexuality by the APA's Nomenclature Task Force on Homosexuality, headed by Dr. Robert L. Spitzer (Columbia University), who had never previously addressed the matter.

The proposed change to the *Diagnostic and Statistical Manual* went to the APA Reference Committee. Socarides and two others, who held out for retaining a scientific rather than an ideologically-driven approach, 'received a hearing immediately preceding the Board of Trustees vote on December 14, 1973'. Socarides was given five minutes to present his case, arguing against something that he saw would become a dogma.

The Board of Trustees voted practically unanimously against us, with two abstentions. It is interesting to note that only two thirds of the members of the Board of Trustees were present, barely enough to constitute a quorum for this important decision. Were some members simply avoiding a confrontation with the majority view already determined and adamant in their conviction? Otherwise, how could one explain their absence on such a critical issue?[36]

Several weeks later, the Board's vote was explained as being based on two items. A few weeks later, the rationale for the deletion of homosexuality as a psychiatric disorder was presented to the medical community. This was in two items: The first was the position paper

---

35   Ibid.
36   Ibid.

of Spitzer's Nomenclature Task Force on Homosexuality, *Psychiatric News* stating that it was 'essentially upon the rationale of Dr. Spitzer's presentation that the Board made its decision'.[37] Ignoring the corpus of material on the subject, Spitzer's conclusion was that of Kinsey's, that homosexuality did not meet the requirements of a psychiatric disorder since it 'does not either regularly cause subjective distress' or is not 'regularly associated with some generalized impairment in social effectiveness or functioning'.[38] Secondly were the conclusions of Drs. Marcel T. Saghir and Eli Robins from their book *Male and Female Homosexuality* (1973). Socarides states that Saghir and Robins had not used psychoanalytic methodology, but rather a survey of homosexuals recruited via homosexual advocacy organisations.

A petition for a referendum on reversing the Board decision was signed by 243 participants at the APA conference in New York. In April 1974, a vote of the APA membership was held. Despite behind-the-scenes lobbying by homosexual activists, of the 10,000 who voted, 40% disagreed with the Board's decision, 'asserting that there were no legitimate scientific reasons for the APA's change in fundamental psychiatric theory'. However, only 25% of those eligible to vote had sent in their papers.[39] It is therefore a myth that a majority of the APA's members voted in favour of the Board's decision.

The importance of the issue was expressed by Abram Kardiner,[40] former Professor of Psychiatry at Columbia University, who wrote to Socarides:

---

37   R. L. Spitzer, 'The Homosexual Decision — A Background Paper', *Psychiatric News* (1974), pp. 11–12.

38   Socarides.

39   Ibid.

40   Kardiner co-founded the Psychoanalytic and Psychosomatic Clinic for Training and Research in the Department of Psychiatry, Columbia University. He was particularly interested in the psychoanalytic study of cultures, and pioneered work on post-traumatic stress disorder.

There is an epidemic form of homosexuality, which is more than the usual incidence, which generally occurs in social crises or in declining cultures when license and boundless permissiveness dulls the pain of ceaseless anxiety, universal hostility and divisiveness. Thus in the Betsileo of Madagascar the incidence of homosexuality was visibly increased at a time when the society was under a state of collapse. Supporting the claims of the homosexuals and regarding homosexuality as a normal variant of sexual activity is to deny the social significance of homosexuality. To do this is to give support to the divisive elements in the community. Above all it militates against the family and destroys the function of the latter as the last place in our society where affectivity can still be cultivated.

Homosexuals cannot make a society, nor keep ours going for very long. Homosexuality operates against the cohesive elements in society in the name of fictitious freedom. It drives the opposite sex into a similar direction. And no society can long endure when either the child is neglected or when the sexes war upon each other.[41]

As Kardiner states, this is one more factor in the deconstruction of the organic social community, 'in the name of a fictitious freedom'. Kardiner opines that homosexuality increases during times of cultural crisis. He provides an example and points out that among the Betsileo homosexuality is a manifestation of social abnormality. There are variables at work. It is poor scholarship that forms a conclusion without considering such variables.

We have considered in some detail the background of the controversy regarding homosexuality within the APA because:

1) the change in stance is cited as proof in a shift of scientific evidence; and the current transgender agenda follows the same pattern,

2) it is a far-reaching example of how science can be hijacked and diverted to serve an agenda.

---

41 Kardiner to Socarides (1973). Emphasis added.

Reconditioning Children

N EW ZEALAND has for a long time been referred to as a 'social laboratory'.[1] Among the first to institute social welfare reforms, labour arbitration, pensions, women's franchise, and much else, many of those reforms, introduced during the late 19th century and into the 1930s by social reformers relatively devoid of dogma, have been of fundamental benefit. However, the takeover and redirection of social reform by the oligarchy, which we have been considering, has taken the necessity for social reform into vastly different directions than the intent of those who had no notion of destroying, but rather restoring, the organic character of social bonds.

Despite present assumptions, fundamental social reform is a necessary element of genuine conservatism,[2] for in order to replenish and invigorate an organism to health, one must be able to weed and prune, and even drastically cut out the dead and the rotting, as Thomas Carlyle pointed out: *'The bough that is dead shall be cut away for the sake of the tree itself. Old? Yes, it is too old ... Let Conservatism that would preserve cut it away'*.[3]

---

1   See for example the note for the seminar: 'New Zealand as a Social Laboratory', School of Government, Victoria University of Wellington, 30 July 2015, https://www.wgtn.ac.nz/sog/about/events/past-events-archived/new-zealand-as-a-social-laboratory2.

2   As distinct from its antithesis, 'Whig' or 'classical liberalism'.

3   Thomas Carlyle, *Past and Present*, 'The Modern Worker', p. 227.

With increasing stridency, backed by the global Establishment and the historic course of modern decay, the present New Zealand Labour Government is empowered to pursue agendas that strike at the roots of what scant remnants there are of traditional organic bonds.

'Gender fluidity' is the primary method of reshaping children, and hence the means by which future generations are being reconstructed. While the suggestion of such an agenda caused outrage in Britain among Muslim parents, in New Zealand the Muslim community has been co-opted by the Establishment and shares platforms with the social engineers in government and their counterparts of the Far Left on the streets, including those of 'gender fluid' orientation. Cognisant of the problems inherent in multiculturalism, the social engineers have laid down guidelines on how objections from more traditionally inclined migrant communities might be overcome.

Indoctrination in the Schools

The focus is on children because they are still going through stages of socio-psychological development, and are therefore most susceptible to social engineering. In 2020, the Ministry of Education issued to primary schools a document touted as an expert study, *Relationships and Sexuality Education: A Guide for Teachers, Leaders and Boards of Trustees — Years 1–8.*[4]

The guide is designed for indoctrinating with a transgender or *gender fluid* bias 5- to 12-year-olds. As with such ideologically driven agendas, there must be a core reference to the Treaty of Waitangi and the customs of sundry ethnic communities, which makes necessary some type of semantic double-dealing for acceptance by those who might not be as acquiescent as White parents.

United Nations intrusion is acknowledged, albeit when such matters are addressed critically, they are condemned as 'Far Right conspiracy theories' and 'false news', as in the case of rightist exposure of

---

4   Margaret Smith, editor (2020).

the UN Compact on Global Migration. In regard to *Relationships and Sexuality Education* (RSE):

> These guidelines also acknowledge Aotearoa New Zealand's international legal commitments to the United Nations Sustainable Development Goals (2015), the United Nations Convention on the Rights of the Child (1989), and the United Nations Convention on the Rights of Persons with Disabilities (2006).[5]

What is 'Relationships and Sexuality Education' (RSE)?

The 'guide' is deemed a necessary update to previous 'guides' (2002, updated 2015) to keep pace with change: *'shifting social norms in relation to gender and sexuality'*; *'global shifts, including trends towards earlier puberty and changing family structures'*; *'continued societal concerns about child protection and abuse prevention'*; *'increasing calls for social inclusion'*, and so forth.[6] *'Changing social norms'* and *'global shifts'* are regarded as primary justifications for imposing those changes onto New Zealand children. It is imposed conformity to the globalist ideological agendas we have been considering here, backgrounded by over a century in social experimentation by the likes of Kinsey, Hirschfeld, and the activists that took over the American Psychiatric Association and enforced their ideologies in the name of 'science', as examined above.

What is implemented is not 'sex education', but *'relationships and sexuality education'* (RSE). 'Sex education' no longer suffices; rather, it must now be eliminated as reactionary and antithetical to the new 'sexuality', as the former sex education was still predicated on traditional *binary gender*.

Throughout the 'guide', it is claimed that RSE accords with the insights of new scientific evidence.[7] We have seen the character

---

5   Ibid. p. 8.

6   Ibid.

7   Ibid., p. 12.

and development of this 'new evidence', and 'science' in the previous chapter. Rather, the reason why children are targeted so early is because that is when attitudes can be conditioned like Pavlov's dogs, with rewards and punishments, at an age range that lacks developed critical faculties. Yet the 'guide' states that children will be taught to exercise critical judgement. Nonsense. They will be told how to think. Children will not be able to critically judge the supposed 'new evidence' that is presented to them by RSE, nor would the Ministry wish them to do so. And how can the 'evidence' be weighed up anyway, if contrary studies are not included? Children are led along a course that conforms to liberal-globalist doctrines emanating from the UNO and elsewhere, so that they are moulded into 'world citizens' of the type required by globalisation. The process reaches its apex at a tertiary level, where critical thought that challenges left-liberal orthodoxy, whether by students or faculty, is punished as heresy, to the point of censuring and purging miscreants.

The 'guide' links RSE with 'climate change' and other agendas in what the Left calls *intersectionality*, but also claims that RSE proceeds from questions posed by children, rather than being imposed from outside bodies such as the UNO, despite having previously stated, as we have seen, that the programmes are designed to accord with various UN requirements:

> Families are now more diverse than ever before, and **children and young people are questioning** gender norms and binaries. Climate change continues to impact how young people view their worlds and their relationship with others and with the environment.[8]

One such source is identified as the UN Convention of the Rights of the Child, where the 'guide' states, '**Children and young people have the right to engage in critical inquiry** *about relationships, gender, and sexuality as part of meaningful learning*'.[9] What youngster of the age

---

8   Ibid., p. 12, emphasis added.

9   Ibid., p. 12, emphasis added.

range being targeted has the ability to '*engage in critical inquiry*'? The youngster is under the thrall of the teacher's authority as a substitute parent figure. If a child does have the genuine independence and courage to reject what is being imposed, he or she will be regarded as a problem to be corrected. The parents will be called by the school and questioned as to the attitudes they have imparted to their child. There is no room for nonconformity. As we have seen, according to *Critical Theory,* parents are the first of the *primary ties* from which the individual must be 'liberated', and the traditional family is the germ-cell of *Fascism.* The large corpus of literature produced by *Critical Theorists, Kinseyans, and others* is the origin for what our current mind manipulators call the 'latest research'.

Revolution in Morals

Just how far-ranging RSE is can be gauged from the stated aims:

> *Quality RSE policies and programmes enable young people to:*
>
> • *challenge homophobia, transphobia, sexism, and gender-based violence*
>
> • *interrogate the ongoing effects of colonisation*
>
> • *study the environmental impacts of changes in population growth and of related issues such as people's use and disposal of menstrual products*
>
> • *engage with mātauranga Māori*
>
> • *gain knowledge about the diversity of cultures in Aotearoa New Zealand — including religious diversity*
>
> • *gain understandings about the strengths of sexual and gender diversity. This learning is vital for children and young people's individual development and overall wellbeing, so it contributes to their academic success. It also enables us to develop more inclusive and positive societies'.*[10]

Again the *intersectional* doctrine of the Far Left is the basis, with key words such as homophobia, transphobia, and sexism conjoined with

10   Ibid., p. 12.

'ongoing colonisation', demographics, multiculturalism, and religious diversity. Double-think — *dialectics* — is required. While traditional Christian attitudes of one's parents can be routinely ridiculed and disposed of, how does one dispose of the traditional attitudes of Muslim parents, without jeopardising the multicultural society? That remains one of the paradoxes of the imposed, rootless System. There is an assurance, however, that RSE accords with Maori and Polynesian customs, and that *'Maori models of sexuality'* will be a premise:

> Sexuality is an element of hauora. Ākonga [students] who are supported in regard to their sexuality are likely to have better overall health, which in turn supports their educational success and strengthens their relationships with whānau and friends.[11]

Analogous to the hijacking of the American Psychiatric Association in 1973 and the redefinition of homosexuality by a militant lobby,[12] recently a long forgotten Maori word, *Takatāpui*, meaning a close bond between males, has been augmented by a few other obscure cultural remnants, and *'reclaimed by Māori in lesbian, gay and trans communities in the 80s. In recent years its definition has expanded to encompass all tāngata whenua with diverse gender identities, sexualities, and sex characteristics — similar to the way the word "queer" is used now'*, according to Maori 'queer' lobbyist Ngahuia Awekotuku.[13] Hence, the social engineers are able to inculcate their ideology by recourse to indigenous custom redefined with modernist interpretations.

Maori (and other Polynesian) medicine and customs on health are 'holistic' and implicitly claimed to be superior to Western medicine, science, concepts of family, and society, which now exist as no more than vestiges within the onslaught of modernism. A sanitised version of Maori and Polynesian precolonial societies is required, which amounts to a return of the 18th century Western liberal doctrine of the

---

11   Ibid., p. 13.

12   Charles W. Socarides (1992).

13   Melody Thomas (2018).

'noble savage', who lived idyllically, unburdened by civilisation; as we have seen, a fallacious model revived by leftist social scientists such as Margaret Mead.

One must also wonder why a child's *'academic success'* is predicated on conformity to the RSE programme?

Deconstruction of Language

To facilitate and encourage 'gender fluidity', whether among staff or children, the prescription includes:

- *ākonga and staff are known, and addressed at school, by their name of choice.*[14]

[One day Mr Jones might show up to class and declare that *'they' is* (sic) now Ms Jones. God help the child who is caught sniggering; that might impact on *'their'* 'academic success' unless confession and penance are shown]

- *School rolls and records use each person's name, gender, and pronoun of choice*

[Johnny decides he is now a girl and is to be called Joanna]

- *all school forms allow for genders in addition to male or female (e.g., gender diverse, nonbinary, takatāpui)*

[Given that there are now more than 120 'genders' and counting, this will be an ever-expanding task]

- *the school has clear and safe procedures for disclosures and complaints*

[Encourage anonymous informants, with all the abuse that entails].

---

14   Smith, op. cit., p. 19.

- *school uniform policies are reviewed so that all the school's uniforms are inclusive and don't reinforce outdated, Eurocentric, and exclusionary notions of gender*

[All children, no matter what discomfort this causes, will be obliged to wear a uniform that is so nebulous as to obliterate genuine identities]

- *procedures for sports are inclusive so that all ākonga can take part, whatever their sexual or gender identities.*

[Striving for excellence is passé and reactionary; inclusion as part of a nebulous blob is the aim]

Imposed and Enforced

For all the cant about consulting the diverse communities, the Ministry of Education unequivocally states that the RSE agenda will be imposed from on high; not subject to reform or rejection by any such community:

The school culture is very powerful. Whether or not they plan to do so, all schools give *ākonga* and their families messages about what is acceptable and what is not, in terms of gender and sexuality. Values are inherent in the practices, policies, and language used by teachers and school leaders.

The New Zealand Curriculum recognises human rights and the values of diversity, equity, and respect. These values ensure the rights of all *ākonga* to self-expression, self-identification, and support. RSE acknowledges and supports diversity among *ākonga*. It is crucial that schools establish and maintain cultures of inclusivity. Schools are encouraged to question gender stereotypes and assumptions about sexuality, including:

• gender norms • gender binaries • gender stereotypes • sex norms, for example, the assumption that sex characteristics at birth are always male or female. School cultures should acknowledge the sexual diversity of Aotearoa New Zealand communities.

The culture should recognise and actively support the rights of those who identify as: • takatāpui, lesbian, gay, bisexual, queer, intersex, transgender •

whakawāhine, tāngata ira tāne • māhū (Tahiti and Hawai'i) • vakasalewale-
wa (Fiji) • palopa (Papua New Guinea) • fa'afafine (Sāmoa and American
Sāmoa) • 'akava'ine (Cook Islands) • fakaleitī or leitī (Tonga) • fakafifine
(Niue and Tokelau) • other sexual and gender identities.[15]

Freedom of opinion is of the type that Marcuse called in *double-think*
'repressive tolerance'. Hence: *'Ākonga should be free to challenge school*
practices (such as rules about uniforms). School leaders and teachers
need to be open and provide spaces for student voices and feedback'.[16]
If Johnny or Mary signify that they are less than comfortable being
forced into participating in these intrusive programmes, they and
their parents will be given corrective treatment. There is no room
provided for challenging this RSE programme, despite supposed as-
surances under the Education Act.

Manipulative techniques to alter the psyche include the obliteration of traditional binary gender roles:

> During play and discovery times, encourage children to engage with a wide
> range of equipment, toys, and play materials. These times offer opportuni-
> ties to discuss and challenge unhelpful stereotypes about girls and boys (for
> example, if ākonga suggest that only girls play dress-ups or that only boys
> play with trucks).[17]

Here again we might discern implicit coercion. Previously we are assured that children must be listened to; now it is that if a child does
not conform to *gender fluid* role-play *'they' is* (sic) to be corrected for
being *'unhelpful'*.

Awareness Raising

If a child comments or laughs when *'they' finds* (sic) it funny that
Johnny is playing dress-up with dolls, this becomes a major issue for
child, parents, and the entire school, if not further:

---

15   Ibid.
16   Ibid., p. 20.
17   Ibid., p. 21.

> When specific issues arise in the school (for example, an incident of homophobic bullying), specific discussions or programmes (in classes, assemblies, or parent and whānau meetings) can **raise awareness** of the school's related support systems and policies. When the whole school community is aware of the issue, all can work together to address it.[18]

Making an example of such a child for not conforming is called an *opportunity* by the social engineers to '*raise awareness*'. *Awareness raising* is a concept that has long been the basis of Marxism. It is also called *consciousness raising*. While originally applied to *class consciousness* among the proletariat, the post-Marxist *Critical Theorists* extended the concept to what is often called *political correctness*. Where Marxism was established as a dictatorship, '*raising awareness*' was maintained by frequent political indoctrination sessions in factory and field. Jim Jones operated a pervasive system to 'raise awareness' at Jonestown, where the aim was perfected Communism. The method involves public confession of guilt, renunciation of one's 'errors', and humiliation for lack of conformity. The method was called *self-criticism*, (USSR = *kritika i samokritika*; Red China = 自我批评, *zìwǒ pīpíng*). This is also used in the human relations field, where it is often called *team-building*.[19]

One might readily envisage a classroom scenario where a child is embarrassed and uncomfortable, being forced to perform roles which call for the class to '*consider plays and role plays that critically investigate gender stereotypes*'. The term being 'outside one's comfort zone' is employed often enough by liberals. What of the child being pushed outside '*their*' (sic) '*comfort zone*' as part of RSE-enforced indoctrination? '*They*' will be subjected to humiliation during a process of '*awareness raising*', and possibly permanent psychological damage for the sake of imposing a fallacious ideology that the Ministry of Education 'experts' dogmatically insist is proven by the latest science.

---

18   Ibid., p. 22.

19   This social engineering technique, widespread in the 'human relations' industry, is examined in the chapter below; 'Behaviour Modification'.

Remoulding Generations

It becomes evident that the aim of RSE is to literally remould children into new, but amorphous beings that will conform to a *brave new world*, behind the façade of pseudo-identity. Modes of thinking will be re-engineered to conform:

> *Ākonga* will make sense of information about growth and development, sexuality, relationships, pubertal change, and societal issues. They will: • reflect critically on that information • examine their own and others' attitudes, values, beliefs, rights, and responsibilities with regard to development, gender, sexuality, and relationships • consider how to solve problems in social situations.[20]

The entire curriculum conforms to RSE. For example, when learning about technology: *'explore symbols linked to the gay and transgender rights movements'*.

> • challenge gender stereotypes in relation to design and materials • explore symbols linked to the gay and transgender rights movements • identify how gender expectations are embedded in technology, for example, in the design and style of power tools and other tools, the range of colours, textures, and designs available for clothing • explore the way toys, apps, and online games and activities are designed for a gendered audience • engage in a gender-neutral design challenge'.[21]

Here we get to the actual aim behind the double-think dialectics: *'engage in a gender-neutral design challenge'*, as with 'gender-neutral' language; gender-neutral clothing, etc. The aim is not to champion identities, but rather to obliterate genuine, organic identities; to manufacture a nebulous being that can be slotted into any circumstance desired by a global technocracy and its plutocratic masters. Every individual will have the potential to become an **interchangeable worker-drone**, and it is being done in the name of 'progress'.

---

20 Smith, p. 24.
21 Ibid., p. 29.

How can an identity be '*neutral*'? How can an identity be '*fluid*'? Identity is premised on **duration**, passed down through generations; not transience based on whim and fashion as defined by social engineers and corporate planners within globalist think tanks, NGOs, and tax-exempt foundations.

No Choice

Parents are reassured that according to the *Education & Training Act* (Section 51) they are able to remove their child from a particular programme, if they present their case in writing, although the school is not required to first seek permission from parents.[22] However, RSE is intended to permeate the entirety of the curriculum, and not just 'health education'. RSE is implemented in technology, mathematics, art, science, English, and sports, that is to say, '**RSE across the curriculum**', as the guidelines state.[23] The reassurances to parents are dishonest. A list of suggestions for teachers to use on parents who express concern is provided, with such examples as, '*Connect back to The New Zealand Curriculum and the established place of relationships and sexuality in the context of the curriculum key competencies*'.[24] Hence, if parents object, they are told that RSE is an **intrinsic part** of the NZ Curriculum, and that their child's learning will suffer unless there is participation.

---

22   Ibid., p. 43.

23   Ibid., pp. 28–20.

24   Ibid., p. 46.

Progressive Regression

Return of the Eunuchs

WHILE THE EMASCULATION of the male, including the 'reas-signment' of genitalia, is acclaimed as 'progressive', as is much else in the name of 'human rights' and 'equality', it has been symptomatic over the course of millennia of civilisations in the epoch of decay, to the extent that the phenomenon had been ritualised and given religious sanction. In Babylonia, Ishtar/Inanna was the goddess of male emasculation, transsexuality and gender ambiguity;

> androgynous, marginal, ambiguous ... She is betwixt and between ... Central to the goddess as paradox is her well-attested psychological and physiological androgyny. Inanna-Ishtar is both female and male ... [in one place stating] 'Though I am a woman I am a noble young man'.[1]

Rivkah Harris, formerly Associate Professor of Religion at Northwestern University, in her study on gender in Mesopotamia describes Ishtar as basically a Communistic icon, symbolising the levelling of all distinctions into an amorphous mass in the name of equality:

> She shattered all gender and socioeconomic distinctions—being both a royal queen and 'the harlot of heaven ... set out for the alehouse'[2] And in

---

1   Rivkah Harris, pp. 160, 163.
2   Ibid., p. 166.

all this she was the role model for her followers. Among her powers was this from a Sumerian poem: 'To turn a man into a woman and a woman into a man are yours, Inanna.'[3]

A hymn to Inanna relates the cross-dressing processions, which culminate in blood-letting:

The people of Sumer parade before you.
They play in the street ala-drums before you.
The people of Sumer parade before you.
I say, 'Hail!' to Inanna, Great Lady of Heaven! …

… The male prostitutes comb their hair before you.
They decorate the napes of their necks with coloured scarves,
They drape the cloak of the gods about their shoulders.
The righteous man and woman walk before you.
They hold the soothing harp by their sides.
Those who follow wear the sword belt.
They grasp the spear in their hands.
The people of Sumer parade before you.
The women adorn their right side with men's clothing.
The people of Sumer parade before you.
I say, 'Hail!' to Inanna, Great Lady of Heaven!
The men adorn their left side with women's clothing.
…The ascending kurgarra priests raise their swords before you.

The priest, who covers his sword with blood, sprinkles blood,
He sprinkles blood over the throne of the court chamber.
The tigi-drum, the sem-drum, and the ala-tambourine resound!
In the heavens the Holy One appears alone.[4]

Harris states of the worshippers:

Their transvestitism simulated the androgyny of Inanna-Ishtar. It was perhaps the inversion of the male/female binary opposition that thereby

---

3   Ibid., p. 160.
4   'The Third Hymn to Inanna: The Holy One', ca. 1974–1953 B.C.

neutralized this opposition. By emulating their goddess who was both female and male, they shattered the boundary between the sexes.[5]

The Canaanites had a fertility cult where the wearing of clothes of the opposite sex and the carrying of implements associated with the opposite sex were used in rituals, probably involving eunuch-priests dressed as females and male and female prostitutes. 'Homosexual activity and bestiality were considered ways of having intercourse with the gods and thus affecting the course of nature'.[6] The Hebrews, surrounded by these practices, were continually drawn to them, hence the many strictures against a variety of cultic activities, such as: 'The implement of a man shall not be borne by a woman, nor shall a man clothe himself in the attire of a woman, for whoever does this is an abomination to Yahweh your God'.[7]

The worship of Ishtar/Inanna spread outward from Sumer, among many nations, and much to the lament of the prophets, was endemic among the Hebrews in periods of religious and cultural regression. However, it seems that the cult of Ishtar/Inanna and associated practices were an aberration even within Babylon, and had originated from Uruk. An ancient text states:

> Babylon a ruin, he turned to Erech,[8] the city of hierodules,[9] courtesans, and sacred prostitutes to whom Ishtar (the goddess of love) was husband and master, the city of eunuchs and sodomites, the merrymakers of Eanna[10] (Ishtar's temple), whose maleness Ishtar had turned to femaleness, in order to terrify man.[11]

---

5   Rivkah Harris, pp. 170–171.

6   H.A. Hoffner Jr., Vol. 85 (1966), pp. 332–333.

7   Deuteronomy 22:5.

8   Sumerian city of Uruk.

9   Temple prostitutes.

10 Temple of Inanna in Uruk.

11 S.N. Kramer, pp. 130 -131. Kramer was a notable authority of Assyria and Sumer.

The transsexual nature of Inanna necessitated a change in outlook among the Babylonians who had previously abhorred the practice. Rome followed a similar pattern.

It is significant that when Rome started morally degenerating amidst the Second Punic War (218–201BC), the Romans resurrected Ishtar worship, centuries after its disappearance, and brought a statue of Cybele (one of many variations) to Rome from distant Phrygia. The statue was paraded through Rome, installed at a temple, and a festival was instituted, in the hope of victory. The cult's priests were eunuchs, which meant they were all foreigners since, until the reign of Claudius, a eunuch could not become a citizen. The priesthood (*galli*) were castrated in honour of Cybele's consort/son Attis, whom she drove mad due to his infidelity, causing him to self-mutilate. A fractured psyche emerged in Rome's later years from a civilisation that had placed honour on manly self-discipline:

> There was a tendency to associate the *galli* with the figure of the *cinaedus*,[12] which, at first, literally meant 'wanton' but, above all, was the name given to the adult man who might display any feminine trait. The association between both falls back on the idea that becoming effeminate would be gradual. Both were effeminate; some because they had in fact been castrated, others because they behaved as if they had been. However, if the presence of the *gallus* was not only permissible, but also, sometimes, esteemed because of his religious services, the *cinaedi* were, in general, execrated. The biggest fear seemed to be associated with those who were willing to take the final step toward the 'abyss' of effeminacy: self-castration. They were then regarded with horror and disdain for making themselves *cinaedi* voluntarily. Invectives and curses contained in the polysemic concept of *cinaedus* were hurled at them: the *galli* were Orientals, dancers, unhinged, weak and inclined to being the ones penetrated (*pathicus*), since they were either unable or unwilling to penetrate anyone.[13]

---

12   Roman derogatory word for effeminate homosexual. The word originally referred to dancers of non-Roman origin.

13   Luciano C. G. Pinto and Renato Pinto, p. 174.

The *galli* and *cinaedi* are honoured today among our 'progressives'.

> Might we speak of a continued oppression of the 'transgressors' of sexual
> norms and gender? The Roman world did not have a conceptual apparatus
> to classify what today is known as 'sexual orientation', much less would the
> individual who might demonstrate a greater inclination towards some kind
> of sexual act in Antiquity earn a specific fixed identity that might charac-
> terize all their social actions.[14]

Yet in normal circumstances, relations outside the male-female family bond were regarded as an abomination. The young Egyptian, for
example, was expected to find a wife and raise children. Daughters
were especially important because inheritance was through the female
line,[15] indicating that patriarchal families do not imply the repression
of women. The abhorrence for the dark god Seth involves the rape of
his brother Horus. The act was '... certainly looked upon as a mark of
ignominy for the sufferer; but it is abominated not as an expression
of triumph by the enemy so much as for the shame attached to the
act itself, just as the eating of excrement is abominated'.[16] Seth was
not only homosexual but was an abortionist,[17] symbolic of Seth as a
god of sexual sterility, an aberration of the divine order. Interestingly,
Seth was regarded by the Egyptians as 'foreign', and his wives Anat
and Astarte were of Canaanite origin.[18]

Toxicity of 'Traditional Masculine Ideology'

The revived cult of the Castrating Goddess proceeds with a scientific
façade; the modern magic. The American Psychological Association
promotes transgenderism as the healthy option to resolve identity confusion, while also promoting that confusion. Not only has

---

14   Ibid., p. 178.
15   M. S. Shaw, pp. 37 — 40.
16   J. G. Griffiths, p. 43.
17   H. Te Velde, p. 55.
18   R. T. Rundle Clark, p. 197.

transsexuality in an ongoing variety become the new 'normal', but traditional maleness has been deemed 'toxic'.

According to official APA ideology, there 'is a particular constellation of standards that have held sway over large segments of the population, including: anti-femininity, achievement, eschewal of the appearance of weakness, and adventure, risk, and violence. These have been collectively referred to as traditional masculinity ideology'.[19] These traditional attitudes are considered to be impacting on physical and mental health, such as the internalisation of emotions causing suicide; hence 'traditional masculine ideology' needs to be eliminated for the welfare of males.

However, reading the APA manifesto, it is apparent that this concern for the welfare of men and boys is a façade. The entirety of the document is infused with a strategy for normalising transgenderism, and for deconstructing the 'patriarchy', using stereotypically leftist jargon:

> When working with boys and men, psychologists can address issues of privilege and power related to sexism in a developmentally appropriate way to help them obtain the knowledge, attitudes, and skills to be effective allies and potentially live less restrictive lives. Male privilege tends to be invisible to men, yet they can become aware of it through a variety of means, such as education.[20]

Men and boys will thus reach happiness when they are liberated from their traditional gender roles; from their responsibility as providers and defenders. Such antiquated 'restrictive' concepts are not required in modern liberal-capitalism. Such a weight of the past can now be lifted from man's shoulders and he too can become an interchangeable

---

19   Fredric Rabinowitz et al., 'APA Guidelines for Psychological Practice with Boys and Men', (American Psychological Association, Boys and Men Guidelines Group, 2018), p. 3; https://www.apa.org/about/policy/boys-men-practice-guidelines.pdf.

20   Ibid., p. 10.

unit. **The male no longer has any sense of purpose. Perhaps that is the actual reason for male health issues?**

Gender is said to be a social construct that is separate from biological sex: 'When trying to understand the complex role of masculinity in the lives of diverse boys and men, it is critical to acknowledge that gender is a non-binary construct that is distinct from, although interrelated to, sexual orientation.'[21]

Further fractures of identity are described as arising among those departing from the traditional norm by forming other sub-group identities: 'Men not meeting dominant expectations often create their own communities within which they develop cultural standards, norms, and values that may depart from dominant masculinity. For instance, in racial and ethnic, youth, or gay communities, boys and men may develop forms of resistance in action and attitudes that challenge the expectations of dominant masculinity...'[22] Hence yet another breakdown in social cohesion that is then expected to recombine through *intersectionality*. Within the subgroups of multiple genders, there are further breakdowns according to race, ethnicity, and age.

Sub-identities form and re-form *ad infinitum* because any identity is a *social construct*, without organic attachments or biological imperatives. Hence, what might have been hardwired in the male and female over tens of millennia as survival mechanisms, maintained by custom, religion, and society, can be discarded like yesterday's clothing for the latest fashion. While the APA speaks of mental and physical health issues of men and boys caused by traditional expectations, such as 'stoicism' and the 'internalisation of emotions', it could be that the causes of problems among males are due to the disparaging and repression of hardwired male traits that are supposed to be discarded on the basis of new ideologies.

---

21   Ibid., p. 6.
22   Ibid., p. 6.

Boys and men who are members of more than one minority group may have an especially difficult time resolving identity-related conflicts. For example, gay boys and men of color may experience racism in the LGBT community, while also experiencing homophobia/heterosexism in their racial/ethnic community and may **choose to turn on and off certain aspects of their identities as they move between different cultural contexts.** Similarly, multiethnic and multiracial boys and men may feel pressure from their families to embrace one portion of their identities while experiencing demands from peers to accentuate different ones. These types of vacillations **can result in identity confusion** and contribute to the development of mental health problems.[23]

The preceding passage indicates a recognition that it is 'identity confusion' that might cause 'mental health problems'. Yet the answer of the APA is to accentuate the mobility of multiple identities, rather than encouraging a sense of permanence and rootedness in belonging to something tangible. All is in flux. Internal conflicts resulting from this multiplicity of identities are to be resolved through therapy, and other forms of social engineering. This is done not by discouraging the multiplication of identities but, on the contrary, by the imposition of their acceptance as the new normal. Here we come to the crux of this issue: the normalisation and reinforcement of the ability to 'turn on and off' identities 'while moving between different cultural contexts'. The role of the psychologist is to

strive to reduce and counter the damaging effects of microaggressions by teaching boys and men from historically marginalized backgrounds skills to cope with racism, homophobia, biphobia, transphobia, ageism, ableism, and other forms of discrimination.[24]

The suppression of *microaggressions* implies the existence of *microidentities*, which means the fracturing of the personality rather than its integration or what Jungian analytical psychology calls *individuation*.

---

23   Ibid., p. 9. Emphasis added.

24   Ibid., p. 9.

Subidentities included above are race, gender, age, and disability. Female disabled in this scenario require their own subidentity and its demands against the male-abled. Black female disabled require their own identity against White male-abled. Black female disabled lesbians and Black disabled transgendered require their own identities contra White hetero-male-abled. Young Black female lesbian/ or transgendered disabled, elderly or middle-aged each surely have their own histories or *herstories* and grievances. What of the need to combat *Achondroplasiaphobia* and associated discrimination and stereotyping? Or is dwarfism a social construct that can be discarded in favour of another identity, and is doing so implicitly insulting? What of *coulrophobia*, particularly relevant to the sensibilities of liberals?

Like all social engineering, it is sold as being for one's own good. The problems cited for resolution are those that have been manufactured or aggravated by the Left and their sponsors. Fundamental solutions are not sought, indeed they must be deflected. The Old Left for example demanded a living family wage; not women's integration into the production process in the name of 'liberation'.

> Sociocultural factors such as increasing rates of women entering the paid labor force and the shifting structure of American families from predominantly married, two-parent households to a wider variety of family compositions may be contributing to the evolution of new fathering behaviors and roles. Many fathers by their own volition have reframed traditional masculinity norms and roles of fathers (e.g., breadwinning) to be stay-at-home fathers or fill more nontraditional roles in the family such as co-parenting. This includes spending more time with their children, assuming more childcare tasks, and filling new paternal roles such as the primary caregiver as a stay-at-home dad.[25]

Just as women were convinced that integration into the workforce would be 'liberating', now the young are to be inculcated with 'progressive' ideas about the obliteration of traditional occupation roles,

---

25   Ibid., p. 12.

again for the sake of economic integration. This works in conjunction with the subverting of binary gender in the interests of 'economic inclusion':

> A particular focus of career education with boys includes encouraging them to explore the full range of career options, not just those that men have traditionally pursued. In addition, psychologists strive to address the difficult barriers and the culture-specific issues impeding the educational and career development of racial and ethnic minority, immigrant, boys with cognitive disabilities, and low-income boys by creating partnerships with schools, health care facilities, social service agencies, and businesses to provide them with mentors to guide and inspire educational striving. ...[26]

In commenting on the APA manifesto, Stephanie Pappas, a science writer at Stanford University Medical School, quotes Ryon McDermott, psychologist at the University of South Alabama, who co-authored the APA document, stating: 'What is gender in the 2010s? It's no longer just this male-female binary. If we can change men, we can change the world'.[27]

In critiquing the manifesto, Dr. Rob Whitley[28] calls it an 'ideological document', driven by 'social ideologies' rather than 'the best available scientific evidence'.

> ... This is especially so in fields such as psychiatry, which have been historically tainted by political abuse. For example, Soviet psychiatrists invented a fake category of mental illness named 'sluggish schizophrenia' which was used to label and confine anti-communist political dissidents.
>
> Sadly, the APA document appears to be driven by a similarly ideological approach in its continuous pathologization of 'traditional masculinity',

---

26   Ibid., p. 14.

27   Stephanie Pappas, 'APA Issues First-Ever Guidelines for Practice with Men and Boys', *Monitor on Psychology*, APA, Vol. 50, No. 1, 2019.

28   Whitley is Principal Investigator of the Social Psychiatry Research and Interest Group, Douglas Hospital Research Center; and Associate Professor, Department of Psychiatry, McGill University.

while ignoring considerable evidence that aspects of traditional masculinity can be beneficial for men's mental health.

So, far from such factors in 'traditional masculinity' as 'achievement', 'adventure', 'risk', and 'success, power and competition' having been 'shown to limit males' psychological development', such traits form the basis of *cognitive-behavioral therapy* (CBT), where clients are encouraged to 'be adventurous and take risks', and to confront 'anxiety-provoking situations'.[29]

Feminism

Among the doctrinal flaws that liberal-capitalism and socialism share is a faith in 'progress'. Marx referred to the 'wheel of history', without seeing that the socialist wagon would fall over a cliff. Liberal historian Francis Fukuyama saw the triumph of the free market and democracy over the world (globalisation) as literally 'the end of history': man would have reached his apex and there would be nothing better to accomplish. Dr. Fukuyama's optimism was reminiscent of that of the 19th century Darwinian who, buoyed by the Industrial Revolution, thought that this was the apex of human achievement. Nothing had been so great in history as that which industrial civilisation had achieved. Auguste Comte, one of the founders of sociology, formulated *positivism* on the basis that humanity went through a procession of epochs ending in the triumph of science and reason over faith. *Positivism* has remained the basis of socialist and capitalist historical and social analyses. The Right sees cycles of rise and fall, and looks at Marx's 'wheel of history' as one on which the spokes gradually fall off the hub.

Hence the tendency to see change as intrinsically 'progressive', whereas the 'change' might — and often is — a symptom of the old age.

---

29 Rob Whitley, 'Why the APA Guidelines for Men's Mental Health Are Misguided', *Psychology Today*, 25 February 2019; https://www.psychologyto-day.com/us/blog/talking-about-men/201902/why-the-apa-guidelines-mens-mental-health-are-misguided.

As we have seen above, the latest 'modern' fad of transgenderism has been around for millennia as an aberration. Likewise, feminism is just another recurrence of a civilisation in decay. We see in prior civilisations the same notions of feminism and egalitarianism as our own.

Mother goddess, moon, phallic and serpent worship are *telluric* cultic manifestations throughout cultures and races across the world. The Dionysian orgies of *telluric* cults dramatise a reversionary, Communistic spirit, where all become one; a nebulous mass, focused on descent to the underworld; a perverse fascination with having humanity crawl back into an amorphous slime.

Politically, one sees the Left embracing the *telluric*. It is politicised *Dionysianism*. Historically, Spartacus, leader of the slave revolt against Rome (73 B.C.), was said to be the incarnation of Dionysus, and the Roman Senate sought to prohibit the Dionysian cult as subversive. Here was Bolshevism two thousand years ago. 'Feminist cultural historian' Professor Lucia Chiavola Birnbaum writes of the Dionysian cults, describing a form of proto-Bolshevism:

> Radical democracy is implicit in celebrations of Dionysus/Bacchus and carnivals: everyone celebrates. ... During Saturnalia slaves became masters, and the people elected a king of the festival... Celebration of all life in dionysian and bacchic rites included the loosening of marital bonds, alarming conservatives, who feared that loosening patriarchal familial ties would lead to the loosening of patriarchal social stratification. ... Bacchanalia were festivals described by a Roman writer as dear to 'proletarians, women, and slaves'.[30]

Birnbaum describes the Dionysian and Bacchanalian rites as 'the ultimate egalitarian festival [which] in authentic manifestation carnival turns everything inside out, bottom to top, front to rear, and unveils, unmasks and uncrowns'.[31] Again, there arises the hatred of the family

---

30   Lucia Chiavola Birnbaum, p. 76.

31   Ibid., p. 77.

and of marriage which makes the reversion of the rites so appealing to 'modern', 'progressive' women.

To Birnbaum and other feminists, the 'Dark Mother' is the origin of religious belief, and 'dark' or 'black' refers both to the soil and to Black African origins, Birnbaum promoting this latter theory in her book *Dark Mother: African Origins and Godmothers*.[32] Hence the notion, popular among feminists, serves to attack not only patriarchy but in particular White patriarchy. The claim is that there existed at the most primordial level a universal egalitarian, pacifistic matriarchy of hunter-gatherers, worshipping a dark goddess. If this were conceded to be historically accurate, it means nothing more than that this was the situation at the most primitive, undifferentiated hunter-gatherer level of existence, and that feminism, like the Left in general, aims to return to a regressive state. This is the paradox of 'progress'.

Anthropologist Professor Joan Bamberger comments on the theory:

> Because no matriarchies persist anywhere at the present time, and because primary sources recounting them are totally lacking, both the existence and constitution of female-dominated societies can only be surmised. The absence of this documentation, however, has not been a deterrent to those scholars and popularists who view in the concept of primitive matriarchy a rationale for a new social order, one in which women can and should gain control of important political and economic roles.[33]

Bamberger traces the theory to 1861 when the Swiss jurist and classical scholar Johann Jakob Bachofen published *Das Mutterrecht* ('Mother Right: an investigation of the religious and juridical character of matriarchy in the ancient world'). Bamberger wrote:

---

32 Lucia Chiavola Birnbaum, *Dark Mother*.

33 Joan Bamberger, 'The Myth of Matriarchy: Why Men Rule in Primitive Society', p. 265; http://radicalanthropologygroup.org/sites/default/files/pdf/class_text_052.pdf.

If anthropologists and scholars of classical jurisprudence no longer read Bachofen, the advocates of the current feminist movement do. They have rediscovered in his theory of mother right a scholarly precedent for the privileged position of females in primitive society.[34]

Bamberger sees as problematic feminist allusions to legends across the world of a pre-historic matriarchy, which also recount that, so far from being idyllic, these societies were brutish and women lost their power when their tyranny became intolerable.[35]

Role of Feminism in Post-Cold War Globalism

Feminism has played a significant role in the globalisation of the former Soviet bloc states. The Network of East-West Women, founded in New York in 1991, is one of many 'gender-focused NGOs', as Susan Zimmerman calls them, spreading through Eastern and Central Europe, backed by Foundations and other globalist agencies, and is part of the offensive against Russia's resistance to globalisation. Among the funders are Ford and Soros, John D. and Catherine T. MacArthur Foundation, United Nations Development Fund for Women, Vanguard Fund.[36] Soros and Ford, the U.S. State Department (Erin Barclay), and the New School for Social Research (Ann Snitow, NEWW chair) are represented on the Board of Directors.[37]

Gender studies aided in the process by subverting the education systems. Susan Zimmermann refers to this as the 'internationalization of gender as part of the neo-liberal transitions package'.[38] Others saw it

---

34 Ibid.

35 Ibid.

36 NEWW, 'About NEWW: Funders'; https://www.neww.org/about/funders.html.

37 Ibid., 'Board of Directors'; https://www.neww.org/about/board.html.

38 S. Zimmermann, 'The Internationalization of Woman and Gender Studies in Higher Education in Central & Eastern Europe & the Former Soviet Union: Asymmetric Politics & the Regional-Transnational Configuration', *East-Central Europe/ECE*, Vols. 34–35, 2007–2008, parts 1–2, pp. 131–160.

as the 'academic Macdonaldization of gender'.[39] Much of the influence is facilitated by opening up to academic international exchanges.[40] Ioana Cirstocea refers to 'entire armies' of feminists arriving in Eastern Europe during the 1990s 'to establish networks, conduct research projects, organize meetings and conferences'. The New School for Social Research assisted Czech sociologist Jirina Siklova to establish the first gender studies department in Prague in 1989.[41]

Cirstocea states that apart from NEWW, the 'gender field' in Eastern Europe 'is mainly structured by the Open Society Institute (OSI)',[42] the omnipresent foundation of George Soros. She points out that OSI had been 'involved in reforming Eastern European public spaces even before the collapse of the communist regimes'. In Yugoslavia, OSI supported the Inter-University Centre, where international feminist conferences were held during the 1980s. OSI's involvement with 'gender issues and feminism' is indicated by the amount of funding it gave to associations during the first post-Soviet decade and by the establishment of gender studies at the Central European University (CEU), founded by Soros, which was a centre for feminist studies, conferences, translations of feminist literature from 'militant resources', and training for the region,[43] prior to being closed by the Hungarian government. Both NEWW and the Soros-sponsored Network Women's Program were particularly involved in the CEU projects.

---

39 J. Butler et al., 'Pour ne pas en finir avec le genre', *Societies and Representations* (2007), pp. 285–306, cited by Cirstocea, p. 66.

40 Quotes from Ioana Cirstocea, 'Transnational Feminism in the Making', in Claudette Fillard, Françoise Oraz (eds.), *Exchanges and Correspondence: Feminism in the Making* (Cambridge Scholars Publishing, 2010), p. 66.

41 Cirstocea, p. 70.

42 Ibid., p. 73.

43 Ibid., p. 74.

Intersectionality — The Politics of Bedlam, or, 'Where Rights Collide'

NTERSECTIONALITY, referred to previously in regard to Germany's state-sponsored Federal Foundation Magnus Hirschfeld, is intended to describe a myriad of identities, some organic and genuine, many contrived and superficial. Unity is forged by targeting 'White patriarchy'. Their activities are known collectively as *identity politics*. The concept is buttressed by *political correctness*, which decrees, often literally via state laws, that criticism of constituent parts of this *rainbow coalition,* as it is called, is *hate speech.*

We have traced over the course of more than a century the development of **new** identities through gender, which added transvestism to homosexuality, and then transgenderism. The 'fluidity of gender' of Hirschfeld and Kinsey increasingly proliferated. First there was the LGB Lesbian/Gay/Bisexual triune. This was supplemented by LGBTTIQ, then by LGBTIQCAPGNGFNBA. One might suppose that there is an in-house joke to utilise every letter of the English alphabet to describe a newly discovered gender. One of the in-crowd describes the variations:

> Ever wondered what does '+' stand for in LGBT+ : *Lesbian*: woman attracted towards a woman; *Gay*: man attracted towards a man; *Bisexual*: person attracted towards both men and women; *Transgender*: person who lives as a member of a gender other than that expected based on sex or gender assigned at birth; *Intersex*: Person both with a combination of

male and female biological characteristics; *Questioning*: person exploring their gender identity and sexual orientation; *Curious*: person who doesn't identify as bisexual but is just curious towards both men and women; *Asexual*: person who does not experience sexual attraction; *Pansexual*: person attracted towards members of all gender identities and expressions; *Gender Nonconforming*: person who either by nature or by choice does not conform to gender-based expectations of society; *Gender-Fluid*: person who does not identify themselves as having a fixed gender; *Non-Binary*: person who does not identify as either man or woman (third gender); *Androgynous*: gender expression with elements of both masculinity and femininity.[1]

Even in the above there are categories that have not been included, such as *Ambonec*: identifying as both man and woman, yet neither at the same time; and *Gyragender*: having multiple genders but understanding none of them.

The roots of *intersectionality* can be found in the calls for a 'New Left' by Herbert Marcuse, when in 1964 he referred to a revolutionary cadre supplanting the proletariat, comprised of youth, gays, feminists and Blacks. While those who promoted this movement assumed it could be a united front against the remnants of traditional society, the result of such a superficial contrivance has been discord. Douglas Murray, gay, conservative, editor of *The Spectator*, writes:

> The advocates of social justice, identity politics and intersectionality suggest that we live in societies that are racist, sexist, homophobic and transphobic. They suggest that these oppressions are interlocked, and that if we can learn to see through this web, and unweave it, we can then finally unlock the interlocking oppressions of our time. After which something will happen. Precisely what this thing is remains unclear. ... We are unlikely to find out.

> Firstly, because the interlocking oppressions do not lock all neatly together, but grind hideously and noisily both against each other and within

---

1   Abhishek Verma, 'Understanding LGBTIQCAPGNGFNBA — Reach for the Rainbow' ; http://sites.tufts.edu/lgbtcommunityinindia/page-2/.

themselves. They produce friction rather than diminish it, and increase tensions and crowd madness more than they produce peace of mind.[2]

Was it to be believed that Blacks would unite with a contrived identity called 'Asian'; that Asians are themselves an identity group without ancestral antagonisms between Chinese and Vietnamese, Chinese and Indians, Indians and Pakistanis…; that ghetto Blacks would welcome as comrades White bourgeoisie student radicals; that Muslims and ghetto Blacks would be forever content with leadership from Jewish intellectuals; and hostility between Hispanics and Blacks, and Blacks and Asians could be obliterated by hatred for Whites? Would centuries of conflict between Shi'ite and Sunni Muslims be resolved by appeals to liberalism? That they could be bought off and tamed with money from oligarchs and organised Jewry, such as that endowed to the NAACP (National Association for the Advancement of Colored People), National Urban League, and Southern Christian Leadership Conference, against the *Identitarianism* of the Black Panthers and Nation of Islam?

Gays vs Queers

Worse still have been the fractures caused by promoting gender fluidity. Murray refers to the divide between 'queers' and 'gays', such as himself. He describes 'queer' as

> … a group of people who believe that being attracted to the same sex should merely be the first stage in a wilder journey. The first step not just to getting on with life but to transgressing the normal modes of life. Whereas gays might just want to be accepted like everyone else, queers want to be recognised as fundamentally different to everyone else and to use the difference to tear down the kind of order that gays are working to get into. It is an almost never acknowledged but completely central divide that has existed as long as 'gay' has been recognised as an identity.[3]

---

2   Douglas Murray, p. 231.
3   Ibid., pp. 36–37.

Murray describes the process by which the 'gay revolution' became part of *intersectionality* during the 1960s, when activists such as Jim Fourrat[4] sought alliances with Blacks and with the Viet Cong, Mao's China (where homosexuals were publically castrated) and Castro's Cuba. The gay movement has kept identifying with revolutionists who seek the overthrow of the society into which gays sought acceptance. 'In every decade that has followed since the 1960s the divide has been replicated in the gay world'.[5]

Fourrat originally regarded transgenderism as a method 'to make gay men and lesbians straight', and therefore as a backward step. The queer movement was perturbed that one of their pioneers could not go further. In May 2000, Fourrat wrote to *The New York Times*. His letter was published with dismay by the National Transgender Advocacy Coalition. Referring to an article in *The Times*, Fourrat wrote:

> ... What is new is we now see gay academics and pop journalists embracing this new push to make gaymen and lesbians straight by leading them to endure painful physical body manipulation and dangerous hormonal injects to take on the topography of the conventional definition of what is male and what is female. Modern medicine is once again trying to cure us of our desire for same sex love. Our gender variant gay and lesbian population is under intense pressure to deny their homosexuality and to take all physical, hormonal and emotional steps in order to be accepted into heterosexual society.

> ... How homophobia both external and more importantly internally puts at risk most homosexuals and lesbians and all gender variant individuals ... How the rush to gender reassign through the wonders of modern medicine has ultimately failed ... where in the sensational picture of a professional skin strutter was there any reference to the 30 year John[s] Hopkins study of sexual reassignment and how ultimately it did not improve the self

---

4   Fourrat, prominent in the music industry, co-founded the Yippies (Youth International Party) with Abbie Hoffman in 1967; one of the most nihilistic of the New Left organisations. In 1969 he co-founded the Gay Liberation Front, and has subsequently been involved with many others.

5   Douglas Murray, p. 37.

image or well being of the subjects in their program. The results of this study caused John[s] Hopkins to cease sexual reassignment as a solution to gender dysfunction. ...[6]

Fourrat described 'queer academics' and mainstream media, such as *The Times*, as 'toxic' and 'anti-gay/lesbian' for promoting 'gender reassignment'. Referring to the celebrated case at the time, the murder of Barry Winchell, boyfriend of celebrity transgender Calpernia Addams, Fourrat asked: 'Why can't Calpernia Sarah Addams dress, act and be himself as a gayman … After all, this construction of "women" is totally informed by gaymale sensibility and has little in reality to do with the essence of being female'.[7] What Fourrat was objecting to was *The Times* stating that Winchell was not actually 'gay' because Addams had become a woman: 'The fact is that Winchell', stated *The Times*, 'killed for being gay, wasn't gay, at least not in the traditional Harvey Fierstein sense of the word. Barry Winchell, who had only ever dated biological women before, was in love with a pre-operative transsexual — a "transgendered woman", as Addams prefers it' …[8]

The problem seems to be that such couplings attempt to **retain traditional** binary gender roles. Even in the case of Dr. Hirschfeld, his partner Karl Giese assumed the female role.[9]

TERFing

So far from such gender complexities being resolved within the Left, they have intensified. While twenty years ago Fourrat was offended by the attempts at gender reorientation by males, regarding them as 'anti-gay', militant feminists now regard the phenomenon as an affront

---

6   Jim Fourrat, letter to the NY Times, 27 May 2000.

7   Ibid.

8   David France, 'An Inconvenient Woman', *The New York Times*, 23 May 2000.

9   Ellen Bækgaard, a member of the committee of the World League for Sexual Reform, described Giese in her memoirs as the 'woman of the house', who enjoyed decorating, needlework, and attending to Hirschfeld's wardrobe. Ralf Dose, p. 28.

to women. A feminist movement called 'TERF' (Trans-Exclusionary Radical Feminist) objects that transgenderism is a form of 'female erasure'. A 2019 *New York Times* column refers to two British women 'storming' 'onto Capitol Hill in Washington for the purposes of ambushing Sarah McBride, the national press secretary of the Human Rights Campaign'. 'Ms. McBride, a trans woman, had just been part of a meeting between the Parents for Transgender Equality National Council and members of Congress'. The British women heckled the meeting, and 'misgendering Ms. McBride, the two inveighed against her supposed "hatred of lesbians", and accused her of championing "the rights of men to access women in women's prison".[10] *TERFs* have split the Left. *The Times* article states:

> The split between the American and British center-left on this issue was thrown into sharp relief last year, when *The Guardian* published an editorial on potential changes to a law called the Gender Recognition Act, which would allow people in Britain to self-define their gender. The editorial was headlined **'Where Rights Collide'**, and argued that 'women's concerns about sharing dormitories or changing rooms with "male-bodied" people must be taken seriously'. Some of *The Guardian's* United States-based journalists published a disavowal, arguing that the editorial's points 'echo the position of anti-trans legislators who have pushed overtly transphobic bathroom bills'.[11]

The Times correspondent, Dr. Sophie Lewis, a 'feminist theorist and geographer', traces *TERFism* to the USA from a radical feminist faction emerging from the 1960s New Left into the 1970s. In Britain during the 1980s, *TERFism* arose among lesbian separatists, from the 'antinuclear protest groups who saw themselves as part of a "feminist resistance" to patriarchal science, taking a stand against nuclear weapons, test-tube babies and male-to-female transsexual surgery alike'.[12]

---

10   Sophie Lewis, 'How British Feminism Became Anti-Trans', *The New York Times*, 7 February 2019.

11   Ibid. Emphasis added.

12   Ibid.

'Just an Exiled Old White Woman'

Due to their non-inclusivity, *TERFs* are confronted by the globalist Establishment with treatment more usually meted out to the Right. Women have been banned from Twitter for tweeting 'men aren't women', and 'what is the difference between a man and a transwoman?', which Twitter deems 'hateful'.[13] Feminist icon Germaine Greer has fallen afoul, having written in her 1999 book *The Whole Woman*, in a chapter titled 'Pantomime Dames', those born men could not be classed as women, and alluded to the 'mutilation' for which transsexuals opt. The reference was unnoticed until 2015, when feminist students objected to Greer lecturing at Cardiff University on 'Women and Power'. She was accused of 'misogynistic views towards trans women', and as 'misgendering trans women'. Her views were 'problematic' (a word often used against an academic or speaker of right-wing persuasion). In a BBC interview, Greer reiterated that she does not think that 'post-operative transgender men are women'.

In 2017, Eve Hodgson wrote in Cambridge University's magazine *Varsity* of Greer as 'just an old, white woman who has forced herself into exile'.[14] This was in reaction to Greer's having called 'ridiculous' the new admission policy of Murray Edwards College, part of Cambridge, the 'widely-applauded policy to allow students who identify as female into their single-sex college'.

> Her [Greer's] theories about transgender people have always been problematic, giving voice to an incredibly harmful, complex strand of modern feminism: what's become known as TERF (that is, trans-exclusionary radical feminism). She refuses to discuss trans people using their proper pronouns. She says that 'just because you lop off your dick… doesn't make you a fucking woman', and that any 'man' who does that is 'inflicting an extraordinary act of violence on himself'.

---

13 Murray, p. 111.

14 Eve Hodgson, 'Germaine Greer Can No Longer Be Called a Feminist', *Varsity*, 26 October 2017. One might be appalled at Hodgson's display of ageism.

Hodgson makes a plea for *intersectionality*, writing, 'Any feminist who claims relevance now has to believe in intersectionality. To ignore the compounded struggle that non-white women, or poor women, or LGBTQ+ women face is to discredit your feminism. If you are willing to drown out those voices with your own privilege, you cannot genuinely claim to care about the advancement of women'.[15]

Muslims vs Gays

It is a paradox when ostensible 'conservatives' and rightists vociferously oppose Muslims as threats to liberal, globalised, secularised, Western society, as if the contemporary West represents in any manner traditional rightist values. Islam is one of the few traditional, conservative remnants in the world. Soros refers to Islam and Russia as the two remaining bulwarks against the *brave new world*. What the oligarchs desire is Muslim immigration to serve as part of their agenda for a globalised economy. However, what they do not want are enclaves of Muslims who retain traditional beliefs and resist liberal, globalist agendas. They want secularised Muslims and hence try to seduce uprooted Muslim youth with the West's culture of decay.[16] They want tamed Muslims like they wanted tamed Blacks, such as Martin Luther King, not Black nationalist ghetto militants.[17]

The problem is, how does a liberal globalist promote an inclusive economy when there is no common outlook among the subjects?

---

15 Ibid.

16 See: Bolton, *Zionism, Islam and the West*, pp. 160–170, on how the U.S. State Department uses pop culture to detach Muslim youths in Europe from their cultural and religious roots.

17 For example, 'it was [Nelson] Rockefeller's representative who secretly provided a suitcase of cash to King's attorney Clarence Jones in the basement of the Chase Manhattan Bank as bail money for those arrested in the Children's March in Birmingham, Ala., in May 1963'. Kevin M. Burke, 'A Close Alliance Between MLK and Nelson Rockefeller Revealed', *The Root*, 11 November 2015; https://www.theroot.com/a-close-alliance-between-mlk-and-nelson-rockefeller-rev-1790858451.

Throwing money at a problem, especially if it involves family, faith and custom, does not always work.

When homosexuality and gender fluidity are taught in schools in Britain, it is the intrinsically conservative Muslims who object, while White indigenes are too cowered or too decadent to react. How then does a liberal defend gender fluidity and inclusivity without offending Muslims? Again, the only method is to detach the young from their parents, and deconstruct the traditional family. Hence, when Muslim parents protested vociferously against compulsory programmes to teach LGBTQ in British schools, the cracks in the inclusive, open society showed. In May 2019, the Muslim parents' protests had spread from Birmingham to schools nationwide. The protests started after pupils at Anderton Park Primary School in Birmingham 'were given books featuring **transgender children** and gay families'. The reaction of the the Department for Education was that primary school children 'should be taught about the society in which they are growing up. These subjects are designed to foster respect for others and for difference, and educate pupils about healthy relationships'.[18] Hence it is a state dogma, into which children must be compulsorily inducted, that transgenderism in children is 'healthy'.

Political Agendas

Intersectionality, like *multiculturalism*, intrinsically means social fracture. The only way global capitalism can rationalise the breakup of society is if this is intended to be *dialectical*; to use *deconstruction* in order to reconstruct society. If the funding of social fracture does not have a dialectical intent, then presumably it means that the financiers who have provided the money for a century to such causes are suicidal. An alternative hypothesis is that the globalist elites are confident of being able to control the forces they unleash, and direct them toward long-term goals. They have a faith in the efficacy of money

---

18 'LGBT School Lessons Protests Spread Nationwide', *BBC News*, 16 May 2019; https://www.bbc.com/news/uk-england-48294017.

for the purpose. The information is not secret; it is readily available by consulting the online annual reports and other documents of the Ford, Rockefeller, Carnegie, Bill Gates, and Soros Foundations, the National Endowment for Democracy, *ad infinitum.* To list the grants in detail is superfluous.[19] I will, however, cite the following as indicative of the important role played by the LGBTQ+ movement, which is explicit in stating that it also serves to undermine states targeted for 'regime change':

> LGBTQ issues have come to the forefront of international human rights and advocacy work, with increased pressure on advocates working for equality and justice for lesbian, gay, bisexual, transgender, queer and intersex groups in places like Uganda, Nigeria, and Russia. At the same time, increased dialogue around LGBTQ issues around the world have created a push for donors—including bilateral, multilateral and private foundations—to look for ways to support NGOs working on these issues. In 2012, US Foundations alone provided over $120 million in support of LGBTQ issues worldwide. Funding support for LGBTQ work is likely to be much higher in the coming years.[20]

What the result will be for the promotion and forcible *intersectionality* of conflicting interests, held together by the artificial bonds buttressed by money, is investable collapse. To paraphrase Marx, this system contains the seeds of its own destruction. To quote Douglas Murray:

> Perhaps they will have their way. Perhaps the advocates of the new religion will use gays and women and those of a different skin colour and trans individuals as a set of battering rams to turn people against the society they have been brought up in. Perhaps they will succeed in turning everyone against the 'cis white male patriarchy' and they will do it before all of their interlocking 'oppressed, victims groups' have torn each other apart. It is

---

19   Many examples are given in Bolton, *Revolution from Above.*

20   'Funding Resources for LGBTQ Issues Worldwide', Funds for NGOs, https://www.fundsforngos.org/lgbtq/funding-resources-lgbtq-issues-worldwide/.

possible. But anyone interested in preventing that nightmarish scenario should search for solutions.[21]

Straight White Leftists

Elements of the Left consider *identity politics* as having fractured opposition to capitalism. They reject the notion of *intersectionality* as a diversion. Historian Jesse Lemisch refers to 'angry white straight men of the Left'. The gay-leftist academic Dr. Martin Duberman, a proponent of *intersectionality*, refers to 'a horde of disgruntled, righteous straight Leftists, eager to join with others who deplored the derailing of class struggle…'.[22]

Duberman contends that 'blue-collar' interests are 'inextricably tied' to 'oppression based on race, gender and sexual orientation'.[23] Attempting to apply classical leftist dialectics, Duberman counters that 'polarization is how social progress takes place'.[24] Duberman condemns certain leftist spokesman, such as columnist and author Michael Tomasky, as 'white, male heterosexuals' 'lecturing the rest of us on the unimportance of our issues', and quotes Tomsky referring to 'narrow concerns' based on 'supposedly oppositional cultures'. 'The word "supposedly" says a lot'. Further, 'Tomasky himself refers to "faux-radical multiculturalism" and its "superficially transgressive ideas"'.[25]

The proletarian revolution has long since been discarded for *intersectionality* between fractured sub-classes. Far from this artificial coalition being a front against the oligarchy, it is held together by its common hatred for the 'White patriarchy', and 'White privilege', in which the White middle and labouring classes are regarded as the

---

21   Douglas Murray, p. 248.
22   Martin Duberman, pp. 415–416.
23   Ibid., p. 417.
24   Ibid., p. 419.
25   Ibid., p. 424.

'enemy', while Messrs. Rothschild, Soros, Rockefeller, Goldman/Sachs et al. proceed unnoticed.

In the New Left discourse that was formalised by Herbert Marcuse and became *identity politics*, the White working class was discarded in favour of bourgeois youth, and ethnic and sexual factions. Marcuse was unequivocal. The 'White patriarchy' became 'the Enemy' around which disjointed factions could unite, and the word *intersectionality* was coined. 'White privilege' means that all White *males* intrinsically benefit in the system of 'White oppression', and 'White supremacy' by virtue of their 'Whiteness' as a *social construct* (in contrast to all other races, which are legitimate entities).

The Myth of 'White Privilege'

THE CURRENT LATE EPOCH of Western civilisation is not the whole of Western culture *per se*; it is a phase of decline. German historicism makes a delineation between *Kultur* and *Zivilisation*, which explains this better than Anglo-French *positivism*:

> '[C]vilization' does not mean the same thing to different Western nations. Above all, there is a great difference between the English and French use of the word, on the one hand, and the German use of it, on the other. For the former, the concept sums up in a single term their pride in the significance of their own nations for the progress of the West and of humankind. But in German usage, *Zivilisation* means something which is indeed useful, but nevertheless only a value of the second rank, comprising only the outer appearance of human beings, the surface of human existence. The word through which Germans interpret themselves, which more than any other expresses their pride in their own achievements and their own being, is *Kultur*.[1]

Engels of British Poverty

The current epoch of Western civilisation, dominated by *money*, as Spengler pointed out, is an affliction on the White. Marx wrote of this as a dialectical process in which the former peasants and artisans, based around the village, were urbanised and proletarianised.

---

1   'Sociogenesis of the Antithesis Between *Kultur* and *Zivilisation* in German Usage', p. 1; http://www.blackwellpublishing.com/content/BPL_Images/ Content_store/Sample_Chapter/9780631221609/Elias_001.pdf.

Whereas precursors of the Right, such as Thomas Carlyle, deplored the process, Marx saw it as a necessary and inevitable historical step in *dialectical materialism*. His collaborator Friedrich Engels, in an early work (1845), wrote of the conditions which do not seem to indicate the proletariat being part of any 'White privilege' or 'patriarchy':

> Every great city has one or more slums, where the working-class is crowded together. True, poverty often dwells in hidden alleys close to the palaces of the rich; but, in general, a separate territory has been assigned to it, where, removed from the sight of the happier classes, it may struggle along as it can. These slums are pretty equally arranged in all the great towns of England, the worst houses in the worst quarters of the towns; usually one- or two-storied cottages in long rows, perhaps with cellars used as dwellings, almost always irregularly built. These houses of three or four rooms and a kitchen form, throughout England, some parts of London excepted, the general dwellings of the working-class. The streets are generally unpaved, rough, dirty, filled with vegetable and animal refuse, without sewers or gutters, but supplied with foul, stagnant pools instead. Moreover, ventilation is impeded by the bad, confused method of building of the whole quarter, and since many human beings here live crowded into a small space, the atmosphere that prevails in these working-men's quarters may readily be imagined. ...

> In the *Edinburgh Medical and Surgical Journal*, Dr. Hennen reports a similar state of things. From a Parliamentary Report, it is evident that in the dwellings of the poor of Edinburgh a want of cleanliness reigns, such as must be expected under these conditions. On the bed-posts chickens roost at night, dogs and horses share the dwellings of human beings, and the natural consequence is a shocking stench, with filth and swarms of vermin. The prevailing construction of Edinburgh favours these atrocious conditions as far as possible.

> ... The great towns are chiefly inhabited by working people, since in the best case there is one bourgeois for two workers, often for three, here and there for four; these workers have no property whatsoever of their own, and live wholly upon wages, which usually go from hand to mouth. Society, composed wholly of atoms, does not trouble itself about them; leaves them to care for themselves and their families, yet supplies them no means of

doing this in an efficient and permanent manner. Every working-man, even the best, is therefore constantly exposed to loss of work and food, that is to death by starvation, and many perish in this way. The dwellings of the workers are everywhere badly planned, badly built, and kept in the worst condition, badly ventilated, damp, and unwholesome. The inhabitants are confined to the smallest possible space, and at least one family usually sleeps in each room. The interior arrangement of the dwellings is poverty-stricken in various degrees, down to the utter absence of even the most necessary furniture. The clothing of the workers, too, is generally scanty, and that of great multitudes is in rags. The food is, in general, bad; often almost unfit for use, and in many cases, at least at times, insufficient in quantity, so that, in extreme cases, death by starvation results. Thus the working-class of the great cities offers a graduated scale of conditions in life, in the best cases a temporarily endurable existence for hard work and good wages, good and endurable, that is, from the worker's standpoint; in the worst cases, bitter want, reaching even homelessness and death by starvation. The average is much nearer the worst case than the best. ...[2]

All putrefying vegetable and animal substances give off gases decidedly injurious to health, and if these gases have no free way of escape, they inevitably poison the atmosphere. The filth and stagnant pools of the working-people's quarters in the great cities have, therefore, the worst effect upon the public health, because they produce precisely those gases which engender disease; so, too, the exhalations from contaminated streams.

Another category of diseases arises directly from the food rather than the dwellings of the workers. The food of the labourer, indigestible enough in itself, is utterly unfit for young children, and he has neither means nor time to get his children more suitable food. ...[3]

In the coal and iron mines which are worked in pretty much the same way, children of four, five, and seven years are employed. They are set to transporting the ore or coal loosened by the miner from its place to the horse-path or the main shaft, and to opening and shutting the doors (which separate the divisions of the mine and regulate its ventilation) for the passage of workers and material. For watching the doors the smallest children are usually employed, who thus pass twelve hours daily, in the dark, alone,

---

2   Engels, *The Condition of the Working Class in England* (1845), 'The Great Cities'.
3   Ibid., 'Results'.

sitting usually in damp passages without even having work enough to save them from the stupefying, brutalising tedium of doing nothing. The transport of coal and iron-stone, on the other hand, is very hard labour, the stuff being shoved in large tubs, without wheels, over the uneven floor of the mine; often over moist clay, or through water, and frequently up steep inclines and through paths so low-roofed that the workers are forced to creep on hands and knees. For this more wearing labour, therefore, older children and half-grown girls are employed.[4]

William Cobbett, the social reformer, stated in Parliament to Wilberforce, the anti-slavery crusader:

You seem to have great affection for the negroes... I feel for the hard-pinched, the ill-treated, the beaten down labouring classes of England, Scotland and Ireland, to whom you do all the mischief that it is in your power to do; because you describe their situation as good, and **because you do, in some degree, at any rate, draw the public attention away from their sufferings.**[5]

The latter comment could apply to the manner by which the Left draws attention away from the actual workings of capitalism and its basis in the debt-finance system, about which the Left have never said much. In regard to government opposition to the Ten-Hour Day Movement, Cobbett stated in Parliament in 1833:

A most surprising discovery has been made, namely, that all our greatness and prosperity, that our superiority over other nations, is owing to 30,000 little girls in Lancashire. If these little girls work two hours less in a day than they do now, it would occasion the ruin of the country.[6]

---

4   Ibid., 'The Mining Proletariat'.

5   William Cobbett, *Cobbett's Weekly Political Register* (London), Vol. 47, 30 August 1823, p. 553.

6   Cobbett cited in Sue Zemka, p. 76.

Redlegs

In the Caribbean, descendants of 'indentured servants' and slaves from Britain and Ireland eke out an existence, while liberal historians and activists attempt to trivialise their plight and claim it is exaggerated and manufactured by 'neo-Nazis', 'racists', 'Holocaust deniers' and 'neo-Confederates'. This is the line taken by the Southern Poverty Law Center when featuring Irish historian Liam Hogan.[7] Yet decades previously *The New York Times,* which is not known to be a neo-Nazi periodical, featured the *Redlegs*:

> Throughout the British West Indies the bottom rung of the socioeconomic ladder is reserved for groups of poor, backward and isolated whites known generally as 'Redlegs.' They are the descendants of men, women and children shipped to the Caribbean islands from Britain from the mid-1600's to the mid-1800's to shore up the labor supply on the profitable sugar plantations. **Some came as slaves:** losers in Protestant-Catholic conflicts, debtors and other convicts or **kidnapping victims**. Others came as **indentured servants, some willingly, some not.** Seventy years ago a Caribbean tourist described their progeny as 'mean whites,' not colonists fallen upon evil days but 'colonists by compulsion who for centuries have enjoyed nothing but a heritage of woe.'
>
> Today the 'Redlegs' — usually identified by complexions which seem almost bleached of all color, straw-like hair and pale blue eyes — are **pariahs,** a subculture unto themselves, aloof from the environment and era. Though their roots in the Caribbean now go back 300 years, they have never assimilated. ...[8]

These people have been put down the memory hole. They are an historic reminder that 'White privilege' is a fanciful myth. The reader

---

7   Liam Hogan, 'How the Myth of the "Irish slaves" Became a Racist Meme Online', SPLC, 19 April 2016; https://www.splcenter.org/hatewatch/2016/04/19/how-myth-irish-slaves-became-favorite-meme-racists-online.

8   Lindsay Haines, 'Poor, Backward and Adamantly White in a Black World', *The New York Times,* 25 February 1973; https://www.nytimes.com/1973/02/25/archives/poor-backward-and-adamantly-white-in-a-black-world-culture-doomed.html. Emphasis added.

is urged to read the full *Times* article. Researchers such as Michael Hoffman, author of *They Were White and They Were Slaves*,[9] are pilloried by liberal academics as 'conspiracy theorists' for claiming that such White history has been deliberately suppressed, yet the Southern Poverty Law Center attempts precisely that.

The Left previously talked of the 'wage slave', whose conditions were carefully documented by Engels, as cited above. Now, by some perverse strangulation of dialectics, the 'wage slave' has become part of the legacy of 'White privilege', and our forefathers have enabled the mass of Whites to become part of an oppressive 'White patriarchy'.

What this 'wage slavery', and the phenomena of the 'Redlegs' and indentured servants, and a host of other historical situations, such as the Highland Clearances, show is that under capitalism there is no common bond between the White industrialists/financiers and White proletarians: there was no kinship of race or even nationality, other than when the White proletarian was needed as cannon fodder for opening up overseas industrial expansion and markets; then a common 'patriotism' was invoked. Yet in the fantasy of the White academic, Whites 'operate as a group to maintain certain advantages and to exclude other groups', 'as the dominant group, politically and economically'.[10]

---

9   Michael A. Hoffman II (1992).

10 Paul Spoonley in Bruce Jesson, Allanah Ryan, Paul Spoonley, p. 127. By 'Right' Spoonley et al. mean Whig liberalism.
    One might suspect that Dr. Spoonley, a sociologist and academic-in-waiting for the news media whenever there is a smear against the Right to be made, is projecting his own 'white privilege'. A Damascus moment came for Spoonley in 1977 when, as a student, he thought he witnessed at Lewisham '4000 National Front members abuse the local non-white community — protected by 5000 police'. Paul Spoonley, 'I Thought There Had Been a Decline in Far Right Politics, I Was Wrong', *Stuff*, 15 March 2020; https://www.stuff.co.nz/opinion/120179211/i-thought-there-had-been-a-decline-in-far-right-politics-i-was-wrong.
    In the real world, there were 500 NF members who attempted to peacefully march through Lewisham while 5000 (some estimates are up to 9000)

The South and the White Worker

Yet surely all Whites in the Southern states of the USA have profited from the exploitation of the Black man's labour under slavery, and that this is the basis of today's 'White privilege'? African slavery in the Southern states was a *cause celebre* for rich Northern Whigs who, like their counterparts in Britain, cared nothing for their fellow Whites bound to wage slavery. However, Hinton Rowan Helper (North Carolina) was an 'abolitionist' because he regarded African slavery as depressing the livelihood of the White worker and retarding the South. Helper spoke as a Southern patriot. He advocated resettlement to Africa of the slaves. Careful to document his position, Helper addressed the position of the common White folk, towards whom Southern oligarchs showed no kinship.

> The lords of the lash are not only absolute masters of the blacks, who are bought and sold, and driven about like so many cattle, but they are also the oracles and arbiters of all non-slaveholding whites, whose freedom is merely nominal, and whose unparalleled illiteracy and degradation is purposely and fiendishly perpetuated. How little the 'poor white trash', the great majority of the Southern people, know of the real condition of the country is, indeed, sadly astonishing. The truth is, they know nothing of public measures, and little of private affairs, except what their imperious masters, the slave-drivers, condescend to tell, and that is but precious little, and even that little, always garbled and one-sided, is never told except in public harangues; **for the haughty cavaliers of shackles and handcuffs will not degrade themselves by holding private converse with those who have neither dimes nor hereditary rights in human flesh.**[11]

Communists and ethnics rioted against the police. Lewisham had a high incidence of mugging, and the NF march was themed against muggers. The riot was organised by the Trotskyite Socialist Workers Party, and had been disapproved by the Communist Party as 'the ritual enactment of vanguardist violence'. This gutless riot is heralded as 'heroism'. (See: Sarah Cox, 'Battle of Lewisham Mural Installed in New Cross', Goldsmiths: University of London, 26 October 2019; https://www.gold.ac.uk/news/battle-of-lewisham-commemorative-artwork-/).

11   Hinton Rowan Helper, pp. 43–44. Emphasis added.

THE ILLITERATE POOR WHITES OF THE SOUTH.

Had we the power to sketch a true picture of life among the non-slave-holding whites of the South, every intelligent man who has a spark of philanthropy in his breast, and who should happen to gaze upon the picture, would burn with unquenchable indignation at that system of African slavery which entails unutterable miseries on the superior race. It is quite impossible, however, to describe accurately the deplorable ignorance and squalid poverty of the class to which we refer. The serfs of Russia have reason to congratulate themselves that they are neither the negroes nor the non-slaveholding whites of the South. Than the latter there can be no people in Christendom more unhappily situated. Below will be found a few extracts which will throw some light on the subject now under consideration.

Says William Gregg, in an address delivered before the South Carolina Institute, in 1851:

'From the best estimates that I have been able to make, I put down the white people who ought to work, and who do not, or who are so employed as to be wholly unproductive to the State, at one hundred and twenty-five thousand. Any man who is an observer of things could hardly pass through our country, without being struck with the fact that all the capital, enterprise, and intelligence, is employed in directing slave labor; and the consequence is, that a large portion of our poor white people are wholly neglected, and are suffered to while away an existence in a state but one step in advance of the Indian of the forest. ... My experience at Graniteville has satisfied me that unless our poor people can be brought together in villages, and some means of employment afforded them, it will be an utterly hopeless effort to undertake to educate them. We have collected at that place about eight hundred people, and as likely looking a set of country girls as may be found — industrious and orderly people, but deplorably ignorant, three-fourths of the adults not being able to read or to write their own names.' ...

Again he asks:

'Shall we pass unnoticed the thousands of poor, ignorant, degraded white people among us, who, in this land of plenty, live in comparative nakedness and starvation? Many a one is reared in proud South Carolina, from birth to manhood, who has never passed a month in which he has not, some part of the time, been stinted for meat. Many a mother is there who will tell you that her children are but scantily provided with bread and much more scantily with meat; and, if they be clad with comfortable raiment, it is at the expense of these scanty allowances of food. These may be startling statements, but they are nevertheless true; and if not believed in Charleston, the members of our legislature who have traversed the State in electioneering campaigns can attest the truth'.[12]

A citizen of New-Orleans, writing in *DeBow's Review*, says:

'At present the sources of employment open to females (save in menial offices) are very limited; and an inability to procure suitable occupation is an evil much to be deplored, as tending in its consequences to produce demoralization. The superior grades of female labor may be considered such as imply a necessity for education on the part of the employee, while the menial class is generally regarded as of the lowest; and in a slave State, this standard is 'in the lowest depths, a lower deep,' from the fact, that, by association, it is a reduction of the white servant to the level of their colored fellow-menials'.[13]

Helper continues:

Last Spring we made it our special business to ascertain the ruling rates of wages paid for labor, free and slave, in North Carolina. We found sober, energetic white men, between twenty and forty years of age, engaged in agricultural pursuits at a salary of $84 per annum — including board only; negro men, slaves, who performed little more than half the amount of labor, and who were exceedingly sluggish, awkward, and careless in all their movements, were hired out on adjoining farms at an average of about $115 per annum, including board, clothing, and medical attendance. Free white men and slaves were in the employ of the North Carolina Railroad Company; the former, whose services, in our opinion, were at least twice as valuable as the services of the latter, received only $12 per month each; the masters of the latter received $16 per month for every slave so employed. Industrious, tidy white girls, from sixteen to twenty years of age, had much difficulty in hiring themselves out as domestics in private families for $40

---

12   Ibid., p. 377.
13   Ibid., p. 380.

per annum — board only included; negro wenches, slaves, of correspond-
ing ages, so ungraceful, stupid and filthy that no decent man would ever
permit one of them to cross the threshold of his dwelling, were in brisk
demand at from $65 to $70 per annum, including victuals, clothes, and
medical attendance. These are facts, and in considering them, the students
of political and social economy will not fail to arrive at conclusions of their
own. …[14]

Helper next described the condition of poor White folk in terms that
would have them classed into what Marx and Engels disparaged as the
lumpenproletariat in Europe:

Poverty, ignorance, and superstition, are the three leading characteristics of
the non-slaveholding whites of the South. Many of them grow up to the age
of maturity, and pass through life without ever owning as much as five dol-
lars at any one time. Thousands of them die at an advanced age, as ignorant
of the common alphabet as if it had never been invented. All are more or
less impressed with a belief in witches, ghosts, and supernatural signs. Few
are exempt from habits of sensuality and intemperance. None have anything like adequate ideas of the duties which they owe either to their God,
to themselves, or to their fellow-men. Pitiable, indeed, in the fullest sense
of the term, is their condition. It is the almost utter lack of an education
that has reduced them to their present unenviable situation. In the whole
South there is scarcely a publication of any kind devoted to their interests.
They are now completely under the domination of the oligarchy, and it is
madness to suppose that they will ever be able to rise to a position of true
manhood, until after the slave power shall have been utterly overthrown.[15]

Where is this legacy of 'White privilege'? The neo-Marxists, just as
much as the bourgeois liberals, say that today's White populations
are living high from the legacy of capitalism. But surely the world pariah, the Afrikaner, until recently lived on such a legacy? Far from it.
During the 19th century, he epitomised the rebel against imperialism
and foreign mining interests. His fall from leftist grace was induced

---

14   Ibid.
15   Ibid., pp. 381–382.

by the change of allegiance from the 'international proletariat' to new-found 'minorities' that could not include even the White proletariat. The rise of Afrikaner nationalism and the foundations of apartheid had their origins in the ongoing conflict with industrial, financial and mining interests, the epochal moment being the violent suppression of the White miner-workers' General Strike on the Rand in 1922.[16] Apartheid was born from White class struggle against mining inter-ests and other oligarchic interests; a struggle which endured until the assumption of Black rule.[17] There was a time when not all Marxists were hoodwinked and clueless. Belfort Bax, of the Social Democratic Federation, Britain's first Marxist organisation, stated during the Second Boer War that Boer legislation to prevent the Blacks from be-ing exploited by *uitlander* capitalists was one of the causes of the war, and he hoped that the Boers would be victorious in forming a 'United Afrikaner Boer Republic'.[18]

---

16   Bolton, *Babel Inc.*, pp. 79–95.
17   Ibid.
18   Quoted by S. F. Kissin, chapter 4.

Population Control

Finally, it is also worth noting that more extreme or controversial proposals tend to legitimate more moderate advances, by shifting the boundaries of discourse.

— Bernard Berelson, Population Council

THE TYPES AND GROWTH of the world's population have long been of primary concern to social engineers. The Left and anti-globalist 'conspiracy theorists' of the libertarian 'American patriot' variety see a 'Fascist conspiracy' in the grants that had been given to eugenics research by Rockefeller and others.

With the question of 'social hygiene' in vogue a century ago, an offshoot of this was the wide popularity of *eugenics*, the aim of up-breeding humans, or weeding out anti-social traits, such as alcoholism, and inherited diseases. The British Eugenics Society was founded in 1907 by Sir Francis Galton, author of the influential *Hereditary Genius* (1869).

It is assumed that eugenics was the preoccupation of upper class Englishmen, seeking to stem the breeding of the genetically inferior proletariat, and hence an intrinsically 'right-wing' — Tory — manifestation that was to be most infamously practised by Nazi Germany. This is incorrect. We have already referred to eugenics being a cause promoted by William Beveridge, regarded as the 'father of the post-1945 welfare state' in Britain. At the beginning of the 20th century,

Beveridge, a liberal politician and director of the London School of Economics, worked with Fabian Society leaders Sidney and Beatrice Webb, and influenced their ideas on social reform.[1]

Beveridge was a member of the Eugenics Society, as were famous Fabian Society authors H. G. Wells and George Bernard Shaw. Prominent geneticist J. B. S. Haldane, a leading member of the British Communist Party,[2] was an avid advocate of eugenics. Charles Merriam, dean of American social science, referred to eugenics when writing that 'control is likely in future to reach a point where it may be possible to breed whatever type of human being it is desired to have. We might even breed strange creatures as beasts of burden and toil...' What type of being might result is the 'chance that the governing group would have to take in such a world'.[3]

While Nazi Germany is assumed to have been uniquely obsessive about *eugenics*, it was Social Democratic Sweden that operated a eugenics policy longer than any other modern state. Sweden's Sterilisation Act was operative from 1934 to 1976, during which time 62,000 (90% women) were forcibly sterilised.

> Teenagers as young as 15 were sterilised, some without their parents' consent, for inadequacies as trivial as shortsightedness or because they allegedly lacked judgment or had 'no obvious concept of ethics'. Pressure was put on orphans and children in special schools and reformatories to have the operation as a condition of release. Pregnant women seeking abortions because their foetus was damaged were told they also had to consent to sterilisation. People could even apply to have problem neighbourhood families sterilised.

---

1   José Harris, p. 98.

2   Haldane, a Communist since the 1930s, joined the party in 1942 and was appointed to the executive committee in 1944. He had, however, served as Chairman of the editorial board of the party newspaper *Daily Worker* from 1940 until 1950, and had been writing a column for the paper since 1937. Ronald Clark, pp. 132, 159, 166, 185.

3   Charles Merriam, pp. 145–157.

As in Britain, where some of eugenics' most enthusiastic supporters were on the political left, liberals and Social Democrats backed the Swedish programme and sustained it for decades.[4]

The principal architect of Sweden's eugenics laws was the sociologist and economist Gunnar Myrdal, who was soon after invited by the Carnegie Corporation to undertake a study on U.S. race relations, which became the seminal *American Dilemma*. Myrdal advocated 'consumption socialism'. His proposals for the reform of abortion laws allowed for abortion on 'eugenics' and 'social-medical' grounds, usually to be accompanied by sterilisation.[5]

The Institute for Human Genetics was established by the Rockefeller Foundation in Denmark, another social democracy, in 1938, and became a department of Copenhagen University.[6] A sterilisation law was passed in Denmark in 1929 under an Agrarian Party government, but with backing from the Social Democrats. Thit Jensen and other feminists supported the law because they assumed it would help birth control, and they regarded it as somehow taking control away from men. Jonathan Leunach, who had co-founded the Magnus Hirschfeld League for Sexual Reform, and the Sexual Reform Party, which was aligned with the Communist Party, supported eugenics because he too saw it as connected with birth control and feminism.[7]

Again, the Left and oligarchy converge. Both want a productive class of drones, in what Alberto Spektorowski and Liza Ireni-Saban call 'welfare-productionism'[8] to explain the early Left's advocacy. They point out that from 1900 to the 1930s, eugenics was not necessarily related to the Right. Eugenics diverged when elements of the Left

---

4   Stephen Bates, 'Sweden Pays for Grim Past', *The Guardian*, 6 March 1999. Emphasis added.

5   Allan C. Carlson, p. 175.

6   Alberto Spektorowski, Liza Ireni-Saban, p. 75.

7   Ibid., p. 73.

8   Ibid., p. 6.

began to focus on this 'welfare-productionism' while elements of the Right (by no means universal) focused on racial biology.

Soviet Eugenics

In Russia, Vasili Florinskii, a gynaecologist, had discussed eugenics since 1866 with the publication of his *Human Perfection and Degeneration*. However, it was not until after the triumph of Bolshevism that the Russian Eugenics Society was founded in Moscow in 1920. Under the direction of Mikhail Volotskoi, an anthropologist, this was intended to promote, in contrast, indeed in opposition to the 'bourgeois eugenics' of Sir Francis Galton, 'proletarian eugenics', also called 'bio-social' eugenics. The concept was implemented by the Soviet authorities at an early stage in marriage laws on the health of prospective spouses. 'Social hygiene' and eugenics became intertwined. Volotskoi was appointed to the 'scientific-consultative group on the biological question' for the State Museum of Social Hygiene (which became the State Institute of Social Hygiene in 1923), established in 1919 by the People's Commissariat of Health Protection.[9]

> The agency's head Nikolai Semashko, a Bolshevik physician, was an active proponent of social hygiene. Indeed, with its focus on the role of social factors in health and disease and its prioritizing of prophylactic over curative approaches to disease, social hygiene became the foundational doctrine of the entire system of health protection created by the Bolsheviks. Furthermore, its proponents defined social hygiene as 'a science of the future, which studies and shapes the facts that promote the biological well-being of humanity', and saw eugenics as 'the ultimate goal of all sanitary-medical activities'.[10]

---

9   Nikolai Krementsov, p. 260. Krementsov is Professor at the Institute for the History and Philosophy of Science and Technology, University of Toronto.

10   Ibid., p. 261. Quoting: T. Ia. Tkachev, *Sotsial'naia gigiena* (Voronezh: Gubzdravotdel, 1924), pp. 11, 153.

Under Stalin this came to a halt in 1930,[11] and not only eugenics but the science of Mendelian genetics was officially repudiated,[12] much to the dismay of pro-Communist geneticists in the West. Professor H. J. Muller, who advocated 'socialist eugenics', wrote to Stalin that '[t]rue eugenics can only be a product of socialism, and will, like advances in physical technique, be one of the means used by the latter in the betterment of life', while reiterating the opposition to Nazi racial eugenics.[13] While the USSR suppressed genetics as intrinsically 'Fascist', Muller continued to promote 'socialist eugenics' in the West, writing in 1939 of heredity and environment 'under the potential control of man [which admits to] unlimited but interdependent progress'. Muller's memorandum was published in *The Journal of Heredity*, and became known as the 'geneticists' manifesto', signed by 21 geneticists.[14] The eagerness to repudiate Stalinism enabled the Institute of Medical Genetics to be established in Moscow in 1969.[15] 'Socialist eugenics' began to be widely discussed again in the USSR from the late 1960s.[16]

Confluence

Social hygiene was indeed a laudable movement, and was not intrinsically the ideological property of any party. Often accompanied by calls for eugenic marriage and birth control programmes — not usually with a racial foundation — the social hygiene doctrine accomplished a great deal for mother and child in states of various ideological and party governance. In New Zealand, for example, the Plunket Society was founded by Dr. Truby King, an advocate of eugenics, and did an excellent job of monitoring the health of generations of babies via

---

11 Nikolai Krementsov, ibid., pp. 17–18.
12 However, Mendelian genetics was not outlawed, despite popular assumptions, and continued to be discussed. See: Nikolai Krementsov, ibid.
13 Muller cited by Krementsov, ibid., pp. 339–340.
14 Muller cited by Krementsov, ibid., p. 343.
15 Krementsov, p. 351–352.
16 Ibid., p. 357.

the Plunket clinics, hospitals and home visits from Plunket nurses, in every community. Originally called the Society for the Promotion of the Health of Women and Children, this was formed in 1907, long prior to the Bolsheviks, Nazis and John D. Rockefeller's Population Council. Plunket's 'domestic hygiene' and 'mothercraft', anathema to today's feminists, educators and liberals, was credited with giving New Zealand the lowest infant mortality rate in the world.

However, social hygiene also became a method of population control and social engineering according to utopian visions on the 'perfectibility of man'. National Socialists thought they would perfect man via racial eugenics, Bolsheviks and Social Democrats through 'proletarian eugenics', and oligarchs through programmes of population control that are in spirit, theory and practice analogous to the Left.

The ideal of the 'perfectibility of man' comes from Enlightenment doctrines, and later from the application of Darwinism to society in Britain. It is here that there was a convergence between socialists, such as the Webbs and Shaw, free traders, and Darwinian scientists, such as Julian Huxley, later to become first director general of UNESCO. The doctrines that began to fester in 18th century Europe erupted in the Jacobin Revolution, the precursor to both British Whig liberalism and Marxism. These doctrines proclaimed the 'perfectibility of man' by the destruction of the traditional institutions. The doctrine of perfectibility entered the social sciences through Boasian cultural anthropology and Critical Theory. The 18th century Order of the Illuminati, the crypto-Masonic precursor of revolutionary movements up to the present, were known as the *Perfectibilists*. The socialism of Marx and the free frade doctrine of Adam Smith both arose within a British society that was dominated by industrialisation and the notion that this was the age of unprecedented 'progress'. Marx was beholden to Adam Smith for the primary element of his doctrine: the 'labour theory of value'. The *Zeitgeist* arising first in Britain was that of *economics*.

Dr. Carolyn Burdett[17] writes of the manner by which 'social Darwinism' became the scientific rationalisation for free trade economics:

> Many Victorians recognised in evolutionary thinking a vision of the world that seemed to fit their own social experience. The scale of change during the 19th century, and the impact on people's lives of industrialisation, urbanisation and technological innovation, was unprecedented. The idea of a 'struggle for existence' that was central to Darwin's theory of biological evolution was a powerful way to describe Britain's competitive capitalist economy in which some people became enormously wealthy and others struggled amidst the direst poverty.
>
> Traditional liberal ideas valued the independence and autonomy of individuals and argued that, wherever possible, the state should adopt a 'laissez-faire' (or 'leave alone') position. Economically, too, markets should be allowed to operate freely, allowing wealth creation to flourish through competition. Evolution seemed to confirm this view: species compete and struggle and only some — the fittest and best — survive. In fact, Darwin was convinced that cooperation was also important, especially for those creatures, including humans, who live in groups. Others, though, were convinced that competition was the key to development.[18]

'Conservatives, liberals and socialists all embraced eugenic ideas. …' As noted above, there were feminists who saw eugenics as a means of 'emancipation' from customary expectations of motherhood. During the 1890s, the 'New Women', precursors of feminism, saw eugenics as a means of undermining marriage and child-birth traditions. Hence we see another important common factor between the Left and modern capitalism: that economic struggle is the basis of 'progress'. Marx, like the free traders, saw in Darwin's *On the Origin of Species* justification for his doctrine, writing to the German socialist Lasalle: 'Darwin's

---

17   Carolyn Burdett is Senior Lecturer in English Literature and Victorian Studies at Birkbeck, University of London.

18   Carolyn Burdett, 'Post Darwin: Social Darwinism, Degeneration, Eugenics', 15 May 2014, British Library; https://www.bl.uk/romantics-and-victorians/ articles/post-darwin-social-darwinism-degeneration-eugenics.

work is most important and suits my purpose in that it provides a basis in natural science for the historical class struggle...'[19]

Nikolai Krementsov put the question as to why there was a convergence of interest in eugenics as a 'social hygiene' mechanism by Bolsheviks, when it seems — superficially — antithetical to the ideology?:

> Bolshevik Russia appeared the least likely locale for concerns with 'national degeneration', the increasing fertility of 'lower classes', or 'interracial meticization', which held the attention of the Second International Eugenics Congress. Yet the rapid institutionalization, internationalization, as well as active propaganda, of eugenics in the immediate post-revolutionary years was fully funded and enthusiastically endorsed by various agents and agencies of the country's new government. Why would a 'proletarian state', which claimed to be building a classless society and vocally denounced racism and nationalism, become a hotbed of eugenic debates, support eugenic research and institutions, and adopt eugenics-inspired policies?

> At least in part, the answer to this question lies in the confluence between the eugenic vision of 'the self-direction of human evolution', as it was expressed in the motto of the Second International Eugenics Congress, and the Bolsheviks' 'revolutionary dreams' (in U.S. historian Richard Stites's apt characterization) of creating a 'new world', a 'new society', and a 'new man'.[20]

> As Kol'tsov[21] clearly articulated in his 1921 anniversary address, the major goal of eugenics was 'to create [...] a higher type of human, the powerful king of nature and the creator of life'. The Bolsheviks, in the words of one of their leaders Leon Trotsky, believed that with the victory of the Revolution 'humankind, frozen *Homo sapiens*, will enter into radical reconstruction and will become — under its own fingers — an object of most complicated methods of artificial selection and psycho-physical training. [...] Man will

---

19   Marx to Lasalle, *Marx and Engels Collected Works*, 16 January 1851, Vol. 41, pp. 246–47.

20   Krementsov, pp. 269–270; citing Richard Stites, *Revolutionary Dreams: Utopian Vision and Experimental Life in the Russian Revolution* (Oxford: Oxford University Press, 1989).

21   Nikolai Kol'tsov (1872–1940), a founder of Russian genetics.

put forward a goal [...] to raise himself to a new level — to create a higher socio-biological type, an *Ubermensch*, if you will'.[22] Resonance between the eugenic vision of 'a higher type of human' and the Bolshevik dreams of 'a higher socio-biological type' played an important role in the appeal of eugenics to its state patrons, as well as to the numerous followers the fledgling 'biological science of eugenics' attracted in 1920s Soviet Russia.[23]

Here we might discern the 'confluence' between the early Bolsheviks and others of the Left, Fabians, Social Democrats et al., and the oligarchs who also aim to achieve the 'self-direction of human evolution', who see themselves as 'the powerful kings of nature and the creators of life', who aim to 'reconstruct' humanity. It is the age-old *hubris* of man aiming to become God that precedes a fall. For over a century, Andrew Carnegie and John D. Rockefeller, when they established their Foundations, and more latterly George Soros, Bill Gates, et al. have sought to recreate the world in their images: as gods remoulding man and Earth at their will, through their money.

Moreover, the attitude of Marx and Engels towards the proletariat was elitist. They distinguished between the industrial workers as the aristocracy of the revolution, and an underclass of 'scum', for whom Marx coined the word *lumpenproletariat*. To Marx and Engels these were the West's equivalent to the *chandala* caste of India. In the *Communist Manifesto*, Marx and Engels refer to the *lumpenproletariat* as 'the "dangerous class", the social scum, that passively rotting mass thrown off by the lowest layers of old society'. Further, that although it 'may, here and there, be swept into the movement by a proletarian revolution, its conditions of life prepare it far more for the part of a bribed tool of reactionary intrigue'.[24] In *The Class Struggles in France*

---

22 Krementsov, citing Leon Trotsky, *Literatura i revoliutsiia* (M.: Krasnaia nov', 1923), pp. 195–97.

23 Krementsov, p. 271; citing T. I. Iudin, 'Nasledstvennost' dushevnykh boleznei', *REZh*, 1922, Vol. 1, No. 1, pp. 28–39; and V. V. Bunak, 'Evgenicheskie opytnye stantsii, ikh zadachi i plan ikh rabot', ibid., pp. 83–99.

24 Marx, *The Communist Manifesto*, Chapter I: 'Bourgeois and Proletarians'.

1848–1850, Marx wrote that the *lumpenproletariat*, 'in all big towns forms a mass sharply differentiated from the industrial proletariat'; 'a recruiting ground for thieves and criminals of all kinds, living on the crumbs of society, people without a definite trade, vagabonds, *gens sans feu et sans aveu*,[25] varying according to the degree of civilisation of the nation to which they belong, but never renouncing their *lazzaroni*[26] character'.[27] Engels wrote in *The Peasant War in Germany*:

> The *lumpenproletariat*, this scum of the depraved elements of all classes, which established headquarters in the big cities, is the worst of all possible allies. This rabble is absolutely venal and absolutely brazen. If the French workers, in every revolution, inscribed on the houses: *Mort aux voleurs!* (Death to thieves!) and even shot some, they did it, not out of enthusiasm for property, but because they rightly considered it necessary above all to keep that gang at a distance. Every leader of the workers who uses these scoundrels as guards or relies on them for support proves himself by this action alone a traitor to the movement.[28]

Rockefeller's Population Council

John D. Rockefeller established the Rockefeller Foundation in 1913. Already in 1914 its *Annual Report* referred to a grant for Dr. Charles Davenport's eugenics work: 'May 5, 1914—To Dr. Charles B. Davenport, Cold Spring Harbor, Long Island, New York, for the purpose of providing field workers in eugenics, the institutions or the State paying the maintenance and expenses of the workers in the field. $1350'.[29] Prior to Rockefeller, the Carnegie Institution funded Davenport in 1902 with $45,000 to set up his 'Biological Experiment

---

25 Men without hearth or home.

26 *Lazzaroni*: a contemptuous nickname for declassed proletarians, the word originating from the Kingdom of Naples, referring to those who were repeatedly used in the struggle against the liberal and democratic movement.

27 Marx, (1850), 'Part I: The Defeat of June, 1848'.

28 F. Engels, *The Peasant War in Germany*, 'Preface to the Second Edition' (1870).

29 The Rockefeller Foundation Annual Report 1913–1914, p. 203.

Station for the study of evolution' at Cold Spring Harbor.[30] In 1915, the Eugenic Record Office received $4,050 from Rockefeller,[31] which seems to be the last Rockefeller payment to Davenport. It is on the basis of such funding and that provided to institutions in Germany that a case is made for a collaboration between the U.S. oligarchy and Nazism. American-Jewish academic Edwin Black writes:

> More than just providing the scientific roadmap, America funded Germany's eugenic institutions. By 1926, Rockefeller had donated some $410,000 — almost $4 million in 21st-century money — to hundreds of German researchers. In May 1926, Rockefeller awarded $250,000 to the German Psychiatric Institute of the Kaiser Wilhelm Institute, later to become the Kaiser Wilhelm Institute for Psychiatry.[32]

Such claims are associated with the persistent red herring that Nazism and Fascism are the 'last resort of capitalism'. As we have seen, eugenics was embraced originally more by the Left than by the Right, which does not have any deep ideological antecedents for it. The concept appealed to the Left because it had a faith in the perfectibility of man. The Right had no such illusions. The Right traditionally does not see man on an upward march of Darwinian evolutionary 'progress'. It was Marxism and liberalism that happily embraced Darwin. Where Hitlerism embarked on that path delineates where the imports of Darwin, Galton and Malthus overtook the German idealism of Fichte, Hegel and Goethe, in a great historical irony.

As for Germany, prior to the Nazis Magnus Hirschfeld's institute included a 'eugenic department for mother and child', and purveyed eugenic marriage guidance advice.[33] In 1913, six years prior to the

30 Carnegie Institution of Washington. Washington: Carnegie Institution of Washington; 1902. Year Book No. 1.

31 The Rockefeller Foundation Annual Report (1915), p. 360.

32 Edwin Black, 'The Horrifying American Roots of Nazi Eugenics'.

33 'Institute for Sexual Science, Eugenics, Marriage, and Sex Counselling', https://www.magnus-hirschfeld.de/institute-for-sexual-science-1919-1933/personnel/eugenicists-marriage-and-sex-counsellor/.

formation of what became the Nazi Party, Hirschfeld co-founded the Medical Society for Sexual Science and Eugenics.[34]

In 1952, John D. Rockefeller III took up the challenge of his grandfather in promoting the importance of population control. He convened a conference of scientists at Williamsburg, Virginia, under the auspices of the National Academy of Sciences, to consider problems of population.

Dr. Phyllis Piotrow, an adviser to USAID, among the primary agencies promoting American globalism, wrote a broad history of population control. It should be kept in mind that what she regards as the 'slowness' of the U.S. response was, as she documents, primarily due to a rear-guard fight by the Catholic Church. Piotrow shows the Rockefeller Foundation and other interests behind population control:

> The most eagerly sought and acknowledged funding for professional and scientific activities in the field of population came from the foundations. ... The first large foundations to make grants in the population field were the Rockefeller Foundation and the Carnegie Foundation.[35]

'In November 1952 the Population Council was organized with Rockefeller as chairman of the board', and the USA's leading eugenicist, 'Frederick Osborn as executive vice-president'.[36] Piotrow, having alluded to Margaret Sanger, the founder of the 'family planning' movement,[37] whose approach was still too radical for many, states that

---

34   Kirsten Leng, p. 193.

35   Phyllis T. Piotrow, p. 8. Piotrow was adviser to government and U.N. agencies, former executive director, Population Action International (PAI); Chair, Population and Family Planning, American Public Health Association, and on the Board of Directors, Centre for Development and Population Activities.
PAI promotes abortion and contraception advocacy with feminism and 'civil society'. On the Board of Directors is William H. Draper III, described as 'one of the West Coast's first venture capitalists'. (PAI Board of Directors, https://pai.org/who-we-are/our-board/).

36   Phyllis T. Piotrow, ibid., p. 13.

37   Sanger founded the International Planned Parenthood Federation in the same year that the Population Council was established; 1952.

'[t]he Population Council provided a heretofore-lacking respectable base from which to influence professional and academic norms and to finance a more specifically problem-oriented approach to population'.[38] Aiming to 'avoid and not to provoke controversy', the Council 'was more acceptable for foundation support than were [Sanger's] active birth controllers'. 'The first two Ford Foundation grants of over $500,000 were to the Population Council, which received nearly 80 percent of all Ford population grants in the 1950s'.[39]

During 1955, 1956, and 1957, 'the Population Council sponsored a series of meetings that included Planned Parenthood officials as well as physical and social scientists to develop and define general principles for promoting birth control overseas'.[40] Guidelines were established that would be used to advise the U.S. and other governments, how these would be funded and how 'the masses' would be approached,[41] given that this aspect of universalist and liberal doctrine is an affront to traditions and faiths the world over.

Hugh Moore and International Capitalism

'An important recruit to the activist ranks' was Hugh Moore. Piotrow refers to Moore as the 'enterprising and successful founder of the Dixie Cup Company'. In 1944, he established the Hugh Moore Fund to promote what Piotrow calls 'world peace', overpopulation being considered 'the greatest threat…'[42] What Piotrow does not mention is that he was much more than a paper cups entrepreneur with a philanthropic nature. Moore was an active advocate for internationalism and the expansion of U.S. global hegemony. The Dixie Cup biography states that Moore was:

---

38   Phyllis T. Piotrow, p. 14.

39   Ibid., p. 15.

40   Ibid., p. 14.

41   Ibid., p. 14.

42   Ibid., p. 18.

Chairman of the executive committee of the League of Nations Association (U.S.), 1940–1943; consultant to the State Department at the United Nations Conference, 1945; founding member of the Committee to Defend America by Aiding the Allies, 1940; treasurer of the Committee for the Marshall Plan, 1948; president of Americans United for World Organization, 1944; chairman of the finance committee of the Woodrow Wilson Foundation, 1951–1952; chairman of the fund-raising arm of the UN education program, 1955; and member of the Atlantic Union Committee, 1949–1960; American Association for the United Nations, 1945–1954; U.S. Committee on NATO, 1961–1972.[43]

Despite the qualms of some oligarchs to become publicly involved with Margaret Sanger, Moore became director of the Planned Parenthood Federation of America in 1951, and vice-president of the International Planned Parenthood Federation in 1964.[44] Moore was at the top of the globalist elite. He had been involved with the Rockefellers since 1909 when Percy Rockefeller and several others invested $200,000 in Moore's Individual Drinking Cup Co.[45] His Fund for World Peace was headquartered at the J. P. Morgan Chase National Bank office in New York, with Stewart Ogilvy, an official of the World Federalists, as executive director. In 1981 Ogilvy was advocating compulsion to restrict the birth of the 'stupid':

The growth rate suggests that mere unofficial advocacy and purely volun-tary compliance are far from enough… voluntarism guarantees big families for the ignorant, the stupid, and the consciousless, while it gradually re-duces the proportion of people who, in conscience, limit the size of their families.[46]

---

43   Hugh Moore Dixie Cup Collection, 'Biographical Sketch: Hugh Moore', https://sites.lafayette.edu/dixiecollection/sample-page/.

44   Ibid.

45   Frank Whelan, 'Dixie Days Lafayette College Exhibit Reflects History of First Paper Cup Company', *The Morning Call* (Pennsylvania) 18 April 1994; https://www.mcall.com/news/mc-xpm-1994-04-18-2981742-story.html.

46   Stewart M. Ogilvy, p. 70; cited in U.S. Congressional Subcommittee on Appropriations, p. 832. Ogilvy was a founder of the Friends of the Earth. At the

Piotrow and other eulogists also neglect to mention that Moore was an advocate of eugenic sterilisation, and from the late 1940s started funding the Human Betterment Foundation, founded in 1928, which was primarily involved with compiling data on compulsory sterilisation. The motivation of the Foundation was explained:

> The Human Betterment Foundation had been highlighting this economic solution since its conception. Reviews of Sterilization for Human Betterment, the foundation's first book length publication released in 1929, commended the inoffensive and intelligent record linking the "economic and eugenic problem."[47] In assessing the global economic crisis posed by the feebleminded population, the foundation's book claimed that established public institutions around the world were spending a collective sum totaling over $5,000,000,000 annually to care for society's unfit population.[48]

Sterilisation laws continued to be enforced in the USA long after 1945, on the basis of economic considerations, unwed mothers being a particular target, whereas in Germany unwed mothers had benefited from advanced social welfare services. One criterion was being of the correct race, the other the correct economic situation:

> The laws passed between 1950 and 1967 to address the illegitimacy problem help explain what was considered objectionable about Nazi reproductive policy. For various reasons, eugenic laws had long targeted unwed mothers on public assistance. Some legislators and theorists emphasized the "unnecessary" costs of paying relief to unwed mothers and their children.[49]

---

time of his death in 1985, Ogilvy was a director of the American Movement for World Government.

47 C. Severin Buschmann, Review: 'Sterilization for Human Betterment, by E. S. Gosney and Paul Popenoe', *Indiana Law Journal* (1930), Vol. 5, No. 4.

48 Gosney and Popenoe, *Sterilization for Human Betterment*, viii.

49 Mary Ziegler, 'Reinventing Eugenics: Reproductive Choice and Law Reform after World War II', *Cardozo Journal of Law and Gender*, Vol. 14, No. 319, Winter 2008; p. 326; citing: 'Baltimore Welfare Denounced', *The Washington Post*, 11 December 1947.

Given the infamy that eugenics had undergone due to the Nazi epoch, Hugh Moore recommended that the Human Betterment Foundation change tactics, and promote 'voluntary sterilisation'.

> Human Betterment's emphasis on choice grew out of a long correspond-ence between its leaders and Hugh Moore, the founder of the Dixie Cup Company. A longtime donor to the organization, Moore believed that Human Betterment could not improve the quality of the population solely by funding private sterilization of the socially inadequate.[50] In 1961, Moore wrote to Ruth Proskauer Smith, the executive director of Human Betterment, and suggested a related change of course.[51] Moore recom-mended that less money be used for actual sterilizations, so that more could be spent to rehabilitate the image of sterilization.[52] If this were done, Moore asserted, it would be easier to convince people to be sterilized and to persuade state and federal agencies to support voluntary sterilization.[53] **It was hoped that sterilization might be associated not with Nazism but with human rights and personal choice.**[54]

Here we have the basis of how abortion and population control are sold as 'reproductive rights' in the name of 'feminism'. Under Moore's prompting, the association expanded the name to Human Betterment Foundation for Voluntary Sterilization. However, the same message remained: 'Over-crowded cities, polluted air and water, countless un-wanted and suffering children, skyrocketing taxes for welfare! Half of the babies now born from some cities are from indigent families on relief. Need we say more?'[55] Piotrow mentions that Moore and others in the business world coming into the population control issue were

---

50 Letter from Ruth Proskauer Smith to Hugh Moore (4 April 1956) in The Hugh Moore Papers, MC 313, Box 15, Folder 6, Seeley Mudd Manuscript Library, Princeton University.

51 Ibid.

52 Letter from Hugh Moore to Ruth Proskauer Smith (13 December 1961), ibid.

53 Ibid.

54 Mary Ziegler, pp. 340–341.

55 Human Betterment Foundation, Fundraising Letter (November 1966).

'more concerned with economics than biology'.[56] '[A]s economic
**development lagged and as increasingly persuasive statistics sug-
gested that population growth was a reason for the lag, a few of
these internationally minded businessmen and bankers began to
speak out'.**[57] Here we have the hard reality behind the humanitarian
façade.

Piotrow states that Moore "'spun-off" half a dozen important
organizations or activities that eventually played a role in the establishment of government policy. In each case he would seize an issue
or opportunity before it was respectable, then fund, encourage, and
promote it to a legitimate status. Then just as his flamboyant methods
began to embarrass his own organizational protégés he would move
on to something else'. It was Moore's influence during the 1950s that
prompted business funding for the International Planned Parenthood
Federation. He later directed his attention to environmental issues.[58]

Draper Committee 1959

William H. Draper III, 'one of the West Coast's first venture
capitalists',[59] has played a central role in population control policies. Additional to his many directorships he has been on the boards
of the Atlantic Council,[60] Draper Richards Foundation,[61] Hoover
Institution, Institute of International Studies at Stanford University,

---

56 Piotrow, p. 18.

57 Ibid., p. 19.

58 Ibid., p. 18.

59 Population Action International, 'Board of Directors, William H. Draper III';
    https://pai.org/who-we-are/our-board/.

60 Globalist think tank based around 'U.S. leadership and engagement in the
    world'. Atlantic Council, 'Shaping the Global Future Together'; https://www.
    atlanticcouncil.org/about/.

61 Formed in 2001, now called the Draper Richards Kaplan Foundation, when
    Robert S. Kaplan, former vice-chairman, Goldman Sachs, joined. Draper
    Richards Kaplan Foundation, 'History'; https://www.drkfoundation.org/
    about/history/.

World Affairs Council of Northern California, and the United Nations Association-USA. He is a member of one of the original globalist think tanks, the Council on Foreign Relations, and the President's Council on International Activities, Yale University. Draper is then high in the echelon of the globalist elite.

Draper had been Under-Secretary of the Army, and served as economic adviser to General Lucius Clay during the Occupation Administration in Germany, and as U.S. special representative in Europe directing the European Recovery Program. He was urged by Hugh Moore and President Eisenhower to investigate population problems, and formed the Draper Committee in 1959. The committee was criticised as having too many people from the military. However, this obscures the oligarchic links. The committee included John J. McCloy, who has been called 'chairman of the American Establishment'.[62]

Having visited Japan, Taiwan and Korea, Draper considered that it was sudden population increase that caused economic problems. In 1959, visiting Japan again, he was impressed by the drop in Japan's population (which had suddenly expanded by the return of 6,000,000 from overseas, after the war) for which he credited legalised abortion. 'The example of Japan influenced Draper as it did Rockefeller and others'.[63] This population control was inaugurated in 1948 with the Eugenic Protection Law, which enabled 'induced abortion' on grounds of 'economic hardship', among others. Heavily promoted by the state, legal abortions rose to 1,170,000 in 1955 and continued above 1,000,000 until 1962. Additionally, Health and Welfare Ministries estimate unreported abortions reach between 500,000 and 1,000,000

---

62   See: Kai Bird (1992). McCloy had served on the committee to establish the OSS, predecessor of the CIA, during the war, had been president of the World Bank, U.S. High Commissioner for Germany, and a trustee of the Rockefeller Foundation. While on the Draper Committee, he was chairman of the board of Rockefeller's Chase Manhattan Bank, a trustee of the Ford Foundation, and chairman of the Council on Foreign Relations.

63   Piotrow, p. 38.

annually.[64] Now, as we know, Japan and the rest of the First World have a major crisis regarding aging populations.

In testimony to the Senate Committee on Foreign Relations on 18 May 1959, Draper stated that '[t]he population problem, I'm afraid, is the greatest bar to our whole economic aid program and to the progress of the world'.[65] Be that as it may — or may not — the point is that the whole trend towards population control has been promoted through feminism, 'woman's reproductive rights', and the normalisation of the modern Moloch devouring aborted foetuses, when behind it all is a cynical concern for economic growth, regardless of the customs, faiths and morals it all affronts. The Draper Committee recommended population control pegged to economic aid and development programmes, as a matter of U.N. 'mutual security'.[66]

In May 1960 at a National Conference on the Population Crisis, co-sponsored by the Dallas branch of the globalist Council on World Affairs and *Newsweek* magazine, John D. Rockefeller III reiterated that population issues 'are so great, so important, so ramified and so immediate that only government, supported and inspired by private initiative, can attack them on the scale required. It is for the citizens to convince their political leaders of the need for imaginative and courageous action — action which may sometimes mean political and economic opposition'.[67] Certainly the sentiments of Catholics were not regarded as a legitimate part of this citizenry, as indicated by Piotrow throughout her book. What was the 'political and economic opposition' referred to by John D. Rockefeller? This could only have been the rear-guard activism of Catholics, with dwindling support in government.

---

64 'Japan's Birthrate — The Trend Turns', *The New York Times*, 25 October 1964.

65 Piotrow, p. 39.

66 Draper Committee, President's Committee Report, Task Group IV, 8 May 1959, Vol. 1, pp. 94–97; cited by Piotrow, pp. 40–41.

67 Piotrow, p. 39.

Hugh Moore began organising the World Population Emergency Campaign, forerunner of Population Action International, to raise funds for the International Planned Parenthood Federation to make it into 'a powerful force'. The campaign was headed by Lammot du Pont Copeland, vice-president of DuPont Company,[68] and by Draper.[69]

Piotrow states that behind the scenes ('with equal lack of publicity') the U.S. State Department, Draper, the Population Reference Bureau, Ford Foundation, Fred Jaffe of Planned Parenthood, and John D. Rockefeller III, liaison between them 'grew apace'.[70] Robert A. Barnett had been assigned to the State Department as head of 'a small undercover group'[71] on population control. He had been instructed 'not to put anything in writing'. In May 1962, Barnett spoke at 'an off-the-record' meeting at the Council on Foreign Relations, stating that 'policy advances would be slow, quiet, and undramatic'.[72] In November, Secretary of State Dean Rusk, at the suggestion of Draper, spoke to the executive of 'some thirty large foundations, organised by John D. Rockefeller III, on how government and foundations might co-operate on population control'.[73]

Sanger & Planned Parenthood

Planned Parenthood was started by a nurse, Margaret Sanger, as part of an extreme leftist faction that for decades remained on the fringes. By the 1950s, largely thanks to Hugh Moore, Planned Parenthood had become an international federation with large funding from the Foundations, whose officials were involved in high level meetings. It is now part of the mainstream.

---

68   Manufacturer of chemicals, electronics, pharmaceuticals, plastics.

69   Piotrow, p. 49.

70   Ibid., p. 61.

71   Ibid., p. 60.

72   Ibid., p. 61.

73   Ibid., p. 62.

Sanger was not a 'Communist'; she was an anarchist. Her population control views were influenced by Emma Goldman, a leading anarchist in the USA, who had preceded Sanger as an advocate of birth control in conjunction with feminism. Sanger was a contributor to anarchist periodicals, including Goldman's *Mother Earth*, and *The Blast*, published by Alexander Berkman, the other leading anarchist in the USA. In 1914, Sanger published her own periodical, *The Woman Rebel*, by-lined 'No Gods; no Masters'.

In the first issue of *The Woman Rebel*, she explained:

Why the Woman Rebel?

Because I believe that deep down in woman's nature lies slumbering the spirit of revolt. Because I believe that woman is enslaved by the world machine, by sex conventions, by motherhood and its present necessary child-rearing, by wage-slavery, by middle-class morality, by customs, laws and superstitions. Because I believe that these things which enslave woman must be fought openly, fearlessly, consciously.[74]

Like the latter-day feminists and Critical Theorists, she claimed that motherhood and child-bearing were a part of capitalist exploitation, which she called 'slavery through motherhood' and 'the home'.[75] Emma Goldman wrote against marriage and the aim of 'few and better children',[76] indicating a eugenic preoccupation which was also advocated by Sanger, to the embarrassment of present-day leftists. Benita Locke wrote a feature opposing proposals for a 'state maternity pension' or a weekly family allowance, as a 'capitalist trap'.[77] Locke objected that a family allowance would restrict the employment of women outside the home. Apparently it is preferable that women become factory fodder than be 'imprisoned' to their children; a paradox that remains the basis of feminism, and explains why it has been

---

74 Margaret Sanger, *The Woman Rebel*, Vol. 1, No. 1, March 1914, p. 8.

75 Ibid., p. 1.

76 Emma Goldman, 'Marriage and Love', ibid., p. 3.

77 Benita Locke, 'Mother's Pensions: The Latest Capitalist Trap', ibid., pp. 4–5.

so lavishly funded and promoted by its supposed capitalist enemies. Emile Chaplier appealed to 'working girls' that 'you will want to be a mother only if you are certain that you are not going to be the mother of stupid, half-witted children...'[78]

One might wonder how Sanger rationalised her views about capitalism and motherhood when she was from the start funded and feted by the world's biggest oligarchs. When she was arrested after the police suppression of a public meeting at the Town Hall Theatre, Manhattan, on 13 November 1921, and was questioned about her connections with anarchists such as Emma Goldman and Alexander Berkman, she responded that she also knew Mrs. Andrew Carnegie and John D. Rockefeller Jr.[79] In 1924, Sanger sent a request for funds for her Birth Control League to the Rockefeller Foundation, and John D. Rockefeller Jr. authorised an 'anonymous donation'.[80] Given her comment to police of her knowing Rockefeller since at least 1921, the relationship with oligarchy had been established early.

Equality of Exploitation

In the July 1914 issue of *The Woman Rebel*, Sanger announced the American Birth Control League,[81] which became Planned Parenthood in 1942. Only through 'complete control of the reproductive functions' could women ever achieve equality with men. It is the tune still played about 'women's reproductive rights' by George Soros, Bill Gates, and the same Foundations that started backing Sanger seventy years ago. In a question and answer column in *The Woman Rebel* it was asked 'why should people only have small families?',

78 Emile Chaplelier, 'To Working Girls', *The Woman Rebel*, Vol. 1. No. 2, April 1914, p. 12.

79 Vicki Cox, p. 73.

80 Letter from Raymond Fosdick, Foundation Trustee to John D. Rockefeller Jr., 13 June 1924, Rockefeller Archive Center, Rockefeller Family Boards, RG III 2 K, Box 1, Folder 1.

81 Sanger, 'The Birth Control League', *The Woman Rebel*, Vol. 1, No. 5, July 1914, p. 39.

answered with, 'to avoid overcrowding the labor market and keeping down wages by competition'.[82] Yet why do the globalist elite promote integration of women into the workforce — in the name of an 'inclusive economy' — if not to expand the production process? The eugenic focus on raising 'healthy and strong children' also contradicts the Sangerite opposition to 'breeding' for capitalist production. Even in 1914, Sanger was warning about overpopulation and not enough food.[83] When twenty years later the USA and others went through the Great Depression, mass starvation was not the result of 'overpopulation' from 'large families'. It was a failure of the financial system; where one had the recurring phenomenon of 'poverty amidst plenty', a factor about which the Left generally remains ignorant.

Marx & Malthus

As an anarchist, Sanger was vehemently opposed to orthodox Marxism, which she lambasted for rejecting the overpopulation theories of Malthus. In *The Pivot of Civilization* she wrote:

Marxian Socialism, which seeks to solve the complex problem of human misery by economic and proletarian revolution, has manifested a new vitality. Every shade of Socialistic thought and philosophy acknowledges its indebtedness to the vision of Karl Marx and his conception of the class struggle. Yet the relation of Marxian Socialism to the philosophy of Birth Control, especially in the minds of most Socialists, remains hazy and confused. No thorough understanding of Birth Control, its aims and purposes, is possible until this confusion has been cleared away, and we come to a realization that **Birth Control is not merely independent of, but even antagonistic to the Marxian dogma**. In recent years many Socialists have embraced the doctrine of Birth Control, and have generously promised us that 'under Socialism' voluntary motherhood will be adopted and popularized as part of a general educational system. **We might more logically**

82 Sanger, 'A Little Lesson', ibid., Vol. 1, No. 7, September-October 1914, p. 53.
83 Ibid.

reply that no Socialism will ever be possible until the problem of re-sponsible parenthood has been solved.[84]

Sanger shows herself to be a reductionist, making birth control into a one-dimensional ideology. The title of her book dogmatically states that birth control is the 'pivot of civilization', albeit a declaration at odds with millennia of historical experience suggesting that **birth control is a symptom of a civilisation in its final states of decay.** Oswald Spengler, in his comparative study of civilisations, asserted:

> The last man of the world city no longer wants to live, he may cling to life as an individual, but as a type, as an aggregate, no... That which strikes the true peasant with a deep and inexorable fear, the notion that the family and the name may be extinguished, has now lost its meaning ... and the destiny of being the last of the line is no longer felt as a doom...[85]

Sanger was a representative of the 'last man [and woman] of the world city', when life becomes a question rather than an imperative.

Sanger announced herself as a protagonist for Malthusianism:

> Many Socialists to-day remain ignorant of the inherent conflict be-tween the idea of Birth Control and the philosophy of Marx. The earlier Marxians, including Karl Marx himself, expressed the bitterest antagonism to Malthusian and neo-Malthusian theories. A remarkable feature of early Marxian propaganda has been the almost complete unanimity with which the implications of the Malthusian doctrine have been derided, denounced and repudiated. Any defense of the so-called 'law of population' was enough to stamp one, in the eyes of the orthodox Marxians, as a 'tool of the capitalistic class' ...[86]

Sanger condemns Marx for relegating Malthus to nothing more than a footnote in Volume I of *Das Kapital*, where he states that

---

84 Sanger, *The Pivot of Civilization* (New York: Brentano, 1922), Chapter VII: 'Is Revolution the Remedy?' Emphasis added.

85 Oswald Spengler, *The Decline of the West*, Vol. II, pp. 103–104.

86 Sanger, *The Pivot of Civilization*.

Malthus' '*Principles of Population* was quoted with jubilance by the English oligarchy as the great destroyer of all hankerings after human development'.

Birth Control 'Pivotal'

For novelist and historian H. G. Wells, a Fabian socialist and eugenicist, writing in the 'introduction' to *The Pivot of Civilization*, 'Mrs. Margaret Sanger sets out the case of the new order against the old...' What was of concern to Sanger was that the *lumpenproletariat* (to use Marx's term) were having too many children, which were a drain on society: 'A distinguished American opponent of Birth Control some years ago spoke of the "racial" value of this high infant mortality rate among the "unfit." He forgot, however, that the survival-rate of the children born of these overworked and fatigued mothers may nevertheless be large enough, aided and abetted by philanthropies and charities, to form the greater part of the population of tomorrow. ...'[87] Social Darwinism, the religion of the 19th century English Whig merchants and pastors (as Marx observed), was not sufficiently operative to cull the population of social misfits, and what was not wanted were charitable endeavours to alleviate conditions, nor family allowances. Birth control is the panacea. Sanger writes of the proliferation of the 'feeble-minded', and cites the eugenicist Charles Davenport:

> There is but one practical and feasible program in handling the great problem of the feeble-minded. That is, as the best authorities are agreed, to prevent the birth of those who would transmit imbecility to their descendants. Feeble-mindedness as investigations and statistics from every country indicate, is invariably associated with an abnormally high rate of fertility. Modern conditions of civilization, as we are continually being reminded, furnish the most favorable breeding-ground for the mental defective, the moron, the imbecile. 'We protect the members of a weak strain,' says Davenport, 'up to the period of reproduction, and then let them free upon the community, and encourage them to leave a large progeny

---

87 Ibid., Chapter II: 'Conscripted Motherhood'.

of 'feeble-minded: which in turn, protected from mortality and carefully nurtured up to the reproductive period, are again set free to reproduce, and so the stupid work goes on of preserving and increasing our socially unfit strains'.[88]

However, Sanger saw a danger in eugenics insofar as it also encouraged the mentally and physically most intelligent to sire more children. This also is burdensome and is against the universality of birth control. The aim of birth control is not a sounder population but a smaller population, because the ultimate goal remains the freeing of all women from child, home, and marriage.

> Eugenics seems to me to be valuable in its critical and diagnostic aspects, in emphasizing the danger of irresponsible and uncontrolled fertility of the 'unfit' and the feeble-minded establishing a progressive unbalance in human society and lowering the birth-rate among the 'fit.' But in its so-called 'constructive' aspect, in seeking to reestablish the dominance of healthy strain over the unhealthy, by urging an increased birth-rate among the fit, the Eugenists [sic] really offer nothing more farsighted than a 'cradle competition' between the fit and the unfit. They suggest in very truth, that all intelligent and respectable parents should take as their example in this grave matter of child-bearing the most irresponsible elements in the community.[89]

Sanger's utopia is one wherein humanity has wrested control over Nature. Birth control is the 'pivotal' means by which the primordial sex impulse is able to be harnessed. Science is the method for reshaping humanity and society: 'Mankind has gone forward by the capture and control of the forces of Nature'. Again we come back to the common theme we have seen among Critical Theorists and other social deconstructionists: the path to utopia needs clearing of tradition, morality, faith, custom. The *sublimation* counselled by both Jung and Freud and by Nietzsche, as well as by the great religious faiths, is to be

---

88 Ibid., Chapter IV: 'The Fertility of the Feeble Minded'.

89 Ibid.

discarded as an impediment towards the individual's self-realisation through unbound freedom:

> Restraint and constraint of individual expression, suppression of individual freedom 'for the good of society' has been practised from time immemorial; and its failure is all too evident. There is no antagonism between the good of the individual and the good of society. The moment civilization is wise enough to remove the constraints and prohibitions which now hinder the release of inner energies, most of the larger evils of society will perish of inanition and malnutrition. Remove the moral taboos that now bind the human body and spirit, free the individual from the slavery of tradition, remove the chains of fear from men and women, above all answer their unceasing cries for knowledge that would make possible their self-direction and salvation, and in so doing, you best serve the interests of society at large. Free, rational and self-ruling personality would then take the place of self-made slaves, who are the victims both of external constraints and the playthings of the uncontrolled forces of their own instincts.[90]

Intersectionality with the New Left

During the late 1960s, issues began to coalesce into *intersectionality*. Feminism was also part of the mix. Piotrow states of the time that while the U.S. Government was supporting population control for economic reasons, the matter was taken up by various converging causes, including "[e]cologists, biologists, feminists, and students demanding zero population growth, more contraceptives, and abortion... At first these ideologies had little impact on government population programs but gradually they provided strong reinforcement for existing programs and increased urgency for new ones".[91]

Moore persuaded 'one of his protégé organizations, the Association for Voluntary Sterilization,[92] to cooperate with the National Conference on Conservation in October 1969 for what was billed as

---

90 Ibid., Chapter X: 'Science the Ally'.

91 Piotrow, p. 187.

92 This had split from the advocates of eugenics.

the first joint meeting of conservation and birth control groups. At that session the AVS became the first of the population groups to adopt a resolution favoring the two-child family'.[93] Population control, like many other issues, had to be presented in a palatable manner, which avoided any stigma of coercion or manipulation. Feminism again served an Establishment role, regurgitating what Sanger had advocated over fifty years previously:

> **Easier access to better birth control methods, including repeal of out-moded restrictions, offered a logical and seemingly acceptable alternative to coercion**. That **tactic** coincided with the developing strategies of another movement. Women's liberationists also demanded greater freedom and an end to all measures that forced women into second-class status. In the field of reproduction, a woman's right to choose included not only pills and IUDs but also abortion — legal, safe, and inexpensive. The 'right of marital privacy' proclaimed in the 1965 Supreme Court decision on birth control was translated by a militant feminist movement and sympathetic physicians into the right of women to control their own bodies, the right to avoid 'compulsory pregnancy' by legal, medically protected abortion.[94]

Catchphrases like 'compulsory pregnancy' had been used since Sanger's *Woman Rebel*. The programme was the same, and was adopted across the broad front. 'On the issue of abortion, the environmentalists, the younger generation, the militant women, the family planners, and most of the doctors and demographers could agree. To fulfill Margaret Sanger's demand that women control their own bodies, to reduce the pressures of rapid population growth, to rebut arguments for coercion by ensuring that no unwanted babies be brought into the world, to increase the safety margin of other contraceptives by providing a backstop when they failed'[95]..., abortion became the panacea.

---

93   Piotrow, p. 189.

94   Ibid., p. 191.

95   Ibid., p. 191.

Piotrow enthuses about the steady retreat of the Catholic Church, as states began to liberalise their abortion laws.[96] When Catholic laymen organised to successfully have the New York Assembly and Senate repeal New York's 'liberal abortion law', Governor Nelson Rockefeller used his veto.[97]

Although President Nixon had supported the Catholic efforts in New York, he named John D. Rockefeller III to head the Population Commission in 1969, with representation from the Population Council, Planned Parenthood, Ford Foundation, several bankers, social scientists, et al. Among the recommendations were that the New York abortion law be the model for the rest of the USA, with abortions funded from the public purse. 'The commission also urged that contraceptive services and sex education be fully available to minors and that legal impediments to such services be eliminated by the states'.[98] Nixon was critical of the Commission report, but one might wonder what he expected by appointing John D. Rockefeller III as the chairman:

> ... I consider abortion an unacceptable form of population control. In my judgment, unrestricted abortion policies would demean human life. I also want to make it clear that I do not support the unrestricted distribution of family planning services to minors. Such measures would do nothing to preserve and strengthen close family relationships. ... I believe in the right of married couples to make these judgments for themselves.[99]

96 Ibid., p. 192.

97 Ibid.

98 Ibid., p. 197.

99 Richard M. Nixon, *The New York Times*, 6 May 1972, p. 1. Quoted by Piotrow, p. 197.

Frederick Jaffe Memo

Jaffe was the first president (1968–1978) of the Center for Family Planning Program Development (renamed the Guttmacher[100] Institute), which began as an affiliate of the Planned Parenthood Federation of America. In 1969, he addressed a memo to Bernard Berelson, president of the Population Council, outlining various measures for population control. The Guttmacher Institute objected that '[s]ome anti-choice activists have attempted to falsely link Mr. Jaffe to coercive population control measures by taking out of context parts of a memo he wrote in 1969. However, Mr. Jaffe's memo merely summarized various population control measures others had proposed at the time; he did not endorse or otherwise condone coercive measures...'

However, the memo was headed 'activities relevant to the study of population policy for the United States'. Jaffe begins his covering letter by stating that the memo is in response to Berelson's letter of 24 January, 'seeking ideas on necessary and useful activities relevant to [the] formation of population policy'.[101]

Jaffe opens the memo by alluding to debate on population control having not seriously so far 'grappled with public policies' in various areas that influence 'fertility preferences', 'nor with the predictable political consequences of a major effort to adopt and **enforce an anti-natalist U.S. population policy'**. Jaffe states that population control has not been adequately discussed as 'only one' element of '**a larger field of social planning'**.[102]

Coercive policies are a public relations problem. Obviously voluntary measures are preferable. Jaffe refers to 'a truly contraceptive

---

100 Alan F. Guttmacher, an obstetrician-gynecologist, was PPFA's president until his death in 1974.

101 Jaffe to Berelson, 'Activities Relevant to the Study of Population Policy for the United States, Center for Family Planning Program Development', 11 March 1969; introductory letter, p. 1 (2). Emphasis added.

102 Jaffe, ibid., p. 2.

society' in which 'contraception is efficiently distributed to all', which would go a long way to achieving a 'tolerable rate of growth'. 'If this hypothesis is basically confirmed, it would negate the need for an explicit U.S. population policy **which goes beyond voluntary norms**'.[103]

Jaffe recommended studies to determine whether welfare support and family allowances do in fact impact on birth rates.[104] Jaffe presented no preconceptions on these matters, but the assumption is that if evidence was adduced that state support encouraged birth-rates, this support would have to be re-designed or eliminated. Jaffe noted that women in the labour market increased during full employment, 'which is achieved by higher inflation'. 'The relationship between employment of women and lower fertility seems well established'. Jaffe recommended a study on 'how much inflation could or should be risked to achieve lower fertility'.[105] Here we might begin to realise the far-reaching implications of population control.

The effect of education on women in regard to fertility required studying questions of childbirth, marriage or labour employment.[106] It is crucial that such 'education' should not be perceived as 'indoctrination'.[107] Whether assistance to working mothers with child care encouraged or discouraged fertility required examining. Whether encouraging small home ownership encouraged birth rates needed considering in regard to alternative policies. Of particular importance was to confront the assumption that population growth was needed for economic growth. Economic models needed formulating to assure birth reduction.[108]

Jaffe's concluding chart has been the most controversial, population control proponents contending that 'anti-choice activists' have

---

103 Ibid., p. 4 Emphasis added.

104 Ibid., p. 4.

105 Ibid., p. 6. 'Fiscal and Monetary Policy'.

106 Ibid., p. 6. 'Education Policy (b)'.

107 Ibid., p. 7.

108 Ibid., pp. 6–7.

misrepresented Jaffe as advocating coercion. What the document in its entirety does show is that Jaffe advocated:

1) Population control as part of social planning

2) This social planning would have far-reaching consequences on all facets of society, including economics, education, welfare, employment, home ownership, and implicitly, on religion and family ethics.

3) Population control would be the 'pivot' (Sanger) in shaping these policies, as to whether one gets child allowances, options of home ownership, types of education, etc.

To pretend that none of this amounts to 'coercion' is semantics and obfuscation. Having outlined recommendations for studies aimed at the revolutionising of society, Jaffe provided a chart entitled 'Proposed Measures to Reduce Fertility, by Universality or Selectivity of Impact in the U.S.' The columns included 'universal' and 'selective'; impact of measures necessary; 'social control' mechanisms, and predicted results on fertility. Jaffe headed the chart '**proposed measures**'. However, the reader is required by the social planners to read something other into the title, being assured that, no, these were not measures being proposed by Jaffe et al. According to Abby Johnson, former director of a Planned Parenthood abortion facility in Bryan, Texas, 'When I worked at Planned Parenthood, there was something that we were not allowed to talk about. If we didn't talk about it, then maybe no one else would either. It was called the Jaffe Memo. In 1969, Planned Parenthood was asked by the government to produce some ideas to help with overpopulation. They did just that'.[109]

---

109 Abby Johnson, 'Secretive Planned Parenthood Memo: How to Stop Overpopulation by Discouraging Birth', *Lifesite*, 28 November 2011, https://www.lifesitenews.com/opinion/secretive-planned-parenthood-memo-how-to-stop-overpopulation-by-discouragin.

Bernard Berelson of the Population Council wrote a paper around the time of the Jaffe memo that reflected Jaffe's proposals. Berelson likewise referred to the problems of implementing numerous draconian policies, but stated they are 'perhaps not insurmountable', and need to be 'developed into a workable plan'.[110] These include 'mass use of "fertility control agent" by government to regulate births at acceptable levels, put into water supplies or staple foods'; licenses for child birth; 'temporary sterilization of all girls via time-capsule contraceptives'; 'compulsory sterilisation of all men' with three or more children; financial incentives for 'contracepting couples'; withdrawal of family benefits, and tax on births; 'promotion or requirement of female participation in labor force' to provide roles and interests for women alternative or supplementary to marriage; 'selective restructuring of the family'; 'encouragement of long-range social trends' including industrialisation, '[which] may "break the cake of custom" and lead to social foment [sic]'; 'population control' pegged to U.S. food aid; reorganisation of national and international agencies empowered to take whatever steps necessary to 'establish a reasonable population size'.[111]

Berelson was outlining measures that were intended as more than theoretic examples. He referred to the need for research on developing 'temporary sterilants' and a 'fertility control agent' that could be 'administered voluntarily and individually as well as involuntarily and collectively' through the water supply.[112] While the imposition of such

---

110 Bernard Berelson, 'Beyond Family Planning', *Studies in Family Planning*, Population Council, No. 38, February 1969, p. 6. At the time, the Population Council was chaired by John D. Rockefeller III, and had on its board Eugene Black, former head of the World Bank, vice-president of the Rockefeller Chase National Bank, organiser of the Asian Development Bank; Carlyle Haskins, Carnegie Institution; Lewis L. Strauss, former partner in Kuhn Loeb & Co., financial adviser to the Rockefeller family; Rawleigh Warner Jr., Mobil Oil, et al. Of note is that Berelson was a 'behavioural scientist' whose focus was on shaping public opinion, and was director of the Found Foundation's behavioural sciences division.

111 Ibid., pp. 2–3.

112 Ibid., p. 3.

measures is difficult, it is 'a matter of timing'; of 'several small steps with an occasional large one'.[113] Issues that would need resolving include the means by which peasant men with more than three children can be forcibly sterilised, and what to do with children who are born beyond a quota. Such issues are 'difficult but perhaps not insurmountable'. 'Compulsion could have its effect' where there are those who find ways to 'beat the system'.[114]

Of added interest is that Berelson plainly states that a *dialectical* method is in operation: '**Finally, it is also worth noting that more extreme or controversial proposals tend to legitimate more moderate advances, by shifting the boundaries of discourse**'.[115] This is why the supposed 'enemies of capitalism' are so generously funded by the biggest capitalists: rampaging students, histrionic feminists, rioting Blacks, et al. enable the Establishment to push through its agendas on the pretext of implementing a 'moderate' course.

Whether the population controllers would really resort to such measures might be gauged by the attitude of Guttmacher, president of the Planned Parenthood Federation, when in regard to the safety of IUD use stated to a Population Council conference in 1962 that checking medical backgrounds would be too time-consuming in regard to the goal: 'to apply this method to large populations'. J. Robert Wilson, chair of Obstetrics and Gynaecology at Temple University, agreed, stating at the conference that '[w]e have to stop functioning like doctors, thinking about the one patient with pelvic inflammatory disease, or the one patient who might develop this, that or the other complication from an intra-uterine device', although the incidence of infection 'might be pretty high'. He added that the patient might be expendable, particularly if the result of IUD use is 'sterilizing but not lethal'. Mary Calderone, medical director of Planned Parenthood, was 'thrilled'

---

113 Ibid., p. 5.

114 Ibid., p. 9.

115 Ibid., p. 12.

that clinicians such as Wilson were thinking in terms of contraceptive 'mass distribution'.[116]

Good Club: Buffett, Rockefeller, Gates, et al.

Population control remains one of the top points on the globalist agenda, under euphemistic terms such as 'women reproductive rights' and 'women's health issues'. It is hopefully by now clear that the aim is to 'liberate' women from child and home for integration into the global 'inclusive economy', while allowing globalists to determine the extent and nature of population.

Yet another network was formed by the globalist oligarchy on 5 May 2009, informally called the Good Club. Again the focus is on world population. The meeting was called jointly by Warren Buffett, David Rockefeller, and Bill Gates.[117] It was held at the president's house of Rockefeller University. Attendees included: Eli Broad, George Soros, Ted Turner, Michael Bloomberg et al. This was said to be a secret meeting, and while no organisation was formally created, the aim was to reach a consensus through discussion. *The London Times* reported,

> Taking their cue from Gates they agreed that overpopulation was a priority, [and that] this could result in a challenge to some Third World politicians who believe contraception and female education weaken traditional values.[118]

Clearly, Rockefeller did not have to 'take his cue' from Bill Gates on the issue of population control. *The Wall Street Journal* continued:

---

116 Cited by Matthew James Connelly, pp. 202–203.
117 Maria Di Mento and Ian Wilhelm, 'America's Top Philanthropists Hold Private Meeting to Discuss Global Problems', *The Chronicle of Philanthropy*, 20 May 2009.
118 Robert Frank, 'Billionaires Try to Shrink World's Population, Report Says', *The Wall Street Journal*, 26 May 2009.

Such a stand wouldn't be surprising. Mssrs. Gates, Buffett and Turner have been quietly worrying about Malthusian population problems for years. Mr. Gates in February outlined a plan to try to cap the world's population at 8.3 billion people, rather than the projected 9.3 billion at which the population is expected to peak.[119]

Robert Frank commented,

But some right-leaning blogs have started attacking the billionaires as forming a kind of secret sterilization society or giant ATM to fund abortions. It fed into time-honored fears of the rich using their wealth to reshape mankind in its preferred image. Some are raising the specter of eugenics.[120]

Something of the character of *The Wall Street Journal* could not 'feed into' such 'time honoured right-wing fears', even when reporting an example. Frank also emphasises that the 'Good Club' is not really a 'club' but supposedly a one-off get-together. This is contradicted by the statements made by the event's organiser, Patricia Q. Stonesifer, former chief executive of the Bill & Melinda Gates Foundation, who nonetheless also sought to downplay the meeting: 'It was a really great discussion, and we agreed to continue the dialogue in the future, but there were no specific action items out of the meeting.'[121] Something as high-powered as the annual Bilderberg meetings is also a 'continuing dialogue'. The meeting was 'not secret', just 'private'.

As this chapter has documented, mainly with the unimpeachable testimony of Ms. Piotrow, the 'rich' have indeed sought to 'reshape mankind' using sterilisation, abortion, and eugenics. The primary worry is that, as alluded to above, 'Third World politicians' believe that 'traditional values will be weakened'. While the globalists and their leftist allies object that this is a matter of women's health and rights, the issue intrinsically strikes at the heart of religion, custom

119 Robert Frank, ibid.

120 Ibid.

121 Maria Di Mento and Ian Wilhelm.

and traditional social foundations, by seeking to impose a universal doctrine emanating from the *Age of de Sade* (a.k.a. 'Enlightenment') of late Western civilisation. Again, it is an attempt to impose a universal doctrine that demands global conformity. As we have seen, it is not just the Third World that is subverted. The issue strikes at the heart of Catholicism in Europe and Orthodoxy in Russia. As Piotrow wrote, Catholics in the USA fought a rear-guard action against the population controllers, and lost. When the unborn child can be universally treated as akin to excrement, as de Sade stated, and as abortionists insist more euphemistically, then humanity can be remoulded at will.

Role of the United Nations Organisation

OPPOSITION TO what Piotrow alludes to as United Nations 'Malthusian thinking' on population control came from the Catholic states and the Soviet bloc. Piotrow's observations are reminiscent of Sanger's in regard to Karl Marx on Malthus. She states that the Soviets regarded 'population control [as] a capitalist stratagem to postpone the real solutions — a reorganization of society and redistribution of wealth'.[1] The Soviet position was broadly accurate, and conservative, and it is such a conservative stance on this and many other issues that placed the Soviet bloc in 'Cold War' confrontation with the USA. The Catholic and Soviet states rejected the *World Leaders' Declaration* of December 1967, circulated by John D. Rockefeller III, proclaiming that it is a 'basic human right' to determine the 'number and spacing' of children. The declaration stated, 'We believe that the population problem must be recognized as a principal element in long-range national planning if governments are to achieve their economic goals...'.[2] Yet how does this feigned commitment to 'human rights' accord with population control being part of 'economic planning'? Again references to 'human rights' and 'women's reproductive rights' are pure cant hiding social engineering agendas.

---

1   Piotrow, p. 201.

2   United Nations Office of Public Information, 'Statement by Secretary-General U Thant on Population Problems', Press Release SG/SM/620 Rev. 1, 9 December 1966, p. 3.

The social engineers had to bypass the Catholic and Soviet blocs in the UNO. At the instigation of Draper, on 14 June 1967, a meeting was chaired by U.N. Under-Secretary Phillippe de Seynes. This included Draper, John D. Rockefeller III, Richard Gardner,[3] and senior officials from the International Planned Parenthood Federation, and the Population Council. The aim was to establish a programme for the UNO on international population control. Secretary General U Thant promptly acted on the recommendation to establish a U.N. Fund for Population.[4] This became the United Nations Fund for Population Activities (UNFPA). By 1972, UNFPA was making grants to private organisations, such as the International Planned Parenthood Federation, and drawing on them to assist with projects.[5]

Just how quickly a nation's population can fall was early demonstrated with the previously cited example of Japan. The birth rate fell from 34.3 per 1,000 in 1947 down to 17.2 in 1957. Piotrow states, 'The decline was unprecedented in demographic history. Induced abortion, condemned by demographic, public health, medical, government, civic, and religious leaders as the least desirable birth control technique, was the principal method used. Only later, after 1952, was contraception specifically fostered to reduce the incidence of abortion'. Japan served as a propaganda tool for showing how economic success can be achieved with population decline.[6] When in 1922 Margaret Sanger had been sponsored by the magazine *Kaizo* to visit Japan and offer population control advice, she was called 'Sangai-san'; 'destructive to production'. But in 1965 she was awarded the Order of the Precious Crown of Japan.

---

3   Richard Gardner, U.S. Deputy Assistant Secretary for International Organization Affairs, was, according to Piotrow, a member of the 'small undercover groups' dealing with population control issues in the U.S. State Department (p. 60).

4   Piotrow, p. 204.

5   Ibid., p. 213.

6   Ibid., pp. 33–34.

The Western states having followed the same course as Japan now also have a demographic crisis with an aging population. The answer of the globalists is to compensate the population decline with what the United Nations calls 'replacement migration' from the Third World.

United Nations Global Migration Compact

One of the most significant instruments for the imposition of this 're-placement migration' is *The United Nations Global Compact for Safe, Orderly and Regular Migration*, signed on 19 December 2018 by 164 members of the U.N. General Assembly. Twenty-nine U.N. member states did not sign the compact, including the USA, Hungary, Austria, Italy, Poland, Slovakia, Chile, Israel and Australia. Apologists for the agreement state that it does not undermine national sovereignty, that it will make migration a more ordered, humane process, and eliminate people smuggling. For example, Lord Bates, Britain's Minister of State at the Department for International Development, states: 'The compact "protects every state's right to determine its own immigration policies, including in areas such as asylum, border controls and returns of illegal migrants."'[7]

Nature of U.N. Declarations and Covenants

While the declaration is called 'non-binding' on signatory states, and it supposedly does not subvert national laws, myriad U.N. declarations have become 'international law', and it is 'international law' to which the *Migration Compact* appeals. For example, the human rights and race relations acts, implemented across the world, are the types of 'international law' to which the *Migration Compact* alludes, which were based on the 1948 *U.N. Declaration on Human Rights*. U.N. members are signatories to many U.N. 'covenants' and as such are 'obligated' to report to the U.N. regularly in regard to how these

---

7 'What's the U.N. Global Compact on Migration?', Reality Check Team, *BBC News*, https://www.bbc.com/news/world-46607015.

'covenants' are being implemented. Under 'universal periodic reviews' these include the *International Covenant on Civil and Political Rights*; *International Convention on the Elimination of All Forms of Racial Discrimination*; *Convention Relating to the Status of Refugees*; *United Nations Declaration on the Rights of Indigenous Peoples*, etc. In regard to U.N. conceptions on 'human rights', for example, the New Zealand government explains: 'Under this mechanism, the human rights situation of all UN Member States is reviewed every 5 years.'[8]

That the *Migration Compact* is based around other U.N. 'covenants' that have become 'international law', with U.N. sanctions against those states deemed offenders, is indicated within the *Compact* 'preamble'.[9] As with other U.N. declarations and covenants, much of the *Migration Compact* outlines the monitoring of compliance by signatory states. Sections entitled 'follow-up' and 'implementation' are devoted to this. The International Organization for Migration is the U.N. policing agency for the purpose.

In arguing for an increase of draconian measures against states deemed to be in violation of 'international law', particularly on how 'human rights' is defined by the U.N., an academic paper points out that while the U.N. claims not to intervene in the internal affairs of members states,

[h]umanitarian intervention is based upon the doctrine that there are limits to the freedoms states have in dealing with their own nationals. It should be distinguished from actions to protect a state's own nationals abroad. When this doctrine was defined by Dutch international scholar Hugo Grotius and other 17th century legal scholars, it allowed one or more states to use force to prevent another state from mistreating its own nationals in circumstances so brutal and widespread that they shocked the conscience of the international community. Such interference in a state's domestic

---

8   *Universal Periodic Review 2019*, NZ Ministry of Foreign Affairs and Trade, https://www.mfat.govt.nz/en/peace-rights-and-security/human-rights/universal-periodic-review-2019/.

9   *Global Compact for Migration*, 'Preamble' (2), 11 July 2018; https://refugeesmigrants.un.org/sites/default/files/180711_final_draft_0.pdf.

affairs is defended by the argument that if certain practices continue to take place in a state despite protest and objections by neighboring states, then humanitarian considerations outweigh the prohibition of intervention and justify a decision to interfere.[10]

In calling for an increase in the powers of intervention by the U.N., Buhm Suk Baek, author of the cited paper, concludes, 'Admittedly, humanitarian intervention had been abused in the past by strong states to pursue other political, economic or military objectives'.[11] Baek approvingly cites the example of the way Yugoslavia was targeted in the name of 'human rights':

> Under Security Council Resolution 757, the Council imposed a wide range of economic sanctions on the Federal Republic of Yugoslavia (Serbia and Montenegro) on May 30, 1992. These sanctions are also related to the protection of human rights as the Council announced its concern for the continued expulsion of non-Serb civilians and noted the 'urgent need for humanitarian assistance and the various appeals made in this connection' under the former Resolution.[12]

Serbia is a particularly poignant example of how the 'human rights' ploy was used to dismember a state for the purposes of privatising and globalising its economy, with particular reference to the mining region of Kosovo, where privatisation was made an official war aim. The Rambouillet peace agreement imposed on Serbia states that 'the economy of Kosovo shall function in accordance with free market principles'.[13]

So what does the *Migration Compact* state? The fundamental premises are that (1) humans should have the right to move across the

---

10 Buhm Suk Baek, 'Economic Sanctions against Human Rights Violations', (2008), 2.1.2. Humanitarian Intervention, Cornell Law School Inter-University Graduate Student Conference Papers, Paper 11; Cornell Law School Inter-University Graduate Student Conference Papers.

11 Ibid., p. 19 (2.3).

12 Ibid., p. 31 (3.2.3), 'Sanctions against the Federal Republic of Yugoslavia'.

13 Rambouillet Agreement, Article I (1), 1.

earth without regard to barriers, (2) this is a natural part of the eco-nomic globalisation process, (3) international capital has a significant role to play, (4) the compact is part of 'international law' and 'global governance'.

When the U.N. General Assembly adopted a resolution on global migration in 2017, affirming the *New York Declaration on Refugees and Migrants* in 2016, it did so with the explicit statement that this involves 'global governance', refers to 'actionable commitments', for-malising what appears to be a policing role for the U.N. International Organisation for Migration.[14]

While apologists allude to the compact being 'non-legally binding', it states of this that the compact upholds 'the sovereignty of States and their obligations under international law'.[15] On 'implementation', the *Compact* states that, 'We reaffirm our commitment to international law and emphasize that the *Global Compact* is to be implemented in a manner that is consistent with our rights and obligations under inter-national law'.[16] The first 'vision and guiding principle' of the *Compact* states:

> This Global Compact expresses our collective commitment to improving cooperation on international migration. Migration has been part of the human experience throughout history, and we recognize that it is a source of prosperity, innovation and sustainable development in our globalized world, and that these positive impacts can be optimized by improving migration governance.[17]

---

14   U.N. General Assembly, Resolution Adopted by the General Assembly on 6 April 2017, https://www.iom.int/sites/default/files/our_work/ODG/GCM/A-71_280-E.pdf.

15   *Global Compact for Migration*, (7); https://refugeesmigrants.un.org/sites/de-fault/files/180711_final_draft_0.pdf.

16   Ibid., (41), p. 32.

17   Ibid. (8) 'Our Vision and Guiding Principles'.

> ... We learned that migration is a defining feature of our globalized world, connecting societies within and across all regions, making us all countries of origin, transit and destination. ...'[18]

This is the crux of the issue; the real aim buried among the usual moralising. Economic globalisation is the real reason for open borders, and a primary means of destroying barriers to international capital, not only economically, but socially, culturally and ethnically. This explains why the international oligarchs contrived this *Compact*, under the guise of 'social investment'. While the U.N. refers to the integrity of the states, this is more *double-speak* as it also refers to states as being fluid and without fixity of heritage or destiny, 'making us all countries of origin, transit and destination'.

While 'national sovereignty' is affirmed[19] in Orwellian manner, this is negated with the next passage, 'that the State, public and private institutions and entities, as well as persons themselves are accountable to laws that are publicly promulgated, equally enforced and independently adjudicated, and which are consistent with international law'.[20] These are the repressive laws that have been enacted in many states, based on supposedly 'legally non-binding' U.N. covenants, where criticism of immigration policies can result in the jailing of dissidents for 'hate speech':

> Human rights: The Global Compact is based on international human rights law and upholds the principles of non-regression and non-discrimination. By implementing the Global Compact, we ensure effective respect, protection and fulfilment of the human rights of all migrants, regardless of their migration status, across all stages of the migration cycle. We also reaffirm the commitment to eliminate all forms of discrimination, including racism, xenophobia and intolerance against migrants and their families.[21]

---

18   Ibid., (10) 'Common Understanding'.
19   *Global Compact for Migration*, 'National Sovereignty' (15).
20   Ibid., 'Rule of Law and Due Process'.
21   Ibid., 'Human Rights'.

Any dissent is called 'racism and xenophobia'. The legal prohibitions have long been enacted through race relations and human rights laws, while the news media in all Western states can be relied on to make pariahs out of those who object.

A primary 'objective' is the utilisation of data to promote global migration agendas. The *Compact* also alludes to co-operation between a broad range of 'stakeholders', including trade unions, media, academia, civil society, business in what it calls a 'whole of society approach'.[22] It seems evident that the purpose is mobilisation against the spectre of 'populism'.

The aim of the *Migration Compact* is supposedly to reduce 'refugees' by ensuring they are not compelled by their home states to seek refuge in other states. This is being used to implement another U.N. initiative, the *2030 Agenda for Sustainable Development*. The whole of Objective 2, 'Minimize the adverse drivers and structural factors that compel people to leave their country of origin', is designed to restructure states socially and economically. This means 'private and foreign direct investment' (d), and there can be little doubt that the aim is to allow predatory capital to take over a state's resources and utilities under the guise of 'human rights', 'inclusive economy', 'gender equity', etc.

Labour Market Fodder

The *Compact* refers to using migration to facilitate 'labour market needs', 'labour mobility agreements', 'free movement regimes', 'visa liberalisation', speed up of visa and permit processing,[23] and addressing 'demographic realities', meaning addressing the demographic decline of the European states through migration, through 'consultation with the private sector and other stakeholders', thereby changing the character of the state according to the requirements of global capital.

---

22   Ibid., p. 4 (15).

23   Ibid, 'Objective 5: Enhance availability and flexibility of pathways for regular migration', p. 11.

Objective 16 aims to integrate migrants into host communities, while ensuring their own identities are retained. Hence, there remains the quandary as to whether a society is to be a melting-pot or multicultural. When politicians a few years ago, such as Angela Merkel and David Cameron, realised that multiculturalism was not working, and that ghettoisation or self-segregation was taking place, they started expounding the old American ideal of the melting-pot. The U.N. gets around the quandary by Orwellian *double-speak*. The ultimate aim remains an 'inclusive economy', as the oligarchic think tanks call it, where the laws of social production will level out any dissimilarities between hosts and migrants, especially after several generations, in the hope that a standardised population will have emerged based on production and consumption. 'Labour market integration'[24] is a key aim; and ultimately the real aim.

Indoctrination

Objective 17 aims at the remoulding of the attitudes of the host peoples: 'We commit to eliminate all forms of discrimination, condemn and counter expressions, acts and manifestations of racism, racial discrimination, violence, xenophobia and related intolerance against all migrants in conformity with international human rights law. ...'[25] This is a reiteration of present U.N. covenants, long enacted as human rights and race relations laws in many states. The same passage concludes: 'We also commit to protect freedom of expression in accordance with international law, recognizing that an open and free debate contributes to a comprehensive understanding of all aspects of migration'.[26] This is again Orwellian *double-speak*. Any criticism of open borders and defence of the host people is called 'racism' and

---

24 Ibid., 'Objective 16: Empower migrants and societies to realize full inclusion and social cohesion', p. 23.

25 Ibid., 'Objective 17 (33): Eliminate all forms of discrimination and promote evidence-based public discourse to shape perceptions of migration', p. 24.

26 Ibid.

'xenophobia' by U.N. 'international human rights law'. Under U.N. Covenants there never has been 'freedom of expression' for dissent. There have been jail sentences and crippling fines for speaking out. Paragraph (c) of this section states that there should be indoctrination in the news media to ensure that there is standardised reporting in support of migrant globalisation:

> Promote independent, objective and quality reporting of media outlets, in-cluding internet based information, including by sensitizing and educating media professionals on migration-related issues and terminology, investing in ethical reporting standards and advertising, and stopping allocation of public funding or material support to media outlets that systematically promote intolerance, xenophobia, racism and other forms of discrimina-tion towards migrants, in full respect for the freedom of the media.[27]

How can there be 'independent, objective and quality reporting of media outlets', and 'full respect for the freedom of the media', when the aim is to impose a common standard of journalism and eliminate anything deemed 'racist' or 'xenophobic'? Although the news media in the Western world has long been compliant anyway, it is part of a projected indoctrination programme, aimed at 'awareness-raising campaigns targeted at communities of origin, transit and destination in order to inform public perceptions regarding the positive contribu-tions of safe, orderly and regular migration, based on evidence and facts, and to end racism, xenophobia and stigmatization against all migrants'.[28]

This is Herbert Marcuse's vision of 'repressive tolerance', where freedom is universal other than when it does not accord with leftist dogma, and where this freedom is premised on an informed citizenry thanks to freedom of information, so long as that too conforms to dogma. Another important aspect is the mention above of 'sensitiz-ing and educating media professionals' and of 'awareness-raising

---

27   Ibid., 17. 33 (c), p. 24.
28   Ibid., (f).

campaigns', these phrases referring to the intensive 'group therapy' methods for attitudinal change, to assure conformity, that are discussed in the chapter on 'Behaviour Modification'.

Interference in the internal political process is also urged to suppress and smear any sign of political resistance:

> Engage migrants, political, religious and community leaders, as well as educators and service providers to detect and prevent incidences of intolerance, racism, xenophobia, and other forms of discrimination against migrants and diasporas and support activities in local communities to promote mutual respect, including in the context of electoral campaigns.[29]

Again, this appears to be an appeal to mobilization against political dissidence.

What is Behind the U.N. Global Compact?

The *U.N. Global Migration Compact* is an initiative of global capital. The aim is the free flow of labour, as part of the free flow of resources. The *Migration Compact* refers frequently to the role to be played by private business. In implementing the *Compact*, it is stated:

> We decide to establish a capacity-building mechanism in the United Nations, building upon existing initiatives, that supports efforts of Member States to implement the Global Compact. It allows Members States, the United Nations and other relevant stakeholders, including the **private sector and philanthropic foundations**, to contribute technical, financial and human resources on a voluntary basis in order to strengthen capacities and foster multi-partner cooperation.[30]

The *Migration Compact* originates from the *New York Declaration for Refugees and Migrants*. The *Compact* states: 'This Global Compact presents a non-legally binding, cooperative framework that builds on the commitments agreed upon by Member States in the *New York*

---

29 Ibid., (g), p. 25.
30 *Global Compact for Migration*, 'Implementation', (43), p. 32.

Declaration for Refugees and Migrants'. The International Organisation for Migration (IOM), the monitoring organisation for the *Compact*, also states: '... Annex II of the *New York Declaration* set in motion a process of intergovernmental consultations and negotiations culminating in the planned adoption of the *Global Compact for Migration* at an intergovernmental conference on international migration in 2018'.[31]

The seeding of the *New York Declaration*, and hence the *U.N. Migration Compact*, leads back to a Rockefeller Foundation plan for city crisis management across the world. The planning originates with a concept called '100 Resilient Cities', established in 2013, funded by the Rockefeller Foundation, 'and managed as a sponsored project by Rockefeller Philanthropy Advisors with support from the Brookings Institution'.[32] Resilient Cities explains:

> Heads of state and government gathered at the UN General Assembly in New York last month against the backdrop of a burgeoning refugee crisis in South Asia and a lingering one across the Middle East and Europe. City leaders from across the globe also convened to discuss the role that cities play in providing assistance to refugees.
>
> These discussions were facilitated by two major events. The Brookings Institution — together with the International Rescue Committee and 100 Resilient Cities — Pioneered by The Rockefeller Foundation — convened a high-level working group to elicit best practice recommendations for local communities grappling with displacement-related challenges. At the same time, New York City convened a Global Mayors Summit on Migration and Refugee Policy and Practice designed to uncover how cities overcome obstacles to implementing policies that promote, among other things, refugee integration, rights protection, and empowerment.[33]

---

31 U.N. Migration, U.N. International Organisation for Migration, https://www. iom.int/global-compact-migration.

32 'About Us', Resilient Cities, managed as a sponsored project by Rockefeller Philanthropy Advisors.

33 'Engaging City Leaders in the Global Compact Process: Recommendations for Action', Resilient Cities, 19 October 2017; http://www.100resilientcities.org/ engaging-city-leaders-global-compact-process-recommendations-action/.

Bloomberg reports:

The Global Compact for Safe, Orderly and Regular Migration gets backing from global business community. Numerous leaders of major multinational companies endorsed the Global Compact for Safe, Orderly and Regular Migration (Global Compact for Migration) today at the second annual Bloomberg Global Business Forum, a gathering of more than 70 heads of state and delegation, and 200 of the world's most prominent business leaders, to strengthen economic prosperity and collaborate on trade issues, globalization, innovation, and competition.

In a press conference with the Presidents of Switzerland and Mexico, Alain Berset and Enrique Peña Nieto, whose Permanent Representatives to the United Nations led the negotiations, Michael R. Bloomberg, the Founder of Bloomberg L.P. and Bloomberg Philanthropies, and Mayor of New York City (2002–2013), announced the first wave of support from global business leaders for the Global Compact for Migration. These founding signers include Jim Coulter and Jon Winkelried, Co-CEOs of TPG; Dawn Fitzpatrick, Chief Investment Officer of the Soros Fund Management; Joe Gebbia, Co-founder and Chief Product Officer of Airbnb; Dara Khosrowshahi, CEO of Uber; Rich Lesser, CEO of BCG; Hamdi Ulukaya, Founder, Chairman and CEO of Chobani; and John Zimmer, President and Co-Founder of Lyft.[34]

Bloomberg states the purpose behind the rhetoric, albeit still retaining some of that rhetoric in regards to 'national sovereignty', and the 'rule of law':

Every nation has a role to play in addressing this crisis, and this Compact is designed to help guide them. It provides a framework for how the international community can reap the economic benefits of immigration without sacrificing national sovereignty or rule of law — and I want to

---

34 'Renowned Business Leaders Welcome Landmark Agreement on International Migration', Bloomberg Global Business Forum, Bloomberg Press Release, 26 September 2018; https://gbf.bloomberg.org/news/renowned-business-leaders-welcome-landmark-agreement-international-migration/.

thank all of the government and business leaders who are supporting its implementation.[35]

President Berset of Switzerland, who has combined a career as a financial adviser with that of being a social democratic politician, also stressed the economic motive for migration: 'Without the foreign labor force, many of our industries would not function as they do now. Notwithstanding difficulties, migration must be seen as an enrichment — economically and culturally'.[36]

Universal 'General Will'

What can be seen with such U.N. 'covenants' and declarations, signed by member states and imposed by a contrived 'international law' with an international army, is the creation of a universal 'civil society' on the basis of a 'social contract'. Member states contract to become part of a global society. The ongoing U.N. declarations and covenants that are signed by member states increasingly extend the *'social contract'* (or *compact*). Once a universal creed is agreed to by contracting parties, it becomes the legal expression of a universal *general will*, and anyone who contravenes that *general will* is liable to punishment or elimination.

The legalistic foundations of the UNO in establishing an enforced *general will* in the name of 'liberty, equality, fraternity' (or 'human rights' as it is now called) derive from Jean-Jacques Rousseau. One sees in Rousseau's *social contract* the basis of U.N. powers to ostracise ('sanctions') and punish *rogue states* in the name of the *general will*, and the *international community* (sic). Even states that are not contracting parties to the UNO, such as Rhodesia, will be targeted if they have offended this universal 'general will'. Rousseau wrote of this:

---

35   Ibid.
36   Ibid.

These clauses, properly understood, may be reduced to one—the total alienation of each associate, together with all his rights, to the whole community; for, in the first place, as each gives himself absolutely, the conditions are the same for all; and, this being so, no one has any interest in making them burdensome to others.[37]

Rousseau emphasised what this means in summary: 'Each of us puts his person and all his power in common under the **supreme direction of the general will**, and, in our corporate capacity, we receive each member as an indivisible part of the whole.'[38] This is a modernistic, artificial construct that was intended to replace the traditional organic community. It is the difference between *Gemeinschaft* and *Gesellschaft*, as previously defined. When extended into a so-called '*international community*', it is a travesty. The feeling of a need for written constitutions and declarations to hold a society together, including an *international community*, is a symptom of the decay of instinct for organic community. Under the mantle of 'modern science', the cultural anthropologists, under the direction of Franz Boas, merely resurrected the 18th century notions of Enlightenment philosophers, such as Rousseau, in stating that man is a blank slate on which anything can be written, and by which his development can be directed. One of the most notable of these scientists, Ashley Montagu, wrote of this doctrine in the UNESCO periodical *The Courier* that 'Man is not born evil or good — he is rendered so'.

No organism of the species so prematurely named Homo Sapiens is born with human nature. What human beings are born with is merely a complex set of potentialities ... Being human must be learned ...[39]

---

37 Jean-Jacques Rousseau, *The Social Contract and Discourses* (1761), Chapter VI: 'The Social Compact'.

38 Ibid. Emphasis added.

39 Ashley Montagu, 'Human Nature Cannot Be Changed; False! Says U.S. Anthropologist', *The Courier*, UNESCO, Vol. VI, no. 2, February 1953. P. 14. Reprinted from *Impact of Science on Society*, UNESCO, Winter 1952.

'Man is born without instincts, without those psychological dispositions which cause other animals to respond in a particular manner to a particular stimulus accompanied by a particular emotion.' 'Man is a creature of habit', and those habits are acquired from his culture and society, 'organized around a number of urges, drives, or basic needs, as they have been variously called', such as hunger, sex, rest and sleep, bowel and bladder evacuation, fear, and avoidance of pain. How a person behaves will be based on acquired experiences.[40] This is all a reformulating of Rousseau and other Enlightenment doctrines.

Montague quotes Abraham Maslow, founder of *humanistic psychology*, which became a fad during the 1960s, that 'those human impulses which have seemed throughout our history to be deepest .... are now being discovered more and more to be acquired and not instinctive.' Montague concluded that so far from not being able to change human nature, 'we find that man is the most plastic, the most malleable, the most educable of all living creatures...'[41]

Montague wrote as though such views were the consensus among scientists. Here can be seen the rationale for the UNO, to reconstruct a mass 'humanity' where all undesirable traits would be eliminated through global indoctrination, re-education and the repression of instincts that Montague and a multitude of social scientists and social engineers insist do not exist. The *primary drives*, in reference to Maslow's doctrines, such as fear, pain avoidance, the need for food, shelter and sex, could be manipulated to condition reflexes and change the 'habits' of Man as a 'creature of habit'.

Dr. Glenda Sluga[42] succinctly described the process for the establishment of the UNO and UNESCO and the concept of 'One World':

---

40 Ibid., p. 15.

41 Ibid., p. 16.

42 Professor of International History, Australian Research Council, Kathleen Fitzpatrick, Laureate Fellow, University of Sydney; 2020–2024, seconded as Professor of International History and Capitalism, European University Institute, Florence.

In that curiously utopian moment bracketed by the end of the Second World War and the onset of the Cold War, cosmopolitanism made its debut on the new international stage of the United Nations in its literal translation as 'World Citizenship' (from the Greek *cosmos* or world, and *polites*, or citizen). In the first few years of the UN's operation, delegates and functionaries portrayed world citizenship as the path to permanent world peace, and as a necessary step in the evolution of mankind from tribes to nations, from national consciousness to 'One World'. At the UN special agency, the United Nations Educational, Scientific, and Cultural Organization or Unesco, world citizenship was celebrated as the adjunct of an anti-chauvinist *raison d'etre* and as a cultural manifestation of the **Enlightenment premise** that humanity was evolving socially, politically, technologically, and even psychologically, towards a 'World Community'.[43]

Note that Sluga traces the ideology of the UNO's cosmopolitanism to the *Age of Enlightenment*, the milieu of Rousseau and the *salon* intellectuals who theorised about the 'noble savage', abolishing property, religion, marriage, monarchy and other accoutrements of civilisation. Their legacy is the bloodshed of the Jacobin Revolution, Bolshevism and the globalist wars of the present. Sluga writes of Julian Huxley of UNESCO, as 'often described as the consummate world citizen'; continuing:

In the history of Unesco's early years, Huxley is often depicted as its hero, charting 'the broad course to which the organization became committed', and granting the natural sciences, and scientists, a central place in the shaping of Unesco's internationally-targeted cultural and educational programs — and literally putting the 'S' in Unesco.[44]

---

43 Glenda Sluga, 'Unesco and the (One) World of Julian Huxley' (draft), *Journal of World History*, 21 March 2010. Emphasis added.

44 Ibid., p. 2.

Julian Huxley's Brave New World

JULIAN HUXLEY was a most distinguished Darwinian biologist, and remained a zealous advocate for eugenics as first director of UNESCO, regardless of his own mental instability that required electro-shock treatment. His utopian vision for a world state under United Nations auspices is remarkably close to the dystopia described by his brother Aldous in *Brave New World*, where 'World Controllers' would exercise their power by keeping the world citizenry content through consumerism, childless sex, music and narcotics. Where Aldous saw a nightmare, Julian saw utopia.

Huxley's eugenics, which he called 'evolutionary humanism' places him in a prominent position among the Left of the eugenics movement and population control. Paul Weindling[1] states that Huxley 'adeptly associated eugenics with a range of reformist movements, such as the popularisation of birth control, the decriminalisation of homosexuality and abortion law reform. Biographical factors show how Huxley linked these agendas (often quite detached from eugenics) to eugenic modernisation', and, like other social planners, sought to detach eugenics from race.[2] Weindling describes Huxley as a 'chameleon like figure', who adapted his 'social agenda' to circumstances,

1   Research Professor of the History of Medicine, Oxford Brookes University, Oxford.
2   Paul Weindling, 'Julian Huxley and the Continuity of Eugenics in Twentieth-Century Britain', *Journal of Modern European History*, 1 November 2012, Vol. 10, No. 4, pp. 480–499.

and 'an opportunistic magpie for whatever could support evolutionary humanism', mentally unstable and requiring electro-shock treatment.

Aldous collaborated with H. G. Wells in popularising science as the social panacea for a new world, co-authoring with Wells *The Science of Life* series (1931). During the 1930s, he was notable for his opposition to Nazism and racism, but retained an elitist attitude towards the colonial peoples. Huxley sought a new, science-based, religion: In 1941, he published *Religion without Revelation* as the creed for 'a socially founded humanist religion', since mankind had outgrown old superstitions, and had evolved to a stage when a new religion was needed. Weindling writes that '[a]fter the war, Huxley advocated that science should be a means of social reconstruction'. Of particular interest, Weindling writes of Huxley in regard to his brother Aldous' novel *Brave New World*:

> Julian Huxley's brother, the novelist Aldous, as the author of the prescient novel *Brave New World* (1931) portrayed both the possibilities of an ordered rationalised society based on cloning, and its defects. By 1958 when Aldous wrote *Brave New World Revisited*, he felt, 'The prophecies made in 1931 are coming true much sooner than I thought they would'. Aldous felt intensely how in the 1950s, the world was post-atom bomb and post-Holocaust: 'Death control is something which can be provided for a whole people by a few technicians working in the pay of a benevolent government'. Julian Huxley, who endorsed the Voluntary Euthanasia Society, meant by 'death control' the new medical ability to prolong life. By way of contrast, Aldous Huxley's main fear by then was brain washing and mind control:

> In the *Brave New World* of my fable socially desirable behavior was insured by a double process of genetic manipulation and postnatal conditioning. Babies were cultivated in bottles and a high degree of uniformity in the human product was assured by using ova from a limited number of mothers and by treating each ovum in such a way that it would split and split again, producing identical twins in batches of a hundred or more. In this way it was possible to produce standardized machine-minders for standardized machines. And the standardization of the machine-minders was perfected, after birth, by infant conditioning, hypnopaedia and **chemically induced**

euphoria as a substitute for the satisfaction of feeling oneself free and creative.[3]

Aldous Huxley's nightmare shifted from planned breeding to mind-manipulation:

> Lacking the ability to impose genetic uniformity upon embryos, the rulers of tomorrow's over-populated and over-organized world will try to impose social and cultural uniformity upon adults and their children. To achieve this end, they will (unless prevented) make use of all the mind-manipulating techniques at their disposal and will not hesitate to reinforce these methods of non-rational persuasion by economic coercion and threats of physical violence.[4]

> Julian Huxley was untroubled by this post-Orwellian 1984 nightmare — instead he continued to proselytize for the opposite: the idea of an evolutionary religion, based on objective science rather than revelation.[5]

'Mind manipulating techniques reinforced by economic coercion and threats of physical violence'. This is precisely the way the globalists operate through the U.N.O., NATO and the pervasive 'civil society' of Soros, Rockefeller, Bill Gates, National Endowment for Democracy et al. UNESCO remains the primary means by which to 'impose social and cultural uniformity upon adults and their children'. That was why it was created, and why it is maintained.

During and after his tenure as director of UNESO, Huxley was part of the campaign considered previously in regard to population control. Weindling states of this, alluding to his association with Rockefeller:

---

3   Aldous Huxley, *Brave New World Revisited* (1958). Emphasis added. The reference is to a narcotic that Huxley called soma, used to keep the population docile. In Huxley's brave new world, sex was non-reproductive, and channelled into public 'orgy-porgy' thanks-giving celebrations to the 'World Controllers'.

4   Aldous Huxley, Ibid. Emphasis added.

5   Weindling.

Huxley tried to get population problems onto the agendas of the United Nations as well as onto those of its specialised agencies, not least UNESCO, FAO, WHO as well as supporting the UN Population Commission. He took up population questions while still director general of UNESCO in 1948. **He was aligned with the Rockefeller Foundation, being on good terms with the physical sciences programme officer, Warren Weaver.** On the population front, there were dividends for the population lobby. **The Population Council managed to intrude birth control into the United Nations agenda, and population control came to be regarded as a legitimate part of the politics of international assistance.**[6] Huxley endorsed the strategy of world population control.[7]

Huxley's involvement with the population control offensive included support for abortion legalisation and sterilisation, and legalisation of homosexuality,[8] giving support with his public recognition to the population control projects of the Rockefeller, Ford, Ciba and Gulbenkian Foundations and the Milbank Memorial Fund. Weindling traces the concepts of 'think tanks' and NGOs to this milieu.[9]

UNESCO Doctrine

In 1946, Julian wrote the doctrinal manifesto for the founding of UNESCO. The basis is *humanism*, which 'must be' *world humanism* and *scientific humanism*. In eschewing any specific religion of the great traditional faiths as inherently sectarian and divisive, Huxley instead proposed *scientific humanism* that would have 'spiritual, mental and materialistic aspects', which would be 'truly monistic and

---

6   Paul Weindling, 'Modernising Eugenics: The Role of Foundations in International Population Studies', in: Gemelli Giuliana, MacLeod Roy (eds.) *American Foundations in Europe. Grant-Giving Policies, Cultural Diplomacy and Trans-Atlantic Relations, 1920–1980.* (Brussels: Peter Lang, 2003), pp. 167–180.

7   Weindling, (2012), op. cit.

8   Julian Huxley et al. 'Homosexual Acts, Call to Reform Law', *The Times*, 7 March 1958.

9   Weindling.

unitary'. What was essential for a world state was its underpinning by a syncretic world faith that transcended the traditional faiths. This new faith must uphold Man 'as the sole trustee of further evolutionary progress'. 'Thus the general philosophy of Unesco should, it seems, be a scientific world humanism, global in extent and evolutionary in background'.[10] While Huxley had stated that UNESCO cannot identify with any of the main faiths and must be aloof from division, what he proposed is a creed that affronts the traditional teachings of most faiths.

While Huxley was one of the most prominent Darwinian evolutionists, he advocated not Darwin's biological 'natural selection', but conscious, man-directed social, moral, cultural selection through manipulation: 'Thus the struggle for existence that underlies natural selection is increasingly replaced by conscious selection, a struggle between ideas and values in consciousness'. This would enable the 'speed up' of evolution.[11] '...[I]t is in social organisation, in machines, and in ideas that human evolution is mostly made manifest'.[12]

Global Aesthetics: Formless, Rootless

The key to accelerated evolution is to transcend national boundaries with 'some form of world political unity, whether through a single world government or otherwise...', which would assure universal peace. The role of UNESCO would be to promote this 'world political unity' through its brief in education, science and culture.[13] The role of UNESCO was envisaged to be that of indoctrination. This would include the inauguration of activities that would show how 'nationality and nationalism can be transcended in shared activity'.[14] This would also require a global cosmopolitan aesthetic in the arts; 'a new

10   Julian Huxley, *UNESCO: Its Purpose and Its Philosophy*, pp. 7–8.

11   Ibid., p. 9.

12   Ibid., p. 10.

13   Ibid., p. 13.

14   Ibid.

formulation of aesthetics which will take account of the arts of primitive peoples, the various modern movements in art, the relation of deep psychology to aesthetic expression, and the function and value of art in the life of the individual and in the community'.[15] This is the modernist fad for the primitive and the foreign in the West, for art as an expression of psychoanalysis (*surrealism*), and the use of art as a means of manipulating individual and community ethics. The type of new aesthetics Huxley is advocating is intended to shape a globalist outlook without the perception of place and tradition. It is a cosmopolitan, formless art that draws on the African fetish and the artist as rootless psychotic; the disfigured torsos of a Picasso, and the random paint splattings of Jackson Pollock, and the formlessness of a Henry Moore UNESCO sculpture. Huxley describes the formlessness and rootlessness into which a new global art must descend:

> Nor is art concerned only with representation. That is self-evident for music, but is equally true of the visual arts. The painter may choose to represent; but he may also choose to select, to distort, to symbolise, to transmit emotions, to express ideas, to paint his imaginings instead of reproducing what he sees.[16]

Such art belongs everywhere, and nowhere. The nebulousness of its identity is concomitant with the amorphous mass of 'humanity' that the globalists seek to mould. The globalisation of art means its detachment from an organic tradition. Huxley is candid in his view of art as a method of indoctrination: 'Art has important social functions. It can serve to express, as no other medium can do, the spirit of a society, its ideas and purposes, its traditions and its hopes'…[17] Huxley detailed the type of global, stratified, humanistic, secular society UNESCO aims to create. The type of art, which he indicates would have a pervasive, intrusive presence, would reflect that society

---

15   Ibid., p. 41.

16   Ibid., pp. 48–49.

17   Ibid., p. 49.

as a means of inculcating its cosmopolitan 'spirit, ideas, and purposes'. Huxley waxes lyrical about how there will remain great expressions of national art, yet in *double-think* mode explains that under the global regime these will be subsumed by the rootless aesthetic; 'bound to be to a greater degree part of a super-national movement, less distinctive as expressions of national life'.[18] Huxley frankly states that art has a 'social function' as propaganda or 'public relations'.

> Art is necessary as part of the technique, since for most people art alone can effectively express the intangibles, and add the driving force of emotion to the cold facts of information. ... it remains true that one of the social functions of art is to make men feel their destiny, and to obtain a full comprehension, emotional as well as intellectual, of their tasks in life and their role in the community. Rightfully used, it is one of the essential agencies for mobilising society for action.[19]

Classifying Castes

Huxley points out the propaganda function of UNESCO is utilising the mass media, referring to the UNESCO Constitution as mandating this. He refers to the 'rapid build-up of public opinion' by the use of modern mass communications technology. Even then, however, Huxley was warning of the danger of what is now called 'false news'; information and opinions that conflict with globalist agendas. A focus would be on transcending 'national boundaries'. We do not have to read between the lines, when Huxley unequivocally states:

> Taking the techniques of persuasion and information and true propaganda that we have learnt to apply nationally in war, and deliberately bending them to the international tasks of peace, if necessary utilising them, as Lenin envisaged, to 'overcome the resistance of millions' to desirable change.[20]

---

18   Ibid., p. 52.
19   Ibid., pp. 54–55.
20   Ibid., p. 60.

It is of interest that while the American Right[21] and even U.S. Senate investigations were concerned about UNESCO and other U.N. agencies being subverted and used by the USSR, the Soviets were condemning such 'bourgeois cosmopolitanism' and the 'cosmopolitan idea' of a 'one world government'.[22] The USSR discerned something subversive in the international symposiums of the type promoted by UNESCO, while Huxley stated that, 'With all this Unesco must face the fact that nationalism is still the basis of the political structure of the world, and must be prepared for the possibility that the forces of disruption and conflict may score a temporary victory'.[23] However, Huxley was unable to repudiate the genetic underpinnings of inequality:

> There are instances of biological inequality which are so gross that they cannot be reconciled at all with the principle of equal opportunity. Thus low-grade mental defectives cannot be offered equality of educational opportunity, nor are the insane equal with the sane before the law or in respect of most freedoms. However, the full implications of the fact of human inequality have not often been drawn and certainly need to be brought out here, as they are very relevant to Unesco's task.[24]

Such a quandary placed the progressives in a dilemma, as much of the *raison d'etre* of the UNO was promoted in the aftermath of Nazism, against the doctrine of 'biological inequality'. The globalists and progressives strain to draw distinctions between two notions of eugenics. Was it just semantics? Huxley attempted to explain: 'At the outset, let it be clearly understood that we are here speaking only of biological

---

21 See for example G. Edward Griffin (1964). While the American conservative critique of the UNO was broadly legitimate, analysis was retarded by simplistic Cold War rhetoric about opposition between 'free enterprise and Communism'.

22 F. Chernov, 'Bourgeois Cosmopolitanism and Its Reactionary Role', *Bolshevik* (Central Committee of the Communist Party), No. 5, 15 March 1949, pp. 30–41. See Bolton, *Stalin: The Enduring Legacy*, pp. 38–46.

23 Julian Huxley, *UNESCO: Its Purpose and Its Philosophy*, p. 14.

24 Ibid., p. 18.

inequality — inequality in genetic endowment. Social inequality, due to accident of birth or upbringing, is something wholly different.'[25]

UNESCO's eugenics would be quite different. While writing of the need to maintain 'human variety', this required resisting doctrines of racial purity and extermination. According to Huxley, with some type of alchemy, 'human variety' would be achieved by the aim of 'securing the fullest contribution to the common pool from racial groups which, owing to their remoteness or their backwardness, have so far had little share in it'. Such wide racial crossings would somehow ensure 'genetic variability'.[26] How such 'genetic variability' is maintained within a mix of recessive and dominant genes, according to the Mendelian laws of inheritance, is not explained.

'Human difference' in 'psycho-physical types' is an added dimension, which UNESCO would need to study.

> When the time comes, however, [these differences] will be important. For one thing they will be of great value in job selection, in picking those who are most likely to profit from a particular sort of training or are most suitable for a particular kind of work. Conversely, we shall then be enabled to lay down that certain types of men should be debarred from holding certain types of positions.[27]

Huxley looked to the time when studies of character typology would enable individuals to be classified and slotted into the *brave new world*. He referred, for example, to *asthenics*: 'fanatics and overzealous doctrinaire moralists'. Such types would be disqualified from the professions of justice. Character types could be classified by body-type with a system devised by German psychotherapist Ernst Kretschmer. 'Weaklings, fools, and moral deficients' would need purging. 'Many

---

25 Ibid., p. 19.
26 Ibid., pp. 19–20.
27 Ibid., p. 20.

people are not intelligent nor scrupulous enough to be entrusted with political responsibility'.[28]

The *brave new world* envisaged by Julian Huxley would have to be forcibly stratified, with castes, such as technocrats, administrators, and drones, selected at an early age for the appropriate training and placement. Institutions would have to assume functions that have traditionally been the tasks of parents within the family. If parents were of a certain physical typography, one assumes they would be liable to have their children placed elsewhere. Selection boards (alluding to their creation during World War II to place manpower) could vet those standing for office. UNESCO would cultivate a global elite, with a suspicion of 'the common man that might tend, unless we are careful, towards the promotion of mediocrity'.[29] Covering over 60 pages of rationalisations promoting 'international co-operation' for 'world peace' and the ascent of humanity towards unbound, *Promethean* progress, Huxley states that the '**task is to help the emergence of a single world culture, with its own philosophy and background of ideas, and with its own broad purpose**'.[30] While Huxley referred to 'unity-in-variety', the aim is to 'eventually include a unified common outlook and a common set of purposes'.[31]

Family Remains the Target

Since the family is the building block of an organic community, and the stable male-female pair-bond the starting point of that, these are also the starting points for elimination by those who wish to create a substitute system of authority. Why is it that cult leaders, intrinsically seeking total control over their followers, aim first to obliterate family bonds? One sees it in the Charles Manson commune, literally named 'The Family', and in the Communist utopia of Jim Jones, where

---

28   Ibid., pp. 20–21.

29   Ibid., p. 15.

30   Ibid., p. 61.

31   Ibid., p. 17.

he was called 'Dad'. The early years of the Bolshevik regime attempted to replace the family hearth and home for the factory crèche and communal kitchen and canteen, and called it 'liberation'. The family is where the child forms his character and attitudes. If these are regarded as inimical to a ruling establishment, then it is the parents that must be brought to subordination. Hence when Green Party Member of Parliament and ex-Communist Sue Bradford's so-called 'anti-smacking bill'[32] passed into law in the New Zealand Parliament in 2007, it was done so behind the dubious pretext of stopping 'child abuse'. This hid the actual agenda, albeit briefly alluded to by Bradford: to undermine traditional parental authority. She stated: '**It's a choice between an old psychology which says children are our property. Old New Zealand versus New Zealand**'.[33] Bradford stated that the motive behind her bill was based on ideological concepts of power relationships, and of property relationships. The legislation was enacted on the basis that New Zealand was implementing the *U.N. Convention on the Rights of the Child*, dishonestly conflating decent parents with abusive sociopaths:

> The recent change in the law with the introduction of the Crimes (Substituted Section 59) Amendment Act 2007 and the public awareness campaign against family violence signal that New Zealand does not accept violence towards children, and that we are finally beginning to address **our responsibilities to implement the United Nations Convention on the Rights of the Child**. Article 19 requires that state parties take all appropriate measures to protect children against all forms of violence, injury or abuse, and at last we have begun to take action on this issue.[34]

---

32 Crimes (Substituted Section 59) Amendment Bill.
33 'Feeling the Strain of the Front Line', *Dominion Post*, Wellington, 7 April 2007.
34 Julie Lawrence, Anne Smith, 'A Place Where It is Not Okay to Hit Children', *Social Policy Journal of New Zealand*, No. 34, April 2009.

This is just one of many examples of the manner by which the U.N. continues to pervasively, but usually unobtrusively, reconfigure those states willing to succumb to its *general will*.

For the UNO, the family is the incubator of nationalism and other traditional attitudes that must be suppressed if future generations are going to be 'global citizens', devoid of attachments of duration. In 1948, UNESCO included in a series of books, *Toward World Understanding*, statements from a 1948 international symposium of educators. Amongst growing public concern, a U.S. congressional committee issued a whitewash of UNESCO, and in particular rationalised the statements from the series that had been the most contentious, primarily by stating that the opinions in the series were not 'official'. Particularly scrutinised were statements that '...for the moment it is sufficient to note that it is most frequently in the family that children are infected with nationalism...'[35] The comment is a reiteration of Critical Theory. Such comments are thoroughly in line with UNO and UNESCO doctrine. In 1996, a UNESCO publication was issued that again considers parents as problematic in passing attitudes on to their children that do not conform to globalism:

> The initial teaching of values, the initiation to 'peaceful' attitudes, should logically be the responsibility of the family, as the first link between a young person and society. **Owing to the resignation, shortcomings or inability of parents, however, which may be ascribed to many origins (or causes) and situations, the responsibility for education sometimes rests entirely on the teacher,** who, whether disillusioned or militant, has to replace the first link in the chain of the educational process. On the other hand, parents never, or very rarely, replace the teacher. Some countries have made an effort to improve this situation with **programmes to educate parents,** which include methods of inculcating nearly a sense of democracy in the family. The International Commission on Education for the Twenty-first

---

35 'In the Classroom with Children under Thirteen Years of Age, toward World Understanding', Vol. 5 (UNESCO, 1948), p. 58. Cited in House Committee on Foreign Affairs, Subcommittee on International Organizations and Movements (1956), p. 760.

Century quite rightly recalls the human dimension of those who have the **task of transmitting values, and more particularly the inescapable need to upgrade the role of the teacher.**[36]

While the statements are not as avid as Adorno, Marcuse, Fromm or Wilhelm Reich, it is again the parents who are held accountable if they do not impart the doctrines expected of them. Those parents have 'shortcomings' or 'inabilities' and must be replaced by the teacher, whose role needs 'upgrading' from that of parents, if parents are not susceptible to *re-education*. One of the most significant UNESCO projects towards remoulding attitudes is the revision of history textbooks:

> Research has been started, in conjunction with higher education establishments and specialized non-governmental organizations, **to identify the referents, images, terms and illustrations in history textbooks** which are conducive to the development of prejudice and suggest negative representation of particular individuals or groups. **History programmes are being restructured**, placing more emphasis on complementarity. Courses about the history of humankind are **started much earlier on in the curricula**, simultaneously with national histories. '**We should disarm history**', Federico Mayor [UNESCO director-general] urges, and he adds: 'There are too many battles in history, too much power, generals and soldiers. We must therefore provide our children and peoples with a **different vision of history**.' For countries which have begun to **revise history textbooks**, the aim is to bring up to date the contribution of all peoples to the development of humankind and the participation in that development, and to identify the **cultural interactions** which have resulted and result from exchanges between them. If this **universal history** can ever be finalized, it will enable a turning point between two eras to be marked: that of dominations and that of creative **interdependence**, and it will give expression to the truth that: 'It is in the minds of men that the defences of peace must be constructed.'[37]

---

36 Lucie-Mami Noor Nkaké, p. 11. Emphasis added.
37 Ibid., pp. 22–23. Emphasis added.

The original UNESCO programme has proceeded apace. Here we see the UNESCO agenda of revising textbooks to reflect a contrived and forced 'restructuring' of history, focusing on multiculturalism, decolonisation, Martin Luther King, Nelson Mandela, 'White patriarchy', 'White privilege', *womyn's herstory,* and an invented 'universal history', reflecting what UNESCO director general Federico Mayor called 'universal values at all stages of the learning process'.[38] The UNESCO programmes remain very active. For example, the New Zealand National Commission for UNESCO reports that the focus for the period 2014–2021 is 'Global Citizenship Education' (GCED).[39]

---

38   Ibid., p. 23.

39   'Global Citizenship Education in Aotearoa, New Zealand', National Commission for UNESCO, https://unesco.org.nz/our-work/global-citizenship-education-menu/.

Soros' 'Brave New World'

> In a perfectly open society none of the existing ties are final, and people's relation to nation, family and their fellows depends entirely on their own decisions. Looking at the reverse side of the coin, this means that the permanence of social relationships has disappeared; the organic structure of society has disintegrated to the point where its atoms, the individuals, float around without any roots.
>
> — GEORGE SOROS

GEORGE SOROS is a prominent funder of the New School for Social Research. He has achieved fame or infamy in the name of 'philanthropy', lavishing patronage on 'liberal' causes, and is a significant factor in promoting 'colour revolutions' for 'regime change', particularly in the former Soviet bloc. His significance is such that the leadership of Hungary and of Russia have acted to eliminate Soros' Open Society institutes and numerous fronts and offshoots from their societies. In 2018, Prime Minister Viktor Orbán introduced what was widely called a 'Stop Soros' bill in response to Soros' backing of the Third World population shift to Europe. Because Soros is a nominal Jew, albeit secularised and critical of Israel, exposure of him is often condemned as 'anti-Semitism'. In a feature vehemently condemning Orbán and lauding Soros, Zack Beauchamp, like Soros an alumnus of the London School of Economics, writes in *Vox*:

This week, Hungary passed what the government dubbed the "Stop Soros" law, named after Hungarian-American billionaire George Soros. The new law, drafted by Prime Minister Viktor Orbán, creates a new category of crime, called "promoting and supporting illegal migration" — essentially, banning individuals and organizations from providing any kind of assistance to undocumented immigrants. This is so broadly worded that, in theory, the government could arrest someone who provides food to an undocumented migrant on the street or attends a political rally in favor of their rights.

Hungary's government framed the bill as a check on the influence of Soros, a Jewish Holocaust survivor who funds pro-democracy activism around the world. Orbán has fingered Soros (who is also a favorite villain of the American right) as the source of an international plot to destroy Hungary through migration. He often launches attacks on the billionaire in strikingly anti-Semitic terms.[1]

The globalist commentators need only mention key words such as 'Jewish Holocaust survivor' and 'American right', and that is expected to create a negative reflex. That Orbán is one of the few perceptive statesmen in the world is indicated by his description of the Soros offensive, which is reason enough to be condemned by globalists:

'We are fighting an enemy that is different from us. Not open, but hiding; not straightforward but crafty; not honest but base; not national but international; does not believe in working but speculates with money; does not have its own homeland but feels it owns the whole world', Orban said in a characteristic anti-Soros tirade in March.[2]

In another speech Orbán stated:

We are up against media outlets maintained by foreign concerns and domestic oligarchs, professional hired activists, troublemaking protest

---

1   Zack Beauchamp, 'Hungary Just Passed a "Stop Soros" Law That Makes It Illegal to Help Undocumented Migrants', *Vox*, 22 June 2018, https://www.vox.com/policy-and-politics/2018/6/22/17493070/hungary-stop-soros-orban.

2   Ibid.

organizers, and a chain of NGOs financed by an international speculator, summed up by and embodied in the name George Soros.[3]

Orbán describes Soros and oligarchical globalists with precision. The issue is not as to the accuracy of his description, but that one should not speak ill of a 'Jewish Holocaust survivor'.

In 2020, Soros announced at the World Economic Forum at Davos that he was advancing $1 billion to establish a 'global university to fight authoritarian governments....'[4] Soros' Central European University, located in Budapest, was closed by Orbán in 2018. Now Soros has extended the vision to nothing less than the 'transformation of higher education' worldwide. The Carnegie, Rockefeller and Ford Foundations have been influencing and directing higher education through endowments for a century. Soros, with the support of other oligarchs, envisages establishing his own global university network to imbue generations of policy-makers, advisers and educators with his ideology. Soros is overt in the aims:

> The network, which will operate throughout the world, is named the Open Society University Network (OSUN). It will integrate teaching and research across higher education institutions worldwide. It will offer simultaneously taught network courses and joint degree programs and regularly bring students and faculty from different countries together with in-person and online discussions. The network aims to reach the students who need it the most and to promote the values of open society—including free expression and diversity of beliefs.[5]

---

3   Ibid.

4   Katherine Burton, 'George Soros to Start $1 Billion Fund to Fight Nationalists, Climate Change', *Bloomberg Green*, January 24, 2020; https://www.bloomberg.com/news/articles/2020-01-23/soros-starts-new-global-university-with-1-billion-commitment.

5   Open Society Foundations, 'George Soros Launches Global Network to Transform Higher Education', 23 January 2020; https://www.opensocietyfoundations.org/newsroom/george-soros-launches-global-network-to-transform-higher-education.

Note that the university will:

1) Operate as a worldwide network.

2) Influence other tertiary institutions across the world.

3) Indoctrinate students with an ideology — the 'open society' (liberal-capitalism) — hence making the reference to 'free expression and diversity of beliefs' nothing but *doublethink*.

4) 'Fight authoritarian governments'; that is, governments and statesmen, such as Putin and Orbán, who do not acquiesce to globalisation.

> OSUN will seek to promote rigorous education and reach institutions in need of international partners, as well as neglected populations, such as refugees, incarcerated people, the Roma and other displaced groups. OSUN, with the help of its allies, is ready to start a massive "scholars at risk" program, merging a large number of academically excellent but politically endangered scholars into this new global network.[6]

Meaning:

1) OSUN will seek to control the direction and politicise institutions in states targeted for 'regime change'

2) Indoctrinate and manipulate uprooted populations

3) Sponsor those who have opposed targeted regimes

4) Repeat on a larger scale the 1930s Rockefeller programme of sponsoring political agitators in the name of 'scholarship'

Soros is clear that the OSUN network is designed to globally instil the liberal-capitalist doctrine, and reshape 'civilisation' as he sees it.

> Mr. Soros said: "I believe our best hope lies in access to an education that reinforces the autonomy of the individual by cultivating critical

---

6   Ibid.

thinking and emphasizing academic freedom. I consider the Open Society University Network to be the most important and enduring project of my life and I should like to see it implemented while I am still around."

Mr. Soros, who has given more than $32 billion over the past 30 years to education and social justice causes, added, "We are looking for farsighted partner institutions who feel a responsibility for the future of our civilization, people who are inspired by the goals of OSUN and want to participate in its realization."

"We can't build a global network on our own," said Mr Soros. "I hope that those who share this vision will join us in making it a reality."[7]

The Soros initiative is intended to take over and universalise education, indoctrinate and control future generations of academics, create a leadership cadre that can assume administration in the aftermath of 'regime change', and reshape the world from the top-down. OSUN extends what the London School of Economics and the New School were founded to do.

Soros was educated at the London School of Economics, where he encountered his ideological mentor Karl Popper, author of *The Open Society and Its Enemies*, which inspired the naming of the Soros foundations. In 1980, Soros was awarded an honorary doctorate from the New School.[8]

Ideologically, Soros sees an historical dichotomy between 'open and closed societies', between societies that are 'changeless' and those that are continually changing. Soros calls the 'closed society' 'the organic society'. Organic societies are regarded as static. He describes the 'organic society' in a manner that accords with rightist thinking: the individual exists for the benefit of the 'social whole'. 'The unity of a changeless society is comparable to the unity of an organism.

---

7 Ibid.

8 W. Roszkowski and J. Kofman (eds.) p. 948.

Members of a changeless society are like organisms of a living body. … The functions they fulfil determine their rights and duties.[9]

Where the Right sees the fulfilment of the individual in service to the organic society, Soros — as with the Critical Theorists — sees repression.

However, where Soros errs in his opposition to the 'organic society' is in stating that it is 'changeless'. Again using the physiological analogy, a living organism changes by **growth**, based not on the importation of pathogens (which sicken and kill) but on organic growth from the elements out of which it arose (inheritance, tradition). From the rightist interpretation, the 'open society' is one that leaves the organic society 'open' to pathogens. The 'open society' destroys the immune system of the social organism, allowing 'cultural disease' to enter. It is these cultural, economic, social, and moral pathogens that Soros, and others of the globalist elite, promote. The organic society, so far from being 'changeless', unless prematurely killed by war or natural disaster for example, might organically grow to a high culture, such as the West's early medieval Gothic epoch when, especially during the 13th century, the arts and sciences flourished, and life was far removed from the derisive way it has been portrayed since the Renaissance by 'progressives'.[10]

Where the Right sees a social community, Soros sees restriction. What Soros disdains as the 'social whole', his mentor Karl Popper called 'holism'. When Soros aims to break down the bonds that hold the individual to the 'organic society' through the promotion of a myriad of causes that fracture the individual from *primary ties,* we arrive at the convergence between liberal capitalism and the New Left, Critical Theory and Cultural Marxism. **Here one might perceive how Soros and fellow globalists are in accord with the Critical Theorists, and why liberal-capitalists fund 'socialists'.**

Soros frankly stated:

---

9   G. Soros (1995), pp. 260–261.

10   K. R. Bolton, *The Decline and Fall of Civilisations*, pp. 302–305.

Let me try to carry the open society to its logical conclusion and describe what a perfectly changeable society would look like. Alternatives would be available in all aspects of existence: in personal relations, opinions and ideas, productive processes and materials, social and economic organization, and so on. In these circumstances, the individual would occupy the paramount position. Members of an organic society possess no independence at all; in a less than perfectly changeable society, established values and relationships still circumscribe people's behaviour, but **in a perfectly open society none of the existing ties are final, and people's relation to nation, family and their fellows depends entirely on their own decisions.** Looking at the reverse side of the coin, **this means that the permanence of social relationships has disappeared; the organic structure of society has disintegrated to the point where its atoms, the individuals, float around without any roots.**[11]

Soros and Popper reach convergence with Fromm and Marcuse. Liberal-capitalism synthesises with Cultural Marxism.

Soros explains that the individual will choose what alternative best suits his life by the extension of economics. 'In a world in which every action is a matter of choice, economic behaviour characterizes all fields of activity. All values, including spiritual, artistic and moral, can be reduced to monetary terms'. 'This renders the principles of the market mechanism relevant to such far-ranging areas as art, politics, social life, sex, and religion'. In 'a perfectly changeable society the scope of the market mechanism would be extended to this utmost limit'. The most striking aspect of a perfectly changeable society is 'the decline in personal relationships'. 'Friends, neighbors, husbands, and wives would become, if not interchangeable, at least readily replaceable by only marginally inferior (or superior) substitutes; they would be subject to choice under competitive conditions'. Parents and children would 'presumably remain fixed', but the family bond 'may become less influential'.[12]

---

11   G. Soros, p. 282. Emphasis added.

12   Ibid., pp. 282–283.

Soros claims that such a conclusion is 'less than pleasing', but he has spent a lifetime and a vast fortune promoting precisely those causes that lead to this 'logical conclusion'. Soros states that the primary obstacles to this universal open society are Islamic and Russian 'fundamentalism'. The other major challenges are the return of the organic society via 'an ethnic or religious community'.[13] Hence he expends large amounts against 'populist' statesmen, such as Putin and Orbán.

'Piecemeal Social Engineering'

Both Marx on the Left (*dialectical materialism*) and Spengler on the Right (*historical morphology*) were *historicists*; both postulated **laws** of history and social development. Popper and his pupil Soros reject *historicism*. There is no intrinsic unfolding of history; only what the individual makes at a given time. If that individual has extreme wealth, then he is in a position to substantially alter society. This seems to be a highly relativistic form of social engineering, and one that proceeds by trial and error. The social engineer becomes responsible for changing institutions as the need arises; changing society in stages. The premise is one of perpetual change, Popper writing:

> The politician who adopts this [piecemeal] method may or may not have a blueprint of society before his mind, he may or may not hope that mankind will one day realize an ideal state, and achieve happiness and perfection on earth. But he will be aware that perfection, if at all attainable, is far distant and that every generation of men, and therefore also the living, have a claim...[14]

> One of the differences between the Utopian or *holistic* approach and the piecemeal approach may therefore be stated in this way: while the piecemeal engineer can attack his problem with an open mind as to the scope of the reform, the *holist* cannot do this; for he has decided beforehand that a complete reconstruction is possible and necessary.[15]

---

13   Ibid., p. 295.

14   Karl Popper, *The Open Society and Its Enemies*, Vol. 1, p. 158.

15   Popper, *The Poverty of Historicism*, p. 69.

Additionally, from a tactical viewpoint, the social engineer can subvert a community behind the guise of addressing some specific humanitarian issue:

> In favour of his method, the piecemeal engineer can claim that a systematic fight against suffering and injustice is more likely to be supported by the approval and agreement of a great number of people than the fight for the establishment of some ideal.[16]

Hence, the South African economy might be opened up (the open society) to privatisation and globalisation by the destruction of apartheid in the name of 'social justice', or the mineral wealth of Kosovo in the name of 'democracy'.

---

16   Popper, *The Open Society and Its Enemies*, p. 158.

Social Deconstruction
through Ethnic Diversity

I N 1952, UNESCO issued its statement on race, *The Race Concept*, a supposedly scientific symposium of scientists repudiating the significance of race as a dangerous fallacy, and a primary obstacle to One World. In the introduction it was stated that UNESCO was the organisation best equipped to 'head the campaign against race prejudice and to extirpate this most dangerous of doctrines'.[1] In 1949, the UNESCO Department of Social Sciences assembled a team of scientists. Many scientists criticized the first draft, and it was several years later that the final version appeared, still under criticism, especially from within the biological sciences. Despite being unable to dismiss races as taxonomically classifiable, the crux of the argument was that all races are equally educable, and that there is no difference in capacity for 'intellectual and emotional development', and that all races are hybridised and that all belong to the common stock of *Homo sapiens*. Hence there is no scientific justification for scepticism in regard to the creation of humanity as an amorphous mass under a world state. Among the signatories was the avid eugenicist and Communist Dr. J. B. S. Haldane. Julian Huxley, whose references to the mentally and physically deficient would today be regarded with horror by the politically correct, 'contributed to the final wording'.[2]

---

1   L. C. Dunn, et al., *The Race Concept*, p. 5.
2   Ibid., p. 16.

What was significant about the statement was its support for the globalist premise that 'nationality, language and religion can be changed in a single generation for any person or biological group or race...'[3] Therefore, 'race', however one wishes to define it, has no intrinsic duration,[4] and like today's 'scientific' opinion on gender, anyone can be deconstructed and reconstructed according to fad or fashion, as if purchasing a new commodity. Indeed, as seen previously, the *raison d'etre* of UNESCO and other UN organs is to mould all into 'global citizens'. This was enabled by the presumptuous opinion of the committee of scientists that personality and character are 'raceless'.[5] 'The unity of mankind from both the biological and social viewpoints is the main thing. To recognize this and to act accordingly is the first requirement of modern man'.[6] Quoting Darwin, the statement claims that man strives towards ever greater unity, from tribe to nation to 'all nations and races'.[7]

In finale: '**Lastly, biological studies lend support to the ethic of universal brotherhood**'...[8]

With this *Statement,* and *An American Dilemma* prepared by Gunnar Myrdal, who had also given advice on the *UNESCO Statement,*[9] the ideological foundations for an assault on nationality and ethnicity would give scientific rationalisation for integration, open borders, multiculturalism, 'replacement migration', and a globalised 'inclusive economy'.

While the *UNESCO Statement* assured the world that it is man's historical destiny to unite into One World, this crass revision and restructuring of history crashes on the rocks of reality. Ideologically

---

3   Ibid., p. 91.

4   Spengler defined 'race' as 'duration of character'.

5   L. C. Dunn, et al., p. 101 (text of the Statement of 1950).

6   Ibid.

7   Ibid., p. 102.

8   Ibid., p. 103.

9   Ibid.

multicultural societies, or more specifically globalised 'inclusive economies' are supposed to reflect the natural inclination of mankind as a 'social animal'. According to the globalist doctrine, mankind is historically impelled to assimilate any number of cultures and *ethni* within the same territory on the basis that we are all from the same 'stock'. The concluding passage written by Dr. L. C. Dunn harkened to the 19th century Enlightenment doctrines of equality that inspired the Jacobins to oil the guillotines in the name of 'liberty, equality, fraternity'. Dunn triumphantly concluded that the *UNESCO Statement* is in the spirit of the American and French Revolutions and referred to the *Déclaration des Droits de l'Homme* of 1789.[10] Like Marxism, the globalists herald their aims in the name of historical laws that do not exist. When the utopia does not unfold in the manner assumed by the globalists, a multitude of U.N. drafted laws are imposed on member states, bolstered by mass propaganda and indoctrination issued by UNESCO and a vast network of NGOs.

Reality Not on Side of Globalists

Against the bedrock of reality, multiculturalism is progressively falling apart, and mankind, so far from being historically impelled to embrace 'global citizenship', is retribalising and self-segregating. An extensive 'meta-analytical review' on the impact of ethnic diversity on 'social trust' indicates that there is something gravely amiss about the *social engineering* indoctrination on the supposed benefits of ethnic diversity. The study is called 'Ethnic Diversity and Social Trust: A Narrative and Meta-Analytical Review'. This was published online as a preliminary to being published in the *Annual Review of Political Science* (Volume 23, 2020).[11]

Plain sense, whether by instinct or intuition or anecdotal observation, obliges many to look in askance when experiences contradict

---

10   Ibid., p. 91.

11   Peter Thirsted Dinesen, Merlin Schaeffer, and Kim Mannemar Sønderskov, 'Ethnic Diversity and Social Trust: A Narrative and Meta-Analytical Review'.

dogma. However, the masses are assured that this is only due to their innate racism, which is supposedly indicative of a psychological imbalance that can be fixed by a variety of methods.

Of the latter possibilities, scientists at Oxford University found that 'implicit racial bias' can be reduced by the use of the heart medication propranolol, which blocks 'activation in the peripheral "autonomic" nervous system'. Professor Julian Savulescu of Oxford University's Faculty of Philosophy, a co-author, added: 'Such research raises the tantalising possibility that our unconscious racial attitudes could be modulated using drugs, a possibility that requires careful ethical analysis'.[12]

What seems to be discarded as irrelevant by these scientists is the possibility that such 'implicit racial bias', existing at an unconscious level, is likely to be a survival mechanism descended over millennia. What the Oxford tests do indicate (albeit the number of subjects was small) is that 'implicit racism' is hardwired in the 'autonomic nervous system'.

Putnam Study

Of the many studies cited by the meta-analytical review, one of the most significant and earliest was based on 40 communities and 30,000 individuals in the USA, undertaken by Dr. Robert D. Putnam, political scientist at Harvard University. Putnam's 2007 study found that ethnic diversity causes decrease in community trust, engendering feelings of powerlessness and alienation.[13]

Putnam and other social scientists who do not get the results they would wish for, nonetheless remain optimistic that ethnic diversity

---

12   'Drug "Reduces Implicit Racial Bias," Study Suggests', *University of Oxford News & Events*, 8 March 2012; http://www.ox.ac.uk/news/2012-03-08-drug-reduces-implicit-racial-bias-study-suggests.

13   Robert D. Putnam, 'E Pluribus Unum: Diversity and Community in the Twenty-first Century', *Journal of Scandinavian Political Studies*, Vol. 30, No. 2, June 2007, pp. 137–174.

can be made to work by looking for examples in contrived situations, where common interests might be created that can at least temporarily or partially circumvent the outcomes of normal circumstances. Domesticated cats and dogs raised under special circumstances in a household might 'prove' that there can be a future world where cats and dogs can not only tolerate each other, but can become 'friends' and overcome their primal 'implicit specism'; a world moreover where one day the lamb might lay down with the lion. Putnam gave an optimistic view (from the liberal perspective) that his study of social fragmentation caused by ethnic diversity can yet be circumvented by considering such contrived situations as military and religious institutions:

> In the long run, however, successful immigrant societies have overcome such fragmentation by creating new, cross-cutting forms of social solidarity and more encompassing identities. Illustrations of becoming comfortable with diversity are drawn from the US military, religious institutions, and earlier waves of American immigration.[14]

Such situational communities might in themselves take on the traits of ethnic communities. The situation for the forming of the institution, group, or community itself creates 'in-group' solidarity and identity relative to an out-group, and such traits of an ethnos might indeed transcend a biological 'race'. Hence, the Marine Corps has its own ethos, mythos, structure, history and purpose regardless of its racial composition, relative to non-Marines; as do monks, sports teams, symphony orchestras, and college fraternities.

A 'nation' might be constructed by an amalgam of *ethni* into a new *ethnos*, if the nation- and state-building processes are strong enough, in particular with an in-group ethos relative to a perceived out-group. Jews are a particularly strong example. Yet even Israel, perhaps the best possible state for the developing of an *ethnos* across racial boundaries, among a people that has been formed by amalgamating many

---

14   Ibid., Abstract.

ethni over thousands of years around a strong ethos and mythos, remains divided between Sephardic, Ashkenazic, and Beta Israel.[15] A corporation can develop a similar in-group ethos among its employees, cutting across other bonds. Nation-states might also be built and maintained by developing a sufficiently strong bond through the symbiosis of otherwise separate ethnicities. The historical and social circumstances widely diverge, and that is the point; there is no universal formula. To quote a sociologist from the Right, Joseph de Maistre:

> Now, there is no such thing as 'man' in this world. In my life I have seen Frenchmen, Italians, Russians, and so on. I even know, thanks to Montesquieu, that one can be Persian. But as for man, I declare I've never encountered him.[16]

Discussing the 1795 Constitution of the French Revolutionary epoch, de Maistre made a comment that is especially applicable to the *UN Charter*, *UN Declaration on Human Rights*, and the array of other delectations intended to impose universal laws:

> … This constitution is capable of being applied to all human communities from China to Geneva. But a constitution which is made for all nations is made for none: it is a pure abstraction, a school exercise whose purpose is to exercise the mind in accordance with a hypothetical ideal, and which ought to be addressed to Man, in the imaginary places which he inhabits.[17]

Unity in Diversity?

When under tension, are even the situational communities referred to by Putnam necessarily able to maintain their stability? Putnam mentions the military as an example of a community that can maintain unity within diversity. Is this really so? The loyalty of a military under

---

15   Ethiopian Jews settled in Israel.

16   Joseph de Maistre, *Considerations on France* (1797), Chapter VI: 'Of the Divine Influence in Political Institutions'.

17   Ibid.

tension when drawn from disparate sources has always been a matter of concern for rulers. A paper on the Black experience in Vietnam states:

> One of the least known but most important chapters in the history of America's encounter with Vietnam was the internal rebellion that wracked the U.S. military. From the Long Binh jail in Vietnam, to Travis Air Force Base in California, to aircraft carriers in the South China Sea, the armed forces faced widespread resistance and unrest. Throughout the military morale and discipline sank to record lows. Antiwar committee and underground newspapers appeared everywhere. Unauthorized absence rates reached unprecedented levels: in the Army in 1971 there were seventeen AWOLs and seven desertions for every one hundred soldiers. Harsher forms of rebellion also occurred—drug abuse, violent uprisings, refusal of orders, even attacks against superiors. The cumulative result of this resistance within the ranks was a severe breakdown in military effectiveness and combat capability. By 1969 the Army had ceased to function as an effective fighting force and was rapidly disintegrating. The armed forces had to be withdrawn from Indochina for their very survival. The strongest and most militant resisters were black GIs. Of all the soldiers of the Vietnam era, black and other minority GIs were consistently the most active in their opposition to the war and military injustice. Blacks faced greater oppression than whites, and they fought back with greater determination and anger. The rebellions that shook American cities like Watts, Newark, and Detroit erupted at major military installations just a few years later.[18]

The 'Black experience' in the USA was far removed from being capable of inculcating in Black GIs a kinship with one's White comrades against the ostensible enemy. The enemy to the Black GI was the White GI, and there was a kinship with the Vietcong. The sense of what it meant to be an 'American' was and remains too nebulous to provide any common meaning even in as tightly controlled a structure as the military. If the authority, hierarchy and discipline of the military, even

---

18   David Cortright, 'Black GI Resistance During the Vietnam War', *Vietnam Generation* (1990), Vol. 2 : No. 1, Article 5; https://digitalcommons.lasalle.edu/cgi/viewcontent.cgi?article=1052&context=vietnamgeneration.

when confronted by a hostile 'out-group', is insufficient in maintaining an 'in-group', to what extent will social scientists, politicians and plutocrats resort to a levelling tyranny to achieve their aims?

The Review

The question posed by the review is: 'Does ethnic diversity erode social trust?'[19] There have been many studies on the question over 25 years, with various findings. The meta-analysis aims to find common patterns by analysing data from the literature covering 1001 estimates from 87 studies.[20]

There are several definitions of social trust examined: (1) generalised social trust (strangers); (2) out-group trust; (3) in-group trust; (4) trust in neighbours.[21]

The 'key debates in the literature' are: Debate 1: Why does ethnic diversity erode trust? The question posed is as to why closer proximity with out-groups becomes more consequential for social trust?

A 2015 study by two of the review's authors, Dinesen and Sønderskov, found that 'mere exposure to people of different ethnic backgrounds erodes social trust'. This is related to the concept of out-group aversion. 'Shared norms' and other factors impact on this,[22] and it is shared norms that are a distinctive feature of what defines an ethnos. The utopian aim of reducing everyone to a nebulous universal denominator in the name of 'humanity' seems highly dubious. Is the elimination of out-group aversion even a desirable goal? What are the consequences?

---

19 Dinesen, et al., 'Ethnic Diversity and Social Trust: A Narrative and Meta-Analytical Review', p. 1.

20 Ibid., Abstract.

21 Ibid., pp. 1–2.

22 Dinesen and Sønderskov, 'Ethnic Diversity and Social Trust: Evidence from the Micro-Context', *American Sociological Review*, 80 (3), pp. 550–73; cited in Dinesen et al., ibid., p. 3.

One might question the clichés large businesses and governmental agencies like to purvey about being 'inclusive', 'diverse', and the strength that these provide to corporate structures. If a high-tech corporation in the USA employs a significant number of high-tech specialists from, say, India and then lauds the benefits such 'diversity' has brought to the corporation, can it really be said that this has been caused by ethnic diversity, or by employing those who are especially advanced in the expertise required by the business? Rather than there being 'diversity', there will be a common corporate culture, with shared corporate values and aims. Where Pascal Zachary's 'global me' comes into such situations is through the ease by which individuals with the needed qualifications can be transplanted about the world in accordance with the requirements of global capital and technology. However, even at the workplace, as will be seen, Dinesen found that social trust is eroded by diversity.

The authors also refer to 'in-group trust' increasing when there is a perception of being 'surrounded by more ethnic out-groups'.[23] There might also arise feelings of isolation or alienation; 'constrict theory',[24] as one becomes increasingly surrounded by ethnic aliens, some studies referring to 'people's inherent preference to interact with people like themselves'.[25]

Debate 2: Can contact alleviate the negative effect of ethnic diversity? Here 'contact theory'[26] postulates that we could all get along in a multicultural utopia if we sought friends from different races, and that the positive experiences would destroy any prejudices inherited from the bigoted generations of our parents and grandparents. 'Positive intergroup relations' might be built, and 'negative stereotypes' reduced.[27]

---

23 Dinesen et al., 'Ethnic Diversity and Social Trust: A Narrative and Meta-Analytical Review', p. 3.
24 Ibid.
25 Ibid.
26 Ibid., p. 4.
27 Ibid.

It is here where the propagandists for multiculturalism can be at their most fervent, depicting the joys of having ethnically diverse friends; where the power of friendship overcomes small-town bigotry, etc. Naturally that 'bigotry' is invariably from Whites, and one does not see depictions of the 'implicit racism' of American Blacks, Hasidim, Chinese, or Zulus. What ethni does not regard itself as special and even chosen by God? Certainly the Chinese have done so over millennia, dialectical materialism not having dampened their self-perception as the centre of the world. Mention of the ethnic implications of Judaism seems superfluous.

Such a mythos is the basis of inner strength, without which a people would not survive through millennia. When 'push comes to shove', even liberal democracies resort to war propaganda based on negative stereotypes on 'Huns' or 'Japs'.

The sociologist A. James Gregor had a paper published by The Eugenics Review in 1961, examining the persistent phenomenon of 'racial prejudice' over millennia and over sundry cultures. The antiquity and persistence of 'prejudice' confounds the notions that this is a result of 'White privilege', a white social construct, a feature of a certain era of economics, and a means by which the 'ruling class' divides the proletariat. Gregor pointed out that 'anything more than a casual or temporary contact between widely diverse races, in pre-capitalistic as well as capitalistic times, provokes prejudice and discrimination and a subsequent rationalisation for felt preferences'.[28] This is part of man as a 'gregarious creature'; a social animal, manifesting according to 'historic, social and political circumstances in which the particular human group finds itself'.[29] UNESCO scientists and the like distort the premise of 'man as a social animal' to support their doctrine of universal brotherhood.

---

28 A. James Gregor, 'On the Nature of Prejudice', *The Eugenics Review*, Vol. 52, No. 4, January 1961; I.A.A.E.E. reprint No. 3, New York.

29 Ibid., p. 1.

In Mexico, the natives eliminated the persistent trait of albinism because it departed from the norm established by the gods. In New Guinea, the Papuans held children born of lighter hue over a fire of green branches until the skin became tinted.[30] The Japanese discriminate against the light-skinned Ainu. The Chinese derogatively call the European *gweilo*; 'ghost'. Greeks regarded non-Greeks as 'barbarians'. Koreans refer to Japanese as 'monkeys' (*jjokbari*). In New Zealand, 'Maori' means 'normal', as distinct from all others. None of this is a 'White social construct' to legitimise 'White privilege', or a phase of capitalism.

Interestingly, the authors of the meta-analysis pose the question as to whether 'out-group trust' reduces 'in-group trust'. The implication is that harmonious ethnic diversity subverts in-group solidarity. Is that desirable? For the liberal ideologue, and the corporate CEO, the answer is 'yes'.

Nature of Discrimination

Corporations have a stated policy of 'inclusiveness' and 'diversity' as part of their charter, which now includes not only ethnicity but 'gender' in its increasing myriad of forms. This diversity is claimed to bring dynamism to the corporation. However, as alluded to above, are such contrived, artificial and limited situations really examples of 'diversity', or examples of acculturation within a ready-made corporate culture, into which one cannot enter without a prerequisite background that overrides all other aspects of one's personality? The corporation becomes the 'in-group', and the selection process for admission is at least as stringent as admission into a tribe. The corporate recruiting process is a form of 'prejudice' and 'discrimination', without which there would be chaos. How far would or should an applicant to a symphony orchestra get without any musical background? Should

---

30 Ibid., p. 2.

a paraplegic dwarf not at least get a chance to try out for a football team? Discrimination is basic to society.

Discrimination as Cognitive Development

Inability to discriminate is symptomatic of stunted development. The utopian liberal idyll of Black and White toddlers playing as friends is a retarded image when applied in a generalised and universal way to adults. Perhaps this is why we can discern the retarded character of liberals and leftists who become histrionic in their declamations against 'racists' and 'Fascists', and who are incapable of behaving rationally? The ability to discriminate is a part of childhood cognitive development. It seems that the liberal ideal is for adults to regress to the stage of 'pre-connectional thinking' in 'operational intelligence' that normally exists at the age of two, when the child does not yet have the ability to classify, regarding 'similar objects as though they are identical in a type of muddled categorization; i.e. all men must be "Daddy", all animals are "doggies"... The *preconcept* child cannot hierarchically discriminate between oranges and apples for instance... '[31] **Preconnectional thinking becomes a prerequisite for 'global citizenship'.**

The Corporation Ideal

The meta-study cites a 2019 study by Dinesen, Sønderskov, and Thuesen on ethnic diversity and social trust in the workplace, with a focus on Denmark, where statistics are particularly comprehensive.[32] Dinesen states that ethnic diversity in the workplace has the same

---

31   Lesley Olley, 'Paiget's Model of Cognitive Development', https://www.massey.ac.nz/~wwpapajl/evolution/assign2/LO/piaget.html.

32   Peter Dinesen, K.M. Sønderskov, F. Thuesen, 'Working Together? Ethnic Diversity in the Workplace and Generalised Social Trust', Working Paper, 2019. An interview on this paper with Dinsen can be heard at: Center for the Study of Democratic Citizenship, https://csdc-cecd.ca/event/speaker-series-peter-dinesen/.

negative impact on social trust as in the neighbourhood context. The more diverse the workplace, the more the social distrust, indicating that ethnic diversity has a causal effect on social trust. The study on the workplace took variables into account, such as educational backgrounds and types of work, and the results were consistent.[33]

One becomes a corporate being by detachment from ethnic background, not because of ethnic (or gender) background, and amalgamates into the corporate culture. One ceases to be a male, female, Caucasian, Asian, African, and takes on common traits of a corporate being. That is what corporate planners and their political subordinates aim for on a world scale, the result being the antithesis of 'ethnic diversity'; a universal corporate monoculture where those 'nations' most willing to open their borders will be the most successful in the process of globalisation, and the individuals most successful under globalisation will be those who have become most adapted to the corporate global culture, detached from the organic 'primary ties'.

This is where one should delineate the *Identitarianism* of the Right, and the *identity politics* of the Left and its corporate sponsors, despite being confused by libertarians. Hence those most avid in opposing the 'looming menace' of the 'Alt Right' aim to deconstruct the *primary ties* through a multiplicity of identities that are so nebulous and fractured that the end product will not be an enriched diversity across the world, but the *global citizen* as a new species of humanity designed for the global economy.

When one looks closer at the motives behind the academic condemnation of the Right as a supposed terror threat, and the 'scholarly' repudiation of so-called 'racism' (as it solely applies to Whites), behind the façade of moral rectitude is the promotion of globalist interests. One of the leading figures from academia in this crusade is the New Zealander Dr. Paul Spoonley, a sociologist whose claim to fame is his long redundant thesis on the 'extreme Right' in New

---

33   Dinesen interview, CSDC, ibid.

Zealand,[34] presented by the news media as an 'expert' whenever a smear campaign against rightists (some real, most imagined) is required. However, when stripped of the moral cant, the bottom line is that immigration is good for business:

> Skilled migrants make up 60 per cent of total immigrants. With these new arrivals come new business, new investment and new connections with key export markets. 'We can calculate what they contribute and compare that to what they need in terms of benefits and healthcare,' Spoonley said. 'Immigrants in Auckland contribute much more to taxation and economic benefits. Therefore, their net contribution is higher than the local population.'[35]

Are the 'one nation' self-styled 'conservatives' any different in their outlook than liberal academics such as Spoonley, when the criteria for migration and citizenship are to work, invest, and pay taxes? Behind the liberal idealism stands the crassness of global capital.

Meta Estimated

The authors, having explained the parameters of their study, explain the methodology of the 'meta-analytical approach'. The aim was to go beyond the 'idiosyncrasies' of the 87 individual studies, 'to generate an overall meta estimate summarising the effect…' and to 'provide a meta estimate of the relationship between ethnic diversity and social trust'.[36]

This cross study analysis, which seems to be the first of its kind, although supporting the results of other analyses using different methods, shows that 'the overall meta estimate of the relationship between ethnic diversity and social trust is negative'. The more diverse

---

34 Paul Spoonley (1987).

35 'Immigration Good for NZ Economy, No Need for Xenophobic Politics': Paul Spoonley, *Stuff*, 5 May 2017; https://www.stuff.co.nz/business/92217724/soaring-immigration-levels-positive-for-economy-no-reason-for-xenophobic-politics.

36 Peter Dinesen et al., 'Meta-Analysis…'

the location, the lower the social trust. In most, but not all, studies, the negative impact of diversity on social trust is significant.[37]

Where there are results from a quarter century of testing that show some aspect of ethnic diversity that can be discerned in some manner to have a less than negative effect, this, as one would expect, is utilised as a triumphant example of the 'success' of some multicultural experiment, in some manner and context. As referred to above, artificial contexts do not indicate much, other than that social engineering, indoctrination, and coercion might be able to distort the normal character of relationships. Fortunately, the authors definitively stating that 'ethnic diversity is negatively associated with social trust', and that this applies in varying degrees to all forms of social trust,[38] spare the reader the moral platitudes that social scientists generally seem compelled to attach to papers where the empirical evidence does not accord with their personal biases. For example, the above cited Putnam, whose studies are part of the meta-analysis, despite his having found that ethnic diversity increases social mistrust, as an obvious enthusiast for American liberal-democracy contended in the face of criticism that his studies to the contrary show that there are 'substantial benefits of diversity, including racial and ethnic diversity, to our society'. In 2012, Putnam went as far as to file a lawsuit against several scholars of more 'conservative' persuasion for using his 2007 paper 'E Pluribus Unum: Diversity and Community in the Twenty-First Century' in a legal case involving 'reverse discrimination' in education. Putnam countered that ethnic diversity is not the sole cause of negative social trust, and has also considered other factors, such as the role of technology in undermining 'social capital', causing alienation, and a decline in civic participation. He also asserted that it is primarily neighbourhoods rather than schools, churches and workplaces where

---

37 Ibid., p. 9.
38 Ibid., pp. 9–10.

diversity mainly undermines social trust.[39] These are all positions that the rightist critic can readily accept without having to indulge in strained intellectual acrobatics to somehow discount the ethnic factor. As the meta-analysis of studies, including those of Putnam, showed, the neighbourhood level is indeed where social trust is most eroded by diversity, but contrary to what Putnam later insisted, the negative impact is on all forms of social trust.

In 2015, attempts were made to refute Putnam's paper on diversity and social trust in neighbourhoods, and one suspects that he would have been pleased to have his findings refuted. The paper concluded that it is Whites who feel most distrust in neighbourhoods and that this really means that such distrust merely reflects White 'prejudice'.[40] This 2015 study optimistically affirmed that '[o]ur evidence suggests there is no meaningful relationship between ethnic diversity and measures of trust and cooperation'. Where social distrust is undeniable, 'economic and social factors' are sought. 'Indicators of economic conditions, especially education and economic satisfaction, positively predict several measures of trust'.[41]

The meta-analysis examined the variables argued in the 2015 paper, which is the first source cited in the 'references'. The meta-analysis shows that there is a 'consistent pattern of negative relationships with diversity across social trust', which 'supports Putnam's (2007) anomie (social isolation) mechanism predicting a universal decline in trust

---

39 Tom Bartlett, 'Harvard Sociologist Says His Research Was "Twisted"', *The Chronicle of Higher Education*, 15 August 2012; https://www.chronicle.com/blogs/percolator/robert-putnam-says-his-research-was-twisted/30357.

40 Daisy Grewal, 'Does Diversity Create Distrust? Doubts about a Harvard Professor's Landmark Finding', *Scientific American*, 29 November 2016; https://www.scientificamerican.com/article/does-diversity-create-distrust/.

41 Maria Abascal and Delia Baldassarri, 'Love Thy Neighbor? Ethnoracial Diversity and Trust Reexamined', *American Journal of Sociology*, Vol. 121, No. 3 (November 2015), p. 748; https://static1.squarespace.com/static/50e64c35e4b02b36141d5175/t/564de301e4b082df3a504e1a/1447944961025/2.AbascalBaldassarri_HeterogeneityTrust_AJS2015.pdf.

of all types in ethnically diverse surroundings'.[42] The most consistent finding is the negative impact of ethnic diversity in neighbourhoods. This was seen in the USA, Spain, Britain, Germany, the Netherlands, and Sweden. The closer the proximity of the out-group, the higher the social distrust.[43] This contradicts the dogma that inter-ethnic relations can be improved by personal contact with the out-group. It repudiates the notions of assimilation, and interpersonal projects designed to break down out-group distrust. The notion is also something examined by the authors, as there are several studies that purport to show that proximity with out-groups encourages social trust. The authors refer to these studies as being skewered by 'imprecise and biased self-assessments of contact'.[44]

The meta-analysis also considered the objections raised by the 2015 paper under the category of Debate 3: Is ethnic diversity just a placeholder for social disadvantage? The question relates to whether it is really one of ethnic relations, or of social disadvantage and crime. The answer is managed in this study by 'controlling statistically for potentially confounding factors', at both intellectual and contextual levels. This is difficult because of the age-old quandary of distinguishing between consequence and cause, or as the authors put it, are these factors 'confounders or mediators' of ethnic diversity and social trust? In order to resolve these variables, the authors allowed for social and economic status, 'contextual socioeconomic deprivation', and 'contextual crime'.[45]

---

42 Dinesen et al, 'Meta-Analysis...' p. 10.

43 Ibid., pp. 11–12.

44 Ibid., p. 14.

45 Ibid., p. 6.

Conclusion

Dinesen et al. conclude by asking what policy makers might do to mitigate the erosion of social trust by ethnic diversity. What public policies or institutions are available to curb the 'negative effect'?[46]

One might here wonder whether the authors, like Putnam, are loathe to accept the implications of their own findings, and after such scientific rigour, retreat to ideological preconceptions. What is one to make, for example, of their suggestion that there might be a 'gradual implementation of integration policies within countries as sources of quasi-experimental variation in the moderating variable'?[47] One might wonder why a scientist whose studies consistently show that social trust is eroded by integration is advocating a policy of 'gradualness' as a social experiment. Are the authors suggesting a modified approach to the same failed policies that have resulted in social distrust in the hope that the results will be different? This is the resort of every failed ideology: if only the dogma can be implemented in some different manner, the result will be different; rather than questioning whether the dogma itself is irremediably flawed and will give a negative result regardless of how it is implemented.

---

46 Ibid., p. 18.
47 Ibid.

Behaviour Modification

THE META-ANALYSIS of Peter Dinesen et al. shows that the dogma of ethnic diversity does not proceed according to the utopian vision of UNESCO scientists, Critical Theorists, and 'social investors'. The problem is that there can be no globalised 'inclusive economy' unless the *global citizen* can be created as the new human norm. Among the indoctrination techniques are those derived from humanistic psychology, such as 'group therapy', 'sensitivity training', 'encounter groups', and 'human relations' courses. The focus is on group peer pressure and self-criticism until conformity is attained, and stubborn individuals relent to the group. The group achieves a consensus, which has been predetermined by the facilitators, who direct the group toward that goal, which the group believes to be of their own determination.

The technique is a long-established method of indoctrination. At its most overt it has been brutally used in Mao's China and at Jim Jones' commune. Dissidents are shamed into repudiating their non-conformity with public humiliation. More recently, China has revived the practice. In 2018,

> [m]embers of the Politburo 'were asked to conduct criticism and self-criticism in light of work experience,' at a meeting held on Tuesday and Wednesday, state news agency Xinhua reported. They were also questioned

on 'how they have taken the lead to implement Xi's instructions and key Party regulations and policies,' it added.[48]

The Khmer Rouge used regular self-criticism sessions. Francois Bizot, an anthropologist imprisoned by the Khmer Rouge, described one such session in 1971 in his memoirs:

> Several evenings a week — every evening it didn't rain — the guards gathered for a collective confession. ... I was a privileged witness to these circles, where they would sit on the ground under the direction of an elder. Military homilies alternated with simple, repetitive songs. 'Comrades,' began the eldest, 'let us appraise the day that has passed, in order to correct our faults. We must cleanse ourselves of the repeated sins that accumulate and slow down our beloved revolution. Do not be surprised at this!' 'I,' said the first one, 'should have replaced the rattan rod today, the one north of the first shelter, which we use to dry clothes. I have done nothing about it... on account of my laziness.' The man presiding over the session nodded with a frown, though not severely, only meaning to show that he knew how hard it was to combat inertia, so natural in man when he is not sustained by revolutionary convictions. He passed wordlessly onto the next man, indicating who this should be by pursing his lips in his direction.[49]

The Frankfurt Institute used 'group discussions' as a means of manipulating opinions and gathering data since 1944. Rolf Wiggershaus, in his study on the Frankfurt Institute, describes the method as an example of the way in which it was possible to steer discussions in everyday situations towards specific themes without it being realised. Horkheimer and Adorno utilised the method on their return to Germany as part of their role in the American 're-education' programme, developing it into 'a recognized technique of social research' during the 1950s. 'Spontaneous comments' were encouraged by 'a neutral chairman', after the use of a 'basic stimulus' to start the discussion.

---

48 'Top Chinese Officials Forced to Carry Out Self-Criticisms', *Agence France-Presse*, 27 December 2018; https://www.voanews.com/east-asia/top-chinese-officials-forced-carry-out-self-criticisms.

49 Francois Bizot, pp. 52–54.

The discussions were taped and notes taken of reactions. In the second part of the 'group discussion', the fieldworker would introduce arguments and counter-arguments, then a short questionnaire was completed by participants, based on the questionnaire used for researching *The Authoritarian Personality*.[50] The aim was to determine German 'attitudes to democracy', collective guilt, Jews, the USSR, rearmament, and the American occupation.[51] 'The attitudes were depressing', with most expressing negative opinions towards both the USA and USSR, not showing sufficient enthusiasm towards democracy, and rejecting collective guilt for the Nazi past. The groups most resistant to 're-education' were academics and farmers. Opposition to rearmament was regarded as negative, because the USA was wanting to use Germany in its conflict with the USSR, while the neutralist 'without us' attitude of Germans was 'still popular'.[52]

NTL Institute for Applied Behavioral Science

'Sensitivity training' and 'T-Groups' (Training Groups), intended for training in human relations, began under the social psychologist Kurt Lewin, when he was director of MIT's Research Center for Group Dynamics. Lewin 'was attributed as one of the first psychologists to systematically test human behavior, influencing experiential adult learning, social psychology and human interaction'. Lewin 'began applying his research to the war effort, working for the U.S. government'. In 1946, the United States Office of Naval Research and the National Education Association (NEA) funded a planning group named the National Training Laboratory for Group Development, which became the NTL Institute for Applied Behavioral Science. NTL expanded with 'a major grant from the Carnegie Foundation'.[53] NTL has a pervasive

---

50 Rolf Wiggershaus, p. 437.

51 Rolf Wiggershaus, p. 440.

52 Ibid.

53 National Training Laboratories, 'Lewin's Legacy', https://www.ntl.org/about-us/ntl-legacy/.

influence over human relations development in the public and private sectors. Dr. Warren Bennis, pioneer of 'leadership studies', wrote that the NTL had become by 1967 'an internationally recognised and powerful force affecting almost all of the social institutions in our society'.[54]

The popularity of such 'humanistic' therapies gained during the 1960s. 'T-groups evolved into the Encounter groups', a term coined by the humanistic psychologist Carl Rogers. '[T]he boundaries between education and therapy began to blur. People began to speak of therapy for normal'; that is to say, attempts by individuals to achieve *self-actualisation*, a term popularised by Abraham Maslow and Karen Horney, who collaborated with Erich Fromm.[55] Rogers called group therapy '...perhaps the most significant social invention of the century. The demand for it is utterly beyond belief. It is one of the most rapidly growing social phenomenon in the United States. It has permeated industry, is coming into education, is reaching families, professionals in the helping fields and many other individuals'.[56]

Tavistock Institute of Human Relations

Around the time the NTL was established, the Tavistock Institute of Human Relations was founded in Britain to apply the social sciences to problems and issues in the private and public sectors, including the 'environment in all its aspects on the formation or development of human character or capacity'. Hence, on its own account, Tavistock is involved with reshaping 'human character'. Research is intended

---

54 Cited by Elisabeth Lasch-Quinn, p. 67. Lasch-Quinn is professor of history at Syracuse University, specialising in twentieth-century American social, cultural, and intellectual history. She is the daughter of the renegade Leftist Dr. Christopher Lasch.

55 Mark D. Kelland, *Personality Theory in a Cultural Context*, 8.2: 'Carl Rogers and Humanistic Psychology', 1 May 2020; https://socialsci.libretexts.org/Bookshelves/Psychology/Book%3A_Personality_Theory_in_a_Cultural_Context_(Kelland).

56 Rogers cited by Elisabeth Lasch-Quinn, p. 67.

to shape policy.[57] Like the NTL, the origins of Tavistock begin in the military, where the Tavistock Clinic was established in 1920 by psychiatrists who worked on social psychology in response to the incidence of shell-shock from World War I. The Clinic joined the Directorate of Army Psychiatry in 1941, and was known as the Tavistock Group.[58]

As a non-profit think tank, Tavistock, when attached to the Army, studied the application of psychology to social problems. After World War II, an Interim Planning Committee (IPC) was elected to consider the function of Tavistock in the post-war era. Eric Trist, a founder-member and chairman, states of the time:

> This readiness enabled the IPC in 1945 to attract the attention of Alan Gregg, Medical Director of the Rockefeller Foundation, who was touring the various institutions that had been involved in war medicine. He was interested in finding out if there was a group committed to undertaking, under conditions of peace, the kind of social psychiatry that had developed in the army under conditions of war. So began a process that led the Rockefeller Foundation in I946 to make a grant of untied funds without which the IPC's post-war plan could not have been carried out.
>
> The Rockefeller grant led to the birth of the Tavistock Institute of Human Relations, constituted at first as a division of the Tavistock Clinic. With these funds it became possible to obtain for the then joint organization a nucleus of full-time senior staff who would otherwise have been scattered in universities and hospitals throughout the country and abroad.[59]

Tavistock was the seminal influence in the post-war formulation of family welfare policies through association with the National Health Service; industrial psychology, and projective psychology. On 'sensitivity training', Trist stated:

---

57 Tavistock Institute, 'Who We Are', https://www.tavinstitute.org/who-we-are/.

58 Eric Trist, *The Social Engagement of Social Science: A Tavistock Anthology*, Preface (1989), http://www.moderntimesworkplace.com/archives/ericsess/ sessPreface/sesspreface.html.

59 Trist, 'The Formative Years: The Founding Tradition', ibid.; http://www.moderntimesworkplace.com/archives/ericsess/tavis1/tavis1.html.

Another development during this period was the creation, in collaboration with the University of Leicester, of a U.K. equivalent to the form of **sensitivity training pioneered by the National Training Laboratories for Group Development in the United States...**[60]

A self-described leftist, Trist was regarded as Kurt Lewin's apostle in Britain. The association between Tavistock and the NTL was important for the development of the Institute. Trist states: 'We had to do something to get a reputable name for the Tavistock Institute. Our policy was to establish the journal, *Human Relations*, with Kurt Lewin's group in the United States. His notions of action-research were parallel with our socio-clinical, action-oriented work and I was regarded as his representative in Britain'.[61] During the 1960s, an association was established with UNESCO when Trist became a committee member on Research Trends in the Human and Social Sciences.[62]

'Racial Confrontation as Transcended Experience'

It was from this milieu of 'sensitivity training' that the notion of dealing with race relations through group therapy was conceived by two Black psychiatrists, Price M. Cobbs and William H. Grier, who co-authored the influential book *Black Rage* in 1968. With the book becoming a bestseller, Cobbs initiated 'diversity training seminars' which utilised group therapy. Through Pacific Management Systems, a consulting firm which he had founded in 1967, Cobbs conducted workshops on race relations in schools, police departments, social service agencies, community organisations, and the business world. These were called 'racial confrontation groups'.[63] The basis of the 'therapy' was that the

---

60   Trist, ibid. Emphasis added.

61   Eric L. Trist, *Guilty of Enthusiasm* (1993), http://www.moderntimesworkplace.com/archives/ericbio/ericbiobody/ericbiobody.html.

62   Ibid.

63   Elisabeth Lasch-Quinn, p. 77.

USA was infused 'with the idea of white supremacy', and that this was causing widespread mental illness among Blacks.[64]

In 1967, Cobbs and George Leonard[65] held the first encounter group at the Esalen Institute retreat at Big Sur, with a workshop entitled 'Racial Confrontation as Transcended Experience'.[66] In addition to Cobbs, his wife Vad, and Leonard as facilitators, the participants comprised 35 mostly middle class professionals; Blacks, Whites, and Asians. The 'encounter' took place over three days. The Saturday night session proceeded through without a sleep break, as sleep and other deprivations[67] were considered necessary to break down inhibitions. During physical encounters, reactions included 'loud sobbing and wailing'. In an 'encounter', described by Leonard, between a White schoolteacher, Pam, and a light skinned Negro, Cliff, Pam told Cliff she wanted to be his friend. Her offer was rejected as 'pitiful, condescending overtures'. She pleaded tearfully, '*Please*, what can I do? I'm trying. Please help me'. Cliff responded: 'No, baby, I'm not going to help you. I'm not going to take you off the hook. I want you to feel just what I feel. I want you to feel what I've felt for twenty-one years. Go on. Cry'. Leonard, the facilitator, described the silence that followed

---

64 Ibid.

65 Leonard was president of the Esalen Institute, president of the Association for Humanistic Psychology, and had been a senior editor of the magazine *Look*.

66 Elisabeth Lasch-Quinn, p. 88.

67 Sleep deprivation is basic to brainwashing, and as a torture. The techniques were described in 1950 by journalist Edward Hunter in the *Miami Daily News* in a feature on brainwashing (*xi-nao*, the Mandarin words for wash (*xi*) and brain (*nao*)) in China. 'The process was meant to "change a mind radically so that its owner becomes a living puppet—a human robot—without the atrocity being visible from the outside."' 'For the American soldiers trapped in the Korean prison camps, brainwashing meant forced standing, deprivation of food and sleep, solitary confinement, and repeated exposure to Communist propaganda'. Lorraine Boissoneault, 'The True Story of Brainwashing and How It Shaped America', *Smithsonian Magazine*, 22 May 2017; https://www.smithsonianmag.com/history/true-story-brainwashing-and-how-it-shaped-america-180963400/.

as 'in itself a powerful medium of communication. We began to *know* each other.'[68] Crying became a feature of the encounter. Cobbs later told Leonard, 'We have to take this to the world'.[69]

During the 1970s, Cobbs developed what he called *Ethnotherapy*, and traced the premises to Kurt Lewin.[70]

'Unconscious Bias'

In the democratic West, smears meted out to dissidents, accused of 'racism', 'hate', and 'ignorance', where they become social pariahs, lose jobs and are humiliated by the media, maintain conformity. The public 'jet-planing' of dissidents as in Mao's China is not yet necessary. The media smears do however serve the same purpose as the public shaming during Mao's time, when those out of favour with the regime were paraded with signs and high dunce's hats.[71] Where in Mao's time some hapless schoolteacher might suddenly become a 'class enemy', 'reactionary' or 'landlord', in the West an individual might suddenly be publicly 'named and shamed' as a 'racist', 'White supremacist', 'neo-Nazi'. The media smears use techniques of criticism drafted at well-funded think tanks.

Self-criticism and group conformity are used in business to ensure a compliant workforce, weeding out any non-conformist in the interests of curing 'unconscious bias'. In psychology, self-criticism is usually regarded as a destructive personality trait leading to depression. Yet it has been introduced into human relations programmes among corporate and government employees as a means of purging the individual of Orwellian *thought-crimes;* especially those at the sub-conscious level ('unconscious bias'). What the latter means is that even the most 'liberal' White needs thought-processing as the 'social

---

68   Elisabeth Lasch-Quinn, p. 91.

69   Ibid., p. 94.

70   Ibid., p. 97.

71   See: Jung Chang & John Halliday (2005). Mao found the 'jet-planing' technique of bending the arms backward particularly amusing.

construct' of 'Whiteness' is premised on 'White supremacy', which in turn is the foundation of 'White privilege', from which **all Whites**, no matter what their situation or family legacy, apparently benefit. The White is placed in a no-win situation. For one's peace of mind, acquiescence is the solution in a situation that has no logic.

An article in a human relations training manual explains the concept, beginning by heralding the 'good news': 'Research demonstrates that we all harbor unconscious biases. The good news is that enhanced awareness and training can create an inclusive culture that identifies and helps eliminate these hidden biases'.[72]

Dr. Neal Goodman is a leader in the field of mind alteration. Goodman, as president of Global Dynamics International (GDI), explicitly states that the purpose of the programmes is to provide 'training' for **globalisation**. The GDI purpose and reach are explained:

> GDI's network of Senior Associates, located in every major country and region of the world, gives us a wide global reach enabling GDI to offer services literally anywhere, anytime and in virtually any language. For 25 years leading global corporations have turned to Global Dynamics Inc. for world-class business solutions in over 60 countries.[73]

'Global mobility' is an aspect of the GDI 'culture wise' programme, where a corporate employee is able to uproot and resettle across the world, having first attained a background on the culture into which he is to be transplanted. It is preparation for the *Global Me* heralded by G. Pascal Zachary as the evolutionary future of mankind. The techniques focus on reprogramming the individual through group conformity, ensuring the elimination of 'unconscious bias':

---

72 Neal Goodman, 'Unconscious Bias', *Training*, Official Publication of *Training* Magazine Network, https://trainingmag.com/trgmag-article/unconscious-bias/.

73 Global Dynamics International, 'About Us: Our People', https://global-dynamics.com/about-us/our-people/.

Training maximizes the use of **experiential techniques** as a means of creating a challenging and productive learning experience, including **group discussions, role-plays, assessments, simulations, group tasks**, and short lectures. Topics have immediate relevance to the day-to-day **functional activities of every employee** and lead directly to the development of specific action steps for **immediate on-the-job implementation by each participant.**[74]

The group is put through a process of '[b]uilding intercultural awareness through the examination of individual biases, cultural values and traditions, and the exposure and analysis of cultural myths and stereotypes'.[75] In such a 'group therapy' setting, the individual is confronted and his 'unconscious bias' brought out through a facilitator, who places a burden of guilt on the White participants. The attitudes and experiences of the participant are broken down and the personality is reconstructed according to the requirements of corporate globalism.

'Auditing' to achieve the state of 'Clear' is what Scientology calls such a process. When undertaken by North Koreans on American POWs, it was called 'brainwashing'. Under global capitalism, it is called 'enhanced awareness training'.

Goodman explains that '[p]rejudice and discrimination are detrimental to the success of any organization. Yet research from the Kirwan Institute and others demonstrates that we all harbor prejudices; at a minimum, everyone is subject to their own unconscious bias'.[76]

The Kirwan Institute for the Study of Race and Ethnicity is a multi-disciplinary network that operates at universities, and advises the public and private sectors: education justice, healthcare, etc. In what they call 'implicit bias', individuals can be *debiased* (sic) with techniques such as '[c]ounter-stereotypic training in which efforts focus

---

74 Global Dynamics International, 'Our Approach', https://global-dynamics.com/our-approach/ (Emphasis added).

75 Ibid.

76 Goodman, 'Unconscious Bias'.

on training individuals to develop new associations that contrast with the associations they already hold through visual or verbal cues'; exposure 'to counter-stereotypic individuals' [such as we see on television depictions of Black neurosurgeons, et al.]; 'intergroup contact'; 'education efforts aimed at raising awareness about implicit bias help *debias* the individual'; '**having a sense of accountability, that is, "the implicit or explicit expectation that one may be called on to justify one's beliefs, feelings, and actions to others"**'; 'taking the perspective of others'; '**engaging in deliberative processing ... to constantly self-monitor in an effort to offset implicit biases and stereotypes**'.[77]

One of the measures for *debiasing*, 'having a sense of accountability, that is, "the implicit or explicit expectation that one may be called on to justify one's beliefs, feelings, and actions to others"', is intended as *Mao-esque* public humiliation. 'Engaging in deliberative processing ... to **constantly self-monitor** in an effort to offset implicit biases and stereotypes' is analogous to the self-criticism that was a feature of brainwashing and self-denunciation in Communist states.

Goodman explains that *unconscious bias* is inculcated at birth by the culture one is born into:

> Since many of these prejudices exist beyond the conscious level and are a result of being brought up in a culture that harbors biases, we first must acknowledge that they, in fact, exist. You do not have to be racist or sexist to implicitly support racism or sexism. These unconscious biases are not restricted to any one group, and they differ significantly from open and legislated forms of prejudice and discrimination such as usage of a derogatory name.
>
> ... One of the paradoxes of such unconscious biases is that those who are discriminated against also are likely to discriminate against their own kind, since they have been brought up with the same prejudices as everyone else in the society.[78]

---

77 Cheryl Staats, pp. 20–21. Emphasis added.
78 Neal Goodman, 'Unconscious Bias'.

This becomes a hindrance to universal commerce since '[t]he implications of unconscious bias are that the best and brightest talent often is made to feel unwelcome, invisible, and not important to the success of the organization. This results in employees who are detached and likely to take their talents elsewhere'.[79]

Goodman brings hope where there is despair, through attitudinal change, where even the most liberal, self-hating White employee can be purged of 'unconscious' 'racism' and 'sexism'.

> The good news is that, while no one is immune to their own unconscious bias, through **enhanced awareness and training**, these prejudices can be changed. Organizations are slowly recognizing that they must provide training on unconscious bias to create a more **inclusive culture**. ...[80]

The training programme should be followed up by further sessions that reinforce what has been instilled, and then auditing the corporation's performance, called: 'Metrics that demonstrate changes in behaviour'.[81]

PRISM International Inc. is another global diversity training corporation. 'PRISM's Unconscious Bias Training is designed to help participants override their bias and **rewire their brains**'. In the 'Diversity Council Bootcamp', '[p]articipants are both "called out" and "built up"'.[82]

PRISM is more upfront than GDI. The latter attempts to assure clients that there are no 'guilt-trips', and that 'diversity' is wanted, not 'group think'. What is an 'inclusive culture' if not 'group think'? What are the role-playing techniques and uncovering of 'uncensorious bias' designed to do other than instill guilt? What does the White male become other than a subject who must be cured on the assumption that

---

79   Ibid.

80   Ibid.

81   Ibid.

82   PRISM International, 'Prism's Unconscious Bias Training', https://www.prism-diversity.com/products/unconscious-bias.html (PRISM emphasis).

'unconscious bias' is a sickness rather than an instinctive preference for that which is closest to you? PRISM, on the other hand, unequivocally states that the subject's brain will be *rewired*. This involves a process of being 'called out' and 'built up'. In any other circumstance this would be called brainwashing or indoctrination. The subject is called to account for harbouring sinful thoughts, his *persona* is deconstructed, and reconstructed into a servile being.

Rev. Jones' Socialist Paradise Based on Group Therapy

Rev. Jim Jones, much lauded by the American liberal Establishment as a great civil rights leader, sought to create a socialist paradise in the jungle of Guyana. He convinced over 900 followers to relocate to escape impending earthquakes, drought, Fascist takeover, concentration camps, and the genocide of Afro-Americans. He used fear of false crises as a control mechanism. He used mass group therapy, with a focus on *self-criticism* and *self-humiliation* to purge individuals of 'unconscious bias' and to maintain group-think. He replaced the family with the collective, over which he became the substitute father-figure, 'Dad'. Jones perfected the social control mechanism developed by humanistic psychology. Letters to 'Dad'[83] indicate the role played by *self-criticism* and *self-denunciation*:

February 21, 1978

Dad,

I feel I don't work as hard as I should and I feel I am lazy compared to others here that I've seen work. I feel as a supervisor I ain't shit. I see a lot of shit go on and I fail to write it or report it because I want to look good and I want people to like me. I value friendship too highly that's why I never make any complaints on the people I associate with. I feel that I am too family oriented.

Thank you Dad,

---

83 Source: Alternative Considerations of Jonestown & Peoples Temple, 'Letters to Dad (Part 2)'; https://jonestown.sdsu.edu/?page_id=13231.

Shirley Baisy
September 5, '77

*

Father,

We left the US because we wanted to be free. We came here to be safe from all earthquakes, and to [be] free from concentration camps. I came here to be free from Senate Bill 1427 [1437]. Here I am safe from genocide. I came here because they would kill all black people and would have put in slavery.

Nancy Clay
Nancy Clay by Don Bower for N.C.
PS Also the drought that had come up on us no water.

*

Dear Jim

I am guilty of molesting my own child. I know what I'm doing but I still go ahead and do it.

I not only molest my child but also any other children I come in contact with.

Please pray for me.

Rebecca Beikman

*

Dear Jim,

I would like to tell you about a thing I did in Pennsville back in 1938.

I killed the boy and buried him behind Campbell's barn.

I feel I have to tell you at this time to help clear my conscience.

Jack Barron

*

Dad,

I really screwed up today. I lost my temper with Lula Ruben, a senior, was swearing. Not at her in the sense of name calling, but nevertheless talking loudly and unkindly to her. Such conduct on the part of a white supervisor is not excusable. Several others heard it, and I am sure it went all through. [illegible] Went away saying this was just like the USA… I apologize to her at the time. I am bringing myself up for [illegible] because it will have to be made public to clear the air… whether or not anyone [illegible] brings it to your attention.

By way of explanation, but not excuse, a flu bug has got to my stomach so I haven't been eating much for the last day and a half, my blood sugar was off, and I just lost my self control.

I feel very guilty about the whole episode at war like to work Sunday after-noons for four weeks.

Gene [Chaikin]

*

Father,

I failed you in my work. I do want to go to FL [Freedom Land] and I know I will have to work to get there. I'm willing to work right now. I will do my best to make sure I keep no one from going. I will live up to principle. And do whatever needs to be done from me. And I will set a good example for others to follow.

Candace Cordell

*

Dear Dad,

I used someone else's sheet and did not return it for a while, but now it has been returned.

The House supervisor let me use it as she saw no name on it, but I did and did not tell her. (It was returned in our laundry by mistake) I should've returned it sooner.

Joicy E. Clark

*

25–1–78 (January 25, 1978)

To: Dad

From: Loretta Coomer

Being with you for as many years as I have been with you, I should have a lot more conscientiousness and guilt that I do have. Many times I have thought about the black people in our congregation who have been through so much, suffered so much injustice as a result of being black, and yet somehow managed to avoid the issue. Oh! Yes! I have felt guilty for being the same color of skin as their oppressors and have cried about it because I'm sure I have reminded some beautiful black person of someone they hated. I have lived without ever since I've known you. So much so that he used to irritate me (and still does) when I see some of our lighter skinned people continuously sitting together or more than 2 or 3 sitting together with a room full of black people. You have made me that observant.

I often feel bad because I have to scold or be forceful with black seniors a lot in the food serving line, but also realize they too have been conditioned and sometimes respond only to "white" authority — and that makes me very angry. The black sisters serving can tell some people something and that person gets mad. Then I'll say the same thing and they are very nice and accept it and go on their way. This happens 2 or 3 times a day and it causes some hostility from the other servers.

*

25–1–78 (January 25, 1978)

To: Dad

From: Loretta Coomer

Regarding your request for those who have stolen since they've been here in this beautiful Jonestown, I am writing my apologies for taking advantage of the people and falling into the category of the elitist.

I have not taken anything from any one person in particular, but I have taken what I needed while being trusted to work in the people's warehouse.

I sneaked out a blouse sleeves, one pair of panties, ½ cup Clorox, and a bra. I will not ever do it again because I realize now why we have the problem of so much stealing here and will carry out my part to have it all stopped someday. If I need anything in the future, I will go through the normal procedures which are set up for the benefit of everyone.

Thank you, Dad, for stirring up our conscientiousness.

Loretta Coomer

Jones succeeded for so many years because his doctrine reflected that of the Establishment. When the Peoples Temple campaigned for George Mascone for Mayor of San Francisco and other liberal candidates for council, Mascone thanked Jones, writing:

Your contributions to the spiritual health and well-being of our community have been truly inestimable, and I am heartened by the fact that we can continue to expect such vigorous and creative leadership from the Peoples Temple in the future. By your tireless efforts on behalf of all San Franciscans, you have demonstrated that the unique powers of spiritual energy and civic commitment are virtually boundless, and that our lives would be sadly diminished without your continuing contributions.[84]

During the 1976 presidential campaign, Jones met with Rosalynn Carter, wife of Democratic Party candidate Jimmy Carter, at the latter's urging. Jones also met vice-presidential candidate Walter Mondale in San Francisco. Jones was appointed by Mayor Mascone to the San Francisco Housing Committee, and became its chairman. He was recipient of the Fourth Annual Martin Luther King, Jr. Humanitarian

---

84 Catherine Abbott, 'Communism, Marxism, and Socialism: Radical Politics and Jim Jones', https://jonestown.sdsu.edu/?page_id=64856.

Award in 1977; and was named Humanitarian of the Year by the *Los Angeles Herald*.[85]

The Peoples Temple was the fulfilment of the liberal-globalist doctrine in microcosm, honed to perfection as a social control mechanism; until the psychopathy of its 'Father' reached self-destruct mode. While 'Dad' had the power over life and death of over 900 followers in a remote jungle clearing, *mattoids* with the same doctrine have this power over much of the world, and like Jones' followers, multitudes are manipulated into believing the rhetoric about 'philanthropy' and 'humanitarianism' that obscures the quest for control.

---

85   Ibid.

Transhuman

Assisted reproduction will make it possible for individuals of any sex to reproduce in any combinations they choose, with or without 'mothers' and 'fathers,' and artificial wombs will make biological wombs unnecessary for reproduction.

— Drs. George Dvorsky and James Hughes,
Institute for Ethics & Emerging Technologies

I
S THERE ANYTHING outside the realm of sciencefiction that can possibly go beyond the concept of *gender fluidity?* Sadly yes. Huxley, Merriam and other social scientists had a vision that science could remake humanity into whatever form was required for their world utopia. Julian Huxley was the father of *transhumanism*. He dreamt of man going beyond the merely *human*, not through a Nietzschean self-willed quest to ascend the heights, but through manipulation of genes and technology. Julian Huxley's manifesto for *transhumanism*, a collection of essays entitled *New Bottles for New Wine*, was published in 1957.[1]

The first essay is entitled 'Transhumanism'. Huxley states that through both the biological and social sciences man is enabled to control his own evolution; 'suddenly appointed managing director of the biggest business of all...'[2] Man's next step in this 'cosmic office'

---

1   Julian Huxley (1957).
2   Ibid., p. 13.

is to explore his own nature, and find out what possibilities exist.[3] When the world discovers these possibilities, there will be a universal clamour for the benefits of science, and this will begin as 'unpleasant' but end 'beneficent'.[4] All utopian schemes begin 'unpleasant', but has there yet been one that has ended 'beneficent'? As we have seen, Huxley had assisted in creating the organisation intended to impose world beneficence and establish *world order* amidst anything 'unpleasant'. Such beneficence can only be maintained when humanity transcends itself. Huxley explains,

> The human species can, if it wished, transcend itself—not just sporadically, an individual here in one way, an individual there in another way, but in its entirety, as humanity. We need a name for this new belief. Perhaps *transhumanism* will serve: man remaining man, but transcending himself, but raising new possibilities of and for his human nature.[5]

The human species would become as far removed from its present state as we are now from Peking Man.[6]

Science will replace 'myth', which is to say, religion. This needs obliterating, to start 'building a wholly new scaffolding for the human mind', based on 'naturalistic description and scientific method'.[7]

Julian critically alludes to his brother Aldous as being among the opponents of the 'myth of progress', which Aldous sees as being to 'bully nature' for ends outside what it is to be human. But for Julian, 'progress' is not a 'myth', and will 'replace theology'.[8] Progress is 'inevitable', but requires 'human effort'.[9] Darwinian 'natural selection' has been replaced by social change, and can be directed and accelerated

---

3   Ibid., p. 14.

4   Ibid., p. 16.

5   Ibid., p. 17.

6   Ibid.

7   Ibid., p. 19.

8   Ibid., p. 21.

9   Ibid., pp. 28–29.

by eugenics.[10] 'Nation', 'religion' and 'culture' now become impediments to 'progress'.[11] There will be a universal knowledge that unites humanity in a single direction; 'one single body of knowledge, ideas and attitudes'.[12] Julian insisted that this would emerge 'voluntarily'.[13]

It will be '[o]ne World of all the races, nations, classes, and individuals, past, present and to come…',[14] 'a single organic world society and culture'.[15] However, how can a 'single universal attitude' be imposed and maintained if not by perpetual indoctrination and ultimately by force? Several generations would need to be indoctrinated, and detached from all bonds of family, faith, customs and morals. This is precisely what is being enacted on so many levels as to be pervasive. This is what Julian refers to as *psycho-social evolution*.

'Naturalistic', Universal Religion

Religion will need replacing by 'a truly unitary and unitive ideology', which will be embraced by mankind as his knowledge increases through science.[16] However, what Julian proposes is a substitute religion of science. He knows the intrinsic value of myth and ceremony. Hence, this universal ideology will have its own 'celebrations of human achievement and human possibilities', 'pilgrimages and gatherings', 'ceremonies of participation', 'solemnizations of the steps in individual lives and personal relations'.[17] The latter can only be referring to rites in the nature of funerals, baptisms, and marriages. Julian further proposes new rites that will enable 'salvation', 'self-development' and 'self-transcendence', and 'methods of purgation and

10 Ibid., p. 30.

11 Ibid., p. 39.

12 Ibid., p. 52.

13 Ibid., p. 97.

14 Ibid., p. 124.

15 Ibid., p. 309.

16 Ibid., p. 119.

17 Ibid., p. 126.

for achieving freedom from the burdens of guilt and fear...' '[W]hat new formulations of knowledge and consequent belief?'[18] Julian states that it is the duty of scientists to help '**make possible the emergence of a more universal and more adequate religion**', which he also calls *Evolutionary Humanism*.[19] He suggests what aspect of science will offer personal redemption in this religion: **psychoanalysis**. His brother Aldous wrote twenty-five years previously in his dystopian novel that the 'World Controllers' use Freudian psychoanalysis as a control mechanism where 'Our Freud' is given godlike esteem. Freudianism is used to obliterate family and parents from the world order, where love is replaced by ritualised, impersonal, childless sex, with embryos created scientifically. A World Controller tells a class of children:

> Our Freud had been the first to reveal the appalling dangers of family life. The world was full of fathers—was therefore full of misery; full of mothers—therefore of every kind of perversion from sadism to chastity; full of brothers, sisters, uncles, aunts—full of madness and suicide.
>
> Mothers and fathers, brothers and sisters. But there were also husbands, wives, lovers. There were also monogamy and romance.
>
> 'Though you probably don't know what those are,' said Mustapha Mond.
>
> They shook their heads.
>
> Family, monogamy, romance. Everywhere exclusiveness, a narrow channelling of impulse and energy.
>
> 'But every one belongs to every one else', he concluded, citing the hypnopaedic proverb.
>
> The students nodded, emphatically agreeing with a statement which upwards of sixty-two thousand repetitions in the dark had made them accept, not merely as true, but as axiomatic, self-evident, utterly indisputable.[20]

---

18 Ibid., Emphasis added.

19 Ibid., p. 310.

20 Aldous Huxley, *Brave New World*, Chapter III.

Dr. Jerome Meckier[21] commented on the post-Freudian premises of the World Controllers in *Brave New World*:

> Convinced by Freud that man is basically sick, that is, at the mercy of deep-seated drives, the Controllers fabricate a world mindlessly dedicated to the Pleasure Principle, a stress-free society that allows man's basest drives freest play. Freud's theory that certain psychological hazards during childhood and adolescence are both formative and unavoidable compels the Brave New World to keep its citizens permanently infantile.[22]

In common with many of the movements, doctrines and individuals we have considered, Julian Huxley regarded over-population as 'the problem of our age'.[23] 'People-production' (sic) has to be managed by science. This involves studying the psychological attitudes of different nations and groups towards 'population-control' (sic).[24] The implication can only be that mind-altering methods will be needed to change those psychological attitudes, and again this strikes at the roots of religion, family and custom, with the need to impose a uniform outlook. Huxley states that this requires 'a reconsideration of human values'.[25]

In justifying the inevitability of a scientific world order, Huxley applies the *positivism* of Aguste Comte, father of sociology, in seeing a succession of historical stages unfolding: magical, animistic, theological, until the present stage of science has shown that 'God is becoming an erroneous hypothesis...'[26]

---

21 Emeritus Professor of English, University of Kentucky, editor, *Critical Essays on Aldous Huxley*; co-editor, *Aldous Huxley Annual*.

22 Jerome Meckier, 'Brave New World and the Anthropologists', *Alternative Futures*, No. 1 Spring 1978. The reference to 'anthropologists' in the title relates to the influence of Margaret Mead and the Boasian anthropologists, in addition to Freudianism, in Aldous Huxley's novel.

23 Julian Huxley (1957), p. 168.

24 Ibid., p. 185.

25 Ibid., p. 187.

26 Ibid., p. 272.

Transhumanism is the religion, by whatever name, of the globalist oligarchy, premised on the use of technology to change humanity.

Sarwant Singh, a managing partner in Frost & Sullivan, a global research and consultancy corporation, writes of the 'convergence' of 'technology, behavioral and societal changes, and medical advances' that will 'converge to transform society'. '[S]ignals already point to a future of humanity that will **blur our identities into transhumanism**'. The Visionary Innovation Group, a division of Frost & Sullivan, issued a study for business leaders[27] on the impact transhumanism will have on 'individuals, society, businesses, and government' in the next ten to fifteen years.

'Body augmentation' will include 'increased use of implants ranging from brain microchips and neural lace to mind-controlled prosthesis'...

Eugenics is still on the agenda:

> However, the most powerful body augmentation will come from biological augmentation as a result of increased insight into our genomes, advances in IVF technology that may allow us to select the most intelligent embryos, and powerful CRISPR gene-editing technology which may one day give us the ability to eliminate all heritable diseases.[28]

Implantable brain-machine interfaces (BMIs), being developed by organisations such as Elon Musk's Neuralink, Zuckerberg's Facebook, and DARPA, 'will dramatically alter the ways in which we communicate with each other, as well as digital devices ... enabling communication at the speed of thought in its full, unfiltered state'. How confident are we supposed to be with the uses of this technology when

---

27 Visionary Innovation Group, 'Transhumanism: How Humans Will Think, Behave, Experience, and Perform in the Future, and the Implications to Businesses' (Frost & Sullivan, 2017).

28 Sarwant Singh, 'Transhumanism and the Future of Humanity', *Forbes*, 20 November 2017; https://www.forbes.com/sites/sarwantsingh/2017/11/20/transhumanism-and-the-future-of-humanity-seven-ways-the-world-will-change-by-2030/#28.

it is being developed by Musk, Facebook, and the USA's primary defence research contractor?

'BMIs may also advance our ability to empathize if we are able to understand someone else's full perspective straight from their own brain'.[29] This would also enable instant mind-control, without long processes of indoctrination or brainwashing.

Singh refers to 'widespread and revolutionary technologies [that] come at us from every angle and affect our bodies, thought processes, and behaviors'. He states that, 'Integration of BMI into workplaces ... may see eventual scenarios in which companies are sponsoring nootropic supplements and neurostimulation devices to improve employee focus and increase the speed of new skills acquisition'. He asks: 'Are you ready to be augmented into a super human?'[30]

Alternatively: Are you ready to be augmented into a dehumanised automaton?

The dehumanisation of humans is being acclaimed behind the façade of health, business and consumer benefits. Elon Musk's Neurolink is developing a brain implant for those with brain injury. Yet proceeding from this laudable aim, Musk's ultimate goal is 'symbiosis between humans and Artificial Intelligence (AI)', about which he admits there are dangers.[31]

The Greeks called this *hubris*.

---

29 Ibid.

30 Ibid.

31 Isabel Asher Hamilton, 'Elon Musk Believes AI Could Turn Humans into an Endangered Species like the Mountain Gorilla', *Business Insider Australia*, 27 November 2018; https://www.businessinsider.com.au/elon-musk-ai-could-turn-humans-into-endangered-species-2018-11.

Posthuman

Cyberfeminism & Postgender

TRANSHUMANISM resolves questions of gender and of race by submerging them into the next stage of evolution: the *cyborg*. Man becomes machine and can be tailor-made to the requirements of production. This is being zealously advocated among both high-powered think tanks and by socialists and feminists as the means by which the long-desired aim of a high-functioning nebulous entity can be created without recourse to the odious business of child-bearing and child-rearing. It is referred to as *cyberfeminism* and *postgenderism*.

Kyle Munkittrick, programme director for the influential *transhumanist* think tank the Institute for Ethics and Emerging Technologies (IEET), writes in the *transhumanist* magazine *Humanity Plus* of the importance of transhumanism for feminism and transgenderism. Munkittrick links transhumanism to 'modernism and critical theory', such as the philosophers Michel Foucault and Jürgen Habermas.

IEET defines its philosophy as *technoprogressive*, and traces its origins to Enlightenment doctrine, converging 'technological progress and democratic social change'. IEET places *technoprogress* within the sphere of leftist *intersectionality*, aligning with:

- The movement for reproductive rights, around access to contraception, abortion, assisted reproduction and genomic choice

- The movement for drug law reform around the defense of cognitive liberty

- Sexual and gender minorities around the right to bodily self-determination[1]

In a scenario straight from *Brave New World*, where the masses were kept docile and contended by the mass use of a narcotic called *soma*, IEET advocates 'Decarceration and Decriminalization of Psychoactive Drugs, including cognitive enhancement'. To paraphrase Marx, this would literally be 'the opiate of the people'. *Postgenderism* is another IEET ideal.[2]

Munkittrick refers to Dr. Donna Haraway's *A Cyborg Manifesto: Science, Technology, and Socialist-Feminism in the Late Twentieth Century* (1985) as 'the *locus classicus* of cyberfeminism', in which Haraway writes :

> The cyborg is a creature in a **post-gender world; it has no truck with bisexuality, pre-oedipal symbiosis, unalienated labour, or other seductions to organic** wholeness through a final appropriation of all the powers of the parts into a higher unity. In a sense, the cyborg has no origin story in the Western sense — a 'final' irony since the cyborg is also the awful apocalyptic telos of the 'West's' escalating dominations of abstract individuation, **an ultimate self untied at last from all dependency, a man in space.**

> Unlike the hopes of Frankenstein's monster, the cyborg does not expect its father to save it through a restoration of the garden; that is, through the fabrication of a heterosexual mate, through its completion in a finished whole, a city and cosmos. The cyborg does not dream of community on the model of the organic family, this time without the oedipal project.[3]

---

1   IEET, 'Technoprogressive Declaration', Paris, 21 November 2014; https://ieet. org/index.php/tpwiki/Technoprogressive_Declaration.

2   IEET, https://ieet.org/index.php/IEET2/programs.
The IEET's advocacy of rights for animals is the mitigating factor of the IEET doctrine. How animals would fare better in such a *technoprogressive* world seems problematic.

3   Donna Haraway (1991).

Becoming a cyborg eliminates the need for any 'identity'. 'There is nothing about teeing "female" that naturally binds women'. There is no gender.

Munkittrick promotes *transhumannism* and *cyberfeminism* on the premise that it will liberate the outsider, and create a new normal.

> Transhumanists point to the pinnacle of what it believes humanity could become; where it might be going, and asks, 'why not?' and 'how do we get there?' Cyberfeminists (and postmodernists in general) look at the abject, the debased, the grotesque and the marginalized and ask 'why is it so? How did this become the fringe?' Transhumanism needs cyberfeminism because it functions to expose the way in which defining the 'human,' and in turn, the 'transhuman,' can repress, reject, and otherize those it claims to help.[4]

In claiming to be for the benefit of humanity, and indeed for the benefit of our relationship with the animal world, Munkittrick, like Huxley, and Charles Merriam a century previously, holds out the prospect of a post-human form that is better than human. Organisations such as IEET, with the word *ethics* in the title, insist that this utopia, unlike all previous humanist utopias, will operate for the benefit of everyone: enhancing life expectancy, providing limbs for the limbless, and brains for the brainless, liberating man from work, providing opportunities for creative leisure (or narcotic stupor) and wide, open and clear spaces for animals. This in a world that no longer acknowledges humans as organic beings, so bereft of an organic consciousness that children can be laboratory-manufactured, and raised without the need for the 'restrictions' of the parental bond.

'Postmodernists in general look at the abject, the debased, the grotesque and the marginalized and ask 'why is it so? How did this become the fringe?' So here is the aim beyond 'progress'; to elevate the 'abject, the debased, the grotesque and the marginalized' as the new

---

4   Kyle Munkittrick, 'On the Importance of Being a Cyborg Feminist', *Humanity+*, 21 July 2009; https://hplusmagazine.com/2009/07/21/importance-being-cyborg-feminist/.

504   THE PERVERSION OF NORMALITY: FROM THE MARQUIS DE SADE TO CYBORGS

normal, and that is a process that has been long in the making, with those who object or resist being the real 'marginalised'. Drawing on Foucault, who in his *History Of Sexuality,* rationalising his own homosexuality, drew a historical genealogy of morals, Munkittrick appeals to a new morality that is without an axial point of reference; moral relativity: 'The implications for transhumanism are clear: if Foucault's method of historical genealogy can be used to deconstruct what is seen as "natural" sexuality, then what other "natural" aspects of the human subject can be shown to be equally constructed and open for change, perhaps in the form of augmentation (of body, mind) or elimination (of suffering and death).'[5] Here we see the familiar theme of everything as a 'social construct' that can be deconstructed and rebuilt according to a new design. The question is: who does the designing and for what purpose?

Munkittrick assures us that because 'critical theorists' and feminist theorists have contemplated such matters, *technoprogress* will be taken out of the hands of elitists and placed in the safe hands of some other, unnamed (perhaps 'cyberfeminist'?) body where benevolence and wisdom are certain.

> The transhumanist project, like any technological advancement, will place new tools into the hands of authorities to control and regulate life. Feminist and critical theorists have done immense amounts of work exposing these systems of control and demonstrating the methodology for changing them. The transhumanist model of political change should, unquestionably, be built upon the cyberfeminist model of political change.[6]

Does this then mean that the *technoprogessive cyborgising* of humans will not be in the hands of the techno-giants, but instead be under the direction of a public body? Who will comprise this public body? How will members be chosen? Will it be international, such as being an organ of the U.N.O.? Will the guardians of the *brave new world* be

---

5   Kyle Munkittrick, Ibid.

6   Ibid.

scientists such as those on the Board of IEET? Munkittrick provides an example of how issues would be resolved through the wisdom of *cyberfeminism:*

> For a specific example, we turn to reproductive technology. Be it birth-control, STD prevention, assisted reproductive technologies, abortion methods, ultrasounds, neo-natal care, or a myriad of other technologies that are involved in birth, the politics and ethics around these debates are classic arenas of feminist thought and action. The main reason for this tight coupling is that despite pregnancy's obvious impact on women, women's voices are often silenced or manipulated in the heated political arguments. **Transhumanists are liberal/progressive almost by definition,** supporting as many options for the human body as possible, and tend to support many feminist issues, such as abortion rights, safe-sex education, and birth-control options. **Politically, feminists and transhumanists are often in complete agreement.** Why then, you might ask, should transhumanists make a concerted effort to embrace feminism when both philosophies seem to work together so well as it is? … Cyberfeminism matters for transhumanism because **we cannot overcome the limits of biology without overcoming the limits of society: the latter will always inhibit the former, not the other way around.**[7]

Nature is a burden that needs to be overcome. It is the old quandary of the Critical Theorists in stating that the organic 'primary ties' are a burden which must be eliminated before humanity is free. Again, one might ask how animal-friendly would this *brave new world* really be?

Munkittrick concludes with an appeal to *intersectionality* as essential to the success of the project, with a focus on 'transsexuals and intersexuals':

> For transsexuals and intersexuals, transhumanism is a real, visceral, day-to-day lived philosophy. Yet the technology, while liberating in that it allows better transitions every year and provides better medical support for those who have transitioned and those born in-between, has not changed the social norms that entrap and restrict trans and intersex individuals.

---

7   Ibid.

Because of that failure, **we need a philosophy of social change, one that is built upon the discourse of dissolving cultural norms, of countering social standards and undermining hegemonic power.**[8] Transhumanism can articulate the technologies, the potential selves, the unlimited beings we can be, but it needs cyberfeminism to prepare the way, to **alter the politics and deconstruct the norms of culture and society** that would bind technoscience to mindsets of the past. Transhumanism and cyberfeminism are complimentary philosophies that, when united, are capable of driving the technological development, political change, and societal progress necessary for both to be successful.[9]

Postgender

Drs. George Dvorsky and James Hughes, directors of the IEET, write that the future rests with the transcendence of gender through the imposition of technology:

> Postgenderism is an extrapolation of ways that technology is eroding the biological, psychological and social role of gender, and an argument for why the erosion of binary gender will be liberatory. Postgenderists argue that gender is an arbitrary and unnecessary limitation on human potential, and **foresee the elimination of involuntary biological and psychological gendering in the human species through the application of neurotechnology, biotechnology and reproductive technologies.** Postgenderists contend that dyadic gender roles and sexual dimorphisms are generally to the detriment of individuals and society. **Assisted reproduction will make it possible for individuals of any sex to reproduce in any combinations they choose, with or without 'mothers' and 'fathers', and artificial wombs will make biological wombs unnecessary for reproduction.**

---

8   Undermining hegemonic power is precisely what this will NOT achieve. Such zealots need the illusion that they are rebelling against the status quo when they are rather products of it. The high-level participation in the IEET is itself indicative of that.

9   Kyle Munkittrick, Emphasis added.

Greater biological fluidity and psychological androgyny will allow future persons to explore both masculine and feminine aspects of personality....'[10]

In the name of 'equality' the transhumanists go beyond class, race, age and gender conflicts, in proclaiming that All is One, that the future post-human is so amorphous that there will be the peace and unity of the amoeba, and that even reproduction of the *species*, if it can be called that, will proceed from the transhuman equivalent of cell division. This overcoming of biology is heralded as the epitome of evolution. In such a world there will be no 'male coercion', and patriarchy would be obliterated. The advancements of capitalism and science have already set the process in motion: 'Post-industrial production, contraception and abortion have eliminated most of the rationale for gendered social roles in work and the family, reducing the burden of patriarchal oppression on women'.[11] Technology enables the social doctrines of global uniformity to proceed to completion:

> Postgenderism confronts the limits of a social constructionist account of gender and sexuality, and proposes that the transcending of gender by **social and political means is now being complemented and completed by technological means.**[12]

The authors get to the crux of the issue; the theme we have been considering here throughout:

> Gendered occupational achievement is a case in point. Patriarchal culture contributes to differences in boys' and girls' educational access, career aspirations, and the wage and social status advantage that men enjoy in employment in most (if not all) industrialized nations. But some degree of **gendered occupational stratification is also the inevitable result of the greater burden of childbearing on women**, and the different abilities and

---

10 George Dvorsky and James Hughes, 'Postgenderism: Beyond the Gender Binary', *IEET Monograph Series*, Institute for Ethics and Emerging Technologies, March 2008, p. 2. Emphasis added.

11 Ibid.

12 Ibid.

aspirations coded in the gendered brain. **Women are more impaired in the workforce by pregnancy and childbirth, even with the best child care support.** Men also perform better on some intellectual tasks, such as spatial visualization, while women outperform men on verbal acuity and some forms of symbol manipulation tests. Technological progress is ameliorating these gender differences, but **only the blurring and erosion of biological sex, of the gendering of the brain, and of binary social roles by emerging technologies** will enable individuals to access all human potentials and experiences regardless of their born sex or assumed gender.[13]

Technology can destroy the gender binary roles that burden women with childbirth, thus restraining their full integration into the economic process. Technology allowing for the laboratory conception and presumably childrearing by state or corporate institutions will achieve what socialism of even the most extreme types could not. Women will not differ from men in the production process because such entities will no longer exist.

George Dvorsky and James Hughes draw on the transsexual cults of Cybele and others, which we have considered previously, where the rite of castration was regarded as holy, and when eunuchs fulfilled state functions, to give historical justification to transgenderism. They refer to Magnus Hirschfeld and Alfred Kinsey for pioneering scientific justification.[14] *Postgenderism* proceeds therefrom. Drawing on radical feminist academics, the androgyn was discovered as the entity of the future:

> **The goal of a completely postgender society, instead of just gender equality and tolerance of gender diversity**, emerged among some of the social constructionist feminists and sex radicals of the 1970s. For instance radical psychologists such as Sandra Bem, the developer of the Bem Sex Role Inventory, began to reconceptualize gender traits as a continuum, along which it was healthiest to be in the androgynous range. The androgynous had the highest self-esteem, psychological well-being and emotional

---

13   Ibid.
14   Ibid., pp. 4–5.

intelligence, while **those at the psychological extremes of gender were re-cast as constrained and disabled.**[15]

Again, normality was flipped on its head and the previously abnormal became the new normal, while the traditionally normal, like the subjects scoring high on the Critical Theorists' 'F' several decades previously, have been designated '**constrained and disabled**'.

However, transgendered under *transhumanism* might be regarded as maintaining gender stereotypes. From the 1980s, '[g]radually a new "genderqueer" politics emerged which challenged all gender binaries'.

> Today's transgender movement is a roiling, radical critique of the limits of gender roles, with folks living in totally new categories, such as non-op transsexual, TG butch, femme queen, cross-dresser, third gender, drag king or queen and transboi. These genderqueer activists and theorists advocate postgender attitudes, such as promoting the use of gender-neutral pronouns such as "ze", "per", and "zir", or the terms pansexual or omnisexual instead of the binary "bisexual."[16]

Transhumanist scientists can complete the process, 'to deconstruct the gender binary that Shulamith Firestone[17] articulated in 1971 in favor of artificial wombs as a means to deconstruct the biological basis of patriarchy'.

> At the beginning of the 21st century, however, posthumanist and transhumanist discourses about using technologies to intentionally transcend the limitations of the human body began to address the transcending of gender. Trans- or post-humans would at least be able to transcend the limitations of biological sex, and would eventually be able to transcend the biological altogether into cybernetic or virtual form. ... A post-biological species would by definition — although perhaps not completely in the male transhumanist imaginary — be a post-gendered entity. ...'[18]

---

15   Ibid., p. 6.

16   Ibid., p. 7.

17   'Socialist-feminist' author of *The Dialectic of Sex*.

18   George Dvorsky and James Hughes, p. 7.

Here we see the introduction of a new term, *post-biological species*, and becoming a 'cybernetic or virtual form'.

In a type of *transhumanist dialectics*, Dvorsky and Hughes state that the next phase of post-industrial society will proceed from the equalisation process began by post-agricultural, capitalist industrial society. The redefining of marriage, such as 'civil unions' and 'gay marriages' started a process that eliminates traditional marriage. The transhumanist vision is that, '[e]ventually co-housing and co-parenting "civil union" contracts should replace civil marriage. Those contracts would recognize the bonds between small groups of people who have made commitments of some duration. The erosion of dyadic marriage will, in turn, help to erode the gender binary'.[19] As with so much else, the broadening of the legal definition of *marriage* was promoted as just a small measure in the name of 'human rights', which would do no harm; but has opened up the path to the elimination of marriage and family by contractual group arrangements.

The normal male-female pair bond that is hard-wired in the brain will be eliminated by chemical therapy: 'But the final liberation from dyadic, gendered, heteronormative relationships will likely come about through use of drugs that suppress pair-bonding impulses'.[20]

Postgenderism shows precisely how all identities are being obliterated dialectically in the name of 'identity'. From Hirschfeld's and Kinsey's scales of sexuality to dozens of contrived 'genders', the way was opened for the ultimate 'liberation': gender obliteration, and from there into an amorphous mass that will be barely human: post-human.

---

19   Ibid., p. 9.
20   Ibid.

Conclusion

THE FRANKFURT SCHOOL and other forms of social criticism — whatever their anti-capitalist and socialist pretensions — were and remain important to the oligarchy. The social sciences provide a scientific rationale for the destruction of traditional remnants which hinder capitalism from proceeding to its next phase: globalisation and what one of their intellectuals, Francis Fukuyama, calls 'the end of history'.

While much of the world turns to 'populism' and puts up barriers to globalisation in reaction to globalist demands for 'open borders', on the other hand, new identities have been created by detached individuals re-clustering into interest groups that in the name of 'human rights' demand to be fully integrated into the global market economy. Genders, races, families, states, nations, neighbourhoods, as supposedly fluid 'social constructs', can be deconstructed and reshaped at will, and such a fluidity accords with the demands of ever-fluid — expanding — production and consumption. The 'freedom' for which Fromm hoped has become the servitude which he feared, and about which Jung warned. What these new identities demand — *identity politics*, as it is called — is not self-determination or self-help, like the Black nationalism of the Marcus Garvey or Louis Farrakhan type, but 'rights' that necessitate dependence. Hence, the new 'revolutionary' identities envisaged by Herbert Marcuse et al. merely end up as clients of the System.

In states targeted for deconstruction, which persist with some vestiges of tradition, such as Putin's Russia and Shi'ite Islam, identity politics, especially feminism, its concomitant abortion in the name of 'reproductive health', and 'gender fluidity', are promoted by the Open Society global network, USAID, National Endowment for Democracy, Rockefeller, Ford, United Nations agencies, social media corporations and thousands of others, collectively called 'civil society', and 'the international community'.

Are we to suppose that the oligarchs have expended fortunes to fund this process for a century for any other reason than that of control? Are we to suppose that they are too naïve to understand what they are subsidising decade after decade?

This detachment from organic identities and a sense of place and permanence has created what Richard LaPiere foresaw sixty years ago as the emergence of a 'new bourgeoisie'. This new class of what might be aptly termed, to borrow Stalin's phrase, 'rootless cosmopolitans' has become a repository for the functionaries and CEOs of globalisation, lauded by Pascal Zachary as the next stage in evolution.

The sensible predicate for social change is *organic growth* as distinct from artificial 'social engineering', as scientists such as Carl Jung and Konrad Lorenz[1] warned. Jung, from the perspective of analytical psychology, and Lorenz, the founding father of *ethology*, called the problems afflicting modern civilisation *pathological*, and the malfunctioning of instincts.[2]

Contrary to what 'progressives' state in regard to the need for man to be 'liberated' from his organic 'primary ties', and to break free of the traditions and customs by which they are maintained, Lorenz states that 'extreme conservativism' in retaining what has long been tried and tested, 'is a vital property of the apparatus performing, in cultural evolution, a task analogous to that of the genes in species variation'. It is selection that decides what is to be transmitted as 'traditional,

---

1   Konrad Lorenz (1974).

2   Ibid., p. 5.

"sacred" customs and habits'. What is disparaged by the progressives as 'superstition' mostly originated with genuine insights and inventions, which have been maintained over generations by taking on sacred and mythic aspects. 'Retention' is even more important than 'additional acquisition'. What can be discarded as obsolete and useless from a survival perspective and what necessitates preserving as indispensable in the cultural heritage, is not something that should be casually decided.[3]

Mircea Eliade pointed out for the same reasons the importance of enduring myths, sacred places and religious rites and ceremonies, in maintaining a sense of a community's place and purpose in the cosmos.[4] Scorned by the progressives as irrational and useless superstition and 'magic', as Julian Huxley put it, or as a plot by the ruling class to keep the people oppressed in the name of 'God', as Marx put it, there is a religious element to man's psyche that is hardwired and should not be causally rejected in the name of 'progress' and 'science'. Julian Huxley, like the Jacobins with their Cult of Reason, proposed a new cult of science with its own rites and ceremonies that would replace all traditional faiths.

One should look askance at the Critical Theorists and other 'progressives' when they dogmatically state that an institution or custom is 'old fashioned', 'reactionary', 'regressive', and as the cliché goes on so many issues, should not be retained 'in this day and age'. Removing one element from a multiplicity of traditional, cultural interactions might have devastating consequences, as Lorenz pointed out.[5] 'Being enlightened is no reason for confronting transmitted tradition with hostile arrogance...'[6]

---

3   Ibid., pp. 62–63.

4   Bolton, *The Decline and Fall of Civilisations*, pp. 29–31. Mircea Eliade, *The Sacred and the Profane*, passim.

5   Lorenz, p. 63.

6   Ibid., p. 64.

Bibliography

Maria Abascal and Delia Baldassarri, 'Love Thy Neighbor? Ethnoracial Diversity and Trust Reexamined', *American Journal of Sociology*, Vol. 121, No. 3 (November 2015).

Catherine Abbott, 'Communism, Marxism, and Socialism: Radical Politics and Jim Jones', https://jonestown.sdsu.edu/?page_id=64856.

John Abromeit, *Max Horkheimer and the Foundations of the Frankfurt School* (New York: Cambridge University Press, 2011).

Anthony Adamthwaite, *Grandeur and Misery: France's Bid for Power in Europe, 1914–1940* (London: Bloomsbury, 2014).

Brooks Adams, *The Law of Civilisation and Decay* ([1896] London: Black House Publishing, reprint).

T. W. Adorno, Else Frenkel-Brunswik, Daniel J Levinson and R. Nevitt Sanford, *The Authoritarian Personality* (New York: Harper and Brothers, 1950).

Louis Althusser, *Ideology and Ideological State Apparatuses, Lenin and Philosophy and Other Essays* (Monthly Review Press, 1971).

Amanda Amos, Margaretha Hagland, 'From Social Taboo to "Torch of Freedom": The Marketing of Cigarettes to Women', *Tobacco Control*, Vol. 9, No. 1; https://tobaccocontrol.bmj.com/content/9/1/3.

Anne Applebaum, 'How Europe's "Identitarians" are Mainstreaming Racism', *The Washington Post*, 17 May 2019; https://www.washingtonpost.com/opinions/global-opinions/how-europes-identitarians-are-mainstreaming-racism/2019/05/17/3c7c9a6e-78da-11e9-b3f5-5673edf2d127_story.html?noredirect=on&utm_term=.2641dfd32252.

Jerry Avorn et al., *Up Against the Ivy Wall: A History of the Columbia Crisis* (McCleland & Stewart, 1968).

Buhm Suk Baek, 'Economic Sanctions Against Human Rights Violations', (2008), 2.1.2. Humanitarian Intervention, Cornell Law School Inter-University Graduate Student Conference Papers.

Joan Bamberger, 'The Myth of Matriarchy: Why Men Rule in Primitive Society', http://radicalanthropologygroup.org/sites/default/files/pdf/class_text_052. pdf.

Tom Bartlett, 'Harvard Sociologist Says His Research Was "Twisted"', *The Chronicle of Higher Education*, 15 August 2012; https://www.chronicle.com/blogs/percolator/robert-putnam-says-his-research-was-twisted/30357.

Stephen Bates, 'Sweden Pays for Grim Past', *The Guardian*, 6 March 1999.

Zack Beauchamp, 'Hungary Just Passed a "Stop Soros" Law That Makes It Illegal to Help Undocumented Migrants', *Vox*, 22 June 2018, https://www.vox.com/policy-and-politics/2018/6/22/17493070/hungary-stop-soros-orban.

Bernard Berelson, 'Beyond Family Planning', *Studies in Family Planning*, Population Council, No. 38, February 1969.

Edward H. Berman, *The Ideology of Philanthropy* (Albany: State University of New York Press, 1983).

Edward H. Berman, *The Influence of Carnegie, Ford and Rockefeller Foundations on American Foreign Policy* (Albany: State University of New York Press, 1983).

Simone de Beauvoir, *Must we Burn Sade?* ([1951] English ed. 1953).

R. Benedict, 'Nature and Nurture', *The Nation*, No. 118 (1924).

Dan Berger, *Outlaws of America: The Weather Underground and the Politics of Solidarity* (Chico, California: AK Press, 2005).

William H. Beveridge, *The London School of Economics and Its Problems 1919–1937* (New York: Routledge, 2015 [1960]).

Kai Bird, *The Chairman: John J. McCloy and the Making of the American Establishment* (New York: Simon & Schuster, 1992).

Lucia Chiavola Birnbaum, *Black Madonnas: Feminism, Religion & Politics in Italy* (New York: iUniverse, 2000), pp. 76.

Lucia Chiavola Birnbaum, *Dark Mother: African Origins and Godmothers* (San Jose: Authors Choice Press, 2001).

Edwin Black, 'The Horrifying American Roots of Nazi Eugenics', *History News Network*, September 2003; https://historynewsnetwork.org/article/1796.

Casey Blake and Christopher Phelps, 'History as Social Criticism: Conversations with Christopher Lasch', *The Journal of American History*, Vol. 80, No. 4, March 1994.

Sidney Bloch and Peter Reddaway, 'Your Disease Is Dissent', *New Scientist* (July 21, 1977).

Lorraine Boissoneault, 'The True Story of Brainwashing and How It Shaped America', *Smithsonian Magazine*, 22 May 2017; https://www.

smithsonianmag.com/history/true-story-brainwashing-and-how-it-shaped-america-180963400/.

A. Bokern, M. Bolder-Boos, S. Krmnicek, D. Maschek, and S. Page, S. (eds) *TRAC 2012: Proceedings of the Twenty-Second Annual Theoretical Roman Archaeology Conference*, Frankfurt 2012 (Oxford: Oxbow Books, 2012).

K. R. Bolton, *Revolution from Above* (London: Artkos Media Ltd., 2011).

K. R. Bolton, *Stalin: The Enduring Legacy* (London: Black House Publishing, 2012).

K. R. Bolton, 'Marx Contra Marx: A Traditionalist Conservative Critique of the Communist Manifesto', *Anamnesis Journal*, 2 March 2012, http://anamnesis-journal.com/2012/03/kr-bolton/.

K. R. Bolton, *The Psychotic Left: From Jacobin France to the Occupy Movement* (London: Black House Publishing, 2013).

K. R. Bolton, *Zionism, Islam and the West* (London: Black House Publishing, 2014).

K. R. Bolton, *The Decline and Fall of Civilisations* (London: Black House Publications, 2017).

Philip Bounds, 'Just Say No: Herbert Marcuse and the Politics of Negationism', in David Berry (ed.), *Revisiting the Frankfurt School: Essays on Culture, Media and Theory* (New York: Routledge, 2016).

Zbigniew Brzezinski, *Between Two Ages* (New York: the Viking Press, 1970).

Patrick J. Buchanan, *The Death of the West* (New York: Saint Martin's Press, 2002).

Carolyn Burdett, 'Post Darwin: Social Darwinism, Degeneration, Eugenics', 15 May 2014, British Library; https://www.bl.uk/romantics-and-victorians/articles/post-darwin-social-darwinism-degeneration-eugenics.

Kevin M. Burke, 'A Close Alliance between MLK and Nelson Rockefeller Revealed', *The Root*, 11 November 2015; https://www.theroot.com/a-close-alliance-between-mlk-and-nelson-rockefeller-rev-1790858451.

Daniel Burston, *The Legacy of Erich Fromm* (Harvard University Press;1991).

Katherine Burton, 'George Soros to Start $1 Billion Fund to Fight Nationalists, Climate Change', *Bloomberg Green*, January 24, 2020; https://www.bloomberg.com/news/articles/2020-01-23/soros-starts-new-global-university-with-1-billion-commitment.

C. Severin Buschmann, 'Review: Sterilization for Human Betterment, by E. S. Gosney and Paul Popenoe', *Indiana Law Journal* (1930).

J. Butler et al., 'Pour ne pas en finir avec le genre', *Societes and Representations* (2007).

Joseph Campbell, 'The Impact of Science on Myth' (1961).

Allan C. Carlson, *The Swedish Experiment in Family Politics: The Myrdals and the Interwar Population Crisis* (New Brunswick: Transaction Publishers, 1990).

Thomas Carlyle, *Past and Present* (London, 1887).

Andrew Carnegie, 'Wealth', *North American Review*, Vol. CXLVIII, June 1889. Reprinted in Andrew Carnegie, *The Gospel of Wealth and Other Timely Essays*, (Cambridge, Mass.: 1962).

Jung Chang & John Halliday, *Mao: The Unknown Story* (London: Jonathan Cape, 2005).

F. Chernov, 'Bourgeois Cosmopolitanism and Its Reactionary Role', *Bolshevik* (Central Committee of the Communist Party), No. 5, 15 March 1949.

Ronald Clark, *The Life and Work of J. B. S. Haldane* (London: Hodder and Stoughton, 1968).

R. T. Rundle Clark, *Myth and Symbol in Ancient Egypt* (New York: Grove Press 1960).

Adele E. Clarke, *Disciplining Reproduction* (Berkeley: University of California Press, 1998).

William Cobbett, *Cobbett's Weekly Register* (London), Vol. 47, 30 August 1823.

Nathan Cofnas, 'Is Kevin MacDonald's Theory of Judaism "Plausible"? A Response to Dutton' (2018), *Evolutionary Psychological Science*, Vol. 5, (2019) https://doi.org/10.1007/s40806-018-0162-8.

Shari Cohen, 'The Lasting Legacy of an American Dilemma', *Carnegie Results*, Carnegie Corporation of New York, Fall 2004; https://production-carnegie.s3.amazonaws.com/filer_public/98/65/9865c794-39d9-4659-862e-aae1583278a8/ccny_cresults_2004_americandilemma.pdf.

Matthew James Connelly, *Fatal Misconception: The Struggle to Control World Population*, (Cambridge, Mass.: The Belknap Press of Harvard University Press, 2008).

James E. Côté, et al., 'The Mead-Freeman Controversy in Review', *Journal of Youth and Adolescence*, Vol. 29, No. 5, 2000; https://www.academia.edu/27125304/The_Mead_Freeman_Controversy_in_Review.

Stephan Courtois et al., *The Black Book of Communism* (Harvard University Press, 1999).

Sarah Cox, 'Battle of Lewisham Mural Installed in New Cross', Goldsmiths: University of London, 26 October 2019; https://www.gold.ac.uk/news/battle-of-lewisham-commemorative-artwork-/).

Vicki Cox, *Margaret Sanger: Rebel for Women's Rights* (Chelsea House Publishers, 2005).

Benjamin Cunningham, 'Myth over Math', *Aspen Review*, No. 4, 2017; https://www. aspen.review/article/2017/myth-over-math/.

Edwin L. Dale Jr., 'What Vietnam Did to the American Economy', *The New York Times*, 28 January 1973.

Philippa Davies and Shirley Richards, 'Response to Redefining Marriage: U.S. Supreme Court and other related LGBT Decisions by Lord Gifford QC', presented at Council for Legal Education — Continuing Legal Professional Development, 10 December 2016, p. 14; http://www.drjudithreisman.com/ archives/JM_20161210_Richards-Davies.pdf.

Jacques Derrida, 'Force of Law: The Mystical Foundation of Authority', in Cornell et al. (ed.) *Deconstruction and the Possibility of Justice* (Routledge, 1992).

Albert Deutsch, 'The Sex Habits of American Men: Some Findings of the Kinsey Report', *Harper's Magazine*, December 1947.

Peter Thirsted Dinesen, Merlin Schaeffer, and Kim Mannemar Sønderskov, 'Ethnic Diversity and Social Trust: A Narrative and Meta-Analytical Review'; https:// www.researchgate.net/publication/335924797_Ethnic_Diversity_and_Social_ Trust_A_Narrative_and_Meta-Analytical_Review.

Peter Thirsted Dinesen and K. M. Sønderskov, 'Ethnic Diversity and Social Trust: Evidence from the Micro-Context', *American Sociological Review*, 80 (3), 2015.

Peter Dinesen, K.M. Sønderskov, F. Thuesen, 'Working Together? Ethnic Diversity in the Workplace and Generalised Social Trust', Working Paper, 2019. An interview on this paper with Dinsen can be heard at: Center for the Study of Democratic Citizenship, https://csdc-cecd.ca/event/speaker-series-peter-dinesen/.

Z. Dobbs, *The Great Deceit: Social Pseudo-Sciences* (New York: Vertis Foundation, 1964).

Norman Dodd, 'The Dodd Report to the Reece Committee on Foundations', Special Committee of the House of Representatives Investigating Foundations (1954), https://ia800304.us.archive.org/19/items/DoddReportToTheReeceCommittee OnFoundations-1954-RobberBaron/Dodd-Report-to-the-Reece-Committee-on-Foundations-1954.pdf.

Ralf Dose, *Magnus Hirschfeld: The Origins of the Gay Liberation Movement* (New York: Monthly Review Press, 2014).

John Dryden, *The Conquest of Granada* (1672).

Martin Duberman, *Left Out: The Politics of Exclusion* (New York: Basic Books, 1999).

L. C. Dunn, et al., *The Race Concept: The Race Question in Modern Science* (Paris: UNESCO, 1952).

George Dvorsky and James Hughes, 'Postgenderism: Beyond the Gender Binary', *IEET Monograph Series*, Institute for Ethics and Emerging Technologies, March 2008.

Dan Edelstein, *Terror of Natural Right: Republicanism, the Cult of Nature, and the French Revolution* (Chicago: University of Chicago Press, 2009).

Mircea Eliade, *The Sacred and the Profane* (New York: Harcourt Brace, 1959).

Ralph E. Ellsworth and Sarah M. Harris, *The American Right-Wing, A Report to the Fund for the Republic* (Champaign, IL: University of Illinois Graduate School of Library Science Occasional Papers, No. 59, November 1960).

Friedrich Engels, *The Condition of the Working Class in England* (1845).

F. Engels, *The Peasant War in Germany*, Preface to the Second Edition (1870).

F. Engels, *Socialism, Utopian and Scientific* (London: Sonnenschein, 1892).

Julius Evola, *Revolt against the Modern World* (Vermont: Inner Traditions, 1995 [1969]).

Julius Evola, *Men Among the Ruins* ([1972] Vermont: Inner Traditions, 2002).

Julius Evola, *The Path of Cinnabar* (London: Arktos, 2010).

Robert Eringer, *The Global Manipulators* (Bristol: Pentacle Books, 1980).

R. De Felice, *Mussoini il fascista* (Turin, 1966).

Claudette Fillard, Françoise Oraz (eds.), *Exchanges and Correspondence: Feminism in the Making* (Cambridge Scholars Publishing, 2010).

Christian Fleck, 'Heufelder, Argentinischer Krösus', *Serendipities: Journal for the Sociology and History of the Social Sciences*, Vol. 3, No. 1, 2018.

Raymond Fosdick, *The Story of the Rockefeller Foundation* ([1952] New Brunswick: Transactions Publishers, 1989).

Stephen P. Foster, 'Marxism & Behaviorism: Ideological Parallels', Wright State University, *Dialogue*, Vol. 21, No. 1, October 1978.

David France, 'An Inconvenient Woman', *The New York Times*, 23 May 2000.

Robert Frank, 'Billionaires Try to Shrink World's Population, Report Says', *The Wall Street Journal*, 26 May 2009.

D. Freeman, *Margaret Meade and Samoa: The Making and Unmaking of an Anthropological Myth* (Penguin Books, 1984).

William M. Freeman, 'Ex-Magistrate Ploscowe Dies; Criminal-Law Expert Was 71', *The New York Times*, 22 September 1975.

Sigmund Freud, *Civilization and Its Discontents* (Edinburgh: R. & R. Clark, 1930).

S. Freud, Letter to an American Mother, 22 December 1949; 'Historical Notes: A Letter from Freud' in: *The American Journal of Psychiatry*, Vol. 107, No. 10, April 1951.

S. Freud, '"Civilized" Sexual Morality and Modern Nervous Illness', in J. Strachey (ed., trans.), *The Standard Edition of the Complete Psychological Works of Sigmund Freud*, (London: Hogarth Press, 1959 [1908]).

Lawrence J. Friedman, *The Lives of Erich Fromm: Love's Prophet* (Columbia University Press, 2014).

Milton Friedman, 'Washington Spotlight', *The Canadian Jewish Chronicle* (31 May 1963).

Erich Fromm, *Escape From Freedom* (New York: Rinehart & Co., 1941).

Eric Fromm, *The Fear of Freedom* (London: Routledge, 1955).

Eric Fromm, *The Anatomy of Human Destructiveness* (New York: Holt, Rinehart & Winston, 1973).

Francis Fukuyama, *The End of History and the Last Man* (New York: Free Press, 1992).

James W. Fulbright, 'Propaganda Activities of Military Personnel Directed at the Public', Congressional Record (2 August 1961).

Rainer Funk, *Erich Fromm: His Life and Work* (Continuum International Publishing Group Ltd., 2000).

Barry Gewen, 'Irving Kristol, Godfather of Modern Conservatism, Dies at 89', *The New York Times*, September 18, 2009; https://www.nytimes.com/2009/09/19/us/politics/19kristol.html?pagewanted=all.

Gemelli Giuliana, MacLeod Roy (eds.), *American Foundations in Europe. Grant-Giving Policies, Cultural Diplomacy and Trans-Atlantic Relations, 1920–1980* (Brussels: Peter Lang, 2003).

Caroline B. Glick, 'Our World: Soros' Campaign of Global Chaos', *The Jerusalem Post*, 22 August 2016, http://www.jpost.com/Opinion/Our-World-Soross-campaign-of-global-chaos-464770.

C. James Godwin, *A History of Modern Psychology*, (New Jersey: John Wiley & sons, 2015).

Neal Goodman, 'Unconscious Bias', Training, Official Publication of Training Magazine Network, https://trainingmag.com/trgmag-article/unconscious-bias/.

A. James Gregor, 'On the Nature of Prejudice', *The Eugenics Review*, Vol. 52, No. 4, January 1961; I.A.A.E.E. reprint No. 3, New York.

Daisy Grewal, 'Does Diversity Create Distrust? Doubts About a Harvard Professor's Landmark Finding', *Scientific American*, 29 November 2016; https://www.scientificamerican.com/article/does-diversity-create-distrust/.

G. Edward Griffin, *The Fearful Master: A Second Look at the United Nations* (Boston: Western Islands, 1964).

Robert S. Griffin, 'The Tale of John Kasper', *The Occidental Observer*, 15 December 2017; https://www.theoccidentalobserver.net/2017/12/15/the-tale-of-john-kasper/.

J.G. Griffiths, *The Conflict of Horus and Seth from Egyptian and Classical Sources* (New York: Liverpool University Press, 1960).

Andrei Gromyko, *Memories* (London: Hutchinson, 1989).

Lindsay Haines, 'Poor, Backward and Adamantly White in a Black World', *The New York Times*, 25 February 1973; https://www.nytimes.com/1973/02/25/archives/poor-backward-and-adamantly-white-in-a-black-world-culture-doomed.html.

Isabel Asher Hamilton, 'Elon Musk Believes AI Could Turn Humans into an Endangered Species Like the Mountain Gorilla', *Business Insider Australia*, 27 November 2018; https://www.businessinsider.com.au/elon-musk-ai-could-turn-humans-into-endangered-species-2018-11.

Donna Haraway, 'A Cyborg Manifesto: Science, Technology, and Socialist-Feminism in the Late Twentieth Century', in *Simians, Cyborgs and Women: The Reinvention of Nature* (New York: Routledge, 1991).

José Harris, *William Beveridge: A Biography* (Clarendon Press, 1997).

Rivkah Harris, *Gender and Aging in Mesopotamia: The Gilgamesh Epic and Other Ancient Literature* (University of Oklahoma Press, 2003).

Tom Hayden et al., *The Port Huron Statement* (New York: Students for a Democratic Society, 1962).

Tom Hayden, *Reunion: A Memoir* (London: Hamish Hamilton, 1989).

Martin Heidegger, *Martin Heidegger: Basic Writings* (San Francisco: Harper, 1993).

Hinton Rowan Helper, *The Impending Crisis of the South: How to Meet It* (New York: Burdick Brothers, 1857).

Eve Hodgson, 'Germaine Greer Can No Longer Be Called a Feminist', *Varsity*, 26 October 2017.

Michael A. Hoffman II, *They Were White and They Were Slaves* (Wiswell Ruffin House, 1992).

H.A. Hoffner Jr., 'Symbols for Masculinity and Femininity: Their Use in Ancient Near Eastern Sympathetic Magic Rituals', *Journal of Biblical Literature*, Vol. 85 (1966).

Liam Hogan, 'How the Myth of the "Irish Slaves" Became a Racist Meme Online', SPLC, 19 April 2016; https://www.splcenter.org/hatewatch/2016/04/19/how-myth-irish-slaves-became-favorite-meme-racists-online.

M. Horkheimer (ed.), *The Authoritarian Personality* (American Jewish Committee, 1950).

Aldous Huxley, *Brave New World*, (London: Chatto & Windus, 1969 [1932]).

Aldous Huxley, *Brave New World Revisited* (1958).

Julian Huxley, *UNESCO: Its Purpose and its Philosophy*, (London: Preparatory Commission of UNESCO, 1946).

Julian Huxley, *New Bottles for New Wine* (London, Chatto & Windus, 1957).

Julian Huxley et al., 'Homosexual Acts, Call to Reform Law', *The Times*, 7 March 1958.

IEET, 'Technoprogressive Declaration', Paris, 21 November 2014; https://ieet.org/index.php/tpwiki/Technoprogressive_Declaration.

Ben Jacobs, 'Hillary Clinton Calls Half of Trump Supporters Bigoted "Deplorables"', *The Guardian*, 10 September 2016; https://www.theguardian.com/us-news/2016/sep/10/hillary-clinton-trump-supporters--bigoted-deplorable.

Jack Jacobs, *The Frankfurt School, Jewish Lives, and Antisemitism* (New York: Cambridge University Press, 2015).

Frederick S. Jaffe, 'Activities Relevant to the Study of Population Policy for the United States', Center for Family Planning Program Development, 11 March 1969.

Jerome Jamin, 'Cultural Marxism: A Survey', Religion Compass, 2018.

Martin Jay, *The Dialectical Imagination: A History of the Frankfurt School and the New School for Social Research* (University of California Press, 1973).

Stuart Jeffries, *Grand Hotel Abyss: The Lives of the Frankfurt School* (Verso, 2016).

Abby Johnson, 'Secretive Planned Parenthood Memo: How to Stop Overpopulation by Discouraging Birth', *Lifesite*, 28 November 2011, https://www.lifesitenews.com/opinion/secretive-planned-parenthood-memo-how-to-stop-overpopulation-by-discouragin.

James H. Jones, *Alfred C. Kinsey: A Life* (New York: W. W. Norton, 2004).

Carl Jung, *Letters* (Princeton University Press, 1973).

Carl Jung, *Nietzsche's Zarathustra: Notes of the Seminar* (New York: Routledge, 1989).

Carl Jung, *The Psychology of Kundalini Yoga: Notes of the Seminar* (1932) (Princeton University Press, 1996).

Carl Jung, 'Answer to Job', *Collected Works* (Princeton University Press, 2010).

Carlyle, Thomas, *Past and Present* (London: Ward, Lock, & Bowden, 1897).

Mark D. Kelland, *Personality Theory in a Cultural Context*, 8.2: 'Carl Rogers and Humanistic Psychology', 1 May 2020; https://socialsci.libretexts.org/ Bookshelves/Psychology/Book%3A_Personality_Theory_in_a_Cultural_ Context_(Kelland).

Walter Kaufman, *Nietzsche* (Princeton University Press, 1968).

Douglas Kellner, Marcuse, Herbert, The American National Bibliography, http://74.125.155.132/search?q=cache:5_KUmmTtH7QJ:www.uta.edu/english/ dab/illuminations/kell12.html.

Douglas Kellner (ed.) Herbert Marcuse, *The New Left and the 1960s: Collected Papers of Herbert Marcuse* (London: Routledge, 2005).

D. Kellner, 'Cultural Marxism and Cultural Studies' (2013), https://pages.gseis.ucla. edu/faculty/kellner.

Farah Naz Khan, 'A History of Transgender Health Care', *Scientific American*, 16 November 2016, https://blogs.scientificamerican.com/guest-blog/a-history-of- transgender-health-care.

Alfred Kinsey et al., *Sexual Behavior in the Male* (Philadelphia: W. B. Saunders, 1949).

Otto Kirchheimer, Herbert Marcuse, Franz Neumann, *Secret Reports on Nazi Germany: The Frankfurt School Contribution to the War Effort* (Princeton University Press 2013).

S. F. Kissin, *War and the Marxists: Socialist Theory and Practice in Capitalist Wars* (New York: Routledge, 1988).

Joel Kovel, 'From Reich to Marcuse', in Sohnya Sayres (ed). et al., *The 60's Without Apology* (Minneapolis: University of Minnesota Press, 1984).

Steven G. Koven and Frank Götzke, *American Immigration Policy: Confronting the Nation's Challenges* (Springer, 2010).

S.N. Kramer, 'Mythology of Sumer and Akkad', *Mythologies of the Ancient World*, (New York: Doubleday & Co., 1961).

Nikolai Krementsov, *With and Without Galton: Vasilii Florinskii and the Fate of Eugenics in Russia* (Cambridge, UK: Open Book Publishers, 2018).

Ernesto Laclau and Chantal Mouffe, 'Socialist Strategy — Where Next?, *Marxism Today*, January 1981, http://banmarchive.org.uk/collections/mt/pdf/81_01_17. pdf.

Geoffrey P. Lantos, *Consumer Behavior in Action: Real Life Applications for Marketing Managers* (New York: Routledge, 2011).

Richard LaPiere, *The Freudian Ethic* (New York: Duell, Sloan & Pearce, 1959).

Christopher Lasch, *Women and the Common Life: Love, Marriage & Feminism* (W.W. Norton, 1979).

C. Lasch, 'What's Wrong with the Right?', *Tikkun*, No. 1, 1987; https://web.archive.org/web/20040317084407/http://thor.clark.edu/sengland/previous%20features/a_dialogue_with_christopher_lasc.htm.

C. Lasch, 'Why the Left Has No Future', *Tikkun*, https://web.archive.org/web/20040317084407/http://thor.clark.edu/sengland/previous%20features/a_dialogue_with_christopher_lasc.htm.

C. Lasch, *The Culture of Narcissism: American Life in an Age of Diminishing Expectations* (New York: Norton, 2018 [1979]).

C. Lasch, *Revolt of the Elites and the Betrayal of Democracy* (New York: Norton, 1994).

Elisabeth Lasch-Quinn, *Race Experts: How Racial Etiquette, Sensitivity Training, and New Age Hijacked the Civil Rights Revolution* (Maryland: Rowan & Littlefield, 2002).

Julie Lawrence, Anne Smith, 'A Place Where It Is Not Okay to Hit Children', *Social Policy Journal of New Zealand*, No. 34, April 2009.

Bandy X. Lee, *The Dangerous Case of Donald Trump: 27 Psychiatrists and Mental Health Experts Assess a President*, (Thomas Dunne, 2017).

Kirsten Leng, *Sexual Politics and Feminist Science: Women Sexologists in Germany, 1900–1933* (Ithaca: Cornell University Press, 2018).

Sophie Lewis, 'How British Feminism Became Anti-Trans', *The New York Times*, 7 February 2019.

Robert Jay Lifton, 'Goldwater Rule: We Have a Duty to Warn If Someone May Be Dangerous to Others', *Salon*, 19 September 2017; https://www.salon.com/test/2017/09/19/the-dangerous-case-of-donald-trump-robert-jay-lifton-and-bill-moyers-on-a-duty-to-warn_partner/.

John Locke, *Second Treatise of Civil Government* (1690).

Konrad Lorenz, *Civilized Man's Eight Deadly Sins* (1974).

Georg Lukács, 'The Role of Morality in Communist Production' (1919), in R. Livingstone (ed.), *Georg Lukács: Political Writings, 1919–1929* (N.L.B. 1972).

Frank McLynn, *Carl Gustav Jung: A Biography* (London: Bantam Press, 1997).

Matthew MacWilliams, 'The One Weird Trait That Predicts Whether You're a Trump Supporter, And It's Not Gender, Age, Income, Race or Religion', *Politico*

Magazine, 17 January 2016; https://www.politico.com/magazine/story/2016/01/donald-trump-2016-authoritarian-213533.

Kevin MacDonald, *A People That Shall Dwell Alone: Judaism As a Group Evolutionary Strategy, With Diaspora Peoples* (Praeger 1994).

Kevin MacDonald, *The Culture of Critique: An Evolutionary Analysis of Jewish Involvement in Twentieth-Century Intellectual and Political Movements* (Praeger 1998).

Kevin MacDonald, *Separation and Its Discontents: Toward an Evolutionary Theory of Anti-Semitism* (Praeger 1998).

Andrew McGill, 'America's Educational Divide Put Trump in the White House', *The Atlantic*, 27 November, 2018; https://www.theatlantic.com/politics/archive/2016/11/education-put-donald-trump-in-the-white-house/508703/.

S. McMeekin, *The Red Millionaire: A Political Biography of Willi Münzenberg* (New Haven: Yale University Press, 2003).

Joseph de Maistre, *Considerations on France* (1797).

Joseph de Maistre, *Essay on the Generative Principle of Political Constitutions and other Human Institutions*, (1809).

Judith T. Marcus and Zoltan Tar (eds.), *Foundations of the Frankfurt School of Social Research* (New York: Routledge, 2019).

Herbert Marcuse, 'Repressive Tolerance' (1965), https://www.marcuse.org/herbert/publications/1960s/1965-repressive-tolerance-fulltext.htmlhttps://www.marcuse.org/herbert/publications/1960s/1965-repressive-tolerance-fulltext.html.

Herbert Marcuse, *Eros and Civilization — A Philosophical Inquiry into Freud* (Boston: Beacon Press, 1966).

Herbert Marcuse, 'The Problem of Violence and the Radical Opposition, Psychoanalyse und Politik'; Free University of West Berlin, July 1967; https://www.marxists.org/reference/archive/marcuse/works/1967/violence.htm.

Herbert Marcuse, *Soviet Marxism: A Critical Analysis* (New York Columbia University Press, 1969 [1958]).

Herbert Marcuse, *Counterrevolution and Revolt* (1972).

Herbert Marcuse, *One- Dimensional Man* (London: Routledge 2007).

Karl Marx, *The Communist Manifesto* (1848).

K. Marx, *The Class Struggles in France 1848–1850* (1850).

Karl Marx, 'The German Ideology', in Karl Marx, Friedrich Engels: *Collected Works*, (New York: International Publishers, 1976).

K. Marx & F. Engels, *Marx & Engels Collected Works*, Letters 1868–70, Volume 43, (Lawrence & Wishart, 2010); http://www.koorosh-modaresi.com/MarxEngels/V43.pdf.

M. Mead, *Soviet Attitudes Toward Authority* (RAND Corporation, 1951).

Margaret Mead, *The Coming of Age in Samoa* (New York: William Morrow, 1973 [1928]).

Jerome Meckier, 'Brave New World and the Anthropologists', *Alternative Futures*, No. 1 Spring 1978.

Louis Menand, 'A Friend of the Devil', *The New Yorker*, 23 March 2015; https://www.newyorker.com/magazine/2015/03/23/a-friend-of-the-devil.

Maria Di Mento and Ian Wilhelm, 'America's Top Philanthropists Hold Private Meeting to Discuss Global Problems', *The Chronicle of Philanthropy*, 20 May 2009.

Charles Merriam, *New Aspects of Politics* (Chicago: University of Chicago Press, 1931 [1925]).

Ashley Montagu, '"Human Nature Cannot Be Changed"; False! Says U.S. Anthropologist', *The Courier*, UNESCO, Vol. VI, no. 2, February 1953.

M. Morey, 'Rockefeller, Carnegie, and the SSRC's Focus on Race in the 1920s and 1930s', Social Science Research Council, 8 January 2019; https://items.ssrc.org/insights/rockefeller-carnegie-and-the-ssrcs-focus-on-race-in-the-1920s-and-1930s/.

Malcom Muggeridge, 'The Great Liberal Death Wish', *Imprimis*, Hillsdale College, Vol. 8, No. 5, May 1979 ; https://www.orthodoxytoday.org/articles/MuggeridgeLiberal.php.

Kyle Munkittrick, 'On the Importance of Being a Cyborg Feminist', *Humanity+*, 21 July 2009; https://hplusmagazine.com/2009/07/21/importance-being-cyborg-feminist/.

Douglas Murray, *The Madness of Crowds* (London: Bloomsbury Continuum, 2019).

Gunnar Myrdal, *An American Dilemma: The Negro Problem and Modern Democracy* (New York: Harper & Brothers, 1944).

F. Nietzsche, *Twilight of the Idols/The Antichrist* (Penguin Books, 1968).

Lucie-Mami Noor Nkaké, 'Education for International Understanding' (Geneva: UNESCO International Bureau for Education, 1996).

Stewart M. Ogilvy, *Progress As if Survival Mattered* (Friends of the Earth, 1981).

Tom O'Neill, *Chaos: Charles Manson, the CIA & the Secret History of the Sixties* (London: Heinemann, 2019).

Richard Overy, *The Dictators: Hitler's Germany/Stalin's Russia* (London: Allen Lane, 2004).

Mohammad Reza Pahlavi, *The Shah's Story* (London: Michael Joseph, 1989).

Stephanie Pappas, 'APA Issues First-Ever Guidelines for Practice with Men and Boys', *Monitor on Psychology*, APA, Vol., 50, No. 1, 2019.

Roger Pearson, 'The Misuse of the Term "Nation State"', *The Mankind Quarterly*, Volume 44, Numbers 3 & 4, Fall/Winter, 2008.

Luciano C. G. Pinto and Renato Pinto, 'Transgendered Archaeology: The Galli and the Catterick Transvestite', in: A. Bokern, M. Bolder-Boos, S. Krmnicek, D. Maschek, and S. Page, S. (eds.), *TRAC 2012: Proceedings of the Twenty-Second Annual Theoretical Roman Archaeology Conference*, Frankfurt 2012 (Oxford: Oxbow Books, 2012).

Phyllis T. Piotrow, *World Population Crisis: The United States Response* (New York: Praeger Publishers, 1973).

Plato, *The Republic* (Penguin Books, 2007 [357BC]).

Karl Popper, *The Open Society and Its Enemies* (Princeton, New Jersey: Princeton University Press, 1966).

K. Popper, *The Poverty of Historicism* (Routledge, 1994 [1957]).

Dorothy Porter (ed.), *Social Medicine and Medical Sociology in the Twentieth Century* (Amsterdam: Rodopi, 1997).

J. M. Post, 'Notes on a Psychodynamic Theory of Terrorist Behavior', in *Terrorism: An International Journal*, Vol. 7, no. 3, 1984.

David Price, *Cold War Anthropology: The CIA, The Pentagon, and the Growth of Dual Use Anthropology*. (Durham, NC: Duke University Press, 2016).

Robert D. Putnam, 'E Pluribus Unum: Diversity and Community in the Twenty-First Century', Journal of Scandinavian Political Studies, Vol. 30, No. 2, June 2007

Carrol Quigley, *Tragedy & Hope: A History of the World in Our Time* (New York: MacMillan, 1966).

Fredric Rabinowitz et al., 'APA Guidelines for Psychological Practice with Boys and Men', (American Psychological Association, Boys and Men Guidelines Group, 2018); https://www.apa.org/about/policy/boys-men-practice-guidelines.pdf.

Hon. B. Carroll Reece, U. S. Congressional Record, 23 February 1955, A1184.

Wilhelm Reich, *The Mass Psychology of Fascism*, English ed. (New York: Orgone Institute Press, 1946).

Walter and Victor Reuther, 'The Reuther Memorandum to the Attorney General of the United States', (19 December 1961), http://www.scribd.com/doc/31124491/

The-Reuther-Memorandum-Precusor-to-the-Ideological-Organizations-Audit-Project-Created-by-President-John-F-Kennedy-and-Attorney-General-Robert-Kenn.

W. Roszkowski and J. Kofman (eds.), *Biographical Dictionary of Central and Eastern Europe in the Twentieth Century* (New York: Routledge, 2008), 948.

Stanley Rothman, 'Group Fantasies and Jewish Radicalism: A Psychodynamic Interpretation', *The Journal of Psychohistory*, Fall 1978.

Stanley Rothman and S. R. Lichter, *Roots of Radicalism: Jews, Christians and the New Left* (New York: Oxford University Press, 1982).

Jean-Jacques Rousseau, *The Social Contract and Discourses* (1761).

Jerry Rubin, *Growing (Up) At 37* (New York: Warner Books, 1976).

Lillian Rubin, 'A Feminist Response to Lasch', *Tikkun*, op. cit., pp. 89–91; https://web.archive.org/web/20040317084407/http://thor.clark.edu/sengland/previous%20features/a_dialogue_with_christopher_lasc.htm.

Howard A. Rusk, 'Concerning Man's Basic Drive: Sexual Behavior in the Human Male by Alfred S. Kinsey', *The New York Times*, 4 January 1948.

Liza Ireni-Saban, *Politics of Eugenics: Productionism, Population, and National Welfare*, (New York: Routledge, 2013).

Howard Sachar, *The Course of Modern Jewish History* (Vintage Books 1991).

Donatien Alphonse François de Sade, *The 120 Days of Sodom, or the School of Libertinage* (1785). First published 1904.

Donatien Alphonse François de Sade, *Philosophy in the Bedroom* (1795).

M. Sanger, *The Pivot of Civilisation* (New York: Brentano, 1922).

Frances Stonor Saunders, *The Cultural Cold War: The CIA & the World of Arts & Letters* (New York: The New Press, 2000).

Frederick Seelig, *Destroy the Accuser* (1967); https://archive.org/stream/SeeligFrederickDestroyTheAccuser_201610/Seelig_Frederick_-_Destroy_the_accuser_djvu.txt.

Lance Selfa, *The Democrats: A Critical History* (Chicago: Haymarket Books, 2012).

Dennis Sewell, 'How Eugenics Poisoned the Welfare State', *Spectator*, 25 November 2009; https://web.archive.org/web/20101203124517/http://www.spectator.co.uk/essays/all/5571423/part_4/how-eugenics-poisoned-the-welfare-state.thtml.

Myran Sharaf, *Fury on Earth — A Biography of Wilhelm Reich* (London: Andre Deutsch, 1983).

M.S. Shaw, 'Family Life in Ancient Egypt', *Journal of the Manchester Egyptian and Oriental Society*, No. 28 (1933).

Sarwant Singh, 'Transhumanism & the Future of Humanity', *Forbes*, 20 November 2017; https://www.forbes.com/sites/sarwantsingh/2017/11/20/transhumanism-and-the-future-of-humanity-seven-ways-the-world-will-change-by-2030/#28.

B. F. Skinner, *Beyond Freedom and Dignity* (New York: Alfred A. Knopf, 1971).

Glenda Sluga, 'Unesco and the (One) World of Julian Huxley', *Journal of World History*, 21 March 2010.

Margaret Smith (ed.) *Relationships and Sexuality Education: A Guide for Teachers, Leaders and Boards of Trustees, Years 1–8*, Ministry of Education, 2020.

Charles W. Socarides, 'Sexual Politics and Scientific Logic: The Issue of Homosexuality', *The Journal of Psychohistory*, Vol. 19, No. 3, Winter 1992; http://www.geocities.ws/kidhistory/homopolo.htm.

G. Soros, *Soros on Soros* (New York: John Wiley & Sons, 1995).

David W. Southern, *Gunnar Myrdal and Black-White Relations* (Baton Rouge: Louisiana State University Press, 1987), p. 111.

Richard B. Spence, *Wall Street and the Russian Revolution 1905–1925* (Trine Day, 2017).

Oswald Spengler, *The Decline of the West* ([1918, 1926] London: George Allen and Unwin, 1971).

Oswald Spengler, 'Prussianism & Socialism' (1919) in Oswald Spengler, *Prussian Socialism and Other Essays* (London, 2019).

R. L. Spitzer, 'The Homosexual Decision — A Background Paper', *Psychiatric News* (1974).

Paul Spoonley, *The Politics of Nostalgia* (Palmerston North, New Zealand: The Dunmore Press, 1987).

Paul Spoonley in Bruce Jesson, Allanah Ryan, Paul Spoonley, *Revival of the Right: New Zealand Politics in the 1980s* (Auckland: Heinmann Reed, 1988).

Paul Spoonley, 'I Thought There Had Been a Decline in Far Right Politics, I Was Wrong', *Stuff*, 15 March 2020; https://www.stuff.co.nz/opinion/120179211/i-thought-there-had-been-a-decline-in-far-right-politics-i-was-wrong.

Cheryl Staats, 'State of the Science: Implicit Bias Review' (Kirwin Institute, 2014), pp. 20–21; http://kirwaninstitute.osu.edu/wp-content/uploads/2014/03/2014-implicit-bias.pdf.

Harry Stein, 'The Goldwater Takedown', *City Journal*, Autumn 2016; https://www.city-journal.org/html/goldwater-takedown-14787.html.

Peter Stirk, *Max Horkheimer: A New Interpretation* (Landam, MD: Barnes & Noble, 1992).

Richard Stites, *Revolutionary Dreams: Utopian Vision and Experimental Life in the Russian Revolution* (Oxford: Oxford University Press, 1989).

Alan Stone, 'The Psychiatrists' Goldwater Rule in the Trump Era', *Lawfare*, 19 April 2018; https://www.lawfareblog.com/psychiatrists-goldwater-rule-trump-era.

J. Strachey (ed., trans.), *The Standard Edition of the Complete Psychological Works of Sigmund Freud* (London: Hogarth Press, 1932 [1910]).

J. Strachey (ed., trans.), *The Standard Edition of the Complete Psychological Works of Sigmund Freud* (London: Hogarth Press, 1957 [1914]).

Christine Swanton, *The Virtue Ethics of Nietzsche & Hume* (West Sussex: John Wiley, 2015).

Thomas S. Szasz, *Law, Liberty, and Psychiatry: An Inquiry into the Social Uses of Mental Health Practices* (New York: The Macmillan Company, 1963).

Thomas Szasz, *The Manufacture of Madness: A Comparative Study of the Inquisition & the Mental Health Movement* (Syracuse University Press, 1970).

T. Szasz, 'The Shame of Medicine: The Case of General Edwin Walker', 2009; https://fee.org/articles/the-shame-of-medicine-the-case-of-general-edwin-walker/.

'Tax Exempt Foundations, Hearings Before the Select Committee to Investigate Tax Exempt Foundations & Comparable Organizations before the House of Representatives', Washington D.C. (1952).

Melody Thomas, 'Early Maori View on Sexual Fluidity Far More Liberal Than Previously Believed', *Stuff*, 6 July 2018, https://www.stuff.co.nz/life-style/love-sex/105284489/early-mori-view-on-sexual-fluidity-far-more-liberal-than-previously-believed.

Eric Trist, *The Social Engagement of Social Science: A Tavistock Anthology* (1989), http://www.moderntimesworkplace.com/archives/ericsess/sessPreface/sesspreface.html.

Leon Trotsky, *Revolution Betrayed* (New York: Pathfinder, 1937).

Natalia Sedova Trotsky, 'Letter of Resignation from the Fourth International', 9 May 1951; https://www.marxists.org/archive/sedova-natalia/1951/05/09.htm.

H. Te Velde, *Seth: God of Confusion* (Leiden: E.J. Brill, 1977).

Katherine Verdery, 'The CIA Is Not a Trope', *Hau: Journal of Ethnographic Theory* (2016).

Abhishek Verma, 'Understanding LGBTIQCAPGNGFNBA — Reach for the Rainbow'; http://sites.tufts.edu/lgbtcommunityinindia/page-2/.

G. Vico, *The New Science* (Cornell University Press, [1730] 1948).

Val Vinokur, 'What's So 'Jewish' about the New School? Inventing a Parable of Pluralism', Public Seminar, 7 February 2019; https://publicseminar.org/2019/02/whats-so-jewish-about-the-new-school/.

Arthur J. Viseltear, Milton C. Winternitz and the Yale Institute of Human Relations: 'A Brief Chapter in the History of Social Medicine', *Yale Journal of Biology and Medicine*, Vol. 57, No. 5, November-December 1984.

Visionary Innovation Group, 'Transhumanism: How humans will think, behave, experience, and perform in the future, and the implications to businesses' (Frost & Sullivan, 2017).

John. B. Watson, *Behaviourism* (New York: People's Institute Publishing Co., 1924).

Lally Weymouth, 'Foundation Woes: The Saga of Henry Ford II', *The New York Times*, 12 March 1978.

Rob Whitley, 'Why the APA Guidelines for Men's Mental Health Are Misguided', *Psychology Today*, 25 February 2019; https://www.psychologytoday.com/us/blog/talking-about-men/201902/why-the-apa-guidelines-mens-mental-health-are-misguided.

Paul Weindling, 'Julian Huxley and the Continuity of Eugenics in Twentieth-Century Britain', *Journal of Modern European History*, 1 November 2012, Vol. 10, No. 4.

Howard J. Wiarda, *Political Culture, Political Science, and Identity Politics: An Uneasy Alliance* (New York: Routledge, 2014).

Rolf Wiggershaus, *The Frankfurt School — Its History, Theories, Political Significance* (Cambridge, Massachusetts, MIT Press, 1995).

Charles F. Williams, 'Eros in America: Freud and the Counter Culture', PhD thesis, University of Iowa, 2012.

Michael J. Wood, Karen M. Douglas, Robbie M. Sutton, 'Dead and Alive: Beliefs in Contradictory Conspiracy Theories', *Social Psychology & Personality Science*, 25 January 2012, http://m.spp.sagepub.com/content/early/2012/01/18/1948550611434786.full.pdf.

Andrew Woods, 'A Secret Invasion: The University in Exile and Conspiracy Theories', Public Seminar, The New School, 20 May 2019; https://publicseminar.org/essays/a-secret-invasion/.

Andrew Woods, 'The American Roots of a Right-Wing Conspiracy', *Commune*, 20 March 2019; https://communemag.com/the-american-roots-of-a-right-wing-conspiracy/.

Rene A. Wormser, *Foundations: Their Power and Influence* (San Pedro, Ca.: Angriff Press, 1977).

Peter Worsley in Lenora Forestel and Angela Gilliam (eds.), *Confronting the Margaret Mead Legacy: Scholarship, Empire, and the South Pacific* (Philadelphia: Temple University Press, 1992).

G. Pascal Zachary, *The Global Me: New Cosmopolitans and the Competitive Edge: Picking Globalism's Winners and Losers* (New South Wales: Allen & Unwin, 2000).

Sue Zemka, *Time and the Moment in Victorian Literature and Society* (Cambridge University Press, 2012).

Yuri Zhukov, 'Taking Marcuse To The Woodshed', *Atlas*, XVI (Sept., 1958), pp. 33–34.

Yrui Zhukov, 'Werewolves', *Pravda*, 30 May 1968.

Mary Ziegler, 'Reinventing Eugenics: Reproductive Choice and Law Reform after World War II', *Cardozo Journal of Law and Gender*, Vol. 14, No. 319, Winter 2008.

S. Zimmermann, 'The Internationalization of Woman and Gender Studies in Higher Education in Central & Eastern Europe & the Former Soviet Union: Asymmetric Politics & the Regional-Transnational Configuration', *East-Central Europe/ECE*, Vols. 34–35, 2007–2008.

Hub Zwart, 'Conditioned Reflexes and the Symbolic Order: A Lacanian Perspective of Ivan Pavlov's Experimental Practice', *Vestigia (Journal of the International Network of Psychoanalytic Practices)*, Vol. 1, No. 2, Summer 2018.

OTHER BOOKS PUBLISHED BY ARKTOS

SRI DHARMA PRAVARTAKA ACHARYA	*The Dharma Manifesto*
JOAKIM ANDERSEN	*Rising from the Ruins: The Right of the 21st Century*
WINSTON C. BANKS	*Excessive Immigration*
ALAIN DE BENOIST	*Beyond Human Rights*
	Carl Schmitt Today
	The Indo-Europeans
	Manifesto for a European Renaissance
	On the Brink of the Abyss
	The Problem of Democracy
	Runes and the Origins of Writing
	View from the Right (vol. 1–3)
ARTHUR MOELLER VAN DEN BRUCK	*Germany's Third Empire*
MATT BATTAGLIOLI	*The Consequences of Equality*
KERRY BOLTON	*Revolution from Above*
	Yockey: A Fascist Odyssey
ISAC BOMAN	*Money Power*
RICARDO DUCHESNE	*Faustian Man in a Multicultural Age*
ALEXANDER DUGIN	*Ethnos and Society*
	Ethnosociology
	Eurasian Mission
	The Fourth Political Theory
	Last War of the World-Island
	Political Platonism
	Putin vs Putin
	The Rise of the Fourth Political Theory
	The Theory of a Multipolar World
EDWARD DUTTON	*Race Differences in Ethnocentrism*
MARK DYAL	*Hated and Proud*
CLARE ELLIS	*The Blackening of Europe*
KOENRAAD ELST	*Return of the Swastika*
JULIUS EVOLA	*The Bow and the Club*
	Fascism Viewed from the Right
	A Handbook for Right-Wing Youth
	Metaphysics of Power
	Metaphysics of War
	The Myth of the Blood
	Notes on the Third Reich
	The Path of Cinnabar

	Recognitions
	A Traditionalist Confronts Fascism
GUILLAUME FAYE	*Archeofuturism*
	Archeofuturism 2.0
	The Colonisation of Europe
	Convergence of Catastrophes
	Ethnic Apocalypse
	A Global Coup
	Prelude to War
	Sex and Deviance
	Understanding Islam
	Why We Fight
DANIEL S. FORREST	*Suprahumanism*
ANDREW FRASER	*Dissident Dispatches*
	The WASP Question
GÉNÉRATION IDENTITAIRE	*We are Generation Identity*
PETER GOODCHILD	*The Taxi Driver from Baghdad*
PAUL GOTTFRIED	*War and Democracy*
PETR HAMPL	*Breached Enclosure*
PORUS HOMI HAVEWALA	*The Saga of the Aryan Race*
LARS HOLGER HOLM	*Hiding in Broad Daylight*
	Homo Maximus
	Incidents of Travel in Latin America
	The Owls of Afrasiab
RICHARD HOUCK	*Liberalism Unmasked*
A. J. ILLINGWORTH	*Political Justice*
ALEXANDER JACOB	*De Naturae Natura*
JASON REZA JORJANI	*Faustian Futurist*
	Iranian Leviathan
	Lovers of Sophia
	Novel Folklore
	Prometheism
	Prometheus and Atlas
	World State of Emergency
HENRIK JONASSON	*Sigmund*
VINCENT JOYCE	*The Long Goodbye*
RUUBEN KAALEP & AUGUST MEISTER	*Rebirth of Europe*
RODERICK KAINE	*Smart and SeXy*

OTHER BOOKS PUBLISHED BY ARKTOS

Peter King	*Here and Now*
	Keeping Things Close
	On Modern Manners
James Kirkpatrick	*Conservatism Inc.*
Ludwig Klages	*The Biocentric Worldview*
	Cosmogonic Reflections
Pierre Krebs	*Guillaume Faye: Truths & Tributes*
	Fighting for the Essence
Julien Langella	*Catholic and Identitarian*
John Bruce Leonard	*The New Prometheans*
Stephen Pax Leonard	*The Ideology of Failure*
	Travels in Cultural Nihilism
William S. Lind	*Retroculture*
Pentti Linkola	*Can Life Prevail?*
H. P. Lovecraft	*The Conservative*
Norman Lowell	*Imperium Europa*
Charles Maurras	*The Future of the Intelligentsia*
	& For a French Awakening
John Harmon McElroy	*Agitprop in America*
Michael O'Meara	*Guillaume Faye and the Battle of Europe*
	New Culture, New Right
Michael Millerman	*Beginning with Heidegger*
Brian Anse Patrick	*The NRA and the Media*
	Rise of the Anti-Media
	The Ten Commandments of Propaganda
	Zombology
Tito Perdue	*The Bent Pyramid*
	Journey to a Location
	Lee
	Morning Crafts
	Philip
	The Sweet-Scented Manuscript
	William's House (vol. 1–4)
Raido	*A Handbook of Traditional Living* (vol. 1–2)
Steven J. Rosen	*The Agni and the Ecstasy*
	The Jedi in the Lotus
Richard Rudgley	*Barbarians*

OTHER BOOKS PUBLISHED BY ARKTOS

	Essential Substances
	Wildest Dreams
ERNST VON SALOMON	*It Cannot Be Stormed*
	The Outlaws
PIERO SAN GIORGIO	*CBRN: Surviving Chemical, Biological, Radiological & Nuclear Events*
	Giuseppe
SRI SRI RAVI SHANKAR	*Celebrating Silence*
	Know Your Child
	Management Mantras
	Patanjali Yoga Sutras
	Secrets of Relationships
GEORGE T. SHAW (ED.)	*A Fair Hearing*
FENEK SOLÈRE	*Kraal*
OSWALD SPENGLER	*The Decline of the West*
	Man and Technics
RICHARD STOREY	*The Uniqueness of Western Law*
TOMISLAV SUNIC	*Against Democracy and Equality*
	Homo Americanus
	Postmortem Report
	Titans are in Town
ASKR SVARTE	*Gods in the Abyss*
HANS-JÜRGEN SYBERBERG	*On the Fortunes and Misfortunes of Art in Post-War Germany*
ABIR TAHA	*Defining Terrorism*
	The Epic of Arya (2nd ed.)
	Nietzsche's Coming God, or the Redemption of the Divine
	Verses of Light
JEAN THIRIART	*Europe: An Empire of 400 Million*
BAL GANGADHAR TILAK	*The Arctic Home in the Vedas*
DOMINIQUE VENNER	*For a Positive Critique*
	The Shock of History
MARKUS WILLINGER	*A Europe of Nations*
	Generation Identity
ALEXANDER WOLFHEZE	*Alba Rosa*
	Rupes Nigra